Utmost Gallantry

Utmost Gallantry

THE U.S. AND ROYAL NAVIES AT SEA
IN THE WAR OF 1812

Kevin D. McCranie

Naval Institute Press
Annapolis, Maryland

Naval Institute Press
291 Wood Road
Annapolis, MD 21402

Library of Congress Cataloging-in-Publication Data
McCranie, Kevin D.
 Utmost gallantry : the U.S. and Royal Navies at sea in the War of 1812 / Kevin D.
McCranie.
 p. cm.
 Includes bibliographical references and index.
 ISBN 978-1-59114-504-2 (hbk. : alk. paper) — ISBN 978-1-61251-063-7 (ebook) 1.
United States—History—War of 1812—Naval operations. 2. United States. Navy—
History—War of 1812. 3. Great Britain. Royal Navy—History—War of 1812. I. Title.
II. Title: U.S. and Royal Navies at sea in the War of 1812.
 E360.M34 2011
 973.5'2—dc23

                              2011026325
∞This paper meets the requirements of ANSI/NISO z39.48-1992 (Permanence of
Paper).
Printed in the United States of America.

19 18 17 16 15 14 13 12 11   9 8 7 6 5 4 3 2 1
First printing

Contents

ILLUSTRATIONS

MAPS

TABLES

DIAGRAMS

PREFACE

D riving along a rural road in southwestern Georgia on a clear, crisp February day, I was greeted by fields bounded by woods, often of pine. Towns punctuated the vista from time to time. The name of one—Blakely—caught my eye. The historian in me immediately associated the town with Johnston Blakeley, who figures prominently in the following pages as commander of the *Enterprize* and later the *Wasp*. Continuing southeast from Blakely, I entered Decatur County, and then passed through the county seat of Bainbridge. Though a fair distance from salt water where Commodores Stephen Decatur and William Bainbridge defeated British frigates in 1812, the coincidence of Blakely, Georgia, followed by places named for Decatur and Bainbridge demonstrated America's admiration for its navy. Officers like Blakeley, Decatur, and Bainbridge captured America's imagination by fighting for the honor of the young United States against the most powerful navy in the world. There is, however, another side to this story. Britain viewed the War of 1812 on the high seas in the context of its ongoing war against Napoleonic France, and saw the United States Navy as a threat to the sea-lines of communication that were essential for the well-being of its economy and its empire.

In the two centuries since that war, writers have spilled a great deal of ink to explain the bloody encounters between the British and American navies on the oceans. Many of these sources, though, contain one or more of the following weaknesses: an overemphasis on the first six months of the war when the British lost the frigates *Guerriere, Macedonian,* and *Java;* a failure to link the tactical events of the ship-on-ship battles to a broader understanding of the war; an underutilization of British archival and primary sources; and an overreliance on secondary sources, including some that contain erroneous information or distorting nationalistic perspectives. The following pages offer a balanced appraisal of the war based on British and American archival sources, including public and private letters, ships' logs, as well as courts martial records. Where this was not possible, I have relied on published documents to place engagements in a broader operational and strategic context so as to understand the intent of the belligerents, how both sides used their warships, and the broader ramifications of the ship-on-ship battles. Naval warfare involves the interaction of multiple actors; looking critically at all sides, both in battle and in more mundane operations, adds to the narrative of how the war unfolded.

Though this work relies heavily on documents, I have consulted scholarly works as starting points for research, but this does require a notice of caution involving the reference notes. General works on the naval war by authors such as William James, Theodore Roosevelt, Alfred T. Mahan, C. S. Forester, and Robert Gardiner describe nearly every naval engagement in the war; rather than repeat them endlessly in the notes, I have only cited these works where they present unique points.

This book adds to the historical debate, but it is not a complete narrative of the naval war. The following pages only address the war for the lakes between the United States and Canada in a tangential manner. Though manpower constraints caused operations on the Lakes to sap oceanic naval strength, the war on the Lakes was unusually isolated for a naval war and has been divorced from this study. This work also does not assess the contributions by privateers in a critical or detailed manner. Though responsible for the capture of the majority of British merchant vessels and even the occasional, bloody fight, a true analysis of their actions would be a book unto itself. Finally, this study does not claim to assess British operations in the littorals, such as those that occurred in the Chesapeake. Instead, this is a history of the war between the British Royal Navy and the United States Navy on the high seas.

In numbers alone, this was an unequal struggle and should have been a short story of British success that swept the little American navy from the seas, but instead U.S. warships operated from the war's beginning to its end. Why did Britain, with the most powerful navy in the world, find the small American navy so resilient? What does this indicate about well-trained, smaller naval powers with critical asymmetric advantages in geographically expansive and often distant theaters? To the British, it seemed almost ludicrous that the Americans would fight; rather than define victory as defeating the entire British navy, the Americans characterized success as gaining honor while denying it to Britain, and at the same time protracting the war and forcing Britain to expend disproportionate resources to combat the U.S. naval threat. In the end, the Americans proved a nuisance and a nagging threat. Though the British failed to destroy the United States Navy, they largely marginalized it, albeit at high costs in blood, treasure, warships, and time.

A Note on Warship Armaments

The number and type of cannons mounted on warships during the War of 1812 is a nebulous subject. For example, the U.S. frigates *Constitution*, *President*, and *United States* were sister ships, but the armament of each varied slightly and changed slightly during the war. To make this more confusing, all three of the above frigates were rated for forty-four guns, but all carried more guns.

The incongruence between the rated number of guns for a ship and the actual number that ship mounted was owing to several long-term trends. First was the preference of the ship captain. A second reason dealt with mounting guns on previously unarmed portions of the ship. Another factor dealt with the widespread adoption of the carronade. On many warships carronades replaced traditional shipboard guns on a greater than one-for-one basis. These factors contributed to a net gain of six, eight, ten, or even twelve guns per ship.[1] Since ship armament was a moving target, this author has reconciled the problem using a combination of two systems.

The first involves the use of a ship's rated strength. This system was based on historical precedent that had not evolved with the proliferation of guns on warships. Though the rating system was becoming out of date, it had the advantage of consistency, meaning it did not generally change during the war. Particularly with regard to British warships, it provides an approximate indication of a warship's tonnage, broadside weight, and crew strength. Though the three British frigates taken by the Americans in 1812 were all 38-gun frigates and had similar capabilities, each mounted slightly different armaments. Given the very large number of British warships, it is all but impossible to know exact armaments in every case. The British Admiralty in London tried to keep records of ship armaments, but reports from sea at times contradict those records. With the exception of ship-on-ship actions, the rated number is generally accurate enough to provide an approximation of the force. For the United States Navy, several factors have led this author away from the rating system. First, that navy represented a smaller group to track and exact armaments were more often known; in addition, Americans had a tendency to rate warships smaller than similar British ships. For example, the Americans rated the *Congress* as a 36-gun frigate, but it was closer to a British 38-gun frigate in actual armament.

The second means of reconciling the problem of armament involves stating the exact weapons mounted on a ship. Though more accurate than the rating system, this number is not always known. The one time it generally was known, however, was for ship-on-ship actions; at such points in the narrative, this author has provided the best evidence for exact warship armaments.

Acknowledgments

Many people have helped make this book possible. First, the faculty of the Strategy and Policy Department at the United States Naval War College in Newport, Rhode Island, unknowingly served as the book's catalyst. Particularly, I would be remiss if I did not specifically thank Michael Pavković, Jon Scott Logel, and K. J. Delamar for their comments and suggestions. No one could ask for better support than I have received from my department chair, John Maurer. Sara McCranie (my dearest sister) again demonstrated why she is the artist in the family through her superb maps. I also must thank friends and colleagues whose ears I have bent and who I have burdened as I became increasingly engrossed in a war that began almost two centuries ago.

Over the previous four years, I have visited too many libraries and archives to count, and without exception the librarians, archivists, and staff have bent over backward to assist in my research. Several, however, deserve special praise for the manner in which they tolerated my questions and served to facilitate my research. The Navy History and Heritage Command sits at the top of my list. Particularly, Michael J. Crawford, Charles E. Brodine Jr., and Christine F. Hughes have provided immeasurable assistance. In addition, The National Archives at Kew, Richmond; the National Maritime Museum in Greenwich; the Hull History Centre; the Suffolk Record Office in Ipswich; and the National Library of Scotland in Edinburgh deserve special praise.

The positions I am about to express are my own views. I do not represent the Naval War College, Navy, Department of Defense, or the U.S. Government, and my views are not necessarily shared by them.

CHAPTER 1

"Every Appearance of Hastening the Crisis"

The Royal Navy, the United States Navy, and the Background to War

Less than a hundred yards separated the two ships, but darkness obscured their identities. The commander of one, Arthur Bingham, hailed across the water, demanding the name of the other ship. He heard a voice that echoed the same question. Bingham then repeated his demand but received an identical response.

On the other ship, Commodore John Rodgers stood on principle: "Having asked the first question, & of course considering myself entitled by the common rules of politeness to the first answer, after a pause . . . I reiterated my first enquiry of 'What Ship is that'?" Both officers refused to answer as a matter of pride; the dilemma was intensified because one party did not realize the other had spoken first.

At this point one side fired, and in the confused moments that followed, a deluge of iron spewed from both ships. Some minutes later, Rodgers again hailed, "What Ship is that?" A voice responded, "His Britannic Majesty," but the wind swallowed the ship's name. For Rodgers, this answer was enough to discontinue the engagement.

As day broke some fifty miles outside the entrance to Chesapeake Bay on 17 May 1811, the two warships remained in sight. Rodgers sent over a boat with an officer. Bingham identified himself as commander of the British sloop *Little Belt*, and Rodgers' officer stated that he belonged to the U.S. frigate *President*. When Bingham asked why the *President* had fired, the American officer claimed the British had fired first. Bingham railed that this "was positively not the case." To make matters worse, the much larger *President* had completely shattered the *Little Belt*, killing or wounding thirty-two of her crew. Rodgers asserted that such bloodshed "would cause me the most acute pain during the remainder of my life, had I not the consolation to know that there was no alternative left me, between such a sacrifice & one which would have been still greater; namely to have remained a passive spectator of insult to the Flag of my Country, whilst it was confided to my protection."[1]

"The affair of the *President* and *Little Belt*, so contested on the point of fact, but which I believe was unpremeditated at least by the governments on both sides, has every appearance of hastening the crisis," concluded the U.S. ambassador to Russia.[2] The bloody affair was indicative of larger problems involving issues of honor and misunderstandings leading up to the War of 1812.

The heart of the issue was much broader and signaled that the established rules of maritime commerce had deteriorated in an international environment dominated by a series of wars between Britain and France, and at times with Spain or with other European states. In these conflicts spanning the eighteenth century, Britain's survival rested on financial strength, global commerce, and naval power. Victory generally resulted from something more, be it victories on the European continent by British and allied armies or the conquest of colonies. Britain entered the longest, most expensive, and most unlimited of these European wars in 1793. Over the next two decades, Britain fought successive French revolutionary regimes followed by Napoleon and his European allies with only a short pause resulting from the Peace of Amiens. Throughout the conflict, British commercial and naval power grew relentlessly. Britain swept French merchant vessels from the sea and attempted to impose its will on neutrals, including the United States. Concurrently, France obtained stunning land victories over continental challengers. However, the asymmetry between French land power and British sea power meant that neither could strike a decisive blow.

By 1812 Britain possessed half the world's warship tonnage, an unprecedented figure for any state between 1500 and 1850, and its navy arguably stood at the height of its power, having emerged victorious in all its fleet battles since 1793. In smaller actions the British navy looked nearly as impressive. In 1811 no British warship larger than an 18-gun sloop had struck her colors because of combat.[3] Moreover, the missions the Royal Navy undertook were more expansive than any contemporary navy and included policing the oceans, controlling maritime trade, blockading French warships, and supporting land forces.

Though impressive in record and capability, the Royal Navy suffered from a serious flaw. In May 1813 a letter published in an influential British naval journal complained, "Look at our ships, how they are manned at the breaking out of a war, and compare them with the generality of ships now commissioned, and the difference will be most striking: it cannot be otherwise, on account of the vast number of ships at this time in commission, which are now manned by a very small proportion of able seamen, and the remainder filled up with good, bad, and indifferent, *viz.* ordinary seamen, landsmen, *foreigners*, the sweepings of *Newgate*, from the *hulks*, and almost all the prisons in the country."[4]

Naval officers also complained about the manning of their warships. In December 1811 one captain described his crew as "not at all what I would wish them to be, or what they ought to be." The next month, another explained that "such a miserable Crew, I have never before, had the misfortune to command." A third captain wrote in June 1814, "We have not a bad Ships company, tho' a very weak one, as the last supplies of men, . . . were lads much too slight for working Guns of the calibre, this ship is armed with."[5]

Inadequate in quality and quantity, manning the British navy has been described as "its most intractable problem."[6] Skilled seamen took years to train, and without them the wooden warships of the Royal Navy were frankly useless. Attrition suffered in two decades of warfare against Revolutionary and Napoleonic France—and at times Spain, Denmark, and a number of other countries—meant that finding seamen for Britain's warships became ever more difficult, especially since the Royal Navy competed for manpower against more-attractive employment opportunities in merchant ships. Volunteers for the naval service did not prove sufficient, and the navy's leadership resorted to forcible recruitment or impressment. Used in every war of the eighteenth century, it was extraordinarily unpopular in Britain, but the strategic imperative of keeping the Royal Navy operational provided naval leaders with a justification for the questionable practice of impressment.[7]

Manpower deficiencies and the inability to replace human attrition contributed to a decline in the Royal Navy's strength by the time of the War of 1812. The number of ships in operational commands fell from 596 in July 1809 to 515 in July 1812, even though the navy's commitments had not declined proportionately. The 515 ships of July 1812 resulted in a savings of 12,070 men over what was necessary for the 596 ships of 1809.[8] These manpower figures were based on authorized complements, but ships were not always manned to this level.[9] To keep more warships at sea, their authorized complements were reduced to less than optimal numbers, leading one contemporary to write, "The *matériel* and *personnel* were more than ever out of their due proportions."[10]

The British navy consistently had more ships than could be manned, but one should be careful in counting ships. Several studies cite British naval strength at approximately one thousand warships.[11] Though true on paper, this figure included everything from stationary ships to prison hulks; instead, the number of operational ships by the late Napoleonic period varied over time between five hundred and six hundred. In a comparative framework, this was still quite impressive, since the American navy during the War of 1812 had but fifteen to twenty ocean-going warships, and only briefly in July 1812 were even ten at sea simultaneously.[12]

One common assumption is that Britain handily defeated its opponents and recommissioned the captured warships, but the role of captures can be overstated.[13] In July 1812 the British navy had 515 ships in operational commands, 78 percent of them of British construction. Longevity proved more important than commissioning captures. In mid-1812 the average time since the launch date for a deployed frigate was 12.4 years. Ships of the line were even older, with an average launch date of mid-1798.[14] Keeping older ships operational proved key to Britain's naval power. Sustaining such a large and aged fleet demanded superb management, tremendous financial outlays, and harnessing increasing levels of industrialization. In these areas, Britain's early-nineteenth-century capabilities dwarfed its rivals.[15] Ship production and maintenance certainly posed less of a problem than manning them, and, in some respects, Britain's material advantages offset manpower deficiencies.

The Royal Navy had three basic types of warships—ships of the line, frigates, and smaller vessels (see Table 1.1). Ships of the line, sometimes called battleships, were the navy's most imposing ships, designed to stand in a line of battle and trade broadsides in fleet-on-fleet engagements. The largest ships of the line comprised the first and second rates with three full gun decks, rated for ninety or more guns. By late in the Napoleonic period their number had declined, and they played little role in the War of 1812 since the stoutest U.S. warships in 1812 were very large frigates like the *President*.[16] Increasingly, the 74-gun third rate with two full gun decks, possessing a superior ratio between cost, seaworthiness, firepower, speed, and crew size, dominated British ships of the line.[17]

Frigates were capable of nearly everything except standing in a line of battle. Particularly, they could undertake independent missions, and they were excellent for patrol, scouting, and convoy escorts. Frigates required a third to half the men of a ship of the line, and by 1812 British frigates were normally rated for thirty-six or thirty-eight guns. Thirty-six-gun frigates displaced slightly less than one thousand tons, and the 38-gun variety displaced slightly more. Both types generally had a principal armament of 18-pound long guns mounted on a single continuous gun deck running the length of the frigate. Additional lighter cannons and carronades were mounted one deck higher. This was not a continuous gun deck; instead,

Table 1.1. Total Number of Deployed Warships in the Royal Navy, 1 July 1812

	Type	Guns	Number
Ships of the line	First rates	100+	7
"	Second rates	98	6
"	Third rates	64–80	84
	Small two-decked ships	44–50	4
Frigates	Fifth rates	32–44	102
	Sixth rates	20–28	32
Smaller vessels	Sloops / Gun brigs / Cutters / etc.	less than 20	281
	Total		516

Source: Ships in Sea Pay, 1 Jul 1812, ADM 8/100.

Note: The figures for warships from the section listing unappropriated ships have not been included in the table because some of the ships on the list were not fully manned and thus were incapable of immediate operations.

several guns were placed on the forecastle at the bow of the ship, while a larger number of guns were arranged on the quarterdeck toward the stern. There were no guns placed in the middle of the ship in the area known as the waist.[18]

Smaller warships served as the catchall category. At its upper limit, these vessels were used in a manner similar to small frigates, yet each was manned by a third to half as many men and cost significantly less. The largest vessels in this category were the sixth rates; these were ship-rigged with three masts (foremast, mainmast, and mizzenmast), and often looked like miniature frigates, having a quarterdeck and forecastle. More numerous were the two-masted brig sloops. Flush-decked— meaning they did not have a true forecastle or quarterdeck—they were designed as instruments of sea control, to project British sea power. They were generally adequate for patrolling, escorting convoys, and working in the littorals. The most common warship of this type was the *Cruizer* class that displaced just less than four hundred tons with a standard armament of 2 x long 6-pound guns and 16 x 32-pound carronades.[19] Britain also possessed a significant number of gunbrigs, or large gunboats mounting approximately twelve guns. They lacked the endurance of the sloops and were generally used close to bases as well as in the littorals and constricted waters. Not surprisingly many gunbrigs served around the British Isles and in the Baltic. The Royal Navy also had a few cutters and schooners that were used primarily for dispatch and patrol work.[20]

By the War of 1812, the majority of the guns on smaller vessels were carronades. Much lighter than standard guns, they threw a heavy weight of metal, albeit for short distances. The carronade allowed small warships to have the highest broadside-to-tonnage ratio of any type of warship in the Royal Navy. For example, the British originally intended that the lead ship of what became the numerous *Cruizer* class have an armament of 18 x 6-pound long guns, but by substituting carronades, her broadside weight increased from 54 to 262 pounds.[21]

Though this change increased lethality, British carronades had certain design faults, according to William James. As a historian of the Royal Navy and a contemporary of the period, James learned from naval officers that British carronades were lighter than their American counterparts, making them unsteady in action. British carronades also had shorter muzzles and longer breeches, meaning the weapons heated more rapidly with firing; in addition, British rounds did not carry as far as those shot from American carronades. James asserted that design faults were found in all sizes of British carronades but were particularly pronounced in the 18-pound type.[22]

Of the major navies, Britain's made the greatest use of frigates and smaller vessels. This was particularly true after Trafalgar. Though the British took the possibility of a large fleet engagement seriously, the French navy rarely put to sea in numbers, and Britain had to devote increasing attention to policing the seas and attempting to control maritime communications.[23] As the dominant naval power, Britain had to be prepared for potential and developing threats and sustain a presence, especially in strategically important areas. This entailed the need to patrol ever-larger geographic areas and resulted in new commands, including distinct commands off the east coast of South America and at the Cape of Good Hope. Even after the British captured the last French base at Mauritius in 1810 and the last Dutch base at Java in 1811, the British kept eighteen warships, of which ten were frigates, in the Indian Ocean through 1813.[24] Moreover, these were difficult commands to sustain, given their distance from the British Isles. Smaller warships provided Britain an effective means of exercising command of the sea with fewer seamen; however, the use of smaller warships meant they might be lost if the situation in a region deteriorated. In such cases the British attempted to surge reinforcements to reestablish their naval presence. This certainly occurred in several regions during the War of 1812. The complexity of managing near-global deployments and assessing risk made exercising command a far more nuanced and potentially a more difficult aim than gaining command. Moreover, exercising command was an indefinite object that did not end with the war.

Tracking fleet deployments in the first half of 1812 sheds light on Britain's wartime priorities. The principal battle fleets operated in the Mediterranean Sea, the North Sea, and the southern approaches to the English Channel so as to blockade the French naval bases such as Toulon, Antwerp, and Brest. These British battle fleets were needed to confront Napoleon's expansive naval-building program after Trafalgar that emphasized the construction of ships of the line with the object of creating a quantitatively superior fleet. As long as Napoleon sustained a naval-building program, the British had to maintain its blockade squadrons. This imperative drained approximately 70 percent of the Royal Navy's ships of the line and involved defensive deployments where the initiative rested with the French: they could pick the time to sail, whereas the Royal Navy had to maintain a constant presence off French naval ports in all weather conditions. But, as one British admiral put it, "stopping the Enemy's ships in port where they can be so easily confined" was the purpose of the blockading squadrons.[25] However, the British Admiralty worried about "the great and daily increasing force of the Enemy in all their different ports." In June 1812 directions went out to fleet commanders to maintain an ever-more-vigilant blockade. Assessments of long-term trends were even more discouraging, with one Admiralty official questioning "how it will even be possible to keep up the system of Blockade as he increases his force is beyond my comprehension for it is totally impossible to increase our navy in that ratio."[26]

Deploying adequate forces to confront French naval construction had begun to stress the Royal Navy on the eve of the War of 1812, especially since other strategic imperatives also required the precious warships. Deployments in the Baltic during the latter years of the Napoleonic Wars served a two-fold purpose of protecting convoys carrying naval stores essential to Britain's naval survival, and attempting to prevent the Baltic from becoming a lake dominated by France and especially its allies. Off the Spanish and Portuguese coasts, additional deployments supported the land campaign on the Iberian Peninsula being orchestrated by the future Duke of Wellington.[27]

Outside Europe prior to 1812, the British had slowly eliminated all colonies belonging to France and its associates; once these colonies were in British hands, the Admiralty did not recall its naval squadrons. Instead, the British continued to exercise command of the sea since its economic system demanded the maintenance of deployments to protect Britain's colonies and trade routes. Britain's imports more than doubled between 1796 and 1814, while exports increased by a third and re-exports nearly tripled.[28] To safeguard expanding trade, naval squadrons were retooled to reflect threats in their areas of operation. Rather than battle fleets, squadrons on foreign stations served as reminders of British power with limited capabilities to deal with emerging threats. Without exception, the Royal Navy's foreign squadrons were situated along or at the terminus of her sea-lines of communications, inextricably linking trade routes with naval deployments.

The interaction between North Atlantic trade routes and British naval deployments does much to explain the nature of the War of 1812 on the oceans. Wind and currents both impeded and dictated the movement of sailing ships to create a high level of predictability in the path and timing of maritime commerce. Predictability led to vulnerability and the potential for interdiction. To minimize maritime risk, Britain created a convoy system that became increasingly pervasive and sophisticated during the Napoleonic Period.[29]

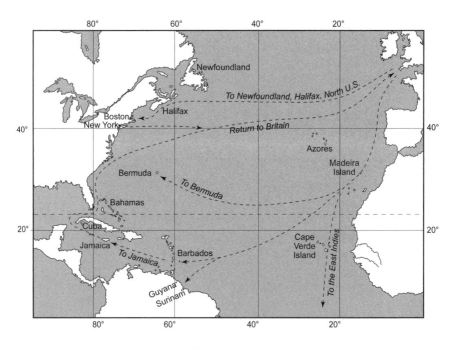

Map 1.1 The North Atlantic Trade Routes

In the Atlantic, currents and winds move in a clockwise pattern. Convoys leaving the United Kingdom stretched south and west toward Madeira. This island could be seen from far off, given its mountainous topography, so it served as a rendezvous for scattered British convoys. Ships continuing toward South America and the East Indies pressed south of Madeira, while ships headed for the Caribbean and

North America followed the current and the wind west across the Atlantic, with convoys occasionally fragmenting as ships broke off for Bermuda and the United States. As convoys approached the Windward Islands, ships for ports in present-day Guyana and Suriname parted company with the convoy, while the convoy continued to the Windward Islands. The remaining ships usually attempted to make Barbados, the most windward of the Windward Islands.[30] On this island the British based its paradoxically named Leeward Islands Station. By 1812 its missions involved patrolling the waters around the Windward and Leeward Islands, as well as the northern coast of South America.[31]

From Barbados, convoys often sailed for Jamaica. Given prevailing conditions, this was an easy voyage, but the same prevailing conditions made the reverse impossible. The inability to sail directly from Jamaica to Barbados led the Admiralty to set up an independent command at Jamaica. In 1812 the tasks of this station included protecting Jamaica and maintaining good order in the Gulf of Mexico, which led to patrols off the mouth of the Mississippi River. Given the currents, the station also included the seas around Cuba, Florida, and the Bahamas. Outbound Jamaica convoys used a favorable current to pass between Florida and Cuba and then between Florida and the Bahamas, picking up the Gulf Stream and rejoining the clockwise wind and currents of the Atlantic.[32]

By 1812 the great majority of the British warships in the Leeward Islands and Jamaica Stations consisted of sloops and other small vessels, reflecting the British Admiralty's assessment of a lack of an imminent naval threat (see Table 1.2). A British government memorandum explained that, in 1811, "nothing occurred to induce the Admiralty to increase this branch of the naval force. The French showed no disposition to push out to the West Indies; both the Haytian [*sic*] Chiefs professed friendship for England; the reception of French privateers in Spanish ports became more improbable; and, though the consideration of possible danger did not cease . . . the Admiralty . . . thought themselves justified in reducing in a small degree the West India force."[33]

Table 1.2. Comparative Strength of British Naval Stations in Total Warships

	1810	1811	1812
Halifax Station	33	23	23
Jamaica Station	34	23	19
Leeward Islands Station	68	48	35
Totals	135	94	77

Source: British Navy in North America, 1810–13, *Castlereagh*, 8:286–87.

Commerce returning to Britain from the Leeward Islands and Jamaica Stations sailed north, paralleling the eastern seaboard of the United States and British Canada before arching eastward into the Atlantic, passing northwest of the Azores, and continuing on toward the southern coasts of England and Ireland.[34] Using the Azores as a waypoint certainly added to the vulnerability of the route, but it also served as an effective rendezvous, similar to Madeira on the way out. To minimize the risk of paralleling the U.S. coast, the British deployed a squadron based out of Halifax and Bermuda. Its assignments were numerous and included the protection of trade, the maritime defense of British Canada and Bermuda, and interactions with the United States. The latter became increasingly significant as American merchant commerce grew, propelled by U.S. neutrality in the French Revolutionary and Napoleonic Wars.

The final British squadron in North America, the Newfoundland Station, was primarily a seasonal deployment. Warships sailed from Britain between March and June to protect the Newfoundland fisheries and commerce passing the Grand Banks. Most of the station's warships wintered in the United Kingdom. Overall, this was the smallest of the North American stations, containing approximately twelve warships during the summer.[35]

Merchant shipping for the Newfoundland fisheries, often Canada, and even the northern United States departed the British Isles and then sailed west along the approximate latitude of 45° N. This was slightly north of the prevailing winds that brought the Jamaica and West Indies trade to Britain. Following the 45° latitude carried ships directly to Newfoundland; taking advantage of favorable currents and winds, ships could make the Gulf of St. Lawrence for the voyage into Quebec, Halifax, and even Boston. The return route tapped into the same prevailing winds and currents that allowed ships returning from the Caribbean to proceed via the Azores.[36]

The sea-lanes that converged on the British Isles concentrated commerce in a finite space, making it vulnerable. Moreover, convoys often scattered as they reached Britain so merchants could gain their respective ports. As a result, the British set up a station at Cork in Ireland to cover the arrival of East and West India convoys. Naval stations dotted England's east coast at Plymouth, Portsmouth, and Yarmouth, while commands at the Downes and Sheerness protected London and the Thames Estuary. A final squadron operated out of Leith (port for Edinburgh) to support trade to the north.[37]

Table 1.3 indicates that the British navy had 515 warships in operational deployments as of 1 July 1812. Of these, a far from insignificant 21 percent were stationed around the British Isles. About half of the navy operated on foreign stations, including those in the Mediterranean and Portugal. The ability to keep 260-plus warships deployed on foreign stations, some as far away as China, demonstrated the

Table 1.3. British Naval Deployments, 1 July 1812

	Ships of the line	Frigates	Smaller vessels	Total
Mediterranean	29	23	36	88
Texel & Scheldt	27	5	21	53
Baltic	10	4	25	39
Channel	14	13	9	36
Portugal	6	3	26	35
East Indies	1	15	6	22
Cape of Good Hope	1	4	3	8
South America	2	1	2	5
Leeward Islands	1	3	23	27
Jamaica	1	4	13	18
North America	1	5	17	23
Newfoundland	0	4	8	12
Ireland	0	4	9	13
Channel Islands	0	1	10	11
Plymouth	0	0	12	12
Portsmouth	4	3	23	30
Downes	0	0	30	30
Sheerness	0	0	5	5
Yarmouth	0	0	6	6
Leith	0	2	11	13
Convoys & Particular Service	0	11	18	29
Totals	97	105	313	515

Source: Ships in Sea Pay, 1 Jul 1812, ADM 8/100.

Note: The column for frigates also contains two-decked 50-gun ships and two-decked 44-gun ships.

complexity of the logistic and administrative systems developed by Britain, especially considering that no other single contemporary navy had so many ocean-going warships in its inventory.[38]

Even with its comparatively large size, Britain's commitments meant that its navy was stretched thin when the United States declared war in June 1812. The Royal Navy continued to fight the existential threat of Napoleonic France. At the same time, the British navy enforced good order at sea on a near-global basis, while the Royal Navy's size had declined from 596 deployed ships in 1809 to 515 in July 1812. Moreover, the United States was a potentially dangerous opponent with many trained sailors and a small navy. In addition, North America was far from the British Isles, presenting logistical and deployment problems. Experience from the American Revolution and an understanding of geography foretold that the war would have a significant naval component. However, Britain's naval leadership lacked the ability to rapidly surge forces to the North American area of operations. Only six ships of the line, six frigates, and eleven smaller warships were in reserve on 1 July 1812, but some were not in a condition for distant deployments and the manning level of these ships varied.[39] Reallocating ships from other commands was an option, but few commands had underutilized assets. Taken together, these factors meant that British leadership faced a high level of uncertainty at the outbreak of hostilities, and the Admiralty lacked the means to rapidly reinforce the commands most affected by the War of 1812.

Whereas Britain dominated the seas in the years before the War of 1812, the United States leveraged its neutral status to facilitate trade with all belligerents. In the process, American exports more than quadrupled between 1793 and 1807. The rising trade led to the merchant marine growing from 558,000 tons in 1802 to 981,000 in 1810, making the United States the largest neutral trading state of the time.[40]

For the United States, the protection of commerce spurred the development of a small navy and led to combat deployments. Between 1798 and 1800 the United States waged an undeclared naval war against France to defend American commercial rights. Known as the Quasi-War, the American navy gained its first victories.[41] Soon after, American warships deployed to the Mediterranean to confront several North African states. Often called the "Barbary pirates," the North Africans used the dislocation of the European conflict to reassert their historical position by preying on the Mediterranean commerce of countries refusing to provide tribute. Rather than pay, the United States sent its navy.[42] Neither the Quasi-War nor problems with the North African states would have occurred as they did if American merchant ships had not plied the oceans, and if the dislocation of the European war had not created maritime instability that led to the harassment of U.S. maritime commerce.

In addition to the above problems, a maritime conflict slowly festered between Britain and the United States over the following three, often overlapping, issues: the impressment of U.S. citizens into the British navy, the free passage of U.S. merchant shipping, and rising naval antagonism between the British Royal Navy and the United States Navy.

Impressment, or forcible recruitment, proved integral for manning the British navy. The Royal Navy asserted its right to stop British and foreign-flagged ships and remove any British subjects for service in the navy. Though British law made it illegal to impress foreigners, those claiming U.S. citizenship caused tremendous difficulties. Augustus Foster, the British minister to Washington immediately prior to the War of 1812, explained, "The inconvenience necessarily resulting from the similarity of habits, language, and manner, between the Inhabitants of the two Countries is productive of Subjects of Complaint and regret."[43] A related problem involved the transfer of citizenship or naturalization. American officials allowed individuals to obtain citizenship after two years of residence in the United States or two years of service on board a ship sailing under the American flag. But, an English official maintained, "If no distinction can be made by the government of the United States, between native and naturalized Citizens; and if every British Seaman who escapes to America may, if he pleases, become a naturalized Subject, it seems to be useless to enter into any discussion or arrangement . . . as it is presumed that we shall never abandon that universally acknowledged maxim in the Law of Nations, that a Subject cannot throw off his allegiance which follows him wherever he goes."[44] The British and American views of naturalization differed; the British only considered those born in the United States or residing there before 1783 as legitimate U.S. citizens. Rudimentary records and documentation further complicated the issue by making it easy to create fraudulent records. Britain's First Lord of the Admiralty lamented in 1801, "Thus it becomes a very difficult point to draw the line, and I have always considered this as the greatest evil arising from the separation."[45]

As with most divisive issues, there were two perspectives. On the one hand, the United States justly demanded respect for its citizens' rights, and to be sure, legitimate U.S. citizens were forced to serve on board British warships. On the other hand, British and American law defined citizenship differently; seamen made pervasive use of fraudulent proofs of U.S. citizenship; and perhaps most important, Britain's war with France demanded a powerful navy for self-preservation. To support the vital interest of British sea power, Royal Navy leadership had no recourse within its existing system but to rely on impressment. Those falsely impressed used diplomatic and other channels to obtain release. British leaders believed they acted liberally, and one Royal Navy officer was probably not far off when he complained in 1806, "Be assured half the men we discharge as Americans are English seamen."[46]

Another vital British national interest involved maintaining the free flow of its commerce while restricting French commercial activities. Whereas the United States supported the free flow of commerce, restrictions on trade contradicted American economic interests. To make the issue more contentious, the French government promoted neutral commerce as a way to work around British naval dominance. Moreover, French regulations made it illegal for American merchants to trade with Britain. In other words, if the United States followed British regulations, the French felt cheated, while the British cried foul when American merchants followed French commercial dictates. American merchants were not innocent, as they parlayed neutrality into economic gain by attempting to trade with both belligerents.[47]

Such shifty maneuvering proved difficult to monitor, but both France and Britain deemed it important to exercise some control over foreign trade. This was particularly true following Trafalgar. Between 1805 and 1807, British naval dominance grew, while France won land victories at Austerlitz, Jena, Auerstädt, and Friedland. The result was a stalemate between the world's greatest land and sea powers. To break the deadlock, both Britain and France turned to economic warfare. Most notably, Napoleon tried the Continental System and the British the Orders in Council. Napoleon's system, an attempt to control maritime commerce without naval power, emerged in late 1806 and was refined during the subsequent years. Napoleon leveraged his land power by forcing most areas of continental Europe to exclude or confiscate trade from Britain, or trade that had passed through the British Isles, or commerce on board merchant vessels visited by British warships. The British Orders in Council demanded that merchant vessels trading with continental Europe obtain an English license. Following British dictates resulted in French confiscation, and following French dictates resulted in capture by British warships.[48]

Since the United States was the largest neutral trading power, the depredations resulting from the French Continental System and the British Orders in Council were keenly felt. Though the actions of both Britain and France economically damaged the United States, President Thomas Jefferson aptly wrote, "We resist the enterprises of England first, because they first come vitally home to us."[49] In this, he referred to the reach of the Royal Navy that allowed greater power of enforcement and created a constant source of friction at sea that proved impossible to ameliorate. One member of the U.S. Congress put it like this: "Not only the safety of her [Britain's] colonies abroad, but that of her very existence as an independent nation depends upon her naval superiority."[50]

Commercial and impressment issues spilled over into a developing naval conflict between Britain and the United States. One example occurred in 1805 when John Rodgers, then commanding the U.S. Mediterranean Squadron, wrote to Captain Thomas Bladen Capel of the 36-gun British frigate *Phoebe* that there were two Americans on board his ship. In response, Capel explained, "The Master of the Vessel they were impressed from, only assured me that *one* was an American, but as their Certificates were not Regular or Clear I had strong grounds for Supposing them English Seamen, but upon any assurance from you that they are really

American Subjects I shall immediately give them up." Capel ended his letter by asking for five British deserters then serving on board the American squadron. This demand incited Rodgers who replied, "Your Letter . . . if impartially dissected will prove that the Flag of the U. States is insulted." Particularly, the British captain had asked for five deserters at the same time Capel had several American deserters on board the *Phoebe*, "which you have not even given yourself the trouble to mention." Rodgers concluded that such issues "will unavoidably end in a dispute between two Nations . . . as to be injurious to both."[51] The crux of the issue involved British hubris and the corollary lack of respect felt by U.S. naval officers. The belief that they were disrespected led one American naval officer to write in 1805, "I wish the British Commanders to observe that our Service is very Independent, and I hope our Commanders will never let slip any Insult which they offer to pass with Impunity."[52]

Such words seemed prophetic only two years later on 22 June 1807, when the U.S. frigate *Chesapeake* under James Baron sailed from Hampton Roads. Just hours later, the British warship *Leopard* bore down on the *Chesapeake* and lowered a boat that went across to the American frigate. A British officer came on board and presented Barron with a letter demanding several supposed British deserters serving on board the *Chesapeake*. Barron refused, but "observ'd some appearance of an hostile Nature." Incredulously, he deduced "that it was possible they were serious." He then quietly ordered his men to quarters, but before this had occurred the *Leopard* fired, killing three men and wounding eighteen. Unready for combat, Barron ordered the *Chesapeake*'s colors struck. The British then removed four supposed deserters but refused to take possession of the *Chesapeake* as their prize.[53]

Barron then returned to Hampton Roads, where his shattered frigate caused an uproar. President Thomas Jefferson asserted "that the British commanders have their foot on the threshold of war." He wrote, "This country has never been in such a state of excitement since the battle of Lexington." The administration attempted to cool public opinion. One way was to avoid an early meeting of Congress, fearing that such a gathering would result in a declaration of war. Instead, Jefferson thought that Congress could do little until "receipt of an answer from Great Britain, before which they could only act in the dark."[54]

Perceptions in Britain painted actions by the U.S. government in a different light. In December 1807 one British observer asserted, "While Mr. Jefferson declaims with great warmth against what He calls the depredations of this country on American commerce, the numerous aggressions of France are passed over without observation. . . . The affair of the *Chesapeake* is mentioned with much irritation."[55] Even so, the British government disavowed the attack and sent reinforcements for the defense of Canada.[56]

Rather than war, the U.S. government attempted economic coercion, and Jefferson commented, "During the present paroxysm of the insanity of Europe, we have thought it wisest to break off all intercourse with her [Britain]."[57] The Americans implemented the Embargo Act of 1807 that forbade its merchant vessels from sailing to foreign ports or French and British vessels from calling at ports in the United States. One American object aimed at restricting British trade, but adverse economic effects were more pronounced in the United States.[58] The story of one American merchant indicates the resulting hardship. He returned from India in early 1808 on board a trading vessel of which he was a half owner. The majority of his cargo consisted of indigo destined for the European market, but the merchant asserted that it "was of course useless during the Embargo, and on the repeal of that measure the rigours of the Continental System and the belligerent depredations were such as to preclude exportation." Eventually, the merchant had to sell the vessel for half her cost. The indigo entered Europe through the port of Archangel in the far north of Russia, but after Napoleon's 1812 invasion of that country, the cargo was sold for a loss.[59] Though perhaps an extreme case, this individual was financially ruined by a combination of trade restrictions and the European war. Fittingly, this book features this merchant. His name was William Jones, and he served as secretary of the navy in 1813–14.

Financial distress led others into smuggling. In early 1809 Jefferson complained that "the unprincipled along our sea-coast and frontiers were fraudulently evading . . . the embargo laws." At the end of the Jefferson administration, smuggling and an economic downturn resulting from the elimination of international commerce led the U.S. government to rescind the Embargo Act.[60]

James Madison, the new president, continued to confront both Britain and France, but the U.S. government found its means limited because it was only a tangential player in the larger European war. Both Britain and France attempted to manipulate the United States so as to obtain their broader policy objectives. In this environment, President Madison had little leverage, but his administration's course of action left the United States vulnerable to European intrigues. The United States, through the Non-Intercourse Act of 1809, reestablished commerce with all states but Britain and France. The following year, trade was reopened with both countries under the condition that if either repealed its trade restrictions, the United States would trade only with that state.[61] Napoleon acted first. Though he seemed to negate the Continental System, in reality it was smoke and mirrors. From Russia, American ambassador John Quincy Adams surmised that France "had laid the trap which she concluded would catch us in an English war."[62]

The United States Navy and the Royal Navy served as tripwires in the increasingly charged international environment following the *Chesapeake* affair. Lingering enmity contributed to the *President* shattering the *Little Belt* in May 1811, but other examples of violence occurred. On 24 June 1810 near the Bahamas the 18-gun British warship *Moselle* fired a single round into the 14-gun *Vixen* of the United

States Navy. It struck less than three feet from where George Poindexter, a member of Congress, stood. Incensed and likely embarrassed, John Trippe, the *Vixen's* commander, sent across an officer for an explanation. The British captain asserted he had not seen the American colors and mistook the *Vixen* for a French vessel. Poindexter concluded, "The character of the affair, however, corresponds with the treatment which we have so often received from the British Naval Commanders, on former occasions." He continued, "The insolence of the transaction is not more remarkable than the meanness displayed by the British Commander." Yet, by Trippe's admission, "On approaching her, a boat put off I supposed, to speak me, about which time she fired a gun. Having a fair wind and all sail set, I determined not to heave to, presuming the English Brig recognized me as an American Vessel of War, but haul'd up so as to permit the officer of the boat to come alongside." Given the *Vixen's* movements, one could argue that it was not unreasonable that the commander of the *Moselle* mistook her for a French vessel and fired a round at her.[63] Though minor in comparison to the *Leopard* and the *Chesapeake* or the *President* and the *Little Belt*, this incident added to the friction. Though the lives of many were at stake, officers on both sides viewed encounters through the prism of their country's honor. Disrespect and injury of this honor, even if only perceived, made relations between Britain and the United States increasingly explosive.

As tensions built, questions about the size and composition of the United States Navy became contentious. President Thomas Jefferson had argued vehemently for a gunboat navy designed for littoral defense as "the only *water* defence which can be useful to us, & protect us from the ruinous folly of a navy."[64] On the oceans Jefferson believed in the extensive use of commerce-raiding privateers as "the most powerful weapon we can employ against Great Britain."[65] Privateers had the distinction of not costing the U.S. government money, since they were procured, fitted, and manned by private citizens as a type of business venture seeking financial gain for capturing commerce of hostile states.

Though the reliance on gunboats and privateers captivated Jefferson, the United States Navy throughout his presidency contained a few ocean-going warships, including several large frigates. In January 1806 the navy counted four frigates and nine smaller ocean-going vessels ready for service, as well as six frigates in need of repair.[66] Scarce funding meant that the United States Navy comprised the same set of frigates at the outbreak of hostilities in 1812 as it had in 1806.

To manage an underfunded navy, Jefferson's successor, President James Madison, chose Paul Hamilton in 1809. A civilian with cabinet rank and the official

Secretary of the U.S. Navy, Paul Hamilton
(Navy History and Heritage Command, Photo # NH 54757-KN)

title of secretary of the navy, Hamilton had little experience in naval matters, but he had previously served as the comptroller and governor of South Carolina. Given the difficult fiscal constraints faced by a peacetime navy, this might not have been a bad résumé for the position. Less than a year after becoming secretary, he wrote, "It appears now very uncertain whether Congress will authorize the repair of frigates, and it becomes proper to take every precautionary measure for the relief of our funds." He concluded, "I have therefore to request that you will *incur no expence whatever* under the head of Repairs of vessels without previous special instructions from me."[67] Between 1809 and 1811 Hamilton repeatedly told Madison that appropriations for the repair of warships were inadequate. Particularly, Congress failed to provide funds to maintain frigates in ordinary (laid up in reserve).[68]

As the prospect of war with Britain increased, influential people called for naval expansion. James Monroe, who would hold the position of secretary of state during much of the War of 1812, argued "that our naval force ought to be increased." Particularly, he "urged that the naval force of the U. States . . . [be augmented] to the strength of the squadrons which they usually stationed in time of war on our coast, at the mouths of our great rivers, and in our harbours. I thought that such a force, incorporated permanently into our system, would give weight at all times to our negotiations with foreign powers, and by means thereof prevent wars and save money."[69]

By 1811 Hamilton, probably influenced by senior naval officers, had become a stalwart believer that Jeffersonian gunboats would not suffice and that large warships were needed.[70] Hamilton clarified, "I am happy in knowing that my little establishment (the navy) is complete as to its present extent—I have no apprehensions ship, gun, and man, when exposed to foreign force—yet I may live to see them overwhelmed by superior force—but if they fall, they will fall nobly—My commanders are of my own choice, and their crews are (as they inform me) equal to their wishes."[71] Though Hamilton believed in his officers or had become enchanted by their spell, he was sanguine enough to realize that his warships were too few in number to do more than die gallantly. To avoid this fate, Hamilton used a November 1811 query from Langdon Cheves, the chairman of the Navy Committee for the House of Representatives, to argue for a larger navy.[72]

Hamilton asked for twelve 74-gun ships of the line and increasing American frigate strength to twenty. This necessitated the navy's sweeping expansion, considering its ocean-going strength in late 1811 comprised five frigates and nine smaller ocean-going warships in service, as well as five frigates in ordinary. By adding ships of the line and new frigates, Hamilton believed that the navy "would be ample to the protection of our coasting trade; would be competent to annoy extensively the commerce of an enemy; and, uniting occasionally in operations with the gunboats already built, if equipped and brought into service, and our fortifications, also afford complete protection to our harbors."[73]

Cheves brought Hamilton's requests before the House of Representatives in January 1812. The House debate over the navy's requests proved contentious, since the proposed naval construction would cut deeply into the scarce funds available to the government; moreover, it showcased regional divisions within the country as to the perception of the navy's utility.[74] Questions were raised on whether a dozen 74-gun ships of the line and twenty frigates would be enough. One speaker explained that he approved of funding the repair of existing frigates but was not "very fond of *water animals* of the size described." He spoke against the new construction, asserting, "If the United States authorized to build these frigates, they could not be done in time for the present emergency."[75] In the end, funding was approved for repairing existing frigates, but new frigate construction was defeated narrowly sixty-two to fifty-nine, and a vote to build only four ships of the line failed by a greater margin. The Senate went a step further by authorizing the repair of only three of the five frigates in ordinary.[76]

Table 1.4. The United States Navy, June 1812

Name of Warship	Rate	Location
President	44	New York
United States	44	New York
Constitution	44	Annapolis
Congress	36	New York
Essex	32	New York
John Adams	20	Boston
Hornet	16	New York
Wasp	16	At Sea
Argus	16	New York
Siren	16	New Orleans
Nautilus	14	Boston
Enterprize	14	New Orleans
Vixen	14	St. Marys
Viper	10	New Orleans

With the congressional debate at an end, Hamilton knew more about the size and funding of the navy as the country moved toward war. Of the frigates in ordinary, Hamilton noted, "Until these vessels shall be opened and thoroughly examined, it is obviously impossible to ascertain, with any degree of precision, . . . what time it would take to repair them."[77] Repair of the three frigates went slowly. Even at the time of the declaration of war, neither the *Constellation* nor the *Chesapeake* was ready.[78] It was reported that the *Adams,* "from her extreme state of decay that to repair her afloat, will be far more expensive than to build a new ship." Since funding was available for her repair, not for building a new warship, she was rebuilt.[79]

Though Hamilton reported on 3 December 1811 that the navy contained five serviceable frigates and nine smaller ocean-going warships, the first half of 1812 was spent trying to make several of these warships combat ready (see Table 1.4). In early 1812 the *United States, Constitution, John Adams,* and *Nautilus,* all supposedly serviceable according to Hamilton's pronouncement of December 1811, underwent significant repairs.[80] Though the *Essex* had been described as being "in good order for service" in February 1812, not four months later on 10 June, only a little more than a week before the declaration of war, the *Essex* had to have her copper cleaned; in the process workers determined that her foremast also required work and she would not be ready for operations until late June.[81] Moreover, the *Constitution* was not ready to sail at the time of the declaration of war owing to the lack of seamen.[82]

At the outbreak of the War of 1812, the largest warships in the United States Navy were three heavy 44-gun frigates. Named the *Constitution, President,* and *United States,* a British Admiralty document later explained that "though they may be called Frigates, [they] are of a size, Complement, and weight of Metal much beyond that Class, and more resembling Line of Battle Ships." The American naval leadership during the War of 1812 labeled them frigates, though, and Theodore Roosevelt in his naval history of the War of 1812 argued, "The American 44-gun frigate was a true frigate."[83] Such statements highlight the controversial nature of these warships that has both clouded and influenced much writing on the War of 1812.

In size, the 44-gun American frigates displaced about 40 percent more than British 38-gun frigates and about 50 percent more than British 36-gun frigates, the two types that dominated Royal Navy deployments. In addition, the heavy American frigates with 24-pound long guns on the gun deck exceeded the firepower of the 18-pound guns of British 36- and 38-gun frigates.[84] Large American frigates were slightly smaller than British 74-gun ships of the line, however, and the broadside of a ship of the line was heavier, particularly in long guns, as indicated by Table 1.5.

Table 1.5. Comparative Strength of British and American Warships

	36-gun frigate	38-gun frigate	36-gun frigate	44-gun frigate	74-gun ship
	Belvidera	Macedonian	Chesapeake	President	Valiant
Tonnage	946	1,081	1,135	1,533	1,718
	Guns	Guns	Guns	Guns	Guns
Lower deck	—	—	—	—	28 x 32lb
Upper deck	26 x 18lb	28 x 18lb	28 x 18lb	30 x 24lb	28 x 18lb
Forecastle and quarterdeck or spar deck	2 x 9lb, 14 x 32lb*	2 x 9lb, 16 x 32lb*	20 x 32lb*	2 x 24lb, 22 x 42lb*	8 x 12lb, 12 x 32lb*
Roundhouse	—	—	—	—	6 x 18lb*
	Broadside	Broadside	Broadside	Broadside	Broadside
Long guns	243lb	261lb	261lb	384lb	748lb
Carronades	224lb	256lb	320lb	462lb	246lb

* Carronades.

Note: For the tonnage of all warships in the table, see Winfield, British Warships in the Age of Sail, 78, 124, 168, 173, 188. In U.S. sources, the tonnage for the President is listed as 1,576 tons and for the Chesapeake as 1,244 tons. See Silverstone, Sailing Navy, 26–27, 30. For these warships, the British tonnage was used in the table because this allowed for a more even comparison. For armament, see ADM 7/556; Chapelle, American Sailing Navy, 132. Guns placed aloft are not included. Chase guns are included in the broadside weight. In addition, some evidence exists that the British pound weighed slightly more than an American one. Roosevelt calculated the British as 7 percent larger; see Roosevelt, Naval War, 66. However, the above numbers consider the British and American pounds to be of the same weight.

In addition to the 24-pound guns on the main gun deck, the large American frigates had either 32- or 42-pound carronades on the deck above. This deck made these frigates unusual. Normal frigates had a forecastle and quarterdeck where guns were mounted; between the forecastle and quarterdeck was an unarmed area known as the waist. This area had become smaller over the years, and by 1812 it was fitted with a gangway linking the forecastle and quarterdeck. The American 44-gun frigates eliminated the waist, creating a ship that looked flush-decked from bow to stern. Often referred to as a spar deck, this made the American frigates distinctive in appearance and gave them more deck space for weapons.[85]

The United States Navy also possessed frigates rated for thirty-six guns. These went by the names *Constellation*, *Congress*, and *Chesapeake*. Apparently, they were scaled-down versions of the 44-gun frigates. They were slightly larger than British 38-gun frigates, but, like them, the American frigates carried 28 x 18-pound long guns along with 32-pound carronades.[86]

The *Essex*, rated for thirty-two guns, was also larger than similar British warships. By 1812 her armament included 40 x 32-pound carronades and 6 x 12-pound long guns. The carronades gave the *Essex* a potent broadside, albeit one with limited range. When the British captured that frigate in 1814, they did away with her carronade-dominated armament and rerated her for thirty-six guns, though her tonnage meant she was small compared with other 36-gun ships.[87]

The design of British and American smaller warships showed strong similarities at the start of the War of 1812. As a rule, smaller warships were brigs with two masts (a mainmast and a foremast). Both the Americans and the British transitioned from brigs of two masts to ships of three masts (with a mainmast, foremast, and mizzenmast) at about the four hundred–ton mark. Three masts gave a ship more redundancy, an important attribute in combat, and also allowed warships to carry more canvas.[88]

Both the British and the Americans generally armed their smaller vessels with carronades in the broadside positions and two long guns in the bow. On the one hand, the latter served well in pursuits, since their longer range could snipe at a fleeing vessel, potentially damaging masts, sails, or rigging to allow the pursuer to come up with her quarry. On the other hand, carronades allowed for very potent broadsides in short-ranged fights and explains why engagements between smaller vessels during the War of 1812 were almost always fought at near pointblank range.

The United States Navy entered the War of 1812 with several advantages. Its warships were large, well built, and heavily armed. In particular, the Royal Navy in 1812 lacked an effective platform for a one-on-one engagement with an American

44-gun frigate. U.S. warships had all-volunteer crews with very few boys, and their ships had larger complements than comparative British warships.[89] The United States Navy, however, suffered from glaring weaknesses as war with Britain approached. Funding was scarce. There were no warships under construction, while the Royal Navy had far more ships building than the Americans had total warships. Moreover, the Americans had to contend with an aging fleet: all U.S. frigates had entered service between 1798 and 1800.[90] From Russia, the U.S. ambassador John Quincy Adams could only watch America's drift to war from afar. He concluded, "The question of a navy is a *great one.*" Penned prior to learning of the declaration of war against Britain, such words succinctly encapsulate lingering questions about what the United States Navy could achieve. Half a year earlier, in January 1812, Adams had accurately assessed that when compared to the British navy, the Americans numbered "scarcely ten to five hundred, and our principal object to contend for is unfortunately on the sea. The position which is not pleasing to acknowledge, but which it behooves us well to know and to consider."[91]

Asserting that the principal object for the United States lay at sea may have been naïve, given expansionist feelings in the United States aimed at British Canada and corollary desires to limit Native American power. Feelings even existed that war would unify the country and Madison's Republican Party.[92] Though numerous reasons led the United States toward hostilities, maritime issues were first among Madison's claims when he asked Congress for a declaration of war on 1 June 1812.[93]

The United States was ill prepared for a naval war, though. Not only were warships still undergoing repair, no warships under construction, and seamen in need of recruitment, but also decisions on how to employ America's small navy were not adequately developed in advance of the war.[94] Endemic of this lack of foresight, Secretary of the Navy Paul Hamilton, only ten days before Madison asked for a declaration of war and less than a month before Congress acquiesced, wrote Commodores John Rodgers and Stephen Decatur, "I request you to state to me, a plan of operations, which, in your judgment, will enable our little navy to annoy in the utmost extent the Trade of Great Britain, while it least exposes it to the immense naval force of that Government."[95]

Decatur responded only ten days before the declaration of war that the best course of action for the United States Navy "would be to send them out with as large a supply of provisions as they can carry, distant from our coast, & singly, or not more than two Frigates in company, without giving them any specific instructions . . . but to rely on the enterprise of the officers." If frigates operated in pairs they would have the strength to attack British convoys and would be unlikely to meet a superior British force. But if such an encounter occurred, "we would not have to regret the whole of our marine crushed at one blow." Decatur wrote, "The advantage of distant cruising would be to relieve our own coast by withdrawing from it a number of the hostile ships, or compelling the enemy to detach from Europe another force in search of us."[96]

Rodgers wrote of the strategic effects that could be realized by deploying a squadron off the British Isles because "it would be menacing them in the very teeth, & effecting the distruction of their commerce in a manner the most perplexing to their Government, & in a way the least expected by the nation generally, including those belonging to the navy: the self styled Lords of the Ocean!!" Rodgers then added his counterargument: "Such a view as I have taken of the subject may, at first sight, appear chymerical; particularly if we reason arithmetically, & take into consideration that we have only a dozen vessels in commission, & they five hundred." He then refuted this point by asserting, "This is the very reason, I think, why such dispersion should be made, as, by the like, it would require a comparatively much greater force to protect their own trade . . . than it would to annihilate ours, & our little navy with it."[97]

On the very eve of war, Hamilton and his uniformed naval leadership embraced active operations, far from American waters, targeting British trade; however, the specific plans had yet to be finalized and Madison had yet to acquiesce. In fact, the options for the United States at sea were quite limited. The United States faced the world's greatest maritime power while lacking a battle fleet for a symmetrical challenge. The extensive coasts of the United States made the nation vulnerable. Defending everywhere was simply impractical. One option involved keeping the United States Navy locked up in a few strongly protected naval bases and forcing the British to incur the cost of blockading or attacking American bases. Given feelings among the U.S. naval officer corps, such a course of action would not avenge the disrespect they believed they had repeatedly sustained from Britain. At least for the uniformed leadership of the navy, a preferred option involved a sort of guerrilla war at sea that targeted Britain's great maritime highways and inflicted losses on its merchant fleet and isolated warships. Britain's dependence on maritime commerce, its ongoing war with France, and its expansive naval commitments, coupled with structural flaws resulting in a shrinking naval establishment, meant that a guerrilla-type war orchestrated by the United States Navy had the potential to land painful blows, at least in the short term. The American navy had never faced an opponent with Britain's capabilities, however.

CHAPTER 2

"'A Little Bit of a Dust' With an English Frigate"

The Opening Naval Campaign, June to September 1812

P resident Madison's administration remained undecided about how to use the United States Navy even after war became a reality on 18 June. This led Secretary Hamilton to inform Commodore Rodgers, who had the navy's main strike force under his direct control, to "remain in such position as to enable you most conveniently to receive further more extensive & more particular orders—which will be conveyed to you through New York." Yet, Hamilton clarified, "It is understood that there are one or more British Cruisers on the coast in the vicinity of Sandy Hook [one entrance to New York harbor], You are at your discretion free to strike at them, returning immediately after into port."[1]

Thinking that Rodgers' command had been placed in something like suspended animation, the Madison administration grappled with possible uses for the navy. Albert Gallatin, the secretary of the treasury, wanted protection for returning merchant vessels that would bring import duties of at least $1 million a week. To obtain this object, Hamilton on 22 June directed two United States Navy commodores, Rodgers and Decatur, to divide the operational warships of the United States Navy between them and cover returning American merchant shipping.[2] The order, however, was never implemented.

Rodgers, upon receipt of Hamilton's 18 June letter apprising him of the declaration of war, had sailed from New York with his frigate, the 44-gun *President*; Decatur's frigate, the 44-gun *United States*; as well as the 36-gun *Congress*; the 18-gun *Hornet*; and the 16-gun *Argus*. To Hamilton, Rodgers wrote, "I shall strictly comply with your orders, but you will perceive, Sir, that I must be governed by circumstances."[3] In a second letter of the same date, Rodgers expounded on what he meant by circumstances: "I am in hopes we shall fall in with some of the British cruisers that lately came on our coast, before they are apprised of the War." But, he maintained, "My principle object, at present, however is to fall in with a large West India convoy, which from the information I have received, is now about S.E. of us, on the edge of the Gulph [*sic*]."[4] Rodgers hoped to take advantage of Britain's ignorance of hostilities, believing that every moment wasted would further limit the United States Navy's ability to combat the massive strength of the Royal Navy. When Rodgers sailed, Hamilton lost control over his primary naval force, but it took several weeks for him to realize he had lost control.

At sea, the five warships of Rodgers' squadron encountered a merchant vessel in the early morning darkness of 23 June 1812. From her master, the Americans received information that four days earlier she had encountered numerous merchant vessels escorted by a frigate and a brig. Thinking this could only be the West India convoy, Rodgers pursued, but only a few hours passed before Rodgers' lookouts descried "a large sail . . . which was soon discovered to be a Frigate."[5] Across the water, Captain Richard Byron of the 36-gun British frigate *Belvidera* also received reports that unknown warships lurked in the distance. Private signals designed to identify friendly warships went unanswered.[6]

Given the superior size of the unknown squadron, Byron fled. During the chase that ensued, he and Rodgers tried to harness every bit of wind throughout the morning and well into the afternoon as the breeze settled. During that time, only the *President* gained on the *Belvidera*: the British frigate proved faster than the other American warships.[7]

On board the *Belvidera*, Byron issued orders to his lieutenants to "prick the Cartridges, but *not* to prime the Guns. Although ignorant of the War, we were of course prepared."[8] Rodgers, however, surmised that his opponent "was training his chase guns, and in the Act (as I supposed) of firing, that the breeze was decreasing, and we now sailed so nearly alike, that to afford him an opportunity of doing the first injury to our Spars and rigging, would be to enable him to effect his escape." Taking no chances, at 4:20 p.m. Rodgers ordered his men to fire.[9]

Rodgers' order still echoed through the decks when the *President*'s bow guns belched the first shots of the War of 1812 on the high seas. Seconds later, with unnerving accuracy, several round shot slammed into the *Belvidera*'s stern. One entered the gun deck, cutting a bloody swath, killing and wounding several. The

Belvidera then returned fire in order to slow the *President*'s pursuit.[10] Ten minutes later, an explosion ripped through the *President*'s bow. As the smoke cleared, a grisly scene emerged. A gun had burst, setting off the ready powder. Sixteen lay dead or wounded and neighboring batteries were "shattered." Though injured in the explosion, Rodgers remained on deck and ordered the undamaged starboard broadside to bear, but it failed to cause significant damage.[11]

Despite the setback, Rodgers pressed his ship and her crew forward. In a desperate bid to close with *Belvidera*, he ordered his men wet the sails to better catch the air. That ploy failed, however, prompting Rodgers to "steer directly after him, and to keep our bow chase guns playing on his Spars and rigging, until our broadside would more effectively reach him." At 5:00 p.m. Rodgers altered course to unmask his broadside, but it did little damage because "the sea was so very smooth, and the wind so light that the injury done was not such as materially to affect his sailing." Afterwards, Rodgers had his frigate regain her position in his opponent's wake, and for the next ninety minutes the *President*'s bow chasers traded shots with the *Belvidera*'s stern guns. By 6:30 p.m. Rodgers had again closed, this time within the range of grape shot, but the *Belvidera*'s fire had done considerable mischief.[12]

As the engagement entered its third hour, damage mounted on board the *Belvidera*, slowing her enough for the other American warships to draw near. The *Congress* opened fire but her shot fell short. In response, Byron ordered his men to lighten his ship by cutting away an anchor. The crew also jettisoned four ship's boats and started fourteen tons of water over the side. As a result, the lightened *Belvidera* quickly left the American squadron well astern.[13] Rodgers later recounted, "I now perceived with more mortification than words can express, that there was little or no chance left of getting within gun shot of the Enemy again."[14] Though bruised, battered, and disappointed, Rodgers did not return to New York as Hamilton had ordered; instead, he sailed in search of his primary object, the West India convoy.

For the British, Byron asserted, "The necessity of retreat was painful to every one on board the *Belvidera*."[15] The Royal Navy was the most powerful in the world with a tradition of victory. Running from an opponent never set well, even when the odds demanded it. One of Byron's fellow British captains, conversely, wrote of "a most honorable action between *Belvidera* & almost all the American navy . . . Their conduct indeed was dastardly . . . as Byron made a steady retreat & with a constant sharp fire on them for three hours whilst they might at once have *crushed him* by closer battle, but they had not spirit to run him alongside." This officer had a point. Prior to Byron lightening his frigate and the *President* sustaining significant damage aloft, Rodgers had the fastest warship in the encounter and the ability and firepower to close with the *Belvidera*.[16] Perhaps the bursting of the gun and Rodgers' wound cooled his ardor, or perhaps he did not want to trade broadsides, being fearful that the damage would prevent him from continuing after the convoy. But for whatever reason, the action served only to betray the existence of hostilities.

The *Belvidera* limped into Halifax four days after encountering Rodgers' squadron. The commander of the British North America Station, Vice Admiral Herbert Sawyer, first considered it "as a *private spiteful attack* of Commodore Rogers [*sic*]," similar to Rodgers' 1811 action against the *Little Belt*. As such, Sawyer sent a vessel under a flag of truce to New York in case the event had been a misunderstanding.[17]

Within a few days, however, additional information confirmed this was no isolated incident, but rather the start of hostilities. This forced Sawyer to act on his own initiative because it took several months for reports of hostilities to cross the Atlantic by ship, be answered by Sawyer's superiors at the Admiralty in London, and the Admiralty's new instructions reach their commander in North America after a second, long ocean transit. In the meantime, Sawyer had to process available intelligence, prepare his forces, and hope that the Americans did not defeat his squadron in detail. His command comprised the 64-gun *Africa*, five frigates (including the *Belvidera*), and seventeen smaller warships.[18] Though this squadron outnumbered the entire United States Navy, its tasks included the patrol of the coastline from the Gulf of St. Lawrence to the Bay of Fundy and south along the eastern seaboard of the United States, as well as the naval defense of Halifax and Bermuda and escorting convoys. Such far-ranging assignments left few warships immediately available for operations against the United States.

At Halifax, Sawyer had only two large warships—the *Africa* and the *Belvidera*. However, on 2 July the 38-gun *Shannon* and the 32-gun *Aeolus* arrived.[19] Sawyer ordered Captain Philip Broke of the *Shannon* to take all four of these warships and "use your utmost endeavours to Capture, or destroy all ships under the American Flag."[20] Sawyer had taken a risk. Dispatching these warships left Halifax unprotected, and he lacked additional vessels to stay in communication with Broke's squadron.

Broke proceeded toward the American coast on 5 July. At sea, four days later, the 38-gun British frigate *Guerriere* joined Broke's squadron. Though his squadron destroyed four American merchant vessels in "hope thus to make the Enemy feel the Evils of the War they have so wantonly began," Broke's main object was the U.S. squadron under Rodgers, but he needed intelligence. With that in mind, Broke had the *Shannon* stand toward the entrance to Long Island Sound, leaving the remainder of his squadron hidden over the horizon. To allay American suspicions, he ordered U.S. colors hoisted. This was an acceptable ruse as long as he did not fire under false colors, and soon two local fishermen came alongside. Broke

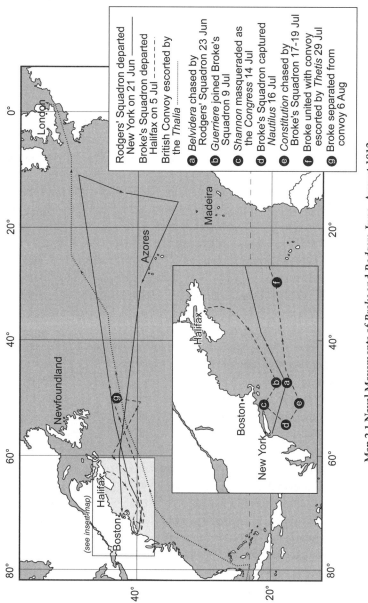

Rodgers' Squadron departed
New York on 21 Jun ——————
Broke's Squadron departed
Halifax on 5 Jul ---------
British Convoy escorted by
the *Thalia* ············

ⓐ *Belvidera* chased by
   Rodgers' Squadron 23 Jun
ⓑ *Guerriere* joined Broke's
   Squadron 9 Jul
ⓒ *Shannon* masqueraded as
   the *Congress* 14 Jul
ⓓ Broke's Squadron captured
   Nautilus 16 Jul
ⓔ *Constitution* chased by
   Broke's Squadron 17–19 Jul
ⓕ Broke united with convoy
   escorted by *Thetis* 29 Jul
ⓖ Broke separated from
   convoy 6 Aug

Map 2.1 Naval Movements of *Broke* and *Rodgers*, June–August 1812

greeted them as the captain of the U.S. frigate *Congress* and asked where he could procure water. It would have taken a skilled eye to know the difference between the *Congress* and *Shannon* since both were virtually identical in size, and Broke thought that the fishermen "were thoroughly deceived." Both fishermen recounted that Rodgers' squadron had sailed after a homeward Jamaica convoy. Broke wrote, "The above mentioned intelligence, will if confirm'd by other information, make a great alteration in my plans." Broke then returned to his squadron, but later in the day, an American revenue schooner "stood near enough to the Squadron to make out the *Africa's* force."[21] Since the Americans did not possess a single ship of the line, Broke had to consider his cover blown.

News that Broke's squadron had sailed from Halifax led Secretary Hamilton to lament, "I have not heard from Commodore Rodgers and consequently I feel unceasing inquietude. . . . In our Navy men I have the utmost confidence, that in equal combat they will be superior in the event but when I reflect on the overwhelming force of our enemy my heart swells almost to bursting, and all the consolation I have is, that in falling, they will fall nobly."[22] Since Hamilton's orders to Rodgers made it clear that he was not to sail very far off the coast, the secretary concluded, "They will all probably be in port very shortly." However, news of Broke's squadron led Hamilton to order the 14-gun *Nautilus* under Lieutenant William Crane to search for Rodgers and warn him, "It is confidently believed that there will be a strong British force on our coast in a few days—be upon our guard—we are anxious for your safe & speedy return into Port."[23]

With haste the *Nautilus* sailed from New York on 15 July. The following morning at daylight, Crane's lookouts sighted five unidentified sail. Crane acted cautiously and attempted to distance his vessel from the unknown ships, but they spotted the *Nautilus*, gave chase, and showed various signals followed by American colors. Crane knew this could mean anything, and countered with his own private signals that only U.S. warships could answer—and received no response.[24] He knew then that he had encountered the British squadron, but Crane found it impossible to out-sail his pursuers because the *Nautilus* could not carry a full press of canvas owing to the fear of carrying away a spar. Moreover, heavy seas favored the larger British ships, allowing the lead British warship to close. In response, Crane had the water started over the side but that did not help his escape. About 9:30 a.m. the first anchor was cut away and a quarter-hour later the second. This helped, but the wind soon moderated. A light breeze and a heavy sea even more decidedly favored the larger British warships, and Crane ordered the lee guns and the round-shot into the watery deep. Still the British continued to close.[25]

Sir Philip Bowes Vere Broke (Naval History and Heritage Command, Photo # NH 72294)

Hoping to find a means of escape, Crane solicited the opinion of his officers who dismally concluded that "every thing had been done to preserve the vessel, and, that no hopes of escape were left." When the *Shannon*, now under her true English colors, closed within short gunshot, Crane gave the painful order "to strike the Flag of the United States." The Americans had sustained their first naval loss of the war. Broke described the encounter as "a smart chace [sic]," and according to reports, he returned Crane's sword "in consequence of his good conduct in endeavoring to save his vessel." This had been a test of seamanship with neither side discharging a weapon in the encounter.[26]

Immediately after capturing the *Nautilus*, Broke had her crew transferred to the *Africa* and in the meantime allowed the *Guerriere*, *Belvidera*, and *Aeolus* to pursue a different vessel. Though they did not come up with their prey, Captain James Dacres of the *Guerriere* decided to investigate yet another sighting.[27] He had unknowingly chanced upon the *Constitution*, which at the outbreak of hostilities was anchored at Annapolis, incapable of operations owing to the lack of men. Secretary Hamilton, however, directed the *Constitution*'s commander, Captain Isaac Hull, to rapidly complete his manning and sail for New York and link up with Rodgers. It was not until 5 July, though, that the *Constitution* sailed, following a second order from Hamilton.[28]

On the afternoon of 16 July the *Constitution* was off New Jersey when her masthead lookouts sighted four sail to the north. Hull made them out as warships and "all sail was made in chase of them, to ascertain whether they were Enemy's Ships, or our Squadron having got out of New York waiting the arrival of the *Constitution*." During the afternoon, a fifth ship was sighted. This ship, the *Guerriere*, remained "too far off to distinguish signals," and, Hull explained, "We could not ascertain before dark, what the Ship in the offing was."[29]

As darkness fell, uncertainty affected both sides, but the wind shifted at sunset, placing the *Constitution* to the windward. This gave Hull an advantage, because he could now work closer to the unknown ships while retaining the ability to flee if they were British. As a result, Hull wrote, "I determined to . . . get near enough to make the night signal."[30] Finally, at 10 p.m., "being within Six or Eight miles of the Strange sail, the Private Signal was made, and kept up nearly one hour, but finding she could not answer it, I concluded she, and the Ships in Shore were Enemy." Hull ordered his ship to haul off. To his chagrin, however, the nearest vessel "hauled off after us . . . occasionally making signals, supposed to be for the Ships in Shore."[31] This was the *Guerriere*, and Dacres tried to maintain contact with the *Constitution* while signaling the rest of the squadron.

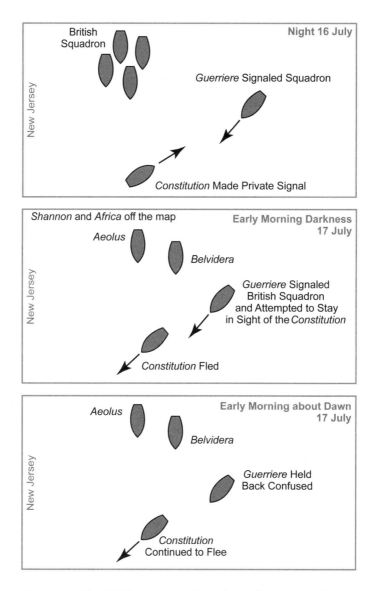

Diagram 2.1 The USS *Constitution* and British Squadron, 16–17 July 1812

Dacres' movements only confused Captain Byron, whose frigate, the *Belvidera*, was the British warship nearest to the *Guerriere*. After tracking both the *Guerriere* and *Constitution* for most of the night, Byron concluded, "Being *near* together, the impression upon my mind was, they were both American Frigates, we saw often Lights on b[oar]d both of them during the Night, and I thought they were making signals to each other."[32] Byron did not realize he had witnessed Hull's attempt to ascertain the identity of the British squadron by showing the night signal and Dacres' attempt to alert the British squadron with additional night signals. These involved lanterns hung aloft. Their location, sequencing, and number allowed rudimentary signaling at night, but in this case, the signals confused Byron and he did not conclude that one set of signals was for him.

Byron remained uncertain of the situation throughout the night. Instead of coming to the *Guerriere*'s aid, he stayed in sight of the *Aeolus* so as to be prepared to encounter two American frigates at daylight. Moreover, Byron worried that signaling the other British warships "might induce the Enemy to make sail from us." With Byron awaiting daylight, Dacres, on board the *Guerriere*, began to second-guess his position. He was almost positive that the *Constitution* was a U.S. frigate, but when the *Belvidera* and *Aeolus* failed to answer his signals, he deduced that they, too, were Americans.[33]

Just minutes before daylight, the *Aeolus* responded to *Guerriere*, but the early morning haze continued to prevent Byron from understanding Dacres' signal. Later, Byron wrote of his "mortification" respecting the events of the night, believing that had he understood the *Guerriere*'s signal he could have closed with the *Guerriere* and potentially brought the *Constitution* to action during the darkness or at daybreak.[34] Instead, daylight found the *Constitution* several miles in advance of Broke's strung-out squadron.

As the morning wore on, the wind stayed with Broke's squadron, while the American frigate lay nearly becalmed. Without wind that would allow for the *Constitution*'s escape, Hull decided his only chance of survival involved towing, so the Americans rigged lines from the boats to the *Constitution* and began the arduous work of rowing her away. The British continued to close, and Hull decided there was "little chance of escaping from them . . . cleared Ship for Action, being determined they should not get her, without resistance on our part." By 8 p.m. "four of the Enemy's Ships [were] nearly within Gun Shot," recalled Hull, who bleakly added, "It soon appeared that we must be taken, and that our Escape was impossible." Sensing their peril, First Lieutenant Charles Morris suggested warping, which involved putting anchors on board the ship's boats and rowing the boat six hundred to eight hundred yards ahead of the *Constitution*, where the anchor was cast into the sea. The anchor retained a cable connecting it to the American frigate, allowing the seamen to pull the *Constitution* to the anchor. By using two anchors, Hull

The Escape of the USS *Constitution* from Captain Broke's British Squadron, 17–19 July 1812 (U.S. Naval Institute Photo Archive)

always had his crew hauling the frigate forward with one anchor, while a boat carried the other anchor well ahead of the frigate to repeat the process. The British soon copied, but they had a great advantage. The *Africa*, the slowest of the British warships, sent forward her boats to assist the more nimble frigates. Thus, the British continued to close.[35]

During the early afternoon, the *Belvidera* and the *Constitution* exchanged fire without effect.[36] The British then sent all their boats to the British frigate nearest the American frigate, but a light breeze filled Hull's sails just enough to keep the lead British frigate from closing. But, even with the breeze, the *Constitution*'s crew continued warping, since three of his opponents were very close. These were the *Belvidera*, *Guerriere*, and *Aeolus*. The *Shannon* was three or four miles astern and the *Africa* still farther behind. Finally, around 11:00 p.m. the wind had built enough so that Hull thought it safe to call in his boats. As the day ended, he ominously recounted, "The Enemy still in chase, and very near."[37]

Broke's ships held their positions throughout the night. As the sun started to peek over the horizon, one of the British frigates passed within gunshot of the *Constitution*, but Hull wrote that the frigate "did not fire on us, perhaps for fear of becalming her as the wind was light." Instead, she tacked so as to fall in behind the *Constitution* and the other British warships followed in her wake.[38] Lieutenant Morris asserted, "Our escape must depend on our superiority of sailing, which we had no reason to hope nor expect." However, the wind began to favor the *Constitution*, and she pulled farther ahead of her pursuers.[39]

As dawn broke on 19 July, only three of the British warships were visible from the masthead. Hull gleefully recounted, "We soon found that we left the Enemy very fast." The British then called off the chase.[40] As the *Constitution*'s surgeon wrote in his journal, "We had many times given over all expectations of making our escape, & had it not been for uncommon exertion we must inevitably have fallen a prey to the superiority of an enemy." Later, Broke stated that "on the 17th, 18th, and 19th we had an anxious [chase] after an American frigate supposed to be the *Constitution*, but she escaped by very superior sailing, tho' the Frigates under my Orders are remarkably fast ships."[41]

❧

Broke failed to take the *Constitution*. He learned later, however, that "Commodore Rogers [*sic*] was gone upon the Grand Bank of Newfoundland to lie [in] wait for our West India Convoys." Broke was well aware of the "vast injury his [Rodgers'] Squadron might do in that point." Sailing the waters of the Grand Banks, the American ships did indeed pose a significant threat to both the British navy and imperial commerce. "It appeared to me the more important duty to abandon the plan we had entered upon of distressing the Enemy trade, for the protection of our own," and Broke "determined accordingly to proceed in quest of the American Squadron instead of waiting their return."[42]

Over the next days, Broke also closed with a British convoy, sighting it in the early hours of 29 July.[43] The seventy-odd ship convoy had sailed from Jamaica four weeks earlier. As for its escorts, the 22-gun *Garland* had parted with the convoy after seeing it to the Florida Strait, leaving the 38-gun *Thetis* as its lone protector.[44] Such a light escort for a large and valuable convoy might at first seem surprising, but, given the strength of expected opposition, this light escort had become the norm. Broke gave Captain William Henry Byam of the *Thetis* his first news that a state of war existed with the United States. Moreover, Broke explained, "This fleet was talked of confidentially in America as the chief object of Commodore Rogers' [*sic*] hazardous enterprize;—we shall at least ensure their safety, and I hope our escorting them may lead to a meeting of the squadron."[45]

A flaw existed in Broke's assessment, though. Rodgers, after engaging the *Belvidera*, had pursued a convoy, but he was not after the *Thetis*' convoy. Rodgers had actually pursued the previous Jamaica convoy that sailed in May and consisted of approximately 120 merchantmen escorted by the 36-gun *Thalia* and the 18-gun *Reindeer*.[46] Such an escort would have proven completely inadequate in an encounter with Rodgers' squadron, and the Americans were close on the convoy's trail. On 29 June Rodgers encountered an American merchant vessel. Her master gave an accurate two-day old position report for the convoy. Then, on 1 July, Commodore Decatur, commanding the *United States,* signaled "that he was passing a number of cocoa nut shells & orange peels." Rodgers determined that this jetsam "indicated that the Convoy were not far distant and we pursued it with zeal."[47] For more than a week no intelligence followed, but on 9 July the squadron captured a British vessel, and from her crew Rodgers learned she had encountered a convoy the previous night. Though the report inflated the size of the escort, the position report was accurate, and Rodgers only called off the pursuit on 13 July near the mouth of the English Channel.[48] This all occurred even before the *Nautilus* had sailed in search of Rodgers, and more than two weeks before Broke fell in with the *Thetis*' convoy. Thus, while Broke escorted the second West India convoy, Rodgers sailed to Madeira and the Azores before shaping a course for home. With few prizes, a midshipman on board the *President* lamented, "It goes damned hard."[49]

Miles away, the *Thetis*' convoy with Broke's squadron in attendance inched closer to England. Broke placed the *Africa*, his slowest warship, with the *Thetis* to defend the convoy while he used his frigates to reconnoiter suspicious sightings.[50] About midday on 6 August lookouts on board the *Thetis* sighted three large ships and a brig closing with the convoy. Broke investigated with the *Shannon, Belvidera,* and *Aeolus*.[51] His opponents turned out to be American merchantmen, and from one, Broke learned that Rodgers was at latitude 46, longitude 22 on 10 July, placing him many hundreds of miles away from the convoy. With that reassuring news, Broke left the *Africa*, *Thetis*, and *Guerriere* to protect the convoy and sailed for the American coast with the *Shannon*, *Belvidera*, and *Aeolus*, intent on "punishing the Americans for their malicious war, by destroying their trade—as we cannot find their *Marauders*."[52]

Several days later the *Belvidera* parted company with the *Shannon* and *Aeolus*. Now with only two frigates, Broke continued toward New York, while the *Belvidera* chanced upon an American merchant vessel. On board were letters from various officers of Rodgers' squadron. With this invaluable information, the *Belvidera* crowded sail, arriving at Halifax on 24 August. When Sawyer read through the captured letters, he concluded, "As far as I can judge from the various conjectures these Letters contain, it [Rodgers' squadron] will . . . probably arrive the latter end of this month, in a different track from the one outwards." Acting on this intelligence, Sawyer sent the 38-gun *Spartan* and the recently arrived 36-gun *Maidstone* to reinforce Broke.[53]

Another British reinforcement was the 38-gun *Statira*. Operating alone off Cape Sable, Nova Scotia, on the afternoon of 26 August, her lookouts sighted Rodgers' squadron. The weather was very thick; several strange sail plied the area, and the American lookouts did not realize one of the strangers was a British frigate.[54] Two afternoons later, this time about 150 miles east of Cape Cod, the *Statira*'s lookouts again sighted Rodgers' squadron. This time the American warships gave chase. For sixteen hours she held off her pursuers, until "the weather coming on thick, the *Statira* lost sight of them." Rodgers had again nearly taken a lone British frigate. Instead, the *Statira* reached Halifax on 31 August, and the information she brought led Sawyer to dispatch three frigates and a sloop in quest of Rodgers. But they sailed too late to influence subsequent events. Instead, Sawyer's best chance rested with the *Maidstone* and *Spartan* joining the *Shannon* and *Aeolus*, giving Broke four frigates off the northeastern coast of the United States.[55]

Rodgers received intelligence about some of these movements.[56] The situation was, however, far more favorable than the commodore realized. Off New York, the *Shannon* and *Aeolus* had separated on 28 August, with the latter in desperate need of water. While sailing toward Halifax, the *Aeolus* fell in with the *Maidstone* and *Spartan*, who provided some water, and the three frigates hurried back toward New York to find the *Shannon*.[57] Rodgers could have overwhelmed Britain's divided forces by prowling the coast in search of an engagement, but an outbreak of scurvy had sickened 150 on board the *United States*, a similar number in the *Congress*, and 50 on board the *President*. As a result, Rodgers thought "it indispensably necessary for us to get into port as soon as possible."[58]

The Americans slipped into Boston on 31 August. Rodgers warned, "The vessels will all require considerable outfit in sails & rigging: they can however, I presume be got ready for sea again in four weeks from this date, or indeed sooner was it not necessary to afford some time to recruit their crews, the Scurvey having made its appearance to an almost alarming degree." Overall, Rodgers went on, "I am sorry to say that our cruise has not been as successful as I had anticipated, having captured only seven merchant vessels, and those not valuable." But, Rodgers asserted, "the only consolation I individually feel on the occasion being derived from knowing that our being at Sea obliged the Enemy to concentrate a considerable portion of his most active force and thereby prevented his capturing an incalculable amount of American property." The closest the commodore came to mentioning his failure to respect Hamilton's orders at the outbreak of hostilities was the following: "I am aware of the anxiety you must have experienced at not hearing from me for such a length of time, but this I am sure you will not attribute in any degree to neglect."[59]

Rather than accusing Rodgers of disobedience or linking his disobedience to the loss of the *Nautilus*, Hamilton echoed Rodgers' conclusions that, "in having kept the sea, you have induced the enemy to concentrate a considerable portion of his most active force, . . . & of course enabled a great number of American vessels which might probably otherwise would have been captured to reach their ports of destination." However, Hamilton did take one jab at Rodgers: "Your next cruise may be more glorious, but I shall consider it particularly fortunate, if it should be attended with more substantial benefit to our country."[60] Rodgers did not escape so lightly in the press, though. One newspaper printed that Rodgers, "instead of protecting commerce of his own country, which was his first duty, he [Rodgers] has pursued *hap hazard* [sic] a fleet of the enemy's merchant ships which was deviating from that duty."[61] More particularly, alternative courses of action existed for the United States Navy, as illustrated by the cruises of the *Constitution*, *Essex*, and *Wasp*.

The *Essex*, under Captain David Porter, was at New York during the last days of peace and should have sailed with Rodgers, but in early June the *Essex* required unexpected repairs.[62] Once completed, Hamilton ordered Porter to join Rodgers' squadron, which was then at sea, but added, "Should you not be able to ascertain where Com. Rodgers is you will then shape your course Southwards as far as St. Augustine." However, Hamilton provided a caveat: "I need not say to you that circumstances may arrise, to justify a departure on your part from the letter of these instructions."[63]

On 3 July the *Essex* sailed without news of Rodgers' whereabouts.[64] About one hundred miles northwest of Bermuda in the early morning darkness of 11 July, the

Essex chanced upon a British convoy. Stealthily, the *Essex* glided among the vessels. Porter determined that he would attack the one ship showing a light, given the probability that she was the escort, but before the attack was to begin someone on board the American frigate accidentally discharged a musket. Mistakenly believing that this alerted the escort, Porter hailed the nearest vessel in the convoy, which turned out to be the *Samuel and Sarah*. Porter "told him if he attempted to make signal my guns were pointed at him, and I would immediately fire a broad side into her." The two ships then stood away from the convoy. When Porter sent a boat over with two midshipmen and six hands to take possession of his prize, they faced a groggy horde comprising three officers and 156 rank and file of the 1st Regiment of Foot, the Royal Scots, along with ten women and nine children. Porter learned that the convoy's other six transports contained the rest of the unit, escorted by the 32-gun frigate *Minerva*. At daylight, Porter tried to lure the *Minerva* away from the convoy, but her captain stayed with his remaining flock and sailed away.[65]

On board the *Essex*, Porter had to dispose of his prize. If he burned her, the soldiers would have to be shifted to his frigate, and they would devour his provisions. If he sent the ship to a port in the United States, the soldiers could easily overwhelm the prize crew. Instead, he ransomed the vessel for bills worth $12,000 while releasing the officers and men on parole "under a solemn agreement not to serve against the United States during the existing war unless first regularly exchanged."[66] Porter then decided to get away from Bermuda, since he believed that three British warships, including the *Guerriere*, were nearby. This intelligence, however, was either incorrect or dated. Only the 18-gun sloops *Recruit* and *Rattler* plied the area at that time.[67]

While still determining his next course of action, Porter captured a British merchantman, and from her crew he learned of the *Thetis'* convoy, and "consequently made every exertion to get off St. Augustine in time to fall in with them." But Porter did not find the convoy, so he sailed north to search on the Banks of Newfoundland. This course of action had an excellent prospect of success, since the convoy and the *Essex* plied the same area at the same time. However, Porter's opportunity evaporated on 29 July when Broke's squadron joined the convoy, increasing the escort well beyond the capabilities of the *Essex*. Though Porter did not find the convoy, he took the merchant vessel *Leander* on 26 July and sent her toward the United States. Only a day later, the British 18-gun *Atalante* recaptured her. Then the *Leander* encountered the *Shannon*, and Broke concluded, "The *Essex* has been making a roving cruize . . . , but a very unsuccessful one."[68]

At this point, Porter's luck changed, and he took five prizes between 2 August and 9 August.[69] Then on the morning of 13 July, the *Essex* fell in with the British sloop of war *Alert*, under Commander Thomas Laugharne, who faced a quandary. In firepower alone, Laugharne faced steep odds, having only 16 x

The Capture of the HMS *Alert* by the USS *Essex*, 13 August 1812 (U.S. Naval Institute Photo Archive)

18-pound carronades and 2 x 6-pound guns to 40 x 32-pound carronades and 6 x 12-pound guns on board the *Essex*. Moreover, the *Alert* may have been the worst-commissioned vessel in the British navy. Originally built as a collier, she had been purchased into British service, and she retained the characteristics of her origin, making her very slow: "Her Bulwarks were exceedingly slight and unlike those of other Ships of War and were incapable of resisting an ordinary Musket Ball." The *Alert* was too slow to escape and too weak to fight. As a result, Laugharne considered his only chance involved pummeling the *Essex* with several quick broadsides in a vain hope of inflicting enough damage to give the *Alert* time to flee before the American could return punishment.[70]

At "short pistol shot" Laugharne unleashed his broadside. Porter cynically observed that it "did us no more injury than the cheers that accompanied it."[71] Laugharne later asserted that his men fired three broadsides before the *Essex* could bring hers to bear, but it made no difference. When the *Essex* did fire, she shattered the *Alert*, dismounting three guns, smashing her bulwark, and cutting her up aloft, but the most serious damage occurred below the waterline, rapidly making the *Alert* waterlogged.[72]

Laugharne then tried to escape, hoping he had severely damaged the *Essex*, but "the Enemy was by this time close on our Lee Quarter, and coming up under easy Sail." Seeing the hopelessness of the situation, the crew of the *Alert* surrounded their commander, beseeching him to strike. Laugharne responded, "He would be damned if he would." The master added that resistance was futile, and Laugharne then asked his men if he had done his duty. Twice they "cried yes."[73] Though one could argue that these men were disaffected and lacked discipline, another argument dealt with the disparity of force. If the *Alert* had fought a sloop of her own size, the men—sensing this to be a fair fight—would likely have fought longer and harder, but battling a larger-class warship, particularly a sloop against a frigate or a frigate against a ship of the line, was seen as asking the men to fight against impossible odds and to uselessly shed their blood. Established custom saw no dishonor in such defeat.

Porter incorrectly determined that the *Alert* was searching for the *Hornet,* writing, "It is a source of regret to me that she did not fall in with that vessel instead of the *Essex*, as the forces would then have been more equal." The United States Navy had something to prove in equal combat. Admiral Sir John Thomas Duckworth, commander at Newfoundland and Laugharne's superior, added, "With respect to the *Alert*, it is a consolation to reflect that the Enemy have not gained either credit in conquering so poor an Adversary or profit in the acquisition of a vessel so little suited to the purposes of war."[74]

Porter and Laugharne agreed that the *Alert* would serve as a cartel, destined for St. John's, Newfoundland, with the prisoners. After delivering up the prisoners, Porter directed that his prize proceed to a port in the United States. When

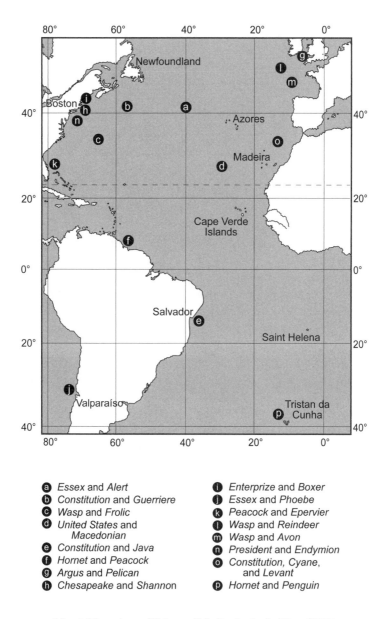

a *Essex* and *Alert*	**i** *Enterprize* and *Boxer*
b *Constitution* and *Guerriere*	**j** *Essex* and *Phoebe*
c *Wasp* and *Frolic*	**k** *Peacock* and *Epervier*
d *United States* and *Macedonian*	**l** *Wasp* and *Reindeer*
e *Constitution* and *Java*	**m** *Wasp* and *Avon*
f *Hornet* and *Peacock*	**n** *President* and *Endymion*
g *Argus* and *Pelican*	**o** *Constitution, Cyane,* and *Levant*
h *Chesapeake* and *Shannon*	**p** *Hornet* and *Penguin*

Map 2.2 Locations of Ship-on-Ship Battles in the War of 1812

Duckworth received the cartel, he honored it because Laugharne had pledged his word, but he considered it to be highly unusual and regrettable. The other mission for Duckworth involved finding the *Essex*, but his command was two schooners short of establishment, and he had been forced to send a sloop with a convoy to England, as well as a frigate with another convoy to Quebec. Needless to say, he lacked the means to search for the *Essex*.[75]

Meanwhile, the *Essex* proceeded toward the United States. On 4 September Porter made out two large warships to the south and a brig of war pursuing what appeared to be a merchant vessel to the north. The *Essex* closed on the brig, but she gave up her pursuit and escaped. Shortly thereafter, Porter came up on the merchantman. He learned she was the American-flagged *Minerva* when he showed his colors, but this betrayed the *Essex* to the ships in the south and they made all sail in chase.[76]

Rather than two large warships as Porter thought, he had encountered the *Shannon* and a prize. In a daring gambit, just at sunset Porter ordered his ship hove about. This took the *Essex* from a northerly to a southeasterly course and placed the *Essex* on an almost perpendicular heading to the *Shannon*. After holding this course for an hour, one of the crew of the *Essex* accidentally discharged a pistol in an act broadly similar to an event that occurred when attacking the troop convoy in mid-July 1812. At the time the pistol fired, Porter later wrote, "we must have been at our shortest distance from them." But the shot solicited no reaction, and at 8:30 p.m. Porter had the *Essex* steer to the southwest. Provided the British ships remained on the same heading observed at sunset, this maneuver took the *Essex* across the *Shannon*'s wake.[77]

Porter called the escape "extraordinary."[78] On board the *Shannon*, Porter's daring maneuver went completely unnoticed, and Captain Broke concluded that "she sailed too well for us . . . he did not like to *fight*, it was well for him he *could run*, & had the night to shade him." As for the *Minerva*, Broke wrote to his wife, "We burn'd the ship *in spite*."[79] Several days later, Porter safely made the Delaware.

Whereas the *Essex* illustrated the single ship cruising alternative to Rodgers' squadron-sized operation, the *Wasp* demonstrated another possible course of action for the United States Navy. The opening of hostilities found the *Wasp* at sea. Under Master Commandant Jacob Jones, she arrived at Newcastle, Delaware, on 10 July from a diplomatic mission to Europe.[80]

In early August Jones received orders to sail in search of a British gunbrig that had been reported off the Delaware. Yet, Hamilton cautioned Jones, "You know that there is a British Squadron on our coast—be on your guard [and] do not make a long cruise." But what was a long cruise? One could argue that this baffled Jones, who replied just a few hours before sailing on 8 August that "if nothing should occur to render it impracticable, shall return to this port in twenty to thirty days, which I presume is as short a cruise as your orders contemplate."[81]

Yet should Jones even have sailed? On 5 August, one day after Hamilton had ordered the *Wasp* to sail but before Jones received the order, he wrote to the secretary of the Navy: "Many vessels arrive here daily from foreign ports & have seen no british [sic] cruisers on our coast, & from the direction in which most of these vessels have come in, I think there can be none of the enemy to the south of the Latitude of 40°."[82] In this case, the officer on the spot had intelligence contradicting Hamilton's assessment. Though Jones could have assumed that Hamilton had better information, it could also be argued that Jones used Hamilton's order as a means of getting to sea.

Jones stretched along the coast as far north as Rhode Island. Even at this point, Jones had exceeded his instructions. As for British warships, he wrote that "none were to be seen or heard of off our ports." This confirmed the intelligence he had obtained before sailing; rather than return to port, however, Jones shaped a course toward Halifax, "believing it probable we should find some of the enemy's Sloops of War there."[83]

Operating in this area courted trouble, since Halifax served as the principal British naval base in North America. On 25 August the *Wasp* recaptured a merchant vessel; however, his prize had only parted with the *Shannon* and the *Aeolus* the day before. In addition, the *Spartan* and *Maidstone* sailed from Halifax on the day Jones took the prize. Moreover, this was the same area where the *Statira* encountered Rodgers' squadron on 26 August.[84] The convergence of five British frigates and Rodgers' squadron made for crowded seas, and in hindsight it was not surprising that the *Wasp*'s lookouts sighted what appeared to be a sloop of war on 27 August. Much to Jones' surprise, "with in about 3 miles of her we discovered she was a thirty gun Frigate. . . . We made sail from her, & night soon coming on we [saw] no more of her." This "frigate" could have been any one of more than a half-dozen warships then in the area. The next morning, Jones peered through thick and squally weather and spied what he thought to be a frigate. His opponent was likely the *Statira*, whose log mentions a strange sail that morning; however, Jones used the weather to mask his escape. Finally, on 11 September the *Wasp* anchored in the Delaware.[85]

Jones had exceeded Hamilton's order, but he did not try to cover it up or explain that he had received information to support his decision. Rather than berating Jones, Hamilton ordered him to prepare for another cruise.[86] When taken together with the actions of other U.S. naval officers, Jones' decisions demonstrate serious inadequacies respecting the command and control of the United States Navy at the opening of the War of 1812. First, Rodgers had acted contrary to his instructions; then, Porter had deviated from his instructions, but at least he argued a reason. Moreover, the wording of his instructions allowed him to do this. Finally, Jones had blatantly exceeded his instructions, and, unlike Porter, his orders did not provide leeway. Hamilton had lost control, and this resulted in the United States Navy fighting Britain in a number of ways that were at best loosely integrated and at worst opportunistic and self-serving.

The *Constitution* epitomized the problems of trying to control the United States Navy while fighting the most powerful navy in the world. After escaping Broke's squadron following a long and anxious chase, Captain Hull decided not to adhere to his orders directing him to join Rodgers' squadron at New York. Instead, he shaped a course for Boston in an effort to avoid another encounter with the British, but his instructions did not account for what he was to do if he had to anchor at Boston. At Boston, Hull quickly restocked his provisions and itched to get back to sea, worried that the British would blockade the *Constitution*.[87]

On 2 August, after only six days in Boston, Hull wrote to Hamilton, "I have determined to run out, having great hopes my Boat which is now at the Post Office, may bring me letters from you. If she does not I shall indeed be at a loss how to proceed, and shall take responsibility on myself." The boat returned without orders, leaving Hull to his own devices. He could sail for New York to comply with Hamilton's directive and potentially encounter British frigates off that port; he could search for Rodgers' squadron, but he had no information of its location; or he could proceed to sea on an independent cruise. Hull chose the last option.[88] Was this taking the initiative or did Hull have knowledge that Hamilton had written the following on 28 July? "On the arrival of the *Constitution* in port I have ordered Com^re. Bainbridge to take command of her." But Bainbridge was in Washington, and Hull's first lieutenant later asserted that Hamilton's order reached Boston one day after the *Constitution* had sailed.[89]

At sea, Hull's lookouts sighted several ships at daylight on 15 August. Hull made them out to be a convoy with an escort. As he closed, the warship fled. She was the 18-gun *Avenger*, and she proved too fast for the *Constitution*. Instead, Hull savaged the convoy, making two prizes and forcing the commander of the *Avenger* to burn the third. Hull learned from his prisoners of six British frigates in the area.[90] Moreover, the commander of the *Avenger* was undoubtedly looking for assistance.

Accordingly, the *Constitution* changed stations, but the seas remained empty until the night of 17 August, when Hull encountered an American privateer. Her captain explained that he had sighted a British warship just hours before, but some thirty-six hours passed before the *Constitution*'s lookouts sighted a ship at 2:00 p.m. on 19 August.[91] Though her identity could not be ascertained, "all sail was instantly made in chace [*sic*]." The *Constitution* quickly closed with the stranger, and at 3:30 p.m. Hull identified her as a frigate. He had chanced upon the *Guerriere*, Captain Dacres commanding.[92]

The maneuvering of each vessel indicated that neither shied from the contest. A lieutenant on board the *Guerriere* asserted, "Made her out to be the United States Frigate *Constitution*, which we had formerly Chased, off New York, but escaped by her superior sailing." With this knowledge, Dacres ordered sails to be taken in so the *Constitution* could close. At 5:05 p.m. he ordered his men to fire the starboard broadside.[93]

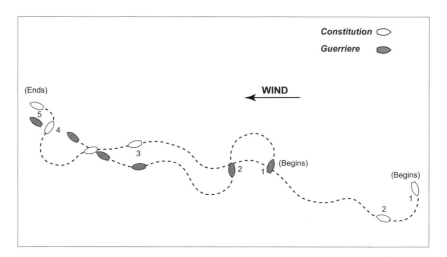

Diagram 2.2 Plan of the Engagement between the *Constitution* and the *Guerriere*, 19 August 1812 (Adapted from Mahan, *Sea Power and its Relations to the War of 1812*, 1:332–33)

The rounds fell short. Immediately, Dacres wore his ship and discharged the larboard broadside. This time two rounds struck the *Constitution*'s hull, while others cut through her rigging. Hull returned fire with as many guns as would bear. Over the next forty-five minutes, both frigates exchanged fire. Captain Hull decided to close, since the *Constitution* was "receiving her shot without being able to return them with effect."[94]

At "less than Pistol Shot," Hull delivered a broadside. A few minutes later, the *Guerriere*'s mizzenmast fell into the sea. In hindsight, this was the critical moment of the engagement. With the mast acting as an anchor, the British frigate lost steerage. Hull used this opportunity to place his frigate off his opponent's bow. In this position, grape and musketry swept the *Guerriere*'s deck while the *Constitution*'s guns raked her.[95] The fire tore the *Guerriere* apart. Her mizzenmast lay across the deck with the masthead dipping into the sea on the starboard side. All the while, a tangled web of shrouds and rigging linked the fallen mast to the frigate.[96]

Over the next minutes the *Guerriere* drifted so that her bowsprit came across the stern of the American frigate and tangled in the *Constitution*'s mizzen rigging.[97] While locked together the most severe fighting took place topside with small arms. Chance again favored Hull, as American fire decapitated the leadership of the *Guerriere*, whose commander on the forecastle fell with severe wounds, while the master was shot in the knee and Dacres suffered a severe wound in his back. In desperation Dacres decided to carry the *Constitution* by boarding.[98]

As the British assembled, First Lieutenant Charles Morris of the *Constitution* attempted to secure the *Guerriere*'s bowsprit to the American frigate, but he suffered a grave wound. Immediately, Lieutenant William S. Bush of the Marines took Morris' place, but "one musket shot entered his face & pass'd into his brains."[99] The British boarding attempt ultimately failed, though, because the sea was too heavy. Moments later, the *Guerriere*'s foremast went over the side, taking her mainmast with it.[100] With the British frigate dismasted and dead in the water, Hull took the conservative action and stood off for about a half-hour so his men could repair damage.[101]

Across the water, amidst the smoke and confusion, the crew of the *Guerriere* worked feverishly to clear the wreckage and prepare to resume the action. The efforts proved in vain. "Having got into the trough of the Sea, she lay there," Dacres later wrote. Another officer added that "she rolled so much . . . the Shot and Shot Boxes on the Quarter Deck were flying from side to side." Owing to the condition of his ship and her crew, Dacres gathered the few surviving officers for counsel. To a man, "they were all of opinion that any further resistance would only be a needless waste of lives."[102] Soon after, *Guerriere* struck her colors.

Unaware of the *Guerriere*'s plight, the crew on board the *Constitution* made hasty repairs then ranged up on the British frigate. Darkness separated the two ships. As a result, Hull wrote, "we could not see whether she had any colours, flying or not." Had she surrendered? To find out, he sent a boat across under a flag of truce, a risky move since British fire could easily have shattered the boat. Twenty minutes later, it returned carrying the bloodied Dacres, signaling an American victory.[103]

Daylight revealed a gruesome scene on board the *Guerriere*, with "pieces of skulls, brains, legs, arms & blood Lay in every direction and the groanes of the

The Engagement between the USS *Constitution* and the HMS *Guerriere* (U.S. Naval Institute Photo Archive)

The Capture of the HMS *Guerriere* by the USS *Constitution*, August 1812 (U.S. Naval Institute Photo Archive)

wounded."[104] She had suffered fifteen dead and sixty-three wounded to her opponent's seven dead and seven wounded.[105] The *Guerriere's* damage was such that Hull did not think he could get her into port, so he ordered the wounded removed and set her afire.[106] According to one onlooker, "She blew up presenting a sight the most incomparably grand and magnificent I have ever experienced, no painter, no poet, or historian could give on canvas or paper any description that could do justice to the Scene."[107] Hull then sailed for Boston.

The first stage of the naval war ended in early September. By numbers the United States had fared well, having taken the *Guerriere* and *Alert* for the loss of the *Nautilus*, especially considering an American's assessment that the British were "hard fellows on salt water."[108] As a percentage of the Royal Navy, however, two losses were almost insignificant. Moreover, American naval operations could have been far more effective than they had been, even when accounting for the fog of war and an extremely capable opponent. The crux of the problem dealt with decisions in the months before the war. The outbreak of hostilities found supposedly operational frigates in port—the *Essex* undergoing repairs and the *Constitution* lacking in seamen. Given the size of the United States Navy, two frigates unavailable for operations hardly proved trifling. In addition, the navy entered the war intellectually unprepared. Only in May did Hamilton seriously begin to develop a strategy. By the outbreak of hostilities, he had yet to issue full orders to key American officers. This was especially important, since a narrow window of opportunity existed at the beginning of the war when the British were unaware of hostilities. A second issue involved the chain of command that placed Hamilton, a civilian with little maritime experience, issuing orders to naval officers. This led to professional friction, and naval officers such as Jones and Rodgers disregarded or modified instructions. Even a very liberal interpretation of Hamilton's intent could in no way account for Rodgers' seventy-day cruise within one day's sail of the English Channel.

Yet did the problems with command and control limit the effectiveness of American naval operations? To determine this, one must first assess American strategy. The clearest statement from Hamilton indicated, "It has been judged expedient so to employ our public armed vessels, as to afford to our returning commerce, all possible protection . . . the safe return of our commercial vessels, is obviously of the highest importance."[109] The sailing of Rodgers' squadron forced Broke to assert that he had to turn "our attention from the *destruction* of the Enemy's trade to the *protection* of our own."[110] Sawyer made a similar choice, sending the *Spartan*, the only frigate not with Broke, to the Bay of Fundy to protect British trade, and dispatching the *Maidstone*, his first wartime frigate reinforcement, on the same mission.[111] The British had few warships off the North American coast during the first six weeks of the war, and rather than focus on American commerce, the British devoted much of their attention to protecting their own trade.

Though Rodgers disregarded orders, his actions led to the government's desired strategic effects, but the same could not be said for the *Essex* and *Wasp*. The *Essex* operated for two months in the Atlantic, capturing eight merchant vessels and the *Alert*. But, there is little evidence that her operations drew off British naval forces. The *Wasp*'s orders to search for a British sloop of war off the Delaware was very much in keeping a strategy of protecting commerce, but her commander took her off Halifax. Such a high-risk cruise did little to protect American commerce.

Finally, a question of risk must be considered. The *Wasp*, *Essex*, and *Constitution* narrowly escaped superior British forces, but the loss of a single ship was much less damaging than the loss of an entire squadron. Placing three frigates and two smaller vessels of war under Rodgers' command potentially concentrated their loss, and sailing almost into the English Channel risked an irreplaceable American instrument of war.

CHAPTER 3

"It Is a Thing I Could Not Have Expected"

The Second Round, September 1812–March 1813

A shabbily dressed man paced the lobby of the House of Commons. Agitated and disgusted, he withdrew into a doorway. Less than sixty seconds passed before a well-dressed and important-looking gentleman walked through the same door. The disheveled man pulled a pistol from his pocket, placed it against the gentleman's side and fired. Mortally wounded, he fell to the floor gasping, "Murder! Murder!" Five minutes later, he was dead. The Sergeant at Arms then walked into the House of Commons and announced, "Mr. Perceval was Assassinated!" Meanwhile, the assassin sat down in the lobby. When approached, he reportedly announced, "I am the man who has done the deed, I don't deny it."[1] He was no more than a disaffected merchant, upset over a failed business venture. His motives were financial and personal, not political, but in his moment of greatest distress he had, on 11 May 1812, assassinated Spencer Perceval, the head of the British government and the greatest supporter of the Orders in Council. Perceval's death masked Britain's drift into war with the United States. For nearly a month Britain lacked an effective government, creating a power vacuum at the very time when President Madison had sent his demands for war to Congress. Finally, on 8 June, a new ministry under Robert Banks Jenkinson, Second Earl of Liverpool, formed.[2]

Liverpool decided to retain the existing First Lord of the Admiralty, Robert Saunders Dundas, the Second Viscount Melville; this action was deceptive, however, because Dundas had only held the position since 25 March. Melville came from a political family with significant links to the navy. His father, Henry Dundas, created First Viscount Melville in 1802, held important positions in the government, where he championed Britain's growing empire and its navy. Particularly, he served as treasurer of the navy from 1792 to 1800 and First Lord during the invasion scare that preceded Trafalgar.[3] This led Captain Broke to write, "I hope he will do them the justice his father intended."[4] The younger Melville faced significant challenges trying to understand the intricacies of the Royal Navy, especially in a rapidly changing strategic environment that witnessed the intensification of war against Napoleonic France and the outbreak of war with the United States.

Unlike Melville, who had limited time in his post, several members of the Admiralty Board had served under previous First Lords, and the secretaries had significant experience. First Secretary John Wilson Croker had held his position since 1809, and John Barrow, the second secretary, had served even longer. Together they wielded much of the Admiralty's power drafting documents, handling day-to-day correspondence, and administering the navy.[5]

Three days after Liverpool formed the new government, Melville warned, "The American Government are proceeding at great lengths in a way of provocation, with a view probably to . . . produce irritation against this country, & undoubtedly such dangerous conduct may involve us in a quarrel."[6] In an effort to ameliorate hostility, the newly appointed government, no longer tied to Perceval's policies, worked to amend the Orders in Council that had placed severe restrictions on American commerce and had proved a major point of conflict. On 23 June the British leadership suspended the Orders, effective 1 August, to allow more room in negotiations. However, the United States had declared war five days earlier.[7]

In the midst of the turmoil stemming from the assassination and the political jockeying over the Orders in Council, the Admiralty quietly prepared for war. Two days before Perceval's death, Croker, in his own hand so as to maintain better security for the sensitive document, sent Admiral Sawyer the government's determination: "To exercise . . . all possible forbearance towards the citizens of the United States." The same document also provided a course of action in the event of war. Following the assassination, the Admiralty continued to function and dispatched three frigates to North America between mid-May and early July. In addition, seven smaller warships escorted convoys to the region.[8] Dispatching ten warships demonstrated the significance of the threat, especially when taken in combination with the Royal Navy's other commitments. However, as events unfolded, these reinforcements served a different purpose from the one intended because they trickled in during the first month and a half of hostilities, giving Sawyer greater means to deal with the developing war.

Though the Admiralty seemed to have a fair grasp of the situation, its relationship with Sawyer cooled because of poor communications. Unofficial accounts detailing the outbreak of hostilities arrived before Sawyer's official dispatch. In part, this was owing to President Madison placing the issue of war before Congress on 1 June; debates in the House and Senate followed. As a result, ships sailing directly from the United States brought news. Moreover, Lloyd's provided the Admiralty with the first quasi-reliable proof of hostilities. As a maritime insurer based in Britain, Lloyd's operated a network of agents and merchants with a global reach, often relaying sensitive information to the Admiralty in order to minimize risk and keep insurance costs low.[9]

Sawyer's official dispatch arrived on board the 16-gun *Julia*, under Captain Valentine Gardner. Its contents added to the Admiralty's unease, leading Croker to write, "Their Lordships command me to express their regret that on a Subject of such extreme importance as that of a declaration of War by America you should not have given their Lordships the particulars of the information which you state yourself to have received, and that you did not send the American official documents upon this subject, which Captain Gardner of the *Julia* reports to have seen at Halifax." Adding to the embarrassment, Sawyer did not order Gardner to detain the mail or passengers on board his warship until the Admiralty received its reports. As a result, the *Julia's* passengers went ashore carrying news of the war, including documentation. This led the Admiralty to complain that by Sawyer's "omission to send the American Documents the Public was in possession of as early, and *more ample* information than His Majesty's Government."[10]

On 3 August, less than a week after officially learning of the war, the Admiralty combined the Halifax, Jamaica, and Leeward Islands Stations.[11] For this command they selected Admiral Sir John Borlase Warren, a fifty-eight-year-old officer who was "above middle size with a pleasing countenance and good figure, and [who] had much the air and appearance of a man of rank and fashion." Though one contemporary voiced concern, asserting, "He was considered more an active and brave man than an officer of any great (particularly practical) professional talent," Warren had significant operational and diplomatic experience. During the 1790s, he had commanded various squadrons and seemed to have a knack for defeating small French squadrons. Warren had experience dealing with Americans, having commanded the British North American Station between late 1807 and January 1811. In addition, Warren had also served previously as ambassador extraordinary to St. Petersburg.[12] The government tried to make use of this background by giving him limited diplomatic powers to terminate hostilities because it was hoped that the U.S. government would negotiate after learning of the suspension of the Orders in Council.[13]

The creation of the unified command, however, set off a firestorm in the British navy, prompting one senior officer to rail in sarcasm, "Why they have excluded the East Indies and the Mediterranean, I know not, for surely they might as rationally have been included in this most unprecedented Command." Sickened by the move, he asserted that it "disgusted the whole service" and speculated that "if it does not set the Navy in a blaze, I know not what could."[14] Much of the disdain surely resulted from Warren's supposed patronage powers to appoint officers and significant pecuniary advantages he would accrue from his share of prize money from all captures made on the enlarged station.

The relationship between Warren and his commanders in the West Indies further highlighted weakness in this new command structure. When he informed Rear Admiral Sir Francis Laforey, his commander in the Leeward Islands, and Vice Admiral Charles Stirling at Jamaica that the Admiralty had appointed him commander in chief, Warren explained that previous orders remained in effect and "comprise the principal duties necessary to be performed." Moreover, Laforey and Stirling would continue to deal with local issues on their own authority, meaning they retained much of the authority, but not the title, of commander in chief of their respective stations.[15] This largely resulted from the extensive size of the command and the slowness of communications.

On 26 September Warren reached Halifax, prompting Broke to suggest that his "arrival makes a *grand revolution* in our government, poor Adm[l] Sawyer is much hurt at the *rude manner* in which the Adm[ty] have deprived him of his chief command."[16] Privately, Warren explained to a fellow admiral that Sawyer was "unwell & I believe it is so & he is very Grumpy also at what he calls being superseded in his Command." Having a disaffected subordinate who had previously been commander in chief was not conducive to effectiveness, and, at Sawyer's request, Warren sent him home.[17] Sawyer had proved able. He had dealt with a very difficult situation at the outbreak of hostilities while mitigating British losses.[18] The Admiralty had lost confidence in him, however, and Warren's arrival meant that Sawyer was essentially a lame duck.

Warren encountered a very different environment from the situation the Admiralty had indicated. Though Warren dispatched a warship under a flag of truce to try and open negotiations to end the hostilities, one of his officers wrote, "*Pacific overtures* were no more likely to check the flames of war—than a mild remonstrance would the raging of a tiger."[19] In addition, Warren had fewer warships than he had been led to believe owing to the loss of five to wreck or enemy action and the loss of four dispatched with convoys. The capture of the *Guerriere* was particularly troubling. In summation, he wrote, "The war . . . seems to assume a new, as well as more active, and inveterate aspect than heretofore."[20] With fewer ships, a more determined opponent, and orders to negotiate an end to hostilities, Warren grew increasingly uncertain and tentative, noted Captain Broke, who confided in his wife, "He [Warren] does not decide very quick."[21]

Like the British, the United States Navy had to prepare for the second stage of the naval conflict. In Boston, Commodore Bainbridge succeeded Captain Hull as commander of the *Constitution*. Though the reason stated related to the death of Hull's brother, earlier correspondence indicated that this had been planned for some time. Across the docks, the *President, United States, Congress, Hornet*, and *Argus* refitted while their crews recovered from scurvy. The *Chesapeake* continued to undergo repairs, but she would not be operational before winter.[22] To the south, the *Essex* and *Wasp* waited in the Delaware.

During the war's first months, American naval operations had proved deceptively encouraging, while the war in other quarters had not gone well. As a result, getting the navy back to sea became a priority. Rather than leave the majority of the force under Rodgers, Hamilton decided to form squadrons under three commodores: Rodgers, Bainbridge, and Decatur. Each squadron would consist of the commodore's own large frigate, a second smaller frigate, and a sloop or brig.[23] This had the benefit of minimizing risk by eliminating the possibility that the Royal Navy could defeat the entire United States Navy in a single engagement. The decision also demonstrated either extreme reverence for the uniformed leadership of the navy or a fear that they again would not follow Hamilton's orders. With respect to the brig or sloop assigned to each squadron, the secretary of the navy decided, "reference must be made to the relative rank of the respective commanding officers." Decatur, the junior commodore, received the *Argus* because her commander was junior among the officers of sloops and brigs, while Rodgers, the senior commodore, received the *Wasp*, leaving Bainbridge with the *Hornet*. Hamilton explained to his officers that Rodgers, Bainbridge, and Decatur would by order of seniority choose their second frigate from among the *Chesapeake, Congress*, and *Essex*. Hamilton, however, admonished his commodores to "consult the good of the service" and pressed his belief that the warships in each squadron should sail nearly alike, be able to carry approximately the same quantity of stores, and be ready for sea at nearly the same time.[24]

One problem quickly emerged—the *Chesapeake* could not sail until the winter, meaning there would not be three squadrons of three ships each but two squadrons of three ships and one of two, comprising the commodores' large frigate and a sloop. Hamilton placed his senior officers in a position to quibble over the one who would command the two-ship squadron.

Rodgers, the senior commodore, chose the *Congress*. This left Decatur and Bainbridge to fight over the remaining operational frigate, the *Essex*. Since the *United States* under Decatur's personal command would be ready before the *Constitution* under Bainbridge's orders, Decatur claimed the second choice given Hamilton's directive that warships should be ready to sail at about the same time. In response, Bainbridge argued, "On mature consideration . . . respecting the three

Frigates to be attached to the respective Squadrons; I am of opinion that I am entitled to the 2nd choice." He chose the *Essex*. To Hamilton, Bainbridge asserted seniority and ranted, "I lay claim to having the Frigate *Essex* attached to my command and as Com. Decatur & myself cannot agree on that point, we both refer to you Sir, for a decision between us."[25] Hamilton, however, had information to which neither Bainbridge nor Decatur was privy. The *Essex* needed an extended refit. Rather than being ready around 1 October when Decatur expected to sail, she would be ready about the same time as the *Constitution*.[26] As a result, Bainbridge emerged victorious.

With command arrangements settled, Hamilton dispatched orders to Rodgers, Bainbridge, and Decatur, directing them to "consider yourself at liberty to proceed to sea wherever you may judge it expedient with the vessels attached to your command. . . . You are to do your utmost to annoy the enemy, & to afford protection to our commerce." Hamilton gave his senior leaders complete geographical latitude. Control of warships at sea during the age of sail was problematic, given the speed of communications that only moved as fast as the ships that carried instructions, and finding warships at sea to deliver new instructions was often like finding the proverbial needle in a haystack. This meant orders had to be carefully reasoned in advance so the instructions contained enough flexibility for the officer to be able to adapt to changing circumstances without recourse to higher authority. In this case, however, Hamilton's orders were too vague. Perhaps this was an admission that the secretary could not control his officers or that he lacked necessary expertise in operational matters. Hamilton demanded only that his commanders provide situation reports so as to avoid a repeat of the embarrassing disappearing act of Rodgers' first cruise.[27]

Rodgers and Decatur's squadrons were ready for sea the first days of October. Rather than have Rodgers proceed with the *President* and *Congress*, and have Decatur sail separately with the *United States* and *Argus*, Decatur asked if they could join forces for the first few days of the cruise so as to have greater combat strength in the event of encountering British warships off Boston. Rodgers thought this a good idea. The *Argus* sailed on 6 October to scout for lurking British warships.[28] This was prudent. At the end of September, a British squadron comprising five frigates had operated in the waters off Boston, but the squadron had broken up during the first days of October, with several of the frigates needing provisions and repairs.[29]

As a result, the commander of the *Argus*, after scouting for two days, reported that the British had disappeared. Taking advantage of this news, the American warships "got under way, from their anchorage opposite the town, and stood out to sea with a fair wind and fine serine [*sic*] weather." Thousands flocked to see the squadron off and "crowded the wharves and covered the hills and houses, and followed with their good wishes."[30]

Two days out, on the afternoon of 10 October, lookouts on board the *United States* sighted the 38-gun British frigate *Nymphe*. The Americans pursued but lost her in the waning light. Several hours later, the *Argus*, under Master Commandant Arthur Sinclair, fell in with a Swedish merchant brig. In need of intelligence, Sinclair had British colors hoisted and played the part of a Royal Navy vessel. The deception worked and the Swede correctly explained that an American squadron had chased a British frigate that afternoon. More ominously, Sinclair learned that the Swedish ship had passed through a British squadron of five frigates about twelve hours before. Still thinking the *Argus* to be British, the Swedes explained that Rodgers' squadron was to sail from Boston on 8 October.[31] The Americans could confirm two of the three pieces of intelligence. The only unconfirmable report was the most dangerous—five British frigates lurked nearby.

The Americans could only assume that the *Nymphe* would warn these frigates. Commodores Rodgers and Decatur also concluded that Admiral Warren would be forced to form powerful squadrons to confront the combined force of the *President*, *United States*, *Congress*, and *Argus*. Concentrating Warren's ships would limit the area they could patrol. Rodgers and Decatur therefore countered by deciding to separate. In fact, Decatur thought it best to allow his squadron to operate as single ships. As for Rodgers, he contemplated detaching the *Congress* but decided not to do so.[32] This was a questionable decision. The *President* and *Congress* were too weak to defeat a Royal Navy squadron sent to confront the combined strength of Rodgers' and Decatur's squadrons, and Rodgers' two frigates would cause single British frigates to flee.

Little did the Americans know that there was no squadron of five frigates in the area; instead, extreme levels of fog and friction beset Warren's command. The 24-gun *Barbadoes* had wrecked off Cape Sable, Nova Scotia; on 3 October, Warren sent the *Shannon* to her rescue.[33] The next day Warren ordered the 74-gun *San Domingo* and the 64-gun *Africa* to protect commerce off the Banks of Newfoundland. By chance, Rodgers' squadron sailed less than a hundred miles south of their cruising ground. Warren claimed to have a frigate squadron off New York or the Delaware, but this squadron had dispersed, with several of the frigates returning to Halifax for supplies and repairs.[34] Between the remnants of this squadron and several others then at sea, Warren did have four frigates off the North American coast, but they were poorly deployed to confront Rodgers. The *Spartan* and *Maidstone* patrolled between New York and the Chesapeake, but the 44-gun *Acasta* and the already-mentioned *Nymphe* operated separately south of the Banks of Newfoundland.[35]

The *Nymphe* made Halifax two days after escaping Rodgers' squadron. Though Warren had no available line of battle ships, there were four frigates and a number of smaller vessels in the harbor. Moreover, two additional frigates arrived just hours

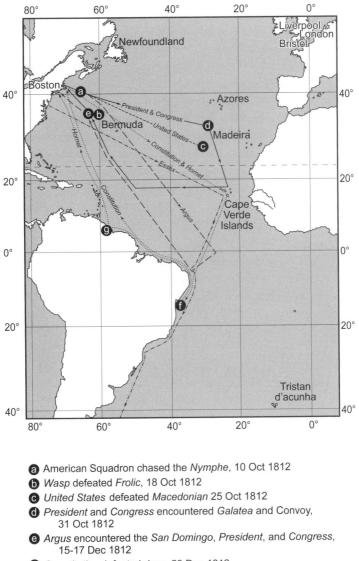

a American Squadron chased the *Nymphe*, 10 Oct 1812
b *Wasp* defeated *Frolic*, 18 Oct 1812
c *United States* defeated *Macedonian* 25 Oct 1812
d *President* and *Congress* encountered *Galatea* and Convoy,
    31 Oct 1812
e *Argus* encountered the *San Domingo*, *President*, and *Congress*,
    15-17 Dec 1812
f *Constitution* defeated *Java*, 29 Dec 1812
g *Hornet* defeated *Peacock*, 24 Feb 1813

Map 3.1 The Cruises of the Three American Squadrons in the Autumn of 1812

after the *Nymphe*.[36] It took six days, however, for Warren to dispatch Broke with the 38-gun frigates *Shannon, Nymphe,* and *Tenedos,* as well as the 18-gun *Curlew,* "with the hope of meeting a Squadron under Commodore Rodgers of three Frigates and a Sloop of War."[37] Serious questions linger over why it took Warren six days to dispatch Broke's squadron. Why send only three frigates when intelligence reports indicated that Rodgers had the *President, United States,* and *Congress* with him? Though the *Congress* was roughly equivalent to a 38-gun British frigate, the *President* and *United States,* in Broke's words were "superior in ship & metal & number of men." Warren most certainly was aware of this, given the evidence presented at the court martial for the loss of the *Guerriere,* held at Halifax on 2 October.[38] One plausible explanation involved showing the Americans that their frigates were not special and the *Guerriere* had been the anomaly.

Across the Atlantic the image of British naval power was bruised when word of the *Guerriere* reached England on early October. Upon hearing the news, one British naval officer exclaimed, "What an unfortunate business the capture of the *Guerrion* frigate! . . . However, there is no doubt the American was superior in men and weight of mettle. . . . It is a thing I could not have expected."[39] If a naval officer could not have expected the loss, the British populace expected it even less and recoiled vociferously. One commentator called it "almost unprecedented in the naval annals of Britain."[40] This stood in stark contrast to British successes along the border between Canada and the United States and led one British official to assert, "The feeling in the British Public in favor of the Navy rendered in their eyes the military triumph no compensation for the Naval disaster."[41] *The Times* of London argued, "Under all the circumstances of the two countries . . . we know not any calamity of twenty times its amount, that might have been attended with more serious consequence to the worsted party." Three days later, *The Times* continued its argument by explaining, "Who does not see how important the first triumph is in giving a tone and character to the war. Never before, in the history of the world, did an English frigate strike to an American."[42]

Such statements led to attacks on the Admiralty. One asserted that Britain should have "at a more early period of the season, sent an effective naval force . . . with orders at once to crush their pigmy fleet."[43] More realistically, Melville wrote, "The *Guerriere* is taken by the *Constitution* American Frigate mounting 56 Guns, heavier metal than ours, & nearly double in number Crew."[44] The result, in his opinion, was not unexpected, given the circumstances. Still, public clamor and accusations placed great pressure on the Admiralty. One newspaper asserted,

"But above all, there is one object, to which our most strenuous effort must be directed,—the entire annihilation of the American navy. Nothing short of this can avenge the disgrace we have suffered by the loss of the *Guerriere*."[45] Instead, a drama with a different ending had already played out to the south of Madeira.

The *Macedonian*, a 38-gun British frigate, escorted a large East India Company ship from England. As per instructions, the ships separated south of Madeira. Several days later, on 25 October, one of the *Macedonian*'s lookouts peering to the leeward at daybreak yelled, "Sail ho!" From the deck, Captain John Surnam Carden demanded, "What does she look like?" The response was, "A square-rigged vessel, sir." Some minutes later, the lookout described her as "a large frigate, bearing down upon us, sir!"[46] Carden ordered his frigate to close with the strange frigate.

The lookout had sighted the *United States*. After parting from Rodgers' squadron, Commodore Decatur pressed toward the rich hunting grounds around the Azores and Madeira. These islands served as a waypoint for British merchantmen and a rendezvous for scattered convoys. Decatur had been hunting merchant vessels but instead had chanced upon the *Macedonian*.[47] As the morning wore on, the two frigates closed. On board the *United States* one midshipman observed, "We had got abreast of him, who not appearing desirous to near us, as was easily in his power, having the weather guage [*sic*], we gave him a starboard broadside from our

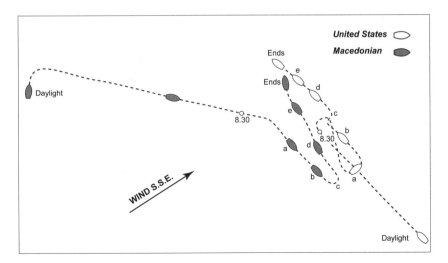

Diagram 3.1 Plan of the Engagement between the *United States* and the *Macedonian*
(Adapted from Mahan, *Sea Power and its Relations to the War of 1812*, 1:418–19)

main deck guns." The rounds, however, fell short. A partial broadside then dribbled from the *Macedonian*, but this was an accident, the product of nervousness on the gun deck.[48]

While the crew reloaded the expended rounds, "We immediately wore after her," wrote the *Macedonian's* master, "and stood for her Larboard Quarter, she wore again we still kept steering for her quarter." A midshipman on board the *United States* thought such movements had the "intention to rake us, but in this he was frustrated." These maneuvers brought the ships nearly abeam, and the *Macedonian* unleashed a broadside with her 18-pound main deck guns, since the distance remained too great for her carronades. The *United States* replied with her heavier 24-pound guns, and the firing soon became general.[49] Over the next hour, the *Macedonian* edged closer to her opponent, but the motion of the sea reduced the accuracy of her guns. Moreover, size mattered: the 18-pound shot of the *Macedonian* did little damage in comparison to the 24-pound shot of the *United States*.[50] Samuel Leech, a common seaman on board the British frigate, related, "I heard the shot strike the sides of our ship; the whole scene grew indescribably confused and horrible; it was like some awfully tremendous thunder-storm . . . strewing the ground with the victims of its wrath."[51] Yet, damage was not confined to the *Macedonian's* hull—her masts, sails, and rigging also suffered, slowing the frigate and limiting her maneuverability.

Soon, the distance had decreased enough for the *United States'* carronades to fire with effect. These smashing weapons accelerated the destruction. In but one example, "A man named Aldrich had one of his hands cut off by a shot, and almost at the same moment he received another shot, which tore open his bowels in a terrible manner. As he fell, two or three men caught him in their arms, and, as he could not live, threw him overboard." Even as the *Macedonian* became a "slaughterhouse," Leech related, "our men fought like tigers," though he admitted, "The large shot came against the ship's side like iron hail, shaking her to the very keel, or passing through her timbers, and scattering terrific splinters, which did more appalling work than even their own death-giving blows."[52]

After giving the British frigate a pounding, the *United States* sailed a short distance off to repair damage, leaving "the *Macedonian* a perfect wreck we having only about one third of the Foresail left to the yard, every other Sail having shot away." Immediately, Carden ordered what was left of his crew to clear the wreckage, and he tried to get his frigate before the wind, but the mizzenmast went over the stern.[53]

The Americans had shattered the *Macedonian*, leaving her partially dismasted and combat ineffective. As Carden viewed his once beautiful frigate, he concluded that further resistance would only waste lives and so he surrendered. On board the *United States*, the men gave "three cheers" and immediately sent a boat over.[54] "When we boarded the prize," one officer recalled, "a most bloody spectacle

The Capture of the HMS *Macedonian* by the USS *United States*, October 1812 (U.S. Naval Institute Photo Archive)

presented to view; mangled bodies, and shattered limbs, the dead laying, and dying wallowing in their gores, the wounded crawling about the decks imploring our assistance, some of them begging to be thrown overboard to terminate their misery." The *Macedonian* had sustained thirty-six killed, thirty-six severely wounded, and thirty-two slightly wounded, meaning that slightly more than one-third of her complement had fallen. The *United States* had lost only five killed and seven wounded (two were mortal wounds), and had received only eight or nine shot in her hull.[55] Decatur wrote, "The fight was all on one side. . . . The damage Sustained by this Ship was not such as to render her return to port necessary, and had I not deemed it important that we should See our prize [in] should have continued our cruise." This was but a half-truth. A lucky round from the *Macedonian* had "spoiled" her mainmast, making arguably the dullest sailing frigate in the United States Navy even slower.[56]

One British naval captain declared, "I am much surprised at Capt. Carden *keeping* so far off." This supported the following court-martial verdict: "The Court is of Opinion that previous to the Commencement of the Action from an over Anxiety to keep the Weather Gage, an Opportunity was lost of closing with the Enemy, and that owing to this circumstance the *Macedonian* was unable to bring the *United States* to close Action until she had received Material Damage." The court considered this hindsight speculation versus negligence, however, and acquitted Carden, his officers, and ship's company.[57] However, the loss of the *Macedonian* caused the cloud over the British navy to grow, leading Melville at the Admiralty to lament, "This is a heavy and most unexpected blow to us, and it proves that we always suspected that the American 44's are greatly an overmatch for our 38's."[58] More damning for Britain, both the *United States* and her prize safely reached the United States in early December.[59]

While the *United States* sailed to her rendezvous with the *Macedonian*, the *President* and *Congress* pressed eastward across the Atlantic, snapping up an official British government packet on 15 October. She was a rich prize with specie on board totaling $150,000 to $200,000.[60] Then, at 7:30 a.m. on 31 October, about three hundred miles south of the Azores, lookouts on board the *Congress* sighted three ships. The Americans had chanced upon two merchant ships and the 36-gun British frigate *Galatea*, homeward bound from the Cape of Good Hope, transporting a substantial sum of money and, of all things, "a very fine Zebra." While the merchantman made all sail, the *Galatea* maneuvered to cover their escape.[61]

The merchant vessels set a full press of sail. About noon this proved too much for one of them, and the wind carried away her foretopmast and her main

Stephen Decatur (Navy History and Heritage Command, Photo # NH 85590-KN)

The Escape of the HMS *Galatea* from the USS *President* and USS *Congress*, 31 October 1812 (U.S. Naval Institute Photo Archive)

topgallant mast. This slowed the merchantman enough for the *Congress* to take her as a prize of war. She proved to be the *Argo*, a British South Sea ship richly laden with whalebone, whale oil, and ebony. Owing to her damage, Captain Smith took her in tow while Commodore Rodgers pursued the *Galatea*. The *President* gained, but the British frigate escaped in the dark. Rodgers concluded, "The chase sailed well, but if we had had four or five hours more daylight, I have no doubt but that we should have come up with her."[62]

Another missed opportunity. Moreover, the *Galatea* continued to England, providing the Admiralty with its first knowledge that Rodgers had put to sea. It led the First Lord to rant, "I have no doubt that the two Frigates which chased *Galatea* . . . under American Colours, were bon a fide Americans whom Sir John Warren has suffered to slip out & try their fortune on another cruise; they should surely be pursued."[63] But this summation occurred six weeks into Rodgers' cruise. Up until this time, his only pursuers had come from North America. Yet, the Admiralty being made aware that Rodgers had sailed did not end his potential success, because sluggish communications hamstrung efforts to find him. A week before information about Rodgers reached the Admiralty, the 36-gun *Phoebe* had sailed on a routine patrol to the area where the *Galatea*'s encounter had occurred. Fearing for the *Phoebe*'s safety, as well as for a West India convoy transiting the area, the Admiralty sent the 74-gun *Elephant* and 20-gun *Hermes*, but this was only the first of four squadrons totaling six 74-gun ships, five frigates, and three sloops that sailed south between late November and the first of the year, chasing outdated intelligence and protecting trade from the phantom-like ships of the United States.[64]

Meanwhile, the *President* and *Congress* circled the North Atlantic, but Rodgers failed to capture another British ship. His movements, however, did lead Captain Broke to conclude, "The Rogue scours about the Atlantic *so wildly* that I doubt we have little chance of catching him." Rodgers reached the area between Bermuda and Halifax in early December, and for the next three to four weeks he searched this well-plied stretch of the ocean "but did not meet with a single Enemy's vessel."[65] However, Rodgers came within a clear day of a different conclusion.

The U.S. brig *Argus* served as the link between Rodgers' squadron and its near encounter with the British in mid-December. Under Master Commandant Arthur Sinclair, the *Argus* had parted company with Rodgers and Decatur in mid-October and then proceeded east of Barbados, through the trade routes linking Britain with South America and the Caribbean. Though Sinclair operated along busy sea-lanes, he took few prizes. Running short of provisions, he sailed home by way of Bermuda.[66]

Northwest of that island on 15 December, the *Argus* fell in with two large ships. An hour later they had closed enough for one of the strangers to signal. Sinclair responded with the private signal, but she failed to answer. Soon after the signal, Sinclair made one of them out to be a ship of the line.[67] He had encountered the 74-gun *San Domingo*, with Admiral Warren on board, and the 38-gun *Junon*. These ships, along with the 38-gun *Statira*, the 20-gun *Wanderer* and four transports, had sailed from Halifax toward Bermuda, but they had been scattered in a gale.[68] The movement of the above British ships as well as others stemmed from the seasonal reorientation of British naval forces, away from the harsher climate of New England and Nova Scotia to the more temperate climes of Bermuda.[69]

It was by coincidence that the *Argus* crossed paths with the *San Domingo* and *Junon*. The former pursued the *Argus*, while the *Junon* chased another unknown vessel.[70] This was still a grim situation for the *Argus*, and nightfall brought no relief. The moon's brightness betrayed the *Argus*, but several hours later the unexpected occurred when "a very black squall of wind and rain came on." Sinclair wrote, "as soon as we were Covered by the rain I went about and past [*sic*] Close under his bow, Carrying a press of Canvas; fortunately he was in the light and we in the dark, so that we saw him and he could not see us." As Sinclair figured, the *San Domingo*'s lookouts had lost the *Argus*.[71]

The next day, the *San Domingo* brought to the *Louisa Cecilia*, an American merchant vessel bound for Lisbon. Apparently, the master and crew kept quiet, and Warren left none the wiser that this vessel had encountered the *President* and *Congress* a mere twelve hours before.[72] What began with the *San Domingo* chasing the *Argus* became a confused series of encounters on 16 December between the *San Domingo*, *President*, *Congress*, and *Argus*, made worse by several merchant vessels, a privateer, and squally weather that severely restricted lines of sight.

At daylight on 16 December Sinclair encountered another warship; soon after, his lookouts sighted yet another large warship. At this desperate hour, Sinclair thought that the unknown warships were attempting to deceive him. Signals shot up the masts of both ships, and then they closed, maneuvering and firing "as if they were enemies coming to an engagement." Sinclair concluded this was a ruse by two British warships. One was acting British and the other was playing the part of an enemy, perhaps an American. Sinclair thought the two British captains were engaged in their act of pretend combat to draw the *Argus* closer to see if either of the ships was an American, but "finding it did not succeed they both made all sail after us."[73]

The reality of the situation proved both different and ironic. Instead of British warships attempting an act of deception, Sinclair had fallen in with Rodgers' squadron. The first ship sighted was the *President*, and the second the *Congress*. Earlier that morning, the *President* had encountered the American privateer *Teazer*. From her crew, Rodgers learned that the *United States* had captured the *Macedonian*. As a result of that American victory, he had signaled to inform the *Congress*.[74] These signals were what Sinclair had witnessed. He was deceived because this looked like the script that occurred when two warships sighted each other. They hoisted private signals, requiring the use of signal flags, and then fired guns for the purpose of signaling identity and intention.

Across the water, neither the lookouts on board the *Congress* nor the *President* identified the *Argus* as one of the several unknown vessels then in sight. Part of this had to do with squally weather, as well as the *Argus* being similar in appearance to a merchant vessel. Moreover, the *Congress* brought yet another merchant vessel to, which distracted her attention.[75]

With the *President* and *Congress* astern, lookouts on board the *Argus* made out a small sail to the south. Then, at 4:30 p.m. a squall cleared, revealing what appeared to be two more large ships to the northwest of the *Argus*. Then, her lookouts descried another large ship dead ahead. "We now found ourselves Compleatly [*sic*] surrounded by the Enemy," recalled Sinclair. He immediately decided his least-worst option involved sailing south toward his smallest opponent. The crew of the *Argus* stood at quarters, prepared for battle. Rather than a small British man of war, she proved to be the *Vansise*, an American merchant schooner that had been abandoned, except for two suspicious individuals with a letter ordering them to Cadiz. Sinclair considered this fishy, so he manned her with a prize crew and sent her to the United States.[76]

Sinclair then resumed his westerly course, but only fifteen minutes later his lookouts sighted two large ships to the northwest. He thought that these were the two ships that had chased him at daybreak, meaning they were the *President* and *Congress*. However, lookouts on board Rodgers' frigates failed to spy the *Argus*, perhaps because of heavy rain and the onset of darkness, or the simplest fact—Sinclair had encountered other ships.[77]

While the *Argus* stumbled upon the American frigates, the *Vansise*, and then several other strange sail, the *San Domingo* had a busy day. After encountering the *Laura Cecilia*, Warren's flagship had captured the American privateer *Teazer*. She had been in company with the *President* earlier in the day, leading Warren to deduce, "I must have passed very near to Commodore Rodgers of whom I had information, and rather believe that the inclemency of the Weather and Snow Storms protected him from my view."[78] Though Warren was tantalizingly close to Rodgers, the *San Domingo* again encountered the *Argus* at about 4:45 a.m. when a squall parted. This time the British warship had the weather gauge, and she quickly closed. With no chance of getting to the windward, the *Argus* ran before the wind.[79]

"At day light [I] saw her to be a line of Battle ship," recounted Sinclair. "She had now commenced her fire on us and it blowing hard, in squalls." Sinclair ordered his men to lighten the ship, but the *San Domingo* drew nearer and a second vessel now appeared. Anchors, spare spars, and the launch went into the water, and the crew began wetting the sails so they could catch the wind more effectively. This allowed the *Argus* to survive. At noon "a very heavy squall came on, . . . and upon its clearing up," Sinclair saw that the *San Domingo* had "given up the chace [*sic*]; and was standing for the other Ship." This proved a poor decision, because she turned out to be a merchant vessel carrying flour to Cadiz.[80]

Only an hour after the *San Domingo* gave up pursuing the *Argus*, Sinclair's lookouts descried another ship. Soon after, two other ships could be seen at various compass points. For a second time in as many days, the *Argus* appeared surrounded. Sinclair thought the sail to the northwest was the smallest and decided "to run through his fire; it being the only possibility of getting off." As the *Argus* neared, Sinclair "discovered he was a very large Merchant Ship full of men. . . . We fired on the ship and pass'd to windward of him." This was likely one of the transports that had sailed from Halifax with Warren. As for the other strangers in this encounter, it is difficult to ascertain their identity. Both the *Junon* and *Wanderer* were nearby and had strangers in sight.[81]

After the *Argus* passed the transport, according to Sinclair, "we were for the first time, for the upwards of fifty hours relieved of the almost certainty of being captured." Sinclair called it a "remarkable chase and wonderful escape," though he failed to realize he had escaped from American warships on at least one occasion.[82]

For Warren, the entire encounter, of which the *Argus* served as the centerpiece, had a tremendous impact on his decision making over the following months. Though the *San Domingo* had captured the privateer *Teazer*, other armed vessels had escaped, including the *Argus* on two occasions. The persistence of Sinclair's command contributed to Warren's negative assessment: "With so many of these Vessels in direct line of my passage hither convinces me how extremely numerous and destructive those Cruisers are and of the impossibility of our Trade navigating these Seas." His remedy involved "a very extensive Squadron . . . to scour the Station, of them."[83] This required reinforcements and put Warren at odds with the Admiralty.

Sinclair, however, had no inkling of his effect on Warren. Soon after losing sight of the British ships, the *Argus'* main topmast gave way, injuring fifteen men and killing one. If this had happened just hours earlier, she would certainly have been captured. Finally, two weeks after the chase, the *Argus* limped into New York in desperate need of a refit.[84]

Whereas Sinclair had survived a hair-raising chase with enemies at every turn and Warren had realized the *President* and *Congress* operated nearby, Commodore Rodgers departed the area completely ignorant of the hell he had caused Sinclair or the danger posed by the *San Domingo*. After making Boston on the last day of the year, Rodgers lamented that he had seen but five vessels and captured two, even though the *President* and *Congress* had sailed nearly eleven thousand miles. To him, not a British ship was at sea, and Rodgers concluded, "I have reason to think that his Commerce is at present infinitely more limited than people are generally aware of."[85] Or, perhaps, Rodgers could not admit that chance had again dealt him a poor hand.

The *Wasp* met a different fate. Secretary Hamilton had assigned the *Wasp* to Rodgers' squadron, but she lay in the Delaware while the rest of the squadron was at Boston. To overcome this problem, Rodgers had set a rendezvous at sea where the *Wasp* would link up with the *President* and *Congress*.[86] Accordingly, the *Wasp* under Master Commandant Jacob Jones sailed on 13 October. Three days later, she encountered a sudden and severe storm. The men raced aloft, desperately trying to shorten sail in the howling wind, but the jib boom was carried away, casting six men into the water. A race with the angry sea saved four of those men.[87]

The next night, with the *Wasp* 250 miles north of Bermuda, lookouts sighted ships in the moonlight. Cautiously, Jones worked to the windward and "steered the remainder of the night the course we had perceived them on." Daylight revealed the same ships to the leeward. Jones pursued and soon made his opponents out to be a convoy escorted by a sloop of war.[88]

Across the water, Commander Thomas Whinyates could only curse his luck. His vessel, the *Frolic*, an 18-gun *Cruizer* class brig, had received orders to escort six merchant vessels, although his crew was eleven men short. The *Frolic* and her convoy encountered a gale on the night of 17 October that sprung her main topmast and carried away her main yard, as well as her topsails. Whinyates spent the morning of 18 October trying to reassemble his vessel, and the *Frolic* remained far from battle-worthy when the *Wasp* appeared. Still, the *Frolic* "dropt astern and hoisted Spanish Colours in order to decoy the stranger under her guns and to give time for the convoy to escape."[89]

By late morning the *Wasp* had closed within half pistol shot before the *Frolic* hauled down her Spanish colors and hoisted the English, followed by a broadside of 32-pound carronades. A heavy swell combined with "the *Frolic* being very light with quick motion and being without Sail, owing to her previous Damages," however, made aiming difficult. Much of the British fire went high, but it appeared deceptively effective, quickly shooting away the *Wasp's* main topmast. Other damaged followed. This led Whinyates to believe, "The superior fire of our Guns gave every reason to expect its speedy termination in our favour." But fire from the *Wasp's* 32-pound carronades soon left the *Frolic* "unmanageable." Jones then took a position opposite the *Frolic's* bow and began to rake his opponent. The *Wasp's* position meant the *Frolic* could not bring her broadside to bear on the American. As a result, the *Frolic* sustained a series of destructive, raking broadsides, while American musketry cut down many of her crew.[90]

Jones then "laid her onboard" with his opponent's bowsprit crossing the *Wasp's* deck between her main and mizzen rigging. This placed the *Frolic* at a right angle to the American ship and still unable to effectively return fire.[91] By this point, the two junior officers remaining on the *Frolic's* deck believed that the time had come to surrender. Whinyates refused, however, deciding to take the *Wasp* by boarding. Instead, the Americans spilled on board the *Frolic*. Whinyates, even though wounded in the leg, went forward to oppose the boarders, but only a few of his men remained unwounded and capable of following. Rather than add needlessly to the bloodshed, he surrendered.[92]

Jones ordered the two vessels disentangled. Minutes later, the British brigs' masts came down. With the *Frolic* dismasted and the *Wasp* having sustained extensive damage aloft, Jones needed the remaining hours of light to get the vessels in a condition to make port. Still, he could be thankful, having but five killed and five wounded. "The slaughter on board the *Frolic* was dreadful," though. The first lieutenant and the master were dead and all the other officers wounded. Of the crew, only fifteen or sixteen were unwounded. One of the *Frolic's* lieutenants aptly concluded, "They were enabled to destroy more men of ours than we could of theirs."[93]

About an hour after the engagement, a sail appeared to the windward. Jones immediately maneuvered the *Wasp* between his prize and the newcomer. Initially, he thought the stranger to be one of the *Frolic's* convoy rejoining her escort. Half an hour later, Jones concluded that the unknown sail was a large warship. He saw his one chance was escape, but this meant abandoning his prize. Jones ordered his men to make sail, but the canvas "was immediately blown to ribbons." The *Wasp* had sustained too much damage aloft—she was doomed. Only three hours after the *Wasp's* victory, Jones surrendered to the *Poictiers*, a 74-gun ship of the line.[94]

Nearly three weeks after Rodgers and Decatur had sailed, Commodore Bainbridge slipped out of Boston with the *Constitution* and the *Hornet* on 27 October. The *Essex* sailed from the Delaware the next day.[95] Again, the Americans benefitted from faulty British intelligence coupled with poor British deployments. The day before Bainbridge put to sea, the 74-gun *San Domingo* and 64-gun *Africa* returned to Halifax. Three 38-gun frigates and a sloop under Broke were too far to the north to intercept Bainbridge. Moreover, Warren expected Bainbridge to sail about a week later than he did and inflated his squadron to include the *Chesapeake* and *Constellation*. Linking the *Constellation*, which was then in Norfolk, to Bainbridge's squadron diluted Britain's naval forces and contributed to Warren's decision to deploy a powerful squadron off Chesapeake Bay, including the 74-gun *Poictiers* and three frigates. With another frigate on a flag of truce mission involved in possible peace negotiations and the *Belvidera* escorting a convoy, Warren lacked the resources to intercept Bainbridge.[96]

The British also failed to account for Bainbridge's decision to operate off the coast of the Portuguese colony of Brazil. Before sailing, the commodore had solicited the opinion of William Jones, a friend with extensive knowledge of the international commerce. Jones was little known outside of select maritime and governmental circles, yet Bainbridge's decision portended the future: Jones would replace Hamilton as secretary of the navy in early 1813. Jones identified the Cape Verde Islands as a place where the *Essex* could rendezvous with the *Constitution* and *Hornet*. In addition, he described the coast of Brazil as an excellent cruising ground.[97]

With such information, Bainbridge, with the *Constitution* and *Hornet* and Captain Porter on board the *Essex*, pressed toward their first rendezvous at the Cape Verde Islands. Bainbridge had a rapid passage and faced a dilemma when he arrived ahead of schedule. Given the limited quantity of provisions warships could carry and the finicky nature of the wind, Bainbridge decided to sail on, hoping to encounter the *Essex* at a subsequent rendezvous. This was a savvy decision, for Porter was ten days behind.[98]

Failing to find Bainbridge at the Cape Verde Islands, Porter pushed on. Several days later, on the afternoon of 11 December, Porter chased a vessel. About 7:00 p.m. the *Essex* came within hail, and the Americans demanded the stranger heave to. Instead, she made sail, and Porter ordered his men to fire a volley of musketry into her stern. Though not as effective as cannons, musketry certainly caused less damage, and in this case it proved just as effective, since the stranger struck her colors. She proved to be the *Nocton*, a British official packet with £11,000 on board.[99]

Three days later the *Essex* made Fernando de Noronha, a small archipelago, just south of the equator and several hundred miles off the Brazilian coast. The islands were controlled by Portugal, a close ally to Britain but neutral in Britain's war with the United States, so Porter acted cautiously by disguising the *Essex* as a British merchant vessel. From the senior Portuguese official, the Americans learned that two British warships had called at the island the previous week. The official explained to the Americans that one was the heavy frigate *Acasta,* under Captain Alexander

Kerr, and the other the ship-sloop *Morgiana*. Porter also learned that Kerr had left a letter for Captain Sir James Yeo of the British 32-gun frigate *Southampton*. Since Fernando de Noronha was off the beaten path, Porter continued his ruse, relating that a gentleman on board his ship knew Yeo, and he would deliver the letter. The Portuguese official handed it over. On board the *Essex*, Porter opened the letter. Though this might seem like a breach of trust, Porter later wrote, "As this was the second rendezvous fixed on by com. [*sic*] Bainbridge I was not at [a] loss to divine whence the letter was from, nor for whom it was intended." Instead of a private letter between two British naval captains, Commodore Bainbridge pretended to be Kerr, and by this means provided Porter with the following information: "Perhaps we may meet at St. Salvadore or Rio Janeiro." By design, this statement sounded like the plan for two old friends to meet for a drink, but instead, Bainbridge had provided Porter with two locations where he hoped to unite with the *Essex*. To clarify, Bainbridge had used invisible ink to scribble, "Go off Cape Frio, to the northward of Rio Janeiro, and keep a look out for me."[100]

The deception required for this letter required substantial knowledge of the British. Kerr in fact commanded the *Acasta*, while Yeo commanded the *Southampton*. The *Acasta* was the British frigate most closely resembling the *Constitution*, the *Morgiana* was similar in appearance to the *Hornet*, and the *Southampton* was a 32-gun frigate like the *Essex*. Porter's only mistake was to act as a British merchant ship instead of the *Southampton*, but by bluffing he negated this issue and obtained the first news of Bainbridge since sailing from the United States, and with this information, he pressed toward Brazil.

On the way, Porter learned that the 20-gun British warship *Bonne Citoyenne*, with a large amount of specie, had anchored at Salvador, a port on the central Brazilian coast. Reports placed Bainbridge off that port. Rather than steer for this location, Porter followed his instructions and continued toward Cape Frio, since he did not know how long Bainbridge could remain off Salvador before a powerful British relief force showed.[101]

Porter's intelligence was correct: the *Constitution* and *Hornet* had arrived off Salvador on 13 December, and Bainbridge sent the *Hornet,* under Master Commandant James Lawrence, into the port to obtain news from the American consul, as well as water and provisions for the two ships. The *Hornet* returned on 18 December with intelligence that the *Bonne Citoyenne* rode there at anchor with $1.2 million on board.[102]

Bainbridge needed to entice the *Bonne Citoyenne* to sail, so he split his squadron with the *Constitution* in the offing and the *Hornet* close in, admonishing Lawrence to respect Brazilian neutrality.[103] On 23 December the *Constitution* chased a vessel running for Salvador, but she escaped. The next morning the *Constitution*'s lookouts sighted what appeared to be the same vessel with the *Hornet* in chase. Though Lawrence closed within musket shot of the unknown vessel, the coast lay only half a mile distant, leading him to call off the chase so as to not further encroach upon Portuguese neutrality. The event developed into an incident. The Portuguese governor maintained that Lawrence had violated the colony's neutrality by his pursuit and particularly by firing so close to the shore. More likely, this was the proverbial straw that broke the camel's back: the *Constitution*'s surgeon commented, "The Portuguese were much irritated at our conduct towards the British merchantmen together with our blockading their port."[104] Bainbridge, for his part, explained, "Had his Excellency [the Portuguese governor] ever been informed of the outrageous manner which *his good Friends* the English cruise on Neutral Coasts, I presume he would have exhibited less temper in his remonstrance to you."[105]

Two wrongs did not make Bainbridge right, however, and he decided not to go into port and instead had the American consul at Salvador send supplies out to the *Constitution* and *Hornet*. While awaiting the arrival of provisions, the *Constitution* took a short cruise, leaving Lawrence to challenge Captain Pitt Burnaby Greene of the *Bonne Citoyenne* to single combat. Both warships mounted 18 x 32-pound carronades and a pair of long guns. The American consul assured Greene that neither the *Constitution* nor any other U.S. warship would interfere.[106] Green, however, declined. The huge quantity of specie on board his ship called for caution, but officially he responded, "The result could not be long dubious and would terminate favorably to the ship which I have the honor to command, but I am equally convinced that Comm. Bainbridge could not swerve so much from the paramount duty he owes to his country as to become an inactive spectator, and see a ship belonging to the very squadron under his orders fall to the hands of an enemy." In response to Green's remarks, Bainbridge retorted, "He certainly was not warranted questioning the sacred pledge I made to him." Moreover, the commodore boasted, "I consider the refusal of Capt Green to meet the *Hornet*, as a Victory gained by the Latter Vessel."[107]

Though the chance of combat eluded Lawrence, that opportunity fell to Bainbridge. At 9:00 a.m. on 29 December his lookouts sighted two strange sail. One of these was the 38-gun British frigate *Java* under Captain Henry Lambert. Sailing for the East Indies, the *Java* had nearly a hundred supernumeraries on board destined for service in other warships on the far side of the world, along with several officers for commands in Asia, including Lieutenant General Thomas Hislop. Though the general could be a liability in action, the extra men meant that for the first time American and British frigates would fight with something approaching similar manning levels. These numbers had a deceptive quality, however, in that many had been accused of ill discipline and only a few had much experience on board a warship.[108]

When Lambert's lookouts sighted the *Constitution*, he ordered his men to cast off the prize he had in tow and close with the American frigate.[109] Bainbridge mistook the *Java* for a ship of the line, however, and kept his distance. Bainbridge tried the private signal to discount the possibility that his eyes had deceived him and she was the *Essex*, but there was no answer. Later, Bainbridge asserted his maneuvers were designed "to draw the strange sail off from the neutral coast."[110]

Regardless of his intention, the *Java* gained on the *Constitution* as the morning passed to afternoon. Bainbridge soon made his opponent out to be a frigate and decided to engage her; Lambert made the same decision.[111] When half a mile separated the frigates, the *Constitution* fired her larboard broadside, but Lambert refused to reply. Meanwhile, the American discharged a second broadside, damaging the *Java* aloft. The British frigate then returned a complete broadside into the *Constitution*'s weather bow.[112] One shot destroyed the *Constitution*'s wheel, killing several men, causing the loss of steerage, and making her drift before the wind.[113]

Bainbridge maintained, "The enemy Kept at a much greater distance than I wished, but [we] Could not bring him to closer action without exposing ourselves to several rakes."[114] This was made all the more complex by the loss of the wheel, resulting in a lack of maneuverability that allowed Lambert to bring the *Java* close under

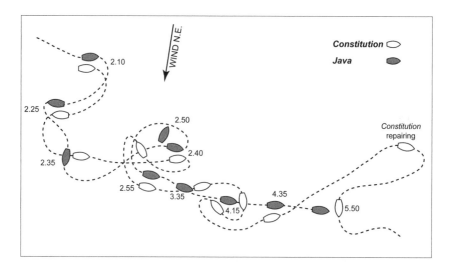

Diagram 3.2 Plan of the Engagement between the *Constitution* and the *Java*
(Adapted from Mahan, *Sea Power and its Relations to the War of 1812*, 2:4–5)

the *Constitution's* stern, raking the American frigate as each gun bore. Though the British inflicted a painful blow, the maneuver also sacrificed the weather gauge, causing the *Java* to slip to the leeward. This placed Bainbridge between the wind and his opponent, making it difficult for Lambert to rake him again and giving Bainbridge the option to rake his opponent. However, only minutes passed before Lambert used his superior maneuverability to regain his former position.[115]

By having the weather gauge, the *Java* remained free of the gunpowder smoke, while the wind caused it to shroud the *Constitution*. Masked in smoke, Bainbridge ordered his frigate to come about. In response, Lambert brought the head of his frigate directly into the wind, putting her in stays "in the hopes of getting round quick and preventing our being raked." But damage to the *Java's* bowsprit slowed this maneuver, causing the British frigate to suffer a raking broadside into her exposed stern.[116]

With a shattered stern and a damaged bowsprit, Lambert again brought the *Java* alongside the *Constitution*, this time at pistol shot. The American musketry picked at the exposed men on the British quarterdeck and forecastle, while grape and round shot splintered her sides. Amidst mounting damage, Lambert decided that his only chance for victory lay with boarding. Just moments before the two ships collided, the *Java's* foremast crashed into the sea and she lost speed and steerage, causing her to fall astern of the *Constitution*. A British officer realized, "We were left at the mercy of the Enemy."[117]

Bainbridge then brought his frigate across the *Java's* bow, raking her at very close range. She lost her main topmast. The *Constitution* then steered down the British frigate's starboard side but received scant return fire, since the battery was covered by a twisted mass of masts, spars, and rigging. Much of the wreckage hung over the side and dipped into the water. This acted like a massive sea anchor and made her unmanageable. Taking advantage, Bainbridge took a position astern and continued to rake his opponent, while musketry from the tops made clearing the wreckage deadly. Notably, a musket ball struck Captain Lambert in the chest. As the mortally wounded captain was carried below, Henry Chads, the senior lieutenant, took command.[118]

For the next forty minutes *Constitution* remained astern, "pouring in a tremendous galling fire."[119] British defenses crumbled. At most the *Java* could bring two or three guns to bear. With casualties mounting, one British officer asserted, "It only remained to uphold the Honor of the British Flag." Then, the mizzenmast went by the board.[120] Within a matter of moments, British fire slackened then stopped, and Bainbridge concluded that his opponent had struck. As a result, he decided to sail out of range so his men could repair damage. While his men worked to right the *Constitution*, Bainbridge discovered that the British flag still flew.[121]

The Capture of the HMS *Java* by the USS *Constitution*, 29 December 1812 (U.S. Naval Institute Photo Archive)

On board the *Java*, the crew worked feverishly to clear the wreckage, but the wreckage limited her steerage, causing her to slip into a trough of the waves and she began to roll heavily. The movement caused the mainmast to fall.[122] Chads received damage reports. The *Java* had lost all three masts and her bowsprit. Moreover, four carronades on the forecastle and six on the quarterdeck, as well as several main deck guns, had been knocked out of action. Finally, he found 110 absent from their quarters, most presumably dead or wounded.[123] With this report in hand, Chads approached Lieutenant General Hislop because, as he later recounted, he thought it his duty to communicate with Hislop the ship's situation and to apprise him that, should the enemy resume a raking position, he feared a continuation of the action would be fruitless. Hislop agreed. About this time, Bainbridge had the *Constitution* stand for the *Java*, leading Chads to strike the British flag.[124]

The action had left the *Constitution* much injured aloft, with nine dead and twenty-seven wounded. For the Americans, this had been the bloodiest and most difficult of the frigate battles to date, but they had plied the *Java* warmly and Chads admitted 22 dead and 102 wounded. The *Java* was nothing more than a dismasted hulk. Unable to patch her up for a journey to the United States, Bainbridge had her set afire.[125]

The *Constitution* then proceeded to Salvador, where Bainbridge deposited the prisoners and linked up with the *Hornet*. Bainbridge decided it was best for the *Hornet* and *Constitution* to "cruise separately, they will have a much better chance to annoy the Enemies Commerce." Leaving the *Hornet* off Salvador, Bainbridge steered north. Soon the commodore determined that a combination of battle damage and general decay necessitated his return to the United States.[126]

South of Bermuda on the morning of 6 February, lookouts made out a brig and schooner to the windward. Soon after, the brig betrayed herself as a warship by signaling the *Constitution*. The *Constitution* had chanced upon the *Dotterel*, an 18-gun British brig under Commander William Daniel, who watched the strange frigate show English colors and hoist a flurry of incomprehensible signals. Smelling a ruse, Daniel fled. About dark, he lost sight of the *Constitution* and had the *Dotterel* sail with all dispatch to Bermuda, arriving on 8 February. The 74-gun *Ramillies* and the 44-gun *Acasta* immediately proceeded, with the *Dotterel* in pursuit of the *Constitution*.[127] The next day proved a busy one for the squadron. In the darkness the ships exchanged numbers with the 32-gun *Narcissus*. She was approaching Bermuda from the south along a track similar to that of the *Constitution*. Just after daybreak the 18-gun *Martin* fell in with the squadron. But most important, in the early afternoon the squadron encountered Captain Broke with the 38-gun frigates *Shannon*, *Tenedos*, and *Nymphe*, and 18-gun *Curlew*. They had been on a long roving patrol and were sailing westward at almost the same latitude that the *Dotterel* had encountered the *Constitution*.[128]

The convergence of these warships occurred just a bit too late: the American frigate had a head start. Then, in the three days before reaching Boston Bay, the *Constitution* encountered a storm, masking her approach and allowing her to slip undetected into Boston.[129]

When the *Constitution* departed the Brazilian coast, Bainbridge left the *Hornet* off Salvador to continue blockading the *Bonne Citoyenne*, but the commodore cautioned Lawrence not to dally, and, particularly, "to be on your guard against the arrival of the *Montague* [sic]."[130] She was the only ship of the line on the British South America Station and was then serving as the flagship for Rear Admiral Manley Dixon. When Dixon learned on 4 January of the *Bonne Citoyenne*'s plight, he rushed north, asserting he would "do my utmost to bring the Enemy to Battle, by which I hope to liberate the *Bonne Citoyenne* and protect her." On his first day out, he fell in with a schooner with a message from the British consul in Salvador. Dated 19 December, it provided Dixon with significant insight into American strength—mentioning the *Constitution*, *Essex*, and *Hornet* by name—and American intentions with respect to the *Bonne Citoyenne*. Dixon hastened onward.[131]

On the morning of 23 January, the *Montagu*'s lookouts sighted several strange ships outside Salvador. One of these was the *Hornet*; however, the American proved nimble, with Lawrence gaining the open sea. Meanwhile, Dixon failed to discern the identity of his opponent; instead, he had *Montagu* anchor at Salvador, rescuing the *Bonne Citoyenne* and her valuable cargo.[132]

Lawrence sensibly shifted his cruising ground, steering northeast and taking one prize on his way to the Demerara River in modern Guyana. Near the river's mouth, the British had a colony that served as a profitable trading center and an outlying terminus for British convoys in the West Indies. The river and colony created favorable conditions for intercepting commerce, but there was also a significant risk of encountering British warships at that location. Lawrence found the area teeming with vessels upon his 23 February arrival. The next morning, his lookouts sighted a sail under English colors. However, the water became quite shallow as Lawrence operated in the shoals around the mouth of the Demerara River, and he decided to call off the pursuit rather than chance running aground. Besides, he had sighted another vessel under British colors. She appeared to be a man of war and Lawrence endeavored to close.[133] The Americans had sighted the *Espeigle*, an 18-gun, *Cruizer*-class brig.

Her crew passed the morning with the captain, second lieutenant, surgeon, and purser ashore. A lookout had spied the *Hornet*, but her first lieutenant discounted the sighting, thinking that she was a British warship or a packet. The lieutenant soon changed his mind and decided the *Hornet* was a merchant ship. Early in the afternoon, the *Espeigle*'s lookouts sighted the *Peacock*, yet another *Cruiser*-class brig, standing down upon the still misidentified *Hornet*.[134]

As the *Peacock*, under Commander William Peake, attempted to close with the *Hornet*, the maneuvers of the two vessels took them away from the *Espeigle*. Lawrence obtained the weather gauge at nearly the last moment. The two vessels then "passed as close as we could on opposite tacks, exchanged broadsides and cheered each other." Peake immediately brought the *Peacock* around, allowing her unengaged broadside to bear, and "the action went on as fast as we could load and fire from both Ships."[135] However, the *Peacock*'s broadsides went high, cutting through the *Hornet*'s sails and rigging. Though one of her lieutenants later asserted, "*Peacock* heeled and rolled more than the *Hornet* from being a shorter vessel," the *Peacock*'s gunner insinuated the poor accuracy stemmed from the failure to train the men at the guns.[136] This inaccuracy was made worse by the inferiority of her armament. The *Peacock* carried 16 x 24-pound carronades, not the 32-pound weapons that were standard for her class, while the *Hornet* mounted 18 x 32-pound carronades.[137]

Lawrence remained largely unaware of his superiority, however, and decided that trading broadsides at close range was the last thing he wished to do. To avoid sustaining further damage, he had the *Hornet* take a position on the starboard quarter of his opponent, "where he poured in a destructive fire from his whole Broadside while we were unable to bring more than two after Guns to bear on him." A round damaged the *Peacock*'s rudder, limiting her maneuverability. Grape ripped across the Peacock's deck, while fire from the *Hornet*'s tops "made every person on the Quarter Deck a Distinct Object." A musket ball and a large splinter wounded Peake, but he remained on deck. Every man at the *Peacock*'s four aft guns was cut down. A double-headed shot then sliced Peake in two. Command devolved upon Lieutenant Frederick Wright, but the *Peacock* was a bloody wreck.[138]

Only a few minutes after Peake's death, the *Peacock*'s carpenter reported "four feet of water in the Hold and the vessel sinking fast from his not being able to stop the Rent." Wright decided nothing more could be done and waved his hat to signal he had surrendered. American fire had cut the *Peacock*'s ensign down.[139]

Lawrence ordered a boat across to take possession of the *Peacock*, but this took several minutes. In the meantime, men on board the British vessel hoisted the colors upside-down to signal distress. The Americans immediately went to work rescuing her crew, but Lawrence lamented that she "sunk in 5 1/2 fathoms water, carrying down thirteen of her crew; and three of my brave fellows." However, four of the thirteen had scrambled aloft as the ship sank and were rescued.[140]

Transferring the crew of the *Peacock* took several hectic hours, made all the more stressful by the presence of the *Espeigle*. Lawrence asserted that she "lay about

6 miles in shore of me, and could plainly see the whole of the action." A window of opportunity existed for the *Espeigle* to come to the *Peacock*'s aid. This would have been a tougher opponent, since she was armed with 32-pound carronades versus the 24-pound ones on the *Peacock*. It took three hours and thirty minutes to repair the *Hornet*'s battle damage, but the *Espeigle* remained at anchor. A subsequent investigation determined that she had lost sight of the *Hornet* and *Peacock* about an hour before the action commenced and no firing was heard.[141]

At 2:00 a.m. the morning after the action, the *Hornet* stood out to sea and set a course for the United States, arriving at New York on 19 March 1813.[142] Only the *Essex*, out of the three American squadrons, remained at sea.

The *Guerriere, Macedonian, Java, Frolic,* and *Peacock* made five warships defeated in single combat by what many considered ships of their class. Though these losses did little to diminish Britain's ability to command the sea, they gave the United States Navy honor and glory that the Royal Navy was not in the habit of conceding. This placed the British on unfamiliar ground and led the Admiralty to demand that Warren see to it that he "vindicated the honor of His Majesty's Arms and the pre-eminence of the Naval Power of the Country."[143] On the North American Station, Captain Broke saw the situation in similar terms and wrote, "*Honor* is a jewel of more value than whole fleets & armies & public prejudice waits not to enquire into the particulars of a defeat where the result is so mortifying."[144]

The actions of the United States Navy served an important purpose. An article in *The New Hampshire Patriot* argued, "These Yankee frigates have again ranged the domain of the pretended Emperor of the Ocean." Of British naval power, the paper continued, the American navy "had the opportunity of putting his omnipo-tency to the test and proving it the groundless boast of overgrown imbecility—they have at least proved that his omnipresence is as ill founded a pretence as his omnip-otence."[145] These boasts were made all the more important given America's poor showing in other theaters of the war. Actions of the United States Navy helped unite a divided nation. Even in New England where support of the war was not strong, one newspaper explained about the sailing of Rodgers and Decatur in October, "Though we abhor the war they are engaged in, yet as they must fight, they have our best wishes for glorious success."[146]

These wishes came to fruition, and an article in *The Times* (London) desired "to give up all the laurels" of Britain's victories on the Canadian border "to have it still to say, that no British frigate ever struck to an American." Captain Broke wrote to his wife, "Had the Americans been as heartily beaten at sea as they have been by land, we might now have retired with honor."[147] Such difficulties encountered by the British at sea, however, should have been expected. In early August 1812 a British newspaper printed a list of the United States Navy warships, with only one sloop and a brig missing from it. The newspaper even gave the correct name of each commanding officer, the rating of each warship, and their locations at the outbreak of hostilities.[148] Four days after the declaration of war, Augustus Foster, the British Minister to Washington, cautioned Sawyer, "Their frigates of the largest rate carry 30 long 24 pounders on the Main Deck and 24 carronades of 32 and 48 pounders on the quarter Deck and Forecastle guns."[149] This warning should not have been required. For years heavy American frigates had operated in the Mediterranean, protecting trade and dealing with the North African states commonly known as the Barbary pirates. This brought the American navy into contact with British warships. Moreover, the *Constitution* had anchored at Portsmouth, England, in 1811. This was the location of a principal British naval base; as one Royal Navy officer put it, "The size and armament of that ship was the subject of much conversation."[150] Admiral Sir Alexander Cochrane, future commander of the British North American Squadron, wrote in January 1813, "These Ships I am told are 1600 tons (I once was on board the *United States*) and carry thirty two guns on each deck with a complement of 450 men, few frigates can stand such a force."[151]

The British possessed significant knowledge about the size of both the United States Navy and its large frigates, but they did not use this knowledge or appreciate American will during the first months of the war. One British naval officer perhaps stated it best: "Accustomed as our Navy had been to triumph on all occasions where a foe was met on anything like equal terms—and sometimes where vastly superior. . . . Our large frigates were in no shape upon a par with theirs."[152]

CHAPTER 4

"If We Could Take One or Two of These D—d Frigates"

Reassessment of Britain's Naval Objectives, 1812–13

In Britain, pressure on the naval establishment increased with each naval reverse. Immediately after news of the *Guerriere* broke in England, the chairman of a powerful merchant interest complained of reports that insurance premiums per voyage had reached 20 to 30 percent compared with the standard prewar rate of about 6 percent for ships sailing between Canada and Bermuda to the West Indies.[1] The public clamored that something had be done to better combat the Americans (see Chapter 3). Then the Admiralty and the British public learned in mid-November that several American frigates had sailed on a second cruise. Rather than receiving this information from Warren, the Admiralty received it from the British frigate *Galatea* on her arrival in Britain, after she had been nearly captured in the mid-Atlantic by the *President* and *Congress*.[2]

The Admiralty blamed Warren for the sailing of the American frigates because "they did not perceive as much vigour of operations as they thought they had a right to expect."[3] In a less than congenial directive dated 18 November, Croker, the secretary of the Admiralty, wrote to Warren, "With the great force which will be thus under your orders, their Lordships are satisfied that you will have ample means for carrying on the war with that degree of vigor and effect which the honor of H. M. Arms, and the character and interests of the country require." Though Warren certainly understood how to uphold the honor of Britain at sea, he lacked the necessary means, and the British government had yet to define the "interests of the country" as they related to the American war. More tactically worrisome, Croker reasoned that "with such ample means as are at your disposal you will not be under the necessity of risking single ships to an attack from the superior forces of the Enemy."[4] The Admiralty failed to take the uncertainty of naval warfare into consideration, writing a script for Warren that supported neither a broader strategy nor the factors of time, space, friction, and interaction.

This placed Warren in a difficult position, but the sluggish speed of communications meant that he did not realize the scope of his emerging problems with the Admiralty. Moreover, the British government piled on additional duties in late November: deciding that negotiations held no prospect for terminating hostilities, the cabinet decided to escalate the maritime war by instituting a blockade of the Chesapeake and the Delaware. Containing major population centers, the national seat of government, and areas with high support of the war, the region was geographically vulnerable to blockade.[5] On the surface this seemed a win-win proposition, but the government's decision did not account for the actual strength of Warren's squadron.

British leadership in London seemed to be making plans as they went. This should not have been surprising, given that the United States, not Britain, had declared war. This had allowed the Americans to obtain the initiative by using knowledge of the war to strike blows against the British navy while the Royal Navy remained unaware of hostilities. This was made worse by the emphasis Britain placed on fighting its ongoing war against France. Moreover, fighting Napoleon, not the American war, posed the greatest danger. Naval defeats at the hands of the United States Navy, however, necessitated the reassessment of the American naval threat in late 1812, but this took time. In the short term the combination of factors made Warren's situation worse by placing him in the difficult position of fighting a war that his political masters had yet to completely assess.

In early December Melville, as First Lord of the Admiralty, set vague rules of engagement for Warren's command as "annoying of the Enemy to the utmost of your power & means, & in every possible mode of legitimate warfare." However, Melville admonished Warren to be risk-averse, adding that he was to undertake only operations "for the success of which a reasonable prospect may be entertained." Doing the utmost to annoy the Americans likely required a willingness to risk warships, but this failed to resonate with Melville. As to Warren's means, Melville considered them adequate and asserted, "In the number of pendants under your orders, we reckon about one seventh of all Sea-going Vessels in the British Navy." Melville could only support this figure, however, by including Warren's forces in the Leeward Islands and at Jamaica, but the objectives outlined by Melville related almost entirely to the portion of Warren's command off the U.S. coast. More specifically, the First Lord wrote, "It is indispensably necessary that our Trade be protected & our Naval superiority be maintained." In this, the First Lord set Britain's initial naval objects and then went on to explain that the means of obtaining the objective would be a naval blockade supported by small squadrons at key locations to make the sailing of American warships "such a hazardous enterprize as may in time produce the same effect upon the Americans as upon the French, in that their Line of Battle Ships & Frigates rarely attempt it, & that their exertions by Sea are chiefly confined to small privateers in the [English] Channel."[6] Though the French navy was larger than the United States Navy, it had taken the British years to obtain a degree of success against the French, even though France was closer to the British Isles and operations against France, even in 1812, required far more than one-seventh of the Royal Navy. Although Melville's assessment held nuggets of wisdom, it also cast Warren's command in a fanciful light; though it was penned in early December, it did not reach Warren until mid-February 1813.[7]

The Admiralty had begun to grow dissatisfied with Warren, but he remained unaware of their discontent owing to delayed communications. In the dark about what he was to do because negotiations with the Americans were not working, Warren wrote the first inklings of an operational plan on 18 November and sent it to the Admiralty. He needed something to guide his operations, and he likely sent this document as a test to determine what resonated with the Admiralty. Warren emphasized amphibious warfare involving the occupation of New Orleans and raids on places like Charleston, Savannah, the Chesapeake, the Delaware, and New York to destroy ships, dockyards, and arsenals. Moreover, he hoped to cause alarm among the inhabitants with these raids. Such operations required ground troops, and Warren asked for 3,100. However, even this small contingent was beyond Britain's means, and Melville cautioned Warren to expect about two thousand soldiers and marines: "[Given] the heavy demands from the Peninsula & Canada, I do not know if more can be spared." For the oceanic war, Warren vaguely outlined a plan to blockade the Chesapeake and station squadrons off the principal American ports "to cut off the Enemy's Commerce and resources." When Melville received this plan, he concurred by asserting that raids, along with a "rigorous blockade of their ports will be the most annoying form of warfare that we can adopt against them." Though Warren asked for naval reinforcements, Melville again cited the lack of available means.[8]

Other commitments meant that Britain lacked the ships and soldiers to implement Warren's proposed amphibious and naval operations. Melville emphasized the destruction of American naval power made necessary by the loss of the *Guerriere,* instead of raids with soldiers and marines and the more commercially oriented blockade advocated by Warren. Though Melville's response differed from Warren's plan, it allowed Warren to begin to clarify his operational concept. In the near term, however, delays in communications continued to negate any beneficial dialogue. For example, Warren wrote his plan on 18 November, but Melville's reply did not reach him until mid-February.[9]

Although the speed of communications proved crippling, the Admiralty thought the contents of Warren's message traffic problematic. Melville in January 1813 wrote to Warren, "We are kept in a very embarrassing state of ignorance on the subject, by having received no disposition of your Fleet."[10] Part of the problem involved finding Warren. Rather than work from a fixed point like Bermuda or Halifax, he was on the move. Additionally, three packet boats carrying letters were captured during this period.[11] The clarity of Warren's dispatches that actually reached the Admiralty left much to be desired. For example, on 5 November he reported, "The Squadron which sailed from Boston on the 5th Ult[imo] under Commodore Rodgers was met with on the 13th Oct. in Latitude 35°06′ N. Longitude 60°00′ W. steering S.E." What Warren meant by "met with" obscured whether the British defeated Rodgers' squadron, turned it back, or just encountered it. Warren did not explain, and the Admiralty needed to know in order to reinforce the necessary stations. To make matters worse, the report arrived in London on 29 December, almost two months after it was written.[12]

Warren's failure to clearly communicate and the Admiralty's failure to balance objectives with the means at Warren's disposal became the nexus of a developing rift between the two parties. The tyranny of distance only made the fracture worse. All the above were internal fissures within the British naval establishment that could have been covered up by naval victories; instead, the United States Navy continued to best British warships in single ship-to-ship combat. In late 1812 one British naval captain stated, "I fear *Macedonian's misfortunes* will be more felt at home than all our *allies' successes*."[13] British newspapers fulfilled this expectation. *The Morning Chronicle*, the mouthpiece of those in opposition to the current British government, ranted, "We hope that the British navy will avoid disgrace; but it is impossible to avoid the ignominy of deserving it: since the total incapacity of the Boards [of Admiralty] . . . must subject us to these disasters." The naval failures they asserted were the result of "the total want of foresight, or of ignorance at the Admiralty Board." A week later, the same newspaper argued, "Much stress has been laid on the size of the American frigates, but though this completely exonerates our officers and sailors . . . , it is no excuse for the Admiralty." Even a more moderate newspaper, *The Times* (London) cast blame: "We have suffered ourselves to be beaten in detail, by a Power that we should not have allowed to send a vessel to sea. We held a stake of millions in our hands, which we could have retained with the grasp of Hercules, and we have hazarded it upon a game at push-pin, played by children."[14]

Just days after these comments appeared in the press, Melville advised Warren, "The capture of the *Guerriere* & *Macedonian* has created a great sensation in this Country, & we look for retribution in the vigorous prosecution of offensive measures & the strict blockade of the Enemy's Ports."[15] The Admiralty demanded: "It is of the highest importance to the Character and interests of the Country that the

Naval Force of the Enemy, should be quickly and completely disposed of." Placing the United States Navy over that of Napoleonic France indicated that emotions had taken control of the Admiralty's war effort. Croker added, "My Lords have thought themselves justified at this moment in withdrawing Ships from other important Services for the purpose of placing under your orders a force with which you cannot fail to bring the Naval War to a termination."[16]

Warren had become a liability for the Admiralty. In an effort to exert better control over naval operations in North America, the Admiralty board in early January 1813 latched onto a demand Warren had made in August 1812 to have a captain of the fleet handle much of the day-to-day business of the fleet. Warren wanted Captain Sir Thomas Hardy, but Melville asserted that he was too junior: the captain of the fleet usually was a rear admiral or a captain senior to all other captains on the station. Several captains had seniority over Hardy, thus his appointment would be improper; instead, the Admiralty dispatched Captain Henry Hotham. Warren considered the Admiralty's comments "respecting the Seniority of Sir Thomas Hardy are very just and conclusive." Though Warren spoke in high terms about Hotham, this did not change the fact that he was not Warren's choice.[17] In addition, the Admiralty sent out Rear Admiral Cockburn, whom Melville considered to be "a very intelligent & enterprizing Officer." Overall, Melville explained to Warren, "We shall hope to hear from you more frequently & regularly than heretofore; more especially as the arrival of Admiral Cockburn & Captain Hotham will have relieved you from a considerable portion of your labor in details of minor importance."[18] The Admiralty placed great hope in these officers, and others held similar views. One of Hotham's fellow officers called him "our leading man in the service one of these days."[19] The Admiralty needed Cockburn and particularly Hotham to better implement Britain's operational requirements in the Americas without the political embarrassment of removing Warren. In fact, before his departure to join Warren's command, Hotham was invited to dine with Melville and other members of the Admiralty for a private conversation about his new appointment.[20]

The need for trusted leadership proved increasingly necessary as criticism mounted over the handling of the war. The Duke of Wellington, then commanding land forces in the Iberian Peninsula, wrote, "I have been very uneasy about the American naval successes. I think we should have peace with America before the season for opening the campaign in Canada, if we could take one or two of these d—d frigates."[21] Inquiries into the war reached the Houses of Parliament in February 1813. In the House of Commons, one member censored the ministers for allowing American warships to sail and privateers to prey on merchant vessels.[22] Another member in the Commons, George Canning, added, "I complain not of the naval department, but of the policy which controlled its operations. I complain that the arm which should have launched the thunderbolt, was occupied in guiding the pen: that Admiral Warren was busied in negotiating, when he ought to have been sinking, burning, and destroying." Canning then asserted that the loss of the *Guerriere* and *Macedonian* "produced a sensation in the country scarcely to be equaled by the most violent convulsion of nature. I do not attribute the slightest blame to our gallant sailors; they always do their duty; but neither can I agree with those who complain of the shock of consternation throughout Great Britain, as having been greater than the occasion justified." As for the war, Canning argued, "I shall not be considered as sanguinary and unfeeling when I express my devout wish that it may not be concluded before we have re-established the character of our naval superiority, and smothered in victories the disasters which we have now to lament."[23]

In the House of Lords, Henry Bathurst, third Earl of Bathurst, then serving as secretary of state for war and the colonies presented the government's arguments. Bathurst's cabinet position placed him in Liverpool's inner circle, responsible for policy decisions relating to military operations and colonial affairs.[24] With a high level of insider knowledge, Bathurst argued that economics was the crucial factor for Britain's apparent lack of aggressiveness during the first months of the war against the United States. The opening of hostilities found valuable British manufactured goods en route to the United States; in addition, American flour was needed for Wellington's army in the Iberian Peninsula, and British colonies in the West Indies depended on foodstuffs from America. One member of the House of Lords countered by citing the naval situation in North America: "An inadequate force was stationed there, and then a parade was made of sending instructions to the admiral to adopt active measures of hostility in the event of a declaration of war, whilst the means of carrying into effect those measures were not placed at his disposal."[25] Melville stated that forces could not be spared from other stations, and Liverpool, the head of the government, added, "If we looked to the greatest naval light of this country (he need hardly mention the name of lord [*sic*] Nelson) . . . that the French fleet twice escaped the vigilance of his pursuit."[26] To better combat accusations of naval failure, a list of actions was drawn up to show how the Admiralty had confronted America since 1810 and in the process cast fault on others.[27]

There was much to blame for Britain's handling of the war in 1812 and early 1813. Warren deserved censure for poor communications, but the government failed to accurately assess the nature of the maritime threat posed by the United States and placed impossible expectations on Warren. Though not an excuse, inexperience was a factor. Melville had been First Lord only since March and Liverpool head of the government since May. War with America served as their first important maritime test, made more severe by the fact that Liverpool's extensive résumé of positions of power in the British government had never included a position in the Admiralty. Added to this, neither Croker nor Melville had ever commanded a warship. Though there were several naval officers on the Admiralty board, none had Warren's experience, and none had been in a command situation as grueling as his current assignment. The Admiralty failed to take into account that Warren had arrived at Halifax less than two weeks before Rodgers and Decatur had sailed on their second cruise. In addition, the government had asked Warren to negotiate an end to hostilities. His initial actions were necessarily tentative to avoid provocation that could adversely affect negotiations. Moreover, his command was an amalgamation of three existing stations: the Jamaica, Leeward Islands, and North America. Given the sluggishness of communications, it took time to develop effective command arrangements.

Warren argued that his command was underresourced in comparison to the area of operations and numerous convoys he had to escort, but he failed to apprise the Admiralty of his deployments or provide accurate lists of the warships he had at his disposal. Because of slow communications, warships could be lost, become inoperable, or be detached from Warren's area of operations for convoys and other missions while the Admiralty remained ignorant.[28] The Admiralty needed better information, not merely appeals for more warships, given the stress that the British navy was under. Between the American war and fighting France, an Admiralty official lamented in mid-January 1813, "We have not at this moment a vessel of any description that we can call disposable."[29] Warren had to make do with the number of warships the Admiralty thought he had. According to February 1813 Admiralty calculations, Warren had significant combat power. Croker argued that his command included a staggering ninety-eight warships, including eleven ships of the line and thirty-four frigates. He added a familiar retort, however—Warren had failed to apprise the Admiralty about his own deployments or the strength of the American navy.[30] This proved particularly irksome, given the country's preoccupation with what one writer labeled the "three overgrown American frigates." This writer added that the British public was "indignant at the bare sound and appearance of a defalcation of our usual superiority on our own element." Another writer argued, "The loss of our ships is a national disgrace, not an individual one."[31]

The Admiralty's opinion of Warren continued to decline. In a scathing secret letter dated 10 February 1813, Croker confronted Warren about what the Admiralty saw as mismanagement. Something needed to be done because "their Lordships are not only not prepared to enter into your opinion that the force on your station was not adequate to the duties to be executed, but they feel that, consistently with what other branches and objects of the public Service require, it may not be possible to maintain on the Coast of America for any length of time a force so disproportionate to the Enemy." Croker then called one of Warren's assertions "exaggerated." He quizzically asked why one of Warren's frigates was refitting at Gibraltar when his command was so weak. As a result, Croker lectured, "the uncertainty in which you left their Lordships in regard to the movements of the Enemy and the disposition of your own force has obliged them to employ" powerful squadrons on distant stations where the Americans might appear. Croker beseeched Warren "to strike some decisive blow" because the Admiralty believed his command adequate to its assigned tasks. Several days later Croker provided the Admiralty's intent for the use of his forces, stating, "In all Cases the full protection of the Trade of His Majesty's Subjects, be considered as the subject of paramount attention and not to be neglected for the no doubt very important but secondary object of distressing the trade of the Enemy."[32]

Protection of British trade might sound one-dimensional, but it entailed interrelated and interlocking layers. Warren had to position squadrons to watch American ports to keep U.S. warships and privateers bottled up or intercept them when they proceeded to sea; he had to deploy roving squadrons along the sea lanes; and he had to deploy convoys for merchant ships, which required escorts strong enough to deal with reasonable threats.

The Admiralty's disgruntlement served an important purpose by forcing a reassessment of the maritime war. Though this had positive long-term ramifications, it had a negative impact on its relationship with Warren. However, Warren remained unaware of the Admiralty's displeasure owing to slow communications. The pivotal Admiralty letter of 18 November that began their critique of Warren's handling of the war only reached him in mid-February, but it spurred him to action. The tenor of his messages to the Admiralty immediately changed: "I am fully aware of the mischief that might result from the American Squadrons being at Sea, and I hope that the disposition of the Force under my orders, the most anxious exertions have been made by me to counteract their depredations to the fullest extent of my means." Warren wrote in thankful terms about the Admiralty's decision to reinforce his command. He acknowledged "their Lordships seem to express great regret at the escape from Port of the American Squadron under Commodore Rodgers," but he asserted, it was "a circumstance that gave me infinite concern, but which was not in my power to prevent." He had arrived on the station only days before Rodgers sailed. He found his command dispersed and worn out from months of active operations. Though he made no mention of Sawyer, the implication was clear—his predecessor left him with a poor hand. Warren took credit for immediately dispatching the 74-gun *Poictiers* to the Chesapeake, though, because on this mission she captured the *Wasp* and recaptured the *Frolic*. One moment of luck occurred on 4 February 1813. While steering into Chesapeake Bay on board his flagship, the 74-gun *San*

Domingo, Warren asserted, "I saw the American frigate *Constellation* . . . but being to Windward she was enabled to get into Hampton Roads before it was possible for me to cut her off."[33] The British had finally prevented an American warship from reaching open water. Overall, Warren focused on his accomplishments, and his problems were beyond his control. Moreover, for the first time since taking command, Warren described his deployments (Table 4.1).[34]

Table 4.1. Proposed Division of British Warships and Their Stations

Stations	Warship Types	Number
Blockade of the Chesapeake	Ships of the line	2
	Frigates	2
	Smaller vessels of war	3
Blockade of the Delaware	Ships of the line	1
	Frigates	1
	Smaller vessels of war	1
Off New York	Ships of the line	1
	Unnamed vessels	1
Off Nantucket Shoals, Block Island, Montauck Point	Frigates	2
Bay of Fundy	Smaller vessels of war	5
For the Protection of Nova Scotia	Frigates	3
Off Charleston, Beaufort, Occacoke, and Roanoke	Frigates	1
	Smaller vessels of war	1
Savannah and St. Augustine	Smaller vessels of war	1
To relieve ships and have a force for contingencies	Ships of the line	2
	Frigates	2
	Smaller vessels of war	2

When Croker and Melville responded to Warren's attempts at damage control in late March, news of the *Java*'s capture had just entered the press. Melville admitted that the loss "excited a considerable sensation here."[35] Again, the press was not kind to the Admiralty, with one newspaper asserting, "Our readers will see with a feeling of great mortification, that another English frigate,—a *third*,—has been captured by the Americans,—who, for their part, have not lost a single one. We say mortification, because were the circumstances owing to any thing but the most culpable folly and neglect on the part of Ministers."[36] One commentator close to the government made the following assessment: "We require success very much: The loss of the *Macedonian* & *Java* frigates . . . having excited a considerable degree of dissatisfaction." However, the commentator continued, "the malcontents know not what to complain of, but bad luck, a kind of desire to complain of the Admiralty."[37] Rather than transfer these complaints to Warren, the Admiralty focused on future operations. Croker reasoned that actions "which should have the effect of crippling the Enemy's Naval force should have a preference."[38] Melville added that this should be done through trade protection and blockading the U.S. coast. To accomplish these missions, the Admiralty increased Warren's command to approximately 120 warships, or nearly one-fourth of the entire deployed strength of the British navy. For the first time in a war that was now nine months old, Warren had been sent clear instructions matching objectives to means.

This situation, however, was not to last. Only three days passed before the British again mismatched objectives and means when the government thought it proper to extend the blockade to include New York, Charleston, Port Royal, Savannah, and the Mississippi River. This was a questionable decision. If the Admiralty's intent was to limit the effectiveness of the United States Navy, New York made sense, given that this was a hub of naval operations, but the other ports listed lacked the facilities to fit out warships for oceanic missions and had difficulty fitting out privateers. The largest benefit of the expanded blockade was commercial, giving the British legal advantages in capturing neutral vessels making these ports. The blockade also communicated to the Americans that the British were willing to escalate the war. In particular, a blockade affected revenue: the U.S. tax system rested on import duties. Melville explained, "We do not intend this as a mere *Paper* blockade, but as a complete stop to all Trade & intercourse by Sea with those Ports."[39]

None of this helped Warren, who remained uncertain if he was to focus on a commercial blockade, a naval blockade, or the defense of British trade. A commercial blockade required ships to be dispersed off all ports and along trade routes. The number of warships was generally more important than size. Whereas a blockade to cripple the United States Navy required larger warships capable of fighting and defeating American warships, and only ports like Boston and New York that could support naval operations required strict blockade. This blockade could be either a close or open blockade. The former was designed to pin warships in port, while the latter was designed to draw warships out to sea so as to be able to eliminate them in combat.[40] The protection of British trade, conversely, placed emphasis on using warships of the Royal Navy as convoy escorts, while a secondary British naval object became the blockade of ports used by American privateers and warships. In attempting to balance these three objectives (trade defense, naval blockade, and commercial blockade), Warren asserted in late April that he had "done all in my power . . . but I have not any ships to relieve those already employed at this critical moment." Warren controlled fewer warships than he thought optimal, but this was not a unique problem. Other British fleet commanders were voicing similar concerns in early to mid-1813.[41]

The Admiralty tweaked Warren's instructions in late April: "His Majesty's Government has *notified* a blockade of certain Ports only, because it is considered that for their purposes your Force will be always adequate, and that it may be concluded that you will be able to maintain throughout the Year such blockade most strictly, but this is by no means intended to interfere with your authority to establish blockades *de facto*, of any other Ports." Understanding the Americans would attempt to circumvent the blockade, the Admiralty explained, "The Enemy will endeavour to turn the Channel of their Trade from the blockaded Ports to others which are not so."[42]

In agreement, Warren replied, "I am persuaded that the Blockade of the Enemies Ports here & the chain of ships established along their whole coasts has already; & will produce most beneficial Effect to our Arms; than any measure whatever." However, a familiar problem still influenced operations on the North American coast, leading Warren to assert that he had "done all in my power . . . but I have not any ships to relieve those already employed at this critical moment." Additionally, Warren lamented, "I am much concerned that notwithstanding every Effort on my part, that it has not been possible to meet & capture any of the Enemies Frigates."[43]

What had been accomplished? Though Warren lacked reliefs, his command now had enough ships to project power along the entire coast. In February his command had prevented the *Constellation* from sailing, leading Captain Broke to exclaim, "This is the *beginning* of naval war to the Americans." As the situation continued to improve, so did Broke's perspective, and the next month he wrote, "Our Blockades are forming—& they will soon learn who commands the ocean."[44] Moreover, the Admiralty and Warren had at last begun to communicate. Though differences remained, naval officers saw the situation improve, leading Broke to state, "*We* are glad to see that old England is at last roused to anger, now the *old Lion* is in wrath & we shall act with energy." He concluded, "Bad luck cannot last forever."[45]

CHAPTER 5

"Cast Away . . . or Taken"

American Naval Failure and Reassessment, June 1812– Early 1813

B ritain suffered a series of naval defeats during the early months of the War of 1812, yet the Americans could count a similar list of failures, particularly as the naval war unfolded in the southern United States. The situation confronted by Lieutenant Johnston Blakeley symbolized America's problems in the south. Concerned and disgusted by the orders he had received, the officer informed Hamilton, "Anxious as I have ever been to render implicit obedience to every order of the Navy department, it is with regret I have to state the total incapacity of the *Enterprize* to carry those arms." It was April 1812—war with Britain appeared only a possibility, and Blakeley had received orders to depart Washington D.C., and sail for New Orleans with his vessel acting as a glorified transport. He ranted, "It would load her up as to disqualify her in every sense of the word as a vessel of war."[1]

Tasking the *Enterprize* to ferry supplies—and, as it turned out, Major General James Wilkinson, the new military commander to New Orleans—was indicative of the geographical complexity and strategic diversity confronting the United States Navy during the War of 1812.[2] The navy needed a developed infrastructure for the maintenance of its ships. North of Norfolk this existed. It was no coincidence that Secretary Hamilton concentrated a large part of the United States Navy at New York immediately prior to hostilities, and returning warships consistently returned to the Delaware, New York, and Boston. Yet, the United States in 1812 counted extensive coastlines south of Norfolk.

When the *Enterprize* sailed in the last days of peace, she proceeded down the Chesapeake, passing the naval base at Norfolk. Over the next weeks the *Enterprize* sailed past the Charleston naval base, under Captain John Dent. Again without

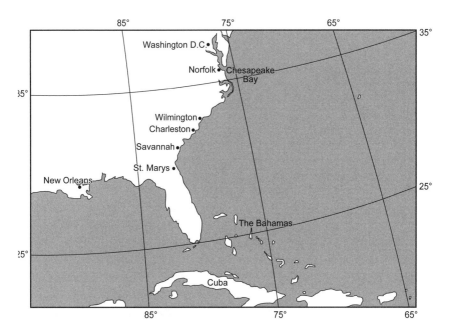

Map 5.1 The Southern United States in 1812

stopping, she continued beyond St. Marys, a naval base on the border between Georgia and Spanish Florida under Captain Hugh Campbell. Next, Blakeley proceeded around Florida, which was not yet part of the United States, and then to the Mississippi River, winding up the difficult channel to New Orleans, where he placed the *Enterprize* under the orders of Captain John Shaw.

One-third of the operational ocean-going warships of the United States Navy operated south of Norfolk at the outbreak of hostilities, but none was larger than a sloop. The *Enterprize* mounted 14 x 18-pound carronades and 2 x long 9-pounders. At New Orleans Hamilton also stationed the *Siren*, with 16 x 24-pound carronades and 2 x long 12-pound guns, and the *Viper*, mounting 12 x 12-pound carronades and 2 x long 6-pound guns. On the eastern seaboard south of Norfolk, only the *Vixen*, armed with 12 x 18-pound carronades and 2 x long 9-pound guns, operated.[3] The day after the declaration of war, Hamilton sent a circular to his uniformed naval leadership in the southern states authorizing them to commence hostilities. He ended, "Be upon your guard—instructions more in detail will be shortly transmitted to you."[4]

When news of hostilities reached New Orleans on 9 July, Captain Shaw immediately reminded Hamilton, "From my former communications . . . it will have been observed, that the force under my command, is by no means adequate to the defence of the extensive coast, which it has to guard, even against pirates and privateers, in a state of peace; and how much less so, must it be, in a time of War!" Although the *Enterprize* had arrived safely in the Mississippi, Shaw lamented that the *Siren* and *Viper* were on peacetime missions and unaware that hostilities existed.[5]

The *Viper* had orders to convoy a U.S. consul to Havana, where news of the war had yet to arrive. While there, a British brig of war called on the port, but the vessel sailed a short time before the *Viper* slipped out to sea on 7 July. Still unaware of hostilities, the American warship pressed for New Orleans. Little did her commander and crew know that reports had appeared in American newspapers of the *Viper*'s capture.[6] This surely added to Secretary Hamilton's concern, because stories telling of her capture appeared at the same time that Rodgers' squadron had vanished at sea after engaging the *Belvidera*. The *Viper*, however, returned to New Orleans on 23 July.[7]

The *Siren* sailed from the Mississippi only one day before news of the declaration of war arrived. Shaw thought it possible to recall the *Siren*, so he dispatched a gunboat after her. But the days turned to weeks, and Shaw was worried: "From the *Siren*, for the safety of which, I entertain considerable apprehension, I have as yet heard nothing."[8]

Meanwhile, the *Brazen*, a British sloop of war mounting twenty-eight guns, appeared off the mouth of the Mississippi.[9] This deployment was the work of Vice Admiral Charles Stirling, the commanding officer at Jamaica, who had acted immediately upon learning of the declaration of war. Taking the initiative did not prove easy: Stirling had at most twenty warships in his command, but he sent the 38-gun frigate *Arethusa* to cooperate with the *Brazen* so as to rapidly bring the war to New Orleans. This led Shaw to worry that the British would snap up the *Siren* upon her return.[10] To prevent this, Shaw worked out a scheme to assist in her safe arrival. He ordered Blakeley to bring the *Enterprize* to the southernmost outpost on the Mississippi at the Balize and take the gunboats there under his orders. Particularly, Shaw directed, "as the Brig *Siren* is now momently [*sic*] Expected at the Balize in the Event of her being attack'd by an Enemy, you will use every Exertion in your Power to Co-operate & render her every aid in your power."[11]

While the *Enterprize* prepared to drop down the Mississippi, the *Siren* anchored off Ship Island. This was the only protected deepwater anchorage between the river and Mobile Bay, and served as a stopping point for vessels trying to enter the Mississippi. On the morning of 17 August the *Brazen*'s lookouts sighted the *Siren*, but her commander decided not to close, given his unfamiliarity with the channel. The next morning, another sail hove into sight, and the *Brazen* pursued.[12]

Before the *Brazen* could return to deal with the *Siren*, events took an unexpected course. On Tuesday 18 August New Orleans baked under sultry heat and humidity, untempered by any kind of breeze. Nightfall brought no relief; but when the inhabitants awoke on Wednesday, both the humidity and the temperature had dropped; and a nice breeze had sprung up. One person noted an ominous sight: "The horizon covered with dark heavy clouds which indicated a storm." As the day wore on, bands of showers lashed the city. The wind built in the darkness and "the rain fell in torrents." About 11:30 p.m. the storm, now hurricane strength, climaxed. A number of merchant vessels detained by the declaration of war "were all, except three, driven from their moorings . . . , [and] were forced across the river and dashed among the vessels at the levee, which caused sad destruction." Three or four of the merchant vessels, being driven by the storm, fouled the *Viper*. Morning found her a hulk, floating amidst masts, spars, and rigging, as well as bales of cotton and the occasional corpse.[13] The hurricane struck while the *Enterprize* was on her way to the Balize and drove her into the muddy riverbank. Shaw described the sight to Hamilton, adding, "Fortunately; however, [it was] without loss of lives, and with little or no injury to her hull." The *Siren* escaped with mild damage.[14]

By the time dawn broke on Thursday 20 August, the tempest had passed. One resident in New Orleans recounted, "The hurricane far surpassed any thing of the kind ever witnessed here before, for violence and consequent destruction of property. Every house in the city is more or less injured—many were dashed to atoms—hundreds of lives were lost on the river, and out of 60 vessels scarcely six are worth repairing."[15]

As for the *Brazen*, her commander had pressed for the open sea as the weather deteriorated, but she did not gain enough sea room before the storm took control of her destiny. From early on she was in trouble, with the hurricane's winds threatening to drive her ashore. The wind blew her sails from her yards; as the hurricane reached its climax, it pushed her westward before the wind. Water stood on her gun deck and each wave caused her to ship more water. Her destruction appeared imminent. Only by cutting away her masts and anchors and throwing her guns and shot over the side did the crew save the ship. Daylight found her but a quarter mile from land. Some two weeks later, she limped into Pensacola for emergency repairs. The *Arethusa* rode out the storm off the Mississippi. Though she preserved her masts, the storm caused her captain to order many of her quarterdeck and forecastle guns, as well as a considerable quantity of shot, heaved into the water. Afterward, she sailed for Vera Cruz, Mexico.[16]

Though both British warships survived, rumors circulated in American newspapers of their loss.[17] This news reached the Admiralty in late October, leading Melville to reminded Warren, "These untoward accidents will have weakened the force on the Jamaica Station, but I conclude that you will have taken immediate measures for reinforcing it."[18] Warren had no forces to send, however, given his other commitments. In Jamaica, Stirling took matters into his own hands and explained to Warren, "The *Narcissus* [thirty-two guns] which brought a convoy from England with orders to join you, will be sent off New Orleans . . . in compliance with your directions to detach a frigate there."[19]

At New Orleans, the American naval force remained combat ineffective until November. The *Siren* became the first operational warship, now under the command of Lieutenant Commandant Joseph Bainbridge, the brother of Commodore William Bainbridge. Joseph received this command on 9 May, but his ship was located at New Orleans and he in Washington. Hamilton allowed him to visit his brother before proceeding to Louisiana, but this delayed his departure until after the declaration of war. Since the war made finding a vessel sailing to New Orleans impossible, he traveled overland, using the river system in a "tedious passage of fifty days, a part of the way in an open Skiff and a Kentucky flatt." This odyssey occurred because of the geographic isolation of New Orleans and the difficulty of moving men and equipment from the eastern United States. Bainbridge arrived in New Orleans on 6 September, but the lack of men and equipment delayed the sailing of his new command. Finally, on 5 November Bainbridge beat out toward open water under a headwind. Around 5:00 p.m. the *Siren* grounded on an unmarked shoal, probably created by the recent hurricane. With "the Ship beating so as to give reason, every moment to expect that she would go to pieces," Bainbridge asked the opinions of his officers, and they all concurred that the *Siren* needed to be lightened. As a result, her crew heaved nine 24-pound carronades and a considerable amount of shot into the water. Considerably lighter, the ship floated, but the loss of much of her armament meant her cruise was over before it even began.[20]

Prior to the hurricane, Blakeley of the *Enterprize* had gone over Shaw's head by writing directly to Secretary Hamilton for orders to return to the Atlantic. The reason he gave dealt with "the little utility which would attend her operations on *this station*. The coast of this country affords no encouragement to a vessel drawing as much water as ours."[21] Alarmed by this pronouncement, Hamilton ordered the *Enterprize* to St. Marys, but this move proved impossible before the end of November, given the damage she had sustained in the hurricane.[22] Shaw, in the meantime, unsuccessfully attempted to have the order revoked, asserting, "Her services being much wanted here; as, in co-operation with the *Siren*, she could not fail of greatly annoying the Commerce of the Enemy in the Gulph [*sic*] of Mexico, and taking many of the Jamaica ships, on their passage round the West end of Cuba."[23]

For Shaw, the first months of the war were a disaster. Moreover, his warships had failed to capture a single British merchant vessel, but another issue loomed. On 7 August Major General James Wilkinson, the senior army officer at New Orleans, presented Shaw an order invoking instructions from the president of the

United States. Wilkinson asserted, "It is Indispensible that you should consider yourself subject to my requisitions and orders only." Affronted, Shaw beseeched Hamilton that he should "forbid the introduction of the precedent,—that a Naval Commander shall consider himself subject to the *orders* of a Military officer." Shaw argued, "Nothing of the kind has ever before been heard, or thought, of; no construction of the existing laws, or of my orders from the Navy-Department, can justify me in fixing on the Naval Service so dangerous and so degrading a precedent. . . . In a word, the Military know nothing about naval affairs." Hamilton only muddied the waters in his response, maintaining on the one hand, "The details however of Your command will not be interfered with," and on the other, that it was "indispensable of having but one head to direct our operations on distant stations."[24] By the end of the year, Wilkinson had turned Shaw into his subordinate.[25]

Wilkinson was not Shaw's only problem. One navy officer in Louisiana concluded, "I cannot forbear expressing my disapprobation of the imbecile measures [*sic*] pursued by those in whom the direction of our Naval affairs here, is vested." This officer lashed out at Shaw: "I cannot but exclaim against the rigour of my destiny, . . . under the controul [*sic*] [of] a *naval officer*, in whose inattintion [*sic*] and cautious timidity, I cannot, in justice to myself acquiesce; and who is himself, in fact, ruled by the arrogant and capricious humour of a *Military* officer, quite unversed in Naval affairs."[26] Other officers on the station had also lost confidence in Shaw. Blakeley had appealed to Hamilton for a reassignment, while Lieutenant John Henley of the *Viper* crafted his own plan. He believed that "this coast affords little or no prospects of success for so small a vessel as the *Viper*." Since Captain Shaw had left it to Henley's discretion where to operate, he pushed the edges of Shaw's intent by deciding to cruise in the Gulf of Mexico before proceeding toward St. Marys or Charleston. Thus, when the *Viper* and *Enterprize* sailed from the Mississippi on 2 January 1813, neither commander intended to return.[27]

The two warships remained together for five days before parting company. The *Enterprize* proceeded toward St. Marys, while the *Viper* continued to search for British merchant ships. The vessel, however, developed a leak that caused Henley to sail for the nearest American port, New Orleans.[28]

As the *Viper* neared the Mississippi early in the afternoon of 17 January, lookouts spied a large ship. Henley soon concluded that the stranger was British, and he decided to sail into the shallows, assuming that his opponent would not risk following into such dangerous waters. However, Captain John Lumley, the commander of the 32-gun frigate *Narcissus*, understood Henley's game and edged his warship between the *Viper* and the coast. This left Henley with only one option—run before the wind. Unfortunately, his opponent proved faster. Lumley hoisted English colors and fired a gun. The *Viper* returned two rounds, but they fell short. The *Narcissus* continued to close, and Henley ordered four guns heaved overboard. "The wind then began to moderate," explained Henley, "which induced me to reserve the other Eight guns, expecting the Ship, had if fallen calm, would have sent her boats." Instead, the wind steadied, allowing the *Narcissus* to draw within range around nightfall, when Lumley had a shot thrown over the *Viper.* Henley, in consultation with his officers, decided that resistance would needlessly waste lives, so he gave the order to strike her colors.[29]

The *Enterprize* reached St. Marys on 18 January; Blakeley found the situation there only slightly more promising than at New Orleans.[30] The station, under the command of Captain Campbell, had several operational gunboats at the outbreak of hostilities. Secretary Hamilton ordered the *Vixen* to join Campbell's command.[31] Under Lieutenant Christopher Gadsden, she was the only vessel of war larger than a gunboat on the Atlantic coast south of Norfolk, but it seemed Hamilton had forgotten her. Nearly two months after the declaration of war, Campbell explained to Hamilton, "Not having received any particular instructions from you relative to the employment of the *Vixen,* I have thought proper to order her to Sea for one month . . . which I hope will meet your approbation."[32]

Off St. Simons Island on 13 August, Gadsden chased an unidentified vessel, but the wind carried away both the *Vixen's* topmasts, sending two men into the water. The chase escaped, while the crew cut away the wreckage and saved one of the men from the ocean. Gadsden surveyed his once beautiful brig and decided to obtain repairs at Charleston.[33] Gadsden's health had been fragile over the previous months, and the stress from the *Vixen's* cruise likely hastened his demise: with her first wartime cruise at an inglorious end, Gadsden died. His death, however, had lingering effects on operations, since Captain John Dent, the senior officer at Charleston, only allowed the *Vixen* to return to St. Marys upon the arrival of her new commander.[34]

Just days after the *Vixen* departed Charleston, a British squadron appeared off that port on 14 October. Comprising the 18-gun *Moselle*, 14-gun *Rhodian*, and 10-gun *Variable*, these warships normally policed the waters around the Bahamas. Given the peculiarities of prevailing winds, currents, and convoy routes, the Bahamas fell into the area of operations for Stirling's Jamaica Station. Though Stirling faced no American frigates and his object involved the accumulation of prize money from captured American commerce, he oversaw the entire naval war against the United States south of the Chesapeake in 1812. Off Charleston, success greeted the British, and Dent lamented, "They have captured within hours nine sail of vessels within three miles of the Bar." The British vessels remained in the offing until a storm forced them to limp off to the Bahamas.[35]

Although the British were gone by the time news of the blockade reached Secretary Hamilton, he did not know it. Not only was South Carolina his home state, he had friends and business relations there. To one such acquaintance, he wrote, "Charleston shall not be forgotten in the dispositions of our small naval means I assure you—Let this assurance be known." Yet, Hamilton did not have much to send. Rodgers and Decatur had sailed on their second cruise. This only left Commodore Bainbridge's squadron. At first, Hamilton thought there were only three British brigs off Charleston, so he ordered the *Essex* to proceed from the Delaware and take care of them. Several days later, Hamilton learned that the British force likely contained a frigate and another brig, so he ordered Bainbridge with the *Constitution* and *Hornet* to sail "for the purpose of clearing the coast of S. Carolina & Georgia of the cruisers of New Providence [Bahamas] which are depredating there." Though Hamilton assured a friend in Charleston that Bainbridge "is an active zealous and brave Commander," the commodore had already sailed from Boston when Hamilton's order arrived.[36]

Meanwhile, the *Vixen* rode at anchor at St. Marys. Campbell lamented the poor utilization of the vessel. Believing that the *Vixen* was too weak to assist Dent in the defense of Charleston, and also unwilling to lose her to that station, Campbell decided to send her to intercept a convoy that had supposedly departed Jamaica on 11 October.[37] She sailed from St. Marys on 22 October under Master Commandant George Washington Reed.

A month at sea passed with no prizes before Reed shaped a return course for St. Marys. At daybreak on 22 November, lookouts at the masthead descried a sail almost on the edge of the horizon, but a combination of distance and morning haze prevented identification. The best Reed could deduce was that she was a large merchant vessel, and he ordered the *Vixen* to close. Around 8:00 a.m. the lookouts determined, "from the cut of her sails, we supposed her to be a man of war." Reed immediately tried to escape, but the *Vixen* had been sighted by the 32-gun British frigate *Southampton*, under Captain Sir James Yeo. Though his frigate had been launched in 1757 and in 1812 was the oldest deployed warship in the Royal Navy, Yeo found the speed to close with the American.[38]

Reed desperately ordered his crew to lighten the ship. Anchors went, the bow guns followed, then the shot, but the *Southampton* continued to gain. On board the *Vixen* one seaman noted of the *Southampton*, "At 3 P.M. her teeth were visible; and at half past 3, coming up with us hand-over-hand, she gave us a shot, which fell short; three quarters past 3 another was sent, which went between our foremast and mainmast." All the *Vixen*'s officers agreed that resistance would be futile, and Reed ordered the colors struck.[39]

Yeo sent a prize crew across and transferred the *Vixen*'s men to the *Southampton*; the vessels proceeded toward Jamaica. Around 11:30 p.m. on 27 November a lookout sighted land. The frigate came about, but a little more than an hour later the frigate struck a reef.[40] Within minutes, the *Vixen* followed. Hopelessly damaged, she was soon abandoned. Yeo thought there was a chance the *Southampton* could be saved. One of the American prisoners commented, "Day-light was anxiously waited for," but dawn revealed the catastrophic extent of her damage. The only consolation was the presence of Conception Island some ten miles to the west, and Yeo dispatched the ship's boats to carry the men there for safety. Meanwhile, Yeo remained with a few seamen to try to keep the *Southampton* afloat until provisions could be brought ashore. Nearly thirty hours after running aground, Captain Yeo came off his dying frigate, leaving her to the wiles of the ocean.[41]

Marooned on Conception Island in the Bahamas, Yeo dispatched boats to New Providence for succor. Finally, on 6 December the *Rhodian*, accompanied by a schooner and cutter, hove into sight. With everyone embarked, the vessels proceeded to Jamaica.[42]

About the *Vixen*'s fate, Captain Campbell at St. Marys wrote in January 1813 that it "induces me to draw the unfortunate conclusion that she is either cast away on some of the Keys or Islands . . . or taken."[43] Correct in both accounts, his conclusions either literally or figuratively fit the *Enterprize*, *Vixen*, and even the *Siren*. Yet American frigate operations were also not without problems, as demonstrated by the 36-gun *Chesapeake*. In the first days of 1812, the U.S. Congress had appropriated funds to repair three frigates in ordinary, so that they would be ready for active operations should war occur. By June none of these warships was ready to sail, and even after the commencement of hostilities, work inched forward.

The *Chesapeake* was the first to become operational, and on 28 November Secretary Hamilton directed Captain Samuel Evans to "weigh anchor & proceed as you have been directed by Com. Decatur, to whose squadron you are attached."[44] Decatur had left Boston on 8 October, though, meaning that Evans' instructions were nearly two months old. As fate would have it, Decatur returned with the *Macedonian* about ten days before the *Chesapeake* sailed, but he did not update Evans' instructions before the *Chesapeake* proceeded to sea on 17 December.[45]

Evans sailed toward the Azores and Madeira, but this course carried significant risks, since the British Admiralty had dispatched squadrons to patrol the very region the *Chesapeake* now approached. The 74-gun *Elephant* and the 20-gun *Hermes* sailed there on 19 November, following news that Commodore Rodgers had pursued and almost taken the *Galatea* on 31 October. The Admiralty sent Captain E. W. C. R. Owen with a ship of the line, a frigate, and a sloop to patrol around Madeira, so as to cover several outbound West India convoys. A second squadron of similar size sailed at the end of November to cover the homeward-bound convoys passing near the Azores. Fragmentary reports that a squadron under Bainbridge might be at sea, coupled with reports of the capture of the *Macedonian*, resulted in the dispatch of two ships of the line, two frigates, and one smaller vessel under Rear Admiral Lord Amelius Beauclerk on 4 January. The Admiralty also ordered Captain William Prowse to take still another squadron (consisting of two ships of the line and a frigate) to St. Helena, so as to strengthen the escort of two returning East India convoys.[46] The *Chesapeake* sailed into danger, but the Americans saw only the potential rewards.

On the last day of 1812, the *Chesapeake* fell in with the *Julia*, an American-flagged merchant vessel sailing under a British license from Lisbon to Boston. Prior to the War of 1812, the British government had issued licenses allowing safe passage to American vessels carrying foodstuffs, particularly grain for Wellington's army that was fighting the French in the Iberian Peninsula. When war with America broke out, many licenses had been issued but not used, and Britain continued to honor them; representatives of the British government even issued new licenses. In part, this paralleled British efforts to negotiate an end to the conflict because it showed goodwill. British leadership also understood that wartime necessity trumped the tax revenue that licensed trade brought the U.S. government. Given the slowness of communications, United States Navy officers at the outbreak of hostilities allowed licensed trade to continue; by late 1812, however, elements in the U.S. government, including President Madison, had accelerated efforts to obtain legislation preventing the use of licenses. By early 1813 the issue remained rather nebulous, which led Evans to send the *Julia* into a U.S. port for further inspection, but darkness fell before he could send her off.[47]

The next morning found the *Chesapeake* and the *Julia* shrouded in a thick mist, but it lifted abruptly.[48] "Two Sails were discover'd in the Winds Eye of us," commented Evans, "standing directly for our weather bow." Hoping these were unwary merchantmen, Evans hove to and let the strangers approach. An hour passed before Evans made them out to be warships. He ordered the *Julia* to the United States, then he had the *Chesapeake* draw the warships after his frigate. He hoped this would allow the *Julia* to escape and give him the opportunity to determine the strength of his opponents. When some distance had opened between the *Julia* and the *Chesapeake*, Evans ordered his men to back his mizzen topsail. This slowed the frigate, letting the strangers approach, but, he recounted, "Finding they bore directly up and that by remaining with it [the sail] aback they would be quite Near us before we could discover their force, I fill'd it again." Evans then altered course, bringing the *Chesapeake* to the windward of his opponents. Now in a position to better control the encounter, Evans only needed his opponents to expose their broadsides so he could determine their force. Before this occurred the weather closed in, causing the *Chesapeake*'s lookouts to lose sight of both the *Julia* and the strangers.[49]

Evans never determined the strength of his opponents. Those on board the *Julia* had a better view and made them out to be a frigate and a brig of war, but who were they?[50] The encounter happened south of the Azores and west of Madeira, but the major British squadrons were several hundred miles away. Three British squadrons were north of the Azores on this day: a first squadron comprising Broke with *Shannon, Tenedos, Nymphe*, and *Curlew*; a second squadron comprising the 74-gun *Colossus*, 38-gun *Rhin*, and 10-gun *Goldfinch*; and a third squadron comprising the 74-gun *Elephant* and 20-gun *Hermes*. A fourth British squadron, under Owen, comprising the 74-gun *Dublin* and 36-gun *Inconstant* was close in with Madeira. On that day they sailed in company with the 36-gun British frigate *Magicienne*.[51] With the British so deployed, the culprits remain uncertain; more important for Captain Evans and the *Chesapeake*, the encounter failed to register with Britain's naval leadership.

The American frigate proceeded south through empty seas, passing the Cape Verde Islands. On 12 January Evans captured the *Volunteer*, a British merchant vessel that had separated from a convoy destined for South America. The convoy had consisted of twelve merchantmen escorted by the 20-gun *Cherub*, under Captain Thomas Tucker. Five days before the *Volunteer*'s capture, one of the convoy signaled distress, and Tucker shortened sail to keep company with the cripple. Though he made signal for the convoy to "close round me," only two of the merchant vessels complied. The *Volunteer* was not one of these; instead, she had pressed on and fulfilled Tucker's following prediction: "I have every reason to suppose that they will be captured by the Enemy."[52]

A dispersed convoy was vulnerable. Rather than a single point of contact in the vast ocean, a dispersed convoy provided as many as the number of the scattered ships. Even with this factor in Evans' favor, his chances were even better than he thought. Not only had ten of the *Cherub*'s merchant vessels separated from their escort, but also a second convoy of six large East India Company ships transited the area.[53] In this target-rich environment, Evans captured another of the *Cherub*'s convoy on 13 January. This time the *Chesapeake* deceptively operated under English colors. It worked, and the master and crew eagerly talked, thinking the *Chesapeake* an English frigate. It was only later that the Americans revealed their true identity. About this time, another sail appeared on the horizon, but she fled into the night.[54]

Rather than continue after the dispersed convoy, Evans decided to remain on his cruising ground because he stood a good chance of encountering another convoy. The valuable East India Company ships in this very area supported Evans' decision, but a second factor loomed: a dangerous fever had appeared on board the *Chesapeake*, killing seven and threatening to be of "epidemical" proportions. Rather than have his command ravaged, Evans decided to conduct a leisurely patrol so the crew could more speedily recover. But, Evans later lamented, "I could scarcely have made a more unhappy determination." More than three weeks passed before the *Chesapeake* captured another British merchantman on 5 February.[55]

Beginning the day of this capture, overcast and squally conditions prevented Evans from obtaining a reliable lunar observation until 23 February, when he determined that the *Chesapeake* had drifted several hundred miles, placing her west of the established trade routes. Given prevailing winds, it would be impossible to regain her station in the time that her provisions allowed, so Evans shaped a course toward South America, arriving off Suriname on 2 March. Unknown to him, the *Hornet* had sailed from this area less than a week earlier, following her successful engagement against the *Peacock*. If the British had responded quickly, the *Chesapeake* would have sailed into a trap, but the British Leeward Islands Station suffered from the lack of warships and the squadron commander only learned of the *Peacock*'s loss some ten days after the *Chesapeake* departed the area. Finally, Evans, while sailing for Boston, recaptured a British prize on 7 April.[56]

At Boston, newspapers descried the appearance of two British frigates in early April. The winter had lulled the Bostonians into a false sense of security because Admiral Warren believed it too dangerous to operate off that port between December and March. As the weather moderated, he ordered Captain Broke to patrol off Boston.[57] With his frigate, the *Shannon*, as well as the *Tenedos*, Broke proceeded into Boston Bay on 2 April, where his command encountered a pilot boat. Her loquacious master reported that the *Constitution*, *Congress*, and *President* were anchored at Boston. Broke confirmed the reports when he sailed within four miles of the harbor on the following day, then he sailed away, encountering the 74-gun *La Hogue* on 6 April, and two days later the 74-gun *Valiant*. The captain of the latter had learned "that the *Chesapeake* was near the coast," and he directed *La Hogue*, *Shannon*, and *Tenedos* off Boston to intercept her.[58]

This did not bode well for Evans, but chance dealt him a good hand. Before Capel could close the trap, Evans slipped into Boston on 9 April, but his arrival did not come without incident. As the *Chesapeake* worked into the harbor, the main topmast gave way, killing three men.[59] This seemed a fitting end to a cruise that had yielded but five prizes and had barely registered with the Royal Navy. The *Shannon* and *Tenedos* again reconnoitered Boston on 11 April, and lookouts sighted the *Chesapeake*. The master of the pilot boat who had previously given information about the American warships in Boston again provided accurate intelligence that the *Chesapeake* "had come in but two days before from a cruise of 115 days in bad condition."[60]

The first months of the War of 1812 proved painful for the United States. Disasters on the Canadian border loomed large. Expansionist moves into Florida failed to yield desired results. Even the navy was not immune, given its inability to rapidly and cheaply commission the frigates in the ordinary. Moreover, neither Hamilton nor his commanders used the warships effectively in the southern stations. By January 1813 one-half of all American naval losses occurred in warships stationed south of Norfolk, though such vessels comprised but one-third of the navy. To make matters worse, vessels of war in the southern stations had failed to take a single prize.

Facing ignominy, President Madison had to be careful when addressing Congress in November 1812. Searching for positive news, he focused on single-ship victories by the *Constitution* and *Wasp*. The president concluded, "On the coasts, and on the ocean, the war has been as successful as circumstances inseparable from its early stages could promise."[61] This speech was steeled by the news that the *Macedonian* had arrived as Decatur's prize. For a country in need of success, this proved just the cure, and it led the chairman of the Naval Committee of the House of Representatives to ask Secretary Hamilton about increasing the naval establishment.[62] Rather than provide his own conclusions, he continued with his habit of deferring to senior officers by asking Captain Charles Stewart, then commanding the frigate *Constellation* at Norfolk, to write up a report. Hamilton latched onto Stewart's comments related to ships of the line, writing, "All things considered, it must be admitted that one 76 gun ship, mounting 86, is equal in combat to three frigates mounting 162 guns." Using this fanciful logic, he hypothesized that one ship of the line would be more cost-effective than three frigates, given manning and construction costs.[63] Moreover, the United States Navy had previously bought many of the heavy ship timbers and cast a proportion of the armament for several ships of the line. Having these on hand reduced both cost and procurement time.[64] Hamilton ended his letter by asking, rhetorically, "We should inquire, what kind of force will, most probably, be brought against us? With what description of force can we meet the enemy with the greatest probability of success, and afford the most effectual protection to our commerce?"[65] To answer these questions, Hamilton referenced and attached Captain Stewart's letter.

Stewart provided a nuanced assessment. Rather than focus heavily on ships of the line, he wrote that a balanced fleet, including ships of the line, frigates, and sloops, could most effectively tangle Britain's operational plans. These Stewart assessed as follows: "Their first object will be to restrain, by ships of the line, our frigates and other cruisers from departing and preying upon their commerce; their next object will be to send their smaller cruisers in pursuit of our commerce; and by having their ships of the line parading on our coast, threatening our more exposed seaport towns, and preventing the departure of our small cruisers, they will be capturing what commerce may have escaped theirs, and recapturing what prizes may have fallen into our hands."[66]

The prize that the British obtained, however, was information from these reports. Printed in the 22 December issue of *The Democratic Press* of Philadelphia, a copy made its way to Admiral Warren. Building ships of the line and new frigates was of little immediate concern, given construction time. Instead, these documents included confidential information as to American intentions, the assessment of British options, as well as the tonnage, manning, and armament of America's heavy frigates.[67] The release of this information to the public demonstrated a significant problem facing the U.S. government. Confidential information reached the British, often through the medium of legitimate newspapers, compromising some of the navy's most particular advantages.

The intended congressional audience also warmly received the letters from Hamilton and Stewart. An easy passage occurred in the Senate, then the House of Representatives took up a bill that would authorize the building of four ships of the line of at least 74-guns and six 44-gun frigates.[68] Representative Elisha Potter of Rhode Island asserted "that the Navy was at this time very popular with all parties, in this House and the nation; that they had done honor to themselves and to their country, while our Army, had in almost every instance, been defeated and disgraced." Moreover, Potter concluded, "there was a kind of popular delusion at this time about a Navy, that he [Potter] found difficult to oppose."[69]

The proposed ships of the line, however, proved controversial. Representative Lemuel Sawyer of North Carolina asked, "But what can we do with four seventy-fours?" He continued, "If we mean merely to annoy her trade, (and he [Sawyer] trusted we meant more,) frigates will do. . . . When the enemy is in search of your forty-fours, if he acts with his frigates you may be sure of being victorious: if for this purpose he selects a higher rate of vessels, he will incur a great additional expense, and give you the chance of out-sailing him, or you will force him to change his present system, and add a new class of vessels to those which he has already adopted."[70] In fact, this is what the British ended up doing. Melville, the First Lord, argued, "We are building two Ships of the same size & force as the large Americans, & shall probably build a third, but I am unwilling at present to introduce a new & cumbersome description of Ships into our Navy to any considerable extent, merely because the Americans have three of them." But the first two of these ships, eventually named the *Leander* and *Newcastle*, would not be operational until 1814. In the meantime, Melville elaborated, "we may more easily supply Line of Battle Ships."[71] Extra 74-gun ships were sent to the American station, some with orders to return after eliminating America's heavy frigates. The Admiralty also ordered the upper works of several small 74-gun ships removed, reducing tonnage and increasing speed. Called razees, these warships mounted 32-pound long guns on their lower gun deck and 42-pound carronades on their upper deck, meaning they threw more metal than America's heavy frigates.[72]

Back on the floor of the House of Representatives, the proposed line of battleships drew considerable fire. On 17 December one motion called for striking them from the bill. Representative William Widgery of Massachusetts maintained, "I cannot feel willing to build seventy-fours, to the exclusion of the smaller ships, of which we are so much in want at this time." Though there was much to be said for the building of smaller vessels, defenders of the bill cited the professional opinions of Stewart, Hull, Morris, and Hamilton, and the existence of timber "which could not be applied to frigates, without great loss." Finally, on 23 December, the bill passed 70 to 56.[73]

Even before the Act to Increase the Navy went before the Senate, a rumor floated that Hamilton was contemplating resignation. One member of the House of Representatives asserted, "Mr. Hamilton's talents have never been estimated above mediocrity. He is much of a gentleman, . . . but a man whatever may be his other qualifications who rarely spends a day without being in a state approaching intoxication, if not absolutely intoxicated, cannot be considered as one of the most fit persons for a high responsible office."[74] Captain Porter made a similar observation in October 1812: "There must be a change in our D[epartmen]t or we never can expect to do any thing except on our own responsibility—there is no energy nor will there be while a pint of whiskey can be purchased in the District of Columbia, it is shameful."[75] At least one historian, however, has questioned the veracity of Hamilton's alleged alcoholism. Perhaps it merely served to cover his ouster, for major problems, particularly financial mismanagement, plagued the Navy Department. Later, the department's chief clerk wrote to Madison, "It is a subject of great regret to me that owing to the very loose manner in which the Books of money warrants & drafts have been kept for some time past, the state of appropriations cannot in any reasonable time be prepared."[76]

Regardless of the reason, influential members of the federal government had decided to replace Hamilton, and the time seemed fortuitous in the last days of 1812. Madison had successfully stood for reelection, and the formation of his new administration allowed certain liberties in the shuffling of the cabinet.[77] Given such conditions, those wishing to replace Hamilton did not wish to stop with him. If anything, the secretary of war, Dr. William Eustis, appeared even less competent. Though Hamilton had proved lacking, his naval officers had demonstrated competence and even brilliance in confronting the Royal Navy. However, Eustis did not have tactical success to mask departmental failings.

At the center of the cabal to oust both secretaries was Representative Jonathan Roberts of Pennsylvania, who explained, "Dr. Eustis gave ground at once . . . he quit it with a magnanimity that has enabled him to carry away a very general respect." Hamilton, though, held onto his position either through ignorance of the forces against him or through the hope of maintaining his position. However, Roberts asserted, "It is now impossible Mr. Hamilton can remain no point was ever more clearly ascertained than that he ought not to remain in office."[78]

One newspaper reported William Jones as Hamilton's probable successor. The article went on to describe Jones as "a man of talents and a practical seaman."[79] Indeed, he was the favored choice, and Senator Roberts explained to Jones, "Be assured sir the vacancy about to occur has not been effected thro' a hope of getting your services but from the impossibility of proceeding with Mr Hamilton." Roberts then beseeched Jones to become secretary of the navy, telling him that the position is "the office which it is wishd you should fill." Jones, however, had declined this very office in 1801, even over the personal appeals of then–president Thomas Jefferson. He had also demurred when first approached in late 1812, but Roberts implored Jones, "The Nation & the Navy point to you as the fittest man to have & what is to become of us if the fittest men cannot come forward in a moment of public danger."[80]

Though Roberts thought highly of Jones, he was an outsider, having served but a single term in Congress (1801–03), and his was far from a household name. One newspaper reported that it had received a letter from Washington indicating that Madison had chosen "Mr. Jones of Philadelphia (I think his name is William) as secretary of the Navy."[81] The position had little appeal for Jones and led one of his correspondents to comment in early 1813, "I could scarcely believe that you would have been drawn into Public life—knowing how little ambitions [*sic*] you are in that pursuit."[82] A second reason existed for not wishing the office. He was at one point a prosperous merchant, but he had been financially ruined between 1808 and 1812 because of the war in Europe and the resulting restrictions placed on American commerce. The embarrassment of financial failure weighed heavily, but against these reasons, Jones asserted "the same indignant feeling which impelled me, not to the 'tented field,' but to the frozen *untented* heights of Princeton, Pluckemin and Morristown, when but just turned of fifteen," stirred his soul, for he was a veteran of the American Revolution and specifically of the brutal winter campaign in New Jersey during 1777. Of the War of 1812, Jones believed "we are engaged in a war more *just and inevitable* than even that of our glorious revolution."[83]

Secretary of the U.S. Navy William Jones
(Navy History and Heritage Command, Photo # NH 66633)

With an heir apparent, Madison met with Hamilton on 29 December. According to one report, "The president then abruptly proceeded to make observations upon the want of confidence which prevailed respecting his administration of the navy department." Hamilton protested, but "the president persisting that an irresistible torrent of opposition to his continuance in office existed" led Hamilton to grudgingly tender his resignation.[84]

Madison selected Jones as his new secretary, and a newspaper reported that he "is by all parties considered to be admirably well qualified."[85] His appointment proved the easiest aspect of his tenure as secretary of the navy, and Jones wrote of "the Herculean task I have to encounter." The war had placed the Navy Department in an unfamiliar situation, but Jones accurately claimed, "My pursuits and studies have been intimately connected with the objects of the department."[86]

Jones found himself "wholly engrossed day and night I may say, by the pressing business of the Department."[87] Although the war accounted for much of what passed across his desk, structural problems added to his workload. Commodore Bainbridge summarized, "You mention the inorganized state of your department—I well know it—And without reflecting on the former heads of it (the last of whom I sincerely esteem for the goodness of his heart) I can say there never was any system in it, and for the want of which great abuses have crept in."[88] Unlike Hamilton, who Bainbridge characterized as good at heart, with the implication that he was an inadequate leader, Jones was savvy enough to recognize that problems existed and was willing to confront them.

One of the first issues facing Jones dealt with preparing the navy for future oceanic operations. The outbreak of hostilities found no warships under construction. Even when war loomed, Congress merely approved funds to commission several frigates in ordinary, but only the *Chesapeake* had sailed before Hamilton's resignation. The *Constellation* sailed during the first days of Jones' tenure as secretary, but a British squadron forced her into Norfolk, and work on the *Adams* inched forward. Legislation in late 1812 provided for four 74-gun ships of the line and six large frigates. Eventually work commenced on three of each, but construction took time. Needing warships sooner, Jones wrote to Burwell Bassett, the chairman of the Naval Committee in the House of Representatives, about procuring six sloops of a class slightly larger than the *Hornet*. Jones even proposed decommissioning some gunboats so as to use their crews and their operating budgets for the sloops.[89]

Bassett pushed the legislation forward. Time was critical if any chance existed in getting the bill approved before the congressional session ended. The House quickly passed the bill on 15 February, and it went to the Senate on the same day.[90] After reading the bill the second time on 16 February, it went to committee, where it languished for nearly two weeks. In the meantime, Jones wrote Senator Samuel Smith of Maryland who chaired the Senate Naval Committee: "Their force is inferior only to a frigate—their cost and expenditure only about one third in actual Service; and in pursuit of the Commerce and light cruisers of the enemy three Sloops of the class proposed may reasonably be expected to produce a much greater effect than a single Frigate."[91] On 2 March the bill emerged out of committee, and one representative tried to reduce the number of sloops from six to two. This measure failed, though only by a margin of 9 to 13. Even with resistance, the bill passed the Senate on 2 March, and Madison quickly signed it into law.[92]

Although Jones sought to obtain new warships, he still had an effective naval force. When he became secretary, the *President* and *Congress* rode at anchor in Boston; the *United States*, *Macedonian*, and *Argus* were at New York; the *Constellation* was in the Chesapeake; the *Enterprize* at St. Marys; and the *Siren* at New Orleans. The *Hornet* returned to New York in March, while the *Constitution* and *Chesapeake* reached Boston in February and April, respectively.

Upon the *Chesapeake's* return, Captain Evans reported on his cruise. Jones' response oozed with a confidence previously lacking in the Navy Department. He wrote, "If, from fortuitous circumstances, your cruize has been less brilliant than your zealous efforts merited, it has not been ineffectual." Jones ordered Evans to prepare the *Chesapeake* for future operations, because "the effect of our limited force depends upon its constant activity and enterprize." As a result, Jones ordered that the *Chesapeake* only undergo absolutely necessary repairs. Particularly, Jones added, "I further trust that in your whole equipment the strictest economy, consistent with real utility, will be strictly observed." To bring his point home, he chided Evans, "The last equipment of the *Chesapeake* was, in many respects highly extravagant; particularly for the luxurious indulgence of the fancy of her commander and officers, much of which will never be allowed by this Department."[93] Economy had been the last nail on the coffin for Hamilton, and Jones understood the United States had a far from unlimited revenue supply.

Even though the new secretary demanded economy, he realized the navy's ships were precious assets. Though he could expect the new sloops to be operational by late 1813, the frigates and ships of the line would take longer to build. As a result, he had to protect his warships, while using them to drive up the cost of the war for Britain.

CHAPTER 6

"Creating a Powerful Diversion"

Secretary Jones and the Naval Campaign of 1813

"Our great inferiority in naval strength, does not permit us to meet them [the British] on this ground without hazarding the precious germ of our national glory.—we have however, the means of creating a powerful diversion," wrote Secretary of the Navy William Jones on 22 February 1813. The statement announced a new oceanic strategy to maximize American naval power by using long cruises with single warships. Jones argued, "If any thing can draw the attention of the enemy, from the annoyance of our coast for the protection of his own rich & exposed commercial fleets, it will be, a course of this nature, & if this effect can be produced, the two fold object, of increasing the pressure upon the enemy, & relieving ourselves will be attained."[1]

While Jones planned for cruises by single warships, Melville, as First Lord of the British Admiralty, wrote to Warren, "It is evident that the Enemy's frigates do not wish to proceed to Sea singly, & we must be prepared accordingly."[2] This was the logical assumption, given American operations in 1812. The expectation of facing U.S. naval squadrons in 1813 led British leaders to employ a defense using powerful squadrons instead of single warships. These would be deployed in depth, beginning with blockade squadrons designed to thwart the sailing of American squadrons; if this failed, these squadrons could pursue and intercept the U.S. squadrons at sea. The possibility of encountering large American frigates led the British to strengthen their blockading squadrons with ships of the line, but Warren made it clear that this was not the most effective use of his limited force. Moreover, he worried that he did not have enough warships, especially when he had to send some into port for repairs and provisions.[3] Warren still lacked the necessary naval means, but Melville prioritized, explaining, "We hope soon to have further accounts from you & to learn that your most important object, the blockading the Enemy's Ships of War in their Ports has been attained, as also the other objects of putting a total stop to their trade, & the annoyance of their Coast." The First Lord added that "any more naval disasters, more especially if they could fairly be ascribed to want of due precaution, would make a strong impression on the public mind in this Country." Stopping American warships had the priority.[4]

Off Boston, Captain Thomas Capel, the British squadron commander, decided on a riskier course of action than the one advocated by Melville. In this, he was spurred on by the earnest desires of Captain Broke, who worried, "My *wooden* wife is very weak & crazy, & must soon be sent home." With little time before the *Shannon* would have to undergo extended repairs, Broke got Capel to keep the majority of his squadron well off the coast, so Broke could challenge Commodore Rodgers to a two-on-two engagement between the 38-gun British frigates *Shannon* and *Tenedos* on one side and the *President* and *Congress* on the other.[5] One of the *Congress*' crew wrote, "Their [*sic*] is two English Frigats in this Bay, which have been insight [*sic*] of us every good day they have sent to inform Commodore Rodgers of their intention of waiting for us." Moreover, Rodgers hoped that Broke would "not change his mind."[6]

Everything seemed set for a battle, but a merchant vessel made Boston on 22 April. Her crew reported that Broke had friends lurking nearby, including a ship of the line, two frigates, two sloops, and a brig. Rodgers correctly sensed a trap. On the day he obtained the information from the arriving merchant vessel, the *Shannon* and *Tenedos* had in fact fallen in with the 74-gun *La Hogue*, the 38-gun *Nymphe*, and the 18-gun sloops *Rattler* and *Curlew*.[7] Captain Capel, the senior British officer and commander of *La Hogue*, explained to Warren, "I have purposely kept *La Hogue* out of sight from the Land with the hope of inducing the Enemy to venture out."[8]

Rodgers decided not to inform the British that the challenge was off and put to sea on 30 April, taking advantage of a wind shift that forced Broke's frigates off the coast.[9] The Americans had surprised the British, and the first inkling the British had that Rodgers had sailed came in the early afternoon of 2 May when the *Curlew*'s lookouts sighted the American frigates. She fled, losing sight of Rodgers in the darkness. One factor improved the *Curlew*'s odds. During the chase, American lookouts spied two large ships, and Rodgers made them out to be *La Hogue* and *Nymphe*.[10] However, these two ships were not in company on this day; instead, Rodgers probably had sighted the *Nymphe* and a merchant vessel she had detained.

Though Rodgers had the strength to engage, he allowed his opponents to disappear in the night.[11]

During the next days, the British acted on the false assumption that Rodgers still meant to accept Broke's challenge. This led Broke to write on 5 May, "I flatter myself they are not gone away, but merely *parading themselves* to prepare for a *field day*." He drew this conclusion even after he learned from two separate merchant vessels that the *President* and *Congress* had sailed.[12] Added to this, Capel determined on 6 May that Rodgers was at sea. Then, after massing most of his squadron on 9 and 10 May, he dispersed it by sending the *Shannon* and *Tenedos* toward Boston for the supposed rendezvous with Rodgers, while keeping the *La Hogue* and *Nymphe* out to sea.[13] Capel hoped that Rodgers was working his command up to fight Broke. The weather made this conclusion more compelling. Early May saw three days of "a furious gale of wind." Broke then explained, "Fogs have now succeeded to the gales, & we are all in the *smoke*."[14] Sighting ships in such weather would be difficult, and the British hoped that Rodgers was merely awaiting better conditions.

Finally, on 11 May Capel concluded that Rodgers had sailed, and wrote Admiral Warren, "It is with great mortification I am to acquaint you, that . . . two of the Enemy's Frigates (the *President* and *Congress*) have escaped." Broke incredulously wrote, "They did not *seek us*—you will hear of their doing mischief . . . *Lord knows where*."[15]

The *President* and *Congress* had slipped though the British blockade, and on 8 May, as planned, the two frigates parted company. Now alone, Rodgers and his frigate the *President* pushed toward the Azores, staying ahead of reports of his escape; he gained little advantage, though, spending five weeks at sea without a prize. Finally, between 9 and 13 June, Rodgers captured five vessels, including the *Duke of Montrose*. After transferring all the prisoners to this vessel and sending her off to England as a cartel, Rodgers steered toward the waters north of Ireland and Scotland, but he lamented, "To my astonishment however in all this route I did not meet with a single vessel." This should not have been astonishing. He was already north of the sea-lanes linking the West Indies and Britain. Moreover, Rodgers' course kept his frigate several hundred miles west of Ireland and the busy waters around that island and Britain. Rodgers' course, however, assumed less risk than sailing closer to Ireland, since it minimized the *President*'s exposure to warships of the Royal Navy. Finally, on 27 June the *President* made the port of Bergen, Norway, but Rodgers found, "to my surprize and disappointment, [that Rodgers] was not able to obtain any thing but water, there being an unusual scarcity of Bread in every part of Norway." Failure to obtain provisions forced a reassessment, and he decided to operate north of Britain until the lack of food necessitated his return to the United States.[16]

John Rodgers (Naval History and Heritage Command, Photo # NH 47060)

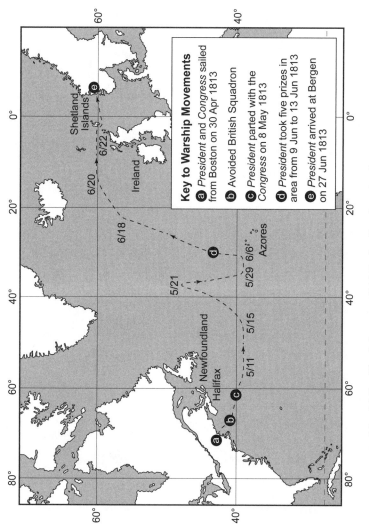

Key to Warship Movements

a *President* and *Congress* sailed from Boston on 30 Apr 1813

b Avoided British Squadron

c *President* parted with the *Congress* on 8 May 1813

d *President* took five prizes in area from 9 Jun to 13 Jun 1813

e *President* arrived at Bergen on 27 Jun 1813

Map 6.1 *President's* Summer 1813 Cruise, Part I, 30 April–27 June 1813

Slow to grasp the situation, Warren had no clue how his command had reacted. Even when Rodgers had been at sea for a month, Warren wrote, "I earnestly hope however that some of our ships will have met or followed him."[17] The problem was one of geography. Warren was at Bermuda and had no admiral at Halifax. The senior officer in the north was Capel, and he spent a good part of May at sea looking for Rodgers; Capel apparently thought he lacked the authority to communicate directly with the Admiralty.[18] These particulars did not bode well, considering Warren's strained relationship with the Admiralty.

Information about the American frigates finally reached the Admiralty in mid-June in the form of an American newspaper taken from a merchant vessel off Lisbon. This was hardly a foolproof piece of intelligence, and, not surprisingly, the Admiralty responded in a tentative manner by asking Warren what had happened.[19] On 23 June the *Duke of Montrose*, serving as Rodgers' cartel, reached England, providing the first public news about the *President*.[20] From several additional snippets of information along with assumptions based on how the Americans had operated in 1812, the Admiralty determined "that all the American Frigates are at Sea" and were "cruizing two or three together." Though erroneous, this led the Admiralty to dispatch a flurry of instructions on 9 and 10 July. The commander of the Newfoundland Station was told to hunt for the Americans. Captain Charles Paget received orders to take a squadron on a cruise stretching from the Azores toward St. Helena to cover homeward-bound convoys. Orders also went to the commander of the Channel Fleet to be especially attentive in the blockade of the French Atlantic ports, in case the Americans tried to slip in for supplies. Another directive went to the commander at Lisbon to dispatch the 64-gun *Stately* and a frigate to search for the Americans. Warren also received an order to prepare for the American frigates when they returned.[21]

The above instructions paled next to a secret directive from the Admiralty. Its genesis can be traced to the loss of the *Java*. When Melville learned of the defeat in March 1813, he decided to minimize risk to his frigates because weathering the storms of public outrage over frigate defeats had become increasingly difficult. The First Lord speculated, "Our Captains of Frigates ought to have a secret hint that they are not only not expected to attack those large American Ships, but that their voluntarily engaging in such an encounter would be considered here in the same light as if they did not avoid an action with a Line of Battle Ship."[22] Several months passed with no Admiralty action, but news that the American frigates were again at sea resulted in a sweeping directive. Dated 10 July, it stated that the Admiralty did "not conceive that any of His Majestys Frigates should attempt to engage, single handed, the larger Class of American Ships, which though they may be called Frigates, are of a size, Complement and weight of Metal much beyond that Class, and more resembling Line of Battle Ships."[23] This circular altered the rules of engagement and went against the image of confidence, and one could dare say the perception of invincibility, that the Royal Navy had developed during the previous two decades of war. Though unknown to the Admiralty, the only large American frigate then at sea was the *President*—and she had begun to captivate the Admiralty.

On the day after issuing the above circular, the Admiralty received a report that the *President* had departed Bergen on 2 July. Immediately discerning the danger posed to the northern whaling fleet and the homeward-bound convoys from the Russian port of Archangel, the Admiralty dispatched the 74-gun *Royal Oak* and the 38-gun *Seahorse* north of Ireland. Orders also went to Admiral William Young, commanding the squadron off the Scheldt, to send several warships toward Bergen. The secretary of the Admiralty explained, "Uninformed as their Lordships are of any particulars they cannot give the officer . . . on this service any specific orders . . . they must therefore trust to exercise of his judgement and discretion on the information he may receive."[24] In compliance, the 74-gun *Norge* sailed north with a sloop, but the latter could not keep up, and the *Norge* continued alone.[25] A ship of the line pursuing a frigate would normally seem like an unequal match, but one of those on board the *Norge* incorrectly believed the *President* had a larger complement and that the *Norge* threw a broadside only nine pounds heavier than the American.[26] Moreover, Admiral Young opined, "The largest two decked ship of the Fleet, looks . . . even the distance at which Ships anchor from each other, so like a Frigate, that it is impossible to persuade one that she is any thing larger. If the *President* saw her she certainly will not avoid her."[27]

Rodgers eluded the *Norge*, *Royal Oak*, and *Seahorse* by pressing into the Arctic. On 18 July, while sailing within sight of North Cape, the *President* fell in with the American privateer *Scourge*. Both were after a lightly escorted convoy from Archangel. At 4:00 p.m. on 19 July, the *President*'s lookouts sighted two large sail. Three hours later, Rodgers identified them as a ship of the line and a frigate.[28] This summation paralleled the character of Young's statement in the previous paragraph: they were the 32-gun frigate *Alexandria* and the 18-gun ship-sloop *Spitfire*.

Rodgers ordered his men to clear for action and issued a triple allowance of spirits. In return, his men pledged to fight until the *President* won or sunk because "the English should never carry the *Precedent* [sic] to England." The men then hoisted two large white flags with black letters. One stated "No Impressment" and the other "This is the Haughty *Precedent* [sic] how do you like her."[29] But rather than engage, Rodgers fled, still thinking that he had encountered a ship of the line and a frigate. Captain Robert Cathcart of the *Alexandria* ordered chase, and Captain John

Ellis of the *Spitfire* accurately concluded that they were in pursuit of a large frigate accompanied by an armed schooner.[30]

The British pursued through the Arctic night (it never becomes completely dark there in July). By morning, the Americans were some ten miles ahead of the British. About 10:30 a.m. the *Scourge* came up within hail of the *President*. Her captain wished Rodgers the best and bore away. The British took no notice of her, and both Cathcart and Ellis continued after the *President*. As the day ended, the wind shifted slightly, allowing the British to gain.[31]

In response, Rodgers had his men wet the sails so they could capture more wind and thus eke out a little more speed. By 3:00 a.m. on the morning of 21 July, the *President* had regained her lead. The weather, being very hazy with sea fog, obscured the ships at various times during the morning. Then in the early afternoon a thick fog descended. The *President* lost sight of the British, and even the *Alexandria* and the *Spitfire* lost sight of each other. When the fog lifted an hour later, six miles separated Rodgers from his pursuers.[32]

On 22 July, the fourth day of the chase, a very propitious wind favored the British, allowing them to close rapidly. Rodgers ordered the men to clear for action and then issued another triple ration of rum. With this, his crew again affirmed that they "had rather sink than be taken."[33] The *Spitfire* closed within one and a half gunshots, while the slower *Alexandria* pressed on, several miles behind. Then, the breeze, which had so favored the British, reached the *President*, and the American frigate pulled away. By evening the *Spitfire* had gotten some eight miles ahead of the *Alexandria*. Rodgers fired a gun and hoisted his colors in hopes he could lure the *Spitfire* under his guns. Given the distance separating the two British warships, Rodgers thought he could defeat them in detail, but Ellis saw through Rodgers' gambit and allowed the *Alexandria* to come up.[34]

As the chase entered a new day, the weather closed in. Around mid-morning a fog descended, and the two sides lost sight of each other. This time, it did not clear.[35] The chase had lasted "*ninety two hours, and a run of four hundred and thirteen miles,*" according to Cathcart's estimates. He described the *President* as "a Frigate of the largest class, whom I judged was an American." Although his actions contradicted the Admiralty order of 10 July directing smaller frigates to avoid combat with the large American frigates, Cathcart had yet to receive the directive.[36] The Admiralty later concluded that they were "highly satisfied with the zeal" of their commanders, but "at the same time they cannot but consider it as fortunate that they were not able to overtake an Enemy of a force so prodigiously greater than that of those two vessels united."[37] Rodgers continued to maintain that he faced a ship of the line and a frigate, however. Nothing could convince him otherwise. In the end, he missed an opportunity to engage an inferior force, but had he fought, the

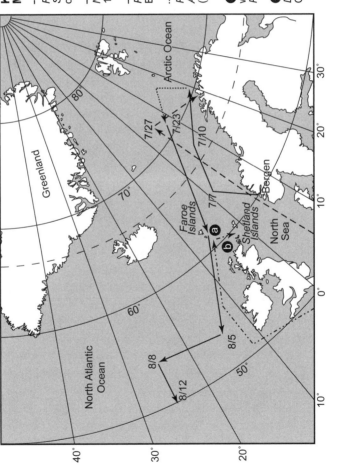

Key to Warship Movements

.... *Royal Oak* (74 guns) and *Seahorse* (38) sailed north on 16 Jul

– – – – *Norge* (74) sailed north on 14 Jul off Bergen on 17 Jul

– – – *President* departed Bergen on 2 Jul

⋯⋯⋯⋯ *President* chased by *Alexandra* (32) and *Spitfire* (18) from 19 Jul to 23 Jul

ⓐ *Royal Oak* and *Seahorse* were within miles of the *President* on 31 Jul

ⓑ *Fortunee* (36) and *Dauntless* (18) off Cape Wrath on 28 Jul

Map 6.2 *President's Summer 1813 Cruise, Part II, 2 July–12 August 1813*

President would likely have sustained damage that would have proved difficult to repair, given the remote location.

In London, the *President* continued to captivate the Admiralty. In addition to dispatching the *Norge, Royal Oak,* and *Seahorse,* the 36-gun *Fortunee* and the 18-gun *Dauntless* joined the hunt off the Orkney Islands, but their force bordered on being too weak to engage the *President.* In another questionable order, the Admiralty sent Captain Cathcart with the *Alexandria* and the *Spitfire* back out to protect the homeward-bound whalers and a convoy from Archangel. Cathcart had orders to join the 20-gun *Bonne Citoyenne.* The Admiralty warned Cathcart, however, that "if with the *Alexandria* and *Spitfire* he should by accident fall in with the *President,* he [Cathcart] is not to bring that ship to action, and if even when joined also by the *Bonne Citoyenne* . . . it is their Lordships opinion that there would not then be such a reasonable prospect of success as should induce Captain Cathcart to *seek* an action."[38] Other than a few American privateers, the *President* posed the principal naval threat in this area, and the Admiralty dispatched three warships lacking the power to engage the American frigate.

At sea, Rodgers needed intelligence and decided to masquerade the *President* as a British warship. When she closed with a merchant vessel on 29 July, she did so under English colors. To further the ruse, a boat carried over a person dressed as a Royal Navy lieutenant who addressed the merchant vessel's master, "stating himself to belong to the *Alexandria* frigate." Since the master knew that the *Alexandria* operated in the area, he was not alarmed. Soon, the master was summoned on board the frigate; "the British Flag was still flying but as soon as he saw the Commander he informed him that he was onboard the *President* . . . and a Prisoner of War, the American Flag was now hoisted, and the British [flag was] struck." The above description was not unique, and Rodgers even visited this ruse on at least one neutral. On 31 July the *President,* again flying British colors, brought a Danish ship to, and "after collecting every information, and after getting some English Newspapers, left her without discovering that he belonged to America, on the contrary he pretended he belonged to Britain, and upbraided the Dane for Carrying as he said Papers to an Enemys Country."[39]

After taking a British whaling vessel on 2 August, Rodgers learned that superior Royal Navy forces lurked in the area. In reality, the danger had passed. The *Royal Oak* and *Seahorse* were within a few dozen miles on 31 July, but by 2 August their course had carried them away from the *President.* Rodgers, however, did not know this and changed stations, steering for the Banks of Newfoundland, where he captured a British merchantman on 30 August. He then passed very close to *La Hogue* and *Tenedos*, probably in thick and foggy weather, on 4 September. Rodgers had unknowingly broken through Warren's first line of defense. Then, on 9 September, he captured the British merchant vessel *Fly*. From her logbook, Rodgers learned that the 74-gun *Bellerophon* and the 36-gun *Hyperion* had boarded the *Fly* the previous morning. These ships, part of the Newfoundland Station, were acting under Admiralty orders to intercept the *President*. Though Rodgers did not know their exact instructions, he could speculate, and so shifted stations. This was wise because the *Bellerophon* and *Hyperion* had made little headway since encountering the *Fly*, and both British warships were still within fifty miles. Fortune continued to favor Rodgers' approach toward the United States, and several other Royal Navy squadrons were unprepared to meet his approach. These included a second squadron from the Newfoundland Station consisting of the 40-gun *Sybille* and 36-gun *Dryad*. These ships had patrolled the area transited by the *President* for much of August, but the squadron anchored in St. John's, Newfoundland, at the end of the month. In addition, Warren had dispatched a squadron comprising the 74-gun *Poictiers*, the 36-gun *Maidstone*, and the 18-gun *Nimrod*, but the squadron had dispersed and did not factor into the hunt.[40] By mid-September Rodgers had eluded all the British squadrons sent to find him in the Atlantic. It only remained for him to slip past the blockade squadrons along the American coast.

⬥⬥⬥

"Commodore Rogers [*sic*] . . . makes himself sure of being taken on the Coast of America," asserted the master of one of the merchantmen he had captured.[41] Given the strength of the Royal Navy and the time the British had to prepare, Rodgers certainly faced a formidable task. Warren would later assert that he had deployed six ships of the line, a razee, eleven frigates, and seven smaller vessels from the Chesapeake to Nova Scotia with a primary purpose of stopping Rodgers.[42]

Yet, synchronizing the movements of so many warships proved difficult, and areas remained uncovered. As a result, Warren had dispatched his tender, the *Highflyer*, under Lieutenant George Hutchinson, to watch Nantucket Shoals. When she encountered a frigate in the haze on 23 September, Hutchinson identified the frigate's distinguishing pendant as belonging to the *Tenedos*, but he lacked private signals to confirm. In haste, Hutchinson went across in a boat and then boarded the frigate. Only after being placed under the guard did he realize his mistake. Rather than the *Tenedos*, he had encountered the *President*. The capture occurred so fast the British did not have time to destroy the logbook, signals, or Warren's orders, and Rodgers used these to assess his opponent's critical vulnerability.[43] The squadron supposedly off Narragansett Bay had returned to Halifax, with the 36-gun

Orpheus having sprung her mainmast; the British commander in the area wrote, "I am sorry to say that Rhode Island has been left quite open."[44] This information virtually assured the *President*'s safe arrival in Newport.

The *President*'s cruise had lasted slightly less than five months, but Rodgers had only captured eleven British merchantmen and a naval tender. Given the expenditure and risk, these appear paltry results, but this belies the overall accomplishment of the cruise. Rodgers had caused the British tremendous disruption on stations from the coast of the United States to the Arctic, and in the process had forced the British to overreact. Of Rodgers, one British newspaper chided, "How flattering it must be to him to learn, that not single ships but squadrons were dispatched after him, and one specifically under the command of *an Admiral*."[45] Such actions had occurred because the Admiralty operated under the imperative of preventing the recurrence of the 1812 frigate defeats. Summing up his success, Rodgers asserted that he had caused disruptions equivalent to "more than a dozen times the force of a single Frigate."[46] Even so, he was probably too modest.

When the *President* departed Boston on 30 April, she sailed in company with the *Congress*. Once at sea, the two frigates separated, with Captain John Smith steering the *Congress* south. In both his previous wartime cruises, Smith had operated with Rodgers. He now had the opportunity to showcase his abilities. On the afternoon of 19 May the *Congress* took a British merchant vessel sailing from Buenos Aires laden with hides, tallow, and copper. This was valuable capture, and one that Smith and his crew would surely have liked to send into port for prize money, but the American captain understood the nature of his mission. Manning prizes depleted his crew, and there was little chance that the prize could safely reach the United States. As a result, Smith ordered his men to transfer the copper and food to the *Congress* before scuttling the prize. Three days later and four hundred miles to the south, the American frigate captured a second British merchant vessel. After dumping her cargo, Smith sent her off with thirty-one men from his two captures.[47]

On 13 June the frigate reached Fortaleza on the northwest coast of Brazil. Over the next few days, Smith obtained water and provisions, as well as information that two British frigates were on the coast and twelve English merchantmen awaited a convoy at Recife.[48] As with most intelligence, it was only partially correct. The convoy existed with the 24-gun *Porcupine* as the escort. The only frigates assigned to the station were the *Aquillon* and *Nereus*, but the latter was off Buenos Aires and the former was preparing to relieve her. Moreover, both were rated for thirty-two guns, making them much inferior to the *Congress*. Perhaps the intelligence about the frigates had misidentified two other British warships on the station, the 20-gun *Cherub* and the 18-gun *Racoon*. The other possibility dealt with the arrival of the 36-gun *Phoebe* at Rio de Janeiro on 10 June, but it was unlikely that information of her presence could have reached Smith in such a short time.[49] However, Smith had to treat the information with respect, at least until he could discount it.

On 19 June the *Congress* departed Fortaleza and sailed to the east, beating against the wind for four hundred miles until she made Fernando de Noronha, a small archipelago just south of the equator. Smith topped off his water and then proceeded eastward, hoping to fall in with a convoy from the East Indies. For nearly two months the *Congress* plied these seas, reaching a point about three hundred miles northwest of Ascension Island. Searching for convoys in this area was like finding the proverbial needle in a haystack. Chance, however, favored the British— they were the ones who almost found such a needle. Warren had ordered Rear Admiral Laforey in the Leeward Islands to dispatch a squadron to look for the American frigates. Consisting of the 38-gun *Rhin*, the 36-gun *Pique*, and the 18-gun *Mosquito*, the squadron nearly crossed paths with the *Congress* in mid-August. Smith never realized his luck. At the same time, his quarry, a large and valuable East India convoy, waited at St. Helena for the arrival of stragglers, as well as the 74-gun *Tigre* that had been dispatched from England to strengthen the escort that already included the 74-gun *Illustrious*. The convoy finally sailed on 1 September, but by this time, the *Congress*, nearly out of water and provisions, had sailed back toward Brazil, leading one exasperated officer on board the *Congress* to recount, "We never saw a vessel."[50] Perhaps Smith was incredibly lucky to dodge a roving squadron, as well as a convoy escorted by two 74-gun ships.

Meanwhile, the British naval commander on the coast of Brazil, Rear Admiral Manley Dixon, had finally learned that the *Congress* had made landfall at Fortaleza in June, and rumors swirled that other American frigates operated along the equator. Dixon particularly feared that the Americans had found out that the 32-gun *Nereus* had orders to transport nearly $1.5 million in specie to Europe. Not wishing to risk such a fortune on board a small frigate, Dixon sent the money to England on board the 74-gun *Montagu*. Dixon also saw fit to reinforce the *Porcupine*'s convoy with the recently arrived 44-gun *Indefatigable*. The convoy and the specie-laden *Montagu* sailed in early August, missing the *Congress* by a wide margin.[51] However, the *Indefatigable* separated from her convoy just south of the equator and sailed east. At the same time, the *Congress* headed west as Smith returned from his long, fruitless search for East India ships. About 17 August the *Congress* passed one to two degrees north of the *Indefatigable*. A week later the American frigate regained Fernando de Noronha. After taking on fresh water, Smith proceeded toward Fortaleza, arriving on 5 September.[52]

Meanwhile, Dixon received more reinforcements on 19 August when the 36-gun *Inconstant* and the 18-gun *Fairy* arrived at Rio de Janeiro. Dixon ordered Captain Sir Edward Tucker to take his frigate, the *Inconstant*, as well as the *Nereus* and *Fairy*, to search for the *Congress*. They made their way up the Brazilian coast, reaching Recife on 5 September before sailing south to Salvador. Off that port on 11 September, Tucker encountered the 38-gun *Rhin*, 36-gun *Pique*, and 18-gun *Mosquito*. After missing the *Congress* in the Atlantic, these warships from the Leeward Islands had reached Salvador on 28 August.[53] After Tucker encountered the roving squadron, his vessels returned to Rio, while the warships from the Leeward Islands Station sailed on a circuitous route for the remainder of September and much of October, patrolling the waters from the coast of Brazil stretching west beyond Fernando de Noronha.[54] Though Tucker never came close to encountering the *Congress*, the ships from the Leeward Islands operated in the same waters that Smith transited on his return to the United States.

Smith never realized the disruption he had caused Dixon or his near encounters with the squadron from the Leeward Islands and the *Indefatigable*. Moreover, the effects of his cruise continued to distract Dixon, even after the *Congress* had sailed toward the United States. At one point, Dixon thought "it probable she may have gone to the Southward to meet with the *Essex*." Even as late as January 1814, Dixon received information that the *Congress* had sailed toward Africa.[55]

Smith had gone home, though. The longer he remained on the Brazilian coast, the riskier his position became. His frigate had been at sea for more than four months, and he needed to reach the United States during the winter when the British found blockade operations more difficult. Finally, on 25 October, Smith captured the British merchant vessel *Rose*. Strangely, Smith took this prize about four hundred miles from the American frigate's previous capture, but nearly five months after the first event had elapsed between the two captures.[56] Smith learned that, three days before her capture, the *Rose* had encountered Paget's British squadron, comprising a ship of the line, a frigate, and a sloop. The Admiralty had dispatched Paget in July when it was thought that U.S. frigates were operating in groups of two or three.[57] Though the Admiralty had an incorrect picture of American movements when this squadron was dispatched, these warships nearly chanced upon the *Congress* three and a half months later.

Only five days after capturing the *Rose*, the *Congress* marked the six-month point of her cruise. Each day the weather became more boisterous, as the autumn marched toward winter and the *Congress* pressed to the north. As November gave way to December, she approached Boston. The cruise had now entered its seventh month, and Smith needed information of the British deployments on the American coast. On 5 December, about five hundred miles east of Boston, he captured a British merchant brig. More important than the prize was the intelligence obtained about a strong force blockading Boston. As a result, Smith sailed for Portsmouth, New Hampshire, arriving there on 14 December.[58]

Four captures in 227 days at sea led one of her officers to call it "a tedious, and I may say, unsuccessful cruise."[59] But Smith had unknowingly disrupted British operations on the South American station. Moreover, at least until early July the Admiralty thought that the *Congress* and *President* operated together. Warren harbored this misassessment even longer. The result was several roving squadrons dispatched into the *Congress'* area of operations, but such deployments only occurred in combination with the *President*—the specific British response to the *Congress* appears paltry, especially considering risk and cost. She returned needing extensive repairs; many of her seamen obtained their discharge, since their two-year term of service had expired during the cruise. Smith lamented that his remaining crew "cannot prepare the Ship for Sea."[60]

The third American warship to sail on a long cruise in 1813 was the *Argus*. Around New Year's Day 1813, she had arrived at New York following a grueling cruise that had rendered her in need of a major refit. Moreover, her commander, Master Commandant Arthur Sinclair, was spent, and he handed over command to William Henry Allen, who had distinguished himself as first lieutenant of the *United States* during her engagement with the *Macedonian*.

In early June Jones provided Allen with instructions. The U.S. government had appointed William H. Crawford minister plenipotentiary to France, and the *Argus* would deliver the diplomat. Afterward, Jones wanted Allen to target trade around Ireland. "This would carry the war home to their direct feelings and interest, and produce an astonishing sensation," argued Jones. He thought that Allen could operate around Ireland for four to six weeks before sailing north to intercept a homeward-bound Archangel convoy.[61] Allen was the perfect commander: young, competent, and impetuous enough to attempt this brash mission.

The *Argus* sailed from Sandy Hook on 18 June. The first morning out, a man of war suddenly appeared out of the rising sun. Allen immediately steered the *Argus* into a fog bank. Then, on the evening of 26 June, Allen encountered a mass of ships that he supposed belonged to a British West India convoy. Rather than close, he proceeded toward France. Attacking a convoy carried great risk, given the strength of the escort, and Allen's orders demanded Crawford's safe passage. The diplomat, however, had a rough voyage and recounted a storm on 30 June: "The guns on the lee side are constantly under water, and every heavy sea washes the deck with its mountain billows. It is impossible to stand on deck without clinging to a rope. . . . The storm raged with increasing violence, the waves swelled into little mountains. . . . The dashing of the ship, its alternate elevations, and depressions excited apprehensions that she might be swallowed up in the immense chasms intervening the billows, or might upset by the violence of the winds."[62]

Every day that the *Argus* plowed through the waters of the Atlantic she drew closer to the French port of Lorient and the interminable blockade of the British Channel Fleet under Admiral George Keith Elphinstone, Lord Keith. However, Keith had been lamenting for months the depleted state of his command.

As early as February the Admiralty had apprised Keith that it would be taking frigates from his fleet with only vague prospects of their replacement, and as summer approached the British government demanded that Keith provide an ever-larger number of warships to support Wellington's Anglo-Portuguese army in Spain. Moreover, the strength of the French navy in the region grew faster than the strength of the British Channel Fleet, meaning that Keith did not have enough warships to adequately blockade all the major French ports in his area of operations.[63] One port left uncovered was Lorient. In mid-July Keith divulged that this caused him considerable apprehension. Particularly, he feared that American frigates would put into the port for supplies, but "I have not the means of increasing the force . . . for the purpose of preventing their entry into Lorient."[64]

One day out of Lorient on 10 July, the *Argus'* lookouts sighted what appeared to be a brig of war mounting eighteen guns, or two less than the Argus. About noon a long gunshot separated the two vessels, but the stranger showed no colors and did not attempt to force an engagement. Crawford related, "The officers were much disappointed in missing a fight." But, the diplomat accurately remarked, "Captain Allen's orders forbid his engaging unless it was unavoidable." The vessel was still visible early in the afternoon when a second warship hove into sight. Allen thought she was a frigate, or even a ship of the line. Suddenly, the brig came about and stood for the *Argus*, but this failed to spur the larger warship to action. Darkness soon obscured both ships. The next day the *Argus* reached the safety of Lorient.[65]

After seeing Crawford ashore, Allen faced a quandary. He needed supplies but Secretary Jones had not provided funds, so he looked to Crawford, who maintained, "I have no authority to draw money from the bankers of the U.S. for the Navy." But, he rationalized, "The supply was necessary—they could not be obtained but on my becoming pay master. This I have done. . . . I am not disposed to see the public Suffer, on account of a little responsibility."[66]

While the *Argus* lay at anchor, the 18-gun British sloop *Royalist* reconnoitered Lorient on 15 July. Her captain noted the presence of the *Argus*. Though he did not identify her by name, he described her as an American brig of war. He even noted she was a naval vessel rather than a privateer. His report, however, took a circuitous route, passing through the hands of two flag officers before reaching the Admiralty in late August.[67] By then, this information was out of date and worthless.

Given the slow reaction of the British Channel Fleet, the *Argus* was able to proceed to sea on 20 July. Three days later, she captured the *Matilda*. Allen decided to disobey orders and send her into a French port, since the *Matilda* had once been an American privateer, making her recaptured American property. Moreover, she could be fitted as a privateer to again attack British shipping. The *Argus* then fell in with the *Susannah* on 24 July. Allen had some of her load of wine transferred to his vessel and then had his men destroy the rest of her cargo. "On account of 2 Lady Passengers we gave her up," sending her into port with the prisoners.[68] The *Susannah* arrived in England on 26 July, providing the first positive intelligence about the *Argus* and her audacious mission. Moreover, the 38-gun English frigate *Revolutionaire* recaptured the *Matilda*. One member of her prize crew talked, providing specific details about the *Argus*.[69] Now apprised of the threat, the British had to determine the most difficult questions—Where was Allen's vessel, and what did he plan to do?

Allen sailed toward Ireland, capturing a British brig on 27 July. At 8:00 a.m. on the next day, his lookout espied a brig and cutter chasing a schooner. As the *Argus* closed, Allen realized his mistake, as all three came about and bore down on the *Argus*. Lacking the force to fight all three, Allen fled. By 3:00 p.m. his vessel had dropped the schooner and cutter well astern, but the brig doggedly followed. Only darkness allowed Allen to lose the last of the pursuers.[70] He then stretched north along the coast of Ireland toward the River Shannon.

On Kerry Head, overlooking the mouth of the Shannon, the British navy had erected a signal station. From this position on the afternoon of 1 August, Lieutenant Robert Fricker spied a brig of war with yellow sides and pierced with nine ports standing into the river under English colors. He also noticed a merchant ship dropping down the river. As the two vessels neared, Fricker stared in disbelief as the brig lowered her English colors and hoisted American colors. She then fired a gun, brought the merchant vessel to, sent a boat over, and boarded her. At 4:00 p.m. Fricker watched the American warship standing out to sea as the merchant vessel burned in the middle of the river. He sent this information off by express to Vice Admiral Edward Thornborough, the commanding officer of the Irish Station, asserting, "I cannot Sir Describe her better then by Informing you I took her to be One of His Majesty's Brigs on the largest Scale."[71] The news reached Thornborough at his headquarters at Cork at 9:00 p.m. the next evening, and he immediately sent the *Jalouse* in quest of the *Argus*. In his directive Thornborough described her as a privateer. The thought that she was a warship of the United States Navy did not

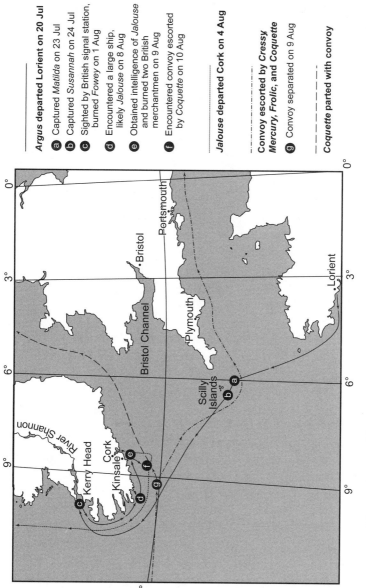

Argus departed Lorient on 20 Jul

- **a** Captured *Matilda* on 23 Jul
- **b** Captured *Susannah* on 24 Jul
- **c** Sighted by British signal station, burned *Fowey* on 1 Aug
- **d** Encountered a large ship, likely *Jalouse* on 8 Aug
- **e** Obtained intelligence of *Jalouse* and burned two British merchantmen on 9 Aug
- **f** Encountered convoy escorted by *Coquette* on 10 Aug

- - - - - - *Jalouse* departed Cork on 4 Aug

Convoy escorted by *Cressy Mercury, Frolic*, and *Coquette*

- **g** Convoy separated on 9 Aug

- - - - - - *Coquette* parted with convoy

Map 6.3 Cruise of the *Argus*, Part I, 20 July–10 August 1813

cross his mind. Still, the *Jalouse*, a ship-sloop mounting twenty-six guns, was more than capable of eliminating the *Argus*.[72]

In the meantime, Allen took another prize on 2 August. The next day, it came to blow, and the foul weather continued for several days, making it impossible to find additional prizes. On the morning of 8 August, the weather had moderated enough for her lookouts to sight a large sail. Allen soon made the stranger out to be a frigate. Taking the only prudent action, he brought his vessel onto a new heading and quickly lost sight of her. This was probably the *Jalouse*. She was in the same area that morning; moreover, she was a large sloop with three masts, as well as a forecastle and quarterdeck, giving her the appearance of a miniature frigate. But if Allen had sighted the *Jalouse*, the *Argus* escaped undetected.[73]

Allen then appeared off Kinsale, Ireland, on 9 August. From a large Russian merchant ship, he obtained information about the *Jalouse*. Since the Russian was neutral, he allowed her to proceed, but several other vessels were in sight. The very light breeze, however, made it impossible for the *Argus* to close with them. Allen therefore ordered out the boats, and his men rowed after these other vessels. Both turned out to be British merchantmen, and Allen ordered them set afire. As night fell, the two burning merchant vessels illuminated the *Argus* as she sailed away.[74]

That night she fell in with four large sail, but Allen decided to wait for sunrise before acting. Day broke in a murky fog, and slowly the four vessels multiplied into a convoy. The elation of the moment was shattered when the Allen realized one of the ships closest to the *Argus* was a warship, and he watched as her crew stowed hammocks. Rather than panic, Allen quickly got his vessel to the windward.[75]

The *Argus* had encountered part of a 160-ship convoy from the Leeward Islands. The escorts comprised the 74-gun *Cressy*, 20-gun *Coquette*, 18-gun *Frolic*, and *Mercury*, a 28-gun frigate fitted as a troopship with much of her armament removed. On the same afternoon that the *Argus'* crew had used their boats to destroy two British merchant ships off Kinsale, the *Coquette* and those merchant vessels proceeding to Ireland, Bristol, and western Scotland had parted from the convoy, while the remainder of the convoy sailed toward England's east coast.[76] These two elements were not far apart when the *Argus* sailed into the *Coquette's* part of the convoy.

In the morning light, the *Coquette's* lookouts sighted the *Argus* within the convoy, but her captain could not close owing to contrary winds. Instead, he signaled to ascertain the *Argus'* identity. Allen saw the signal but did not realize it was for him: he thought it was to alert another escort. Already on edge, Allen made another ship in the convoy out as a brig of war. "We ran nearly close aboard the Brig in perfect silence," stated the *Argus'* surgeon, and "she did not molest us." However, the *Coquette* was the lone escort, and the American likely mistook a merchant brig for a warship. Allen, thinking he had just survived two close calls, let

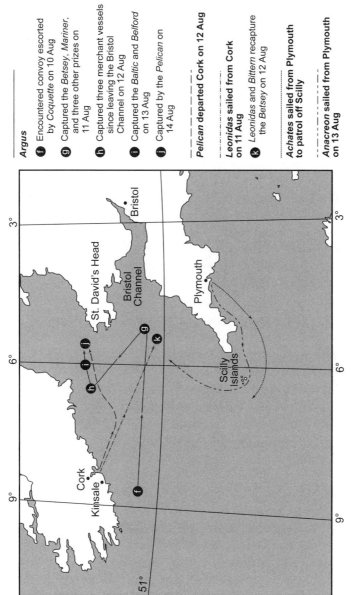

Argus

- **f** Encountered convoy escorted by *Coquette* on 10 Aug
- **g** Captured the *Betsey, Mariner,* and three other prizes on 11 Aug
- **h** Captured three merchant vessels since leaving the Bristol Channel on 12 Aug
- **i** Captured the *Baltic* and *Belford* on 13 Aug
- **j** Captured by the *Pelican* on 14 Aug

Pelican departed Cork on 12 Aug

Leonidas sailed from Cork on 11 Aug

- **k** *Leonidas* and *Bittern* recapture the *Betsey* on 12 Aug

---

Achates sailed from Plymouth to patrol off Scilly

Anacreon sailed from Plymouth on 13 Aug

Map 6.4 Cruise of the *Argus*, Part II, 10–14 August 1813

most of the convoy pass before taking possession of the merchant vessel *Cordelia*. Rather than burn or scuttle her, Allen decided to enhance the shock value of this capture by using the *Cordelia* as a cartel to dispose of the prisoners from his most recent captures. Allen wanted word to spread that he had brazenly attacked a convoy and left his prisoners on board one of its number. Just as he was about to send the *Cordelia* off, the *Coquette* hove into sight. The surgeon related, "The fog clearing a little below we could perceive her hull and ports but not her masts or rigging. She did not observe us."[77]

The next day, Allen fell in with several ships in the Bristol Channel. First, he came up with the *Mariner*, a merchant ship that had parted from the convoy. After taking possession of her, Allen pressed on, because his lookouts reported twelve sail in sight. Later that day, Allen captured the *Betsey*, another large ship once belonging to the convoy. Almost immediately, he also took possession of a pilot boat, a brig, and a cutter. That made five prizes in a day, including two valuable West Indiamen. Allen sent the prisoners into port on board the brig, sent the *Betsey* toward France as a prize of war, and burned the rest.[78] The *Argus* remained in the area. Nightfall allowed the blazing ships to act as beacons. Just before midnight, the *Dinah and Betty*, a merchant ship laden with thirty head of cattle, arrived on the scene. Allen took possession of her and brought three cows across to the *Argus*; a newspaper later proclaimed in horror that Allen "*burned the rest with the vessel!*"[79]

The flames attracted Commander George Augustus Hire of the British naval tender *Bittern*. He saw flames around 10:00 p.m. A little more than three hours later, another blazing ship became visible. As day broke the *Bittern* came up on one of the burned-out vessels. Hire found a sloop already in attendance, and from this vessel he learned that a brig of war had visited the destruction before leaving the area with a prize. This was accurate intelligence about the *Argus* and *Betsey*, and Commander Hire sailed to investigate. About noon, Hire gave chase to the prize. Late in the day, Hire espied a large man of war bearing down on his quarry. This was the 38-gun frigate *Leonidas*, and a short time later she recaptured the *Betsey*.[80]

The *Leonidas* had sailed from Cork with orders from Admiral Thornborough to find the *Argus*. A frigate against a brig was overkill, but Thornborough wrote that the *Argus* "has captured and destroyed many Vessels." Other warships followed, casting a net around Allen's command. On 12 August Thornborough dispatched the *Cruizer*-class brig *Pelican*, under Commander John F. Maples, to search for the American.[81] On the next day Vice Admiral Sir Thomas Byam Martin, the British commander at Plymouth, received an urgent message that an American brig was near the Bristol Channel. He immediately dispatched the *Anacreon*, and, Martin concluded, "From the intelligence being of so recent a date, I flatter myself there is a great probability of the Privateer being fallen in with." Even at this point, the British thought they were dealing with a privateer, but the *Anacreon*, a sister ship of the *Jalouse*, was more than a capable opponent for the *Argus*. Sending the *Anacreon* presupposed by one day an Admiralty order to send the 22-gun *Cossack*. Martin responded by telegraph: "*Cossack* Incapable, *Anacreon* Sailed after *Argus* yesterday morning." Martin also sent the 16-gun *Achates* off Scilly to intercept the *Argus*' prizes as they ran toward French ports.[82]

These movements resulted in a revealing comment from Melville, the First Lord, who queried, "I have the messages . . . that *Cossack* could not go after *Argus*, & that another (*Cretan* [16-guns] I think but probably mistake) is gone. Perchance *Argus* may take the said *Cretan*."[83] In this case, Melville showed a degree of admitted ignorance. The *Cretan* was assigned to the Texel Squadron rather than Plymouth; however, his statement also indicated a developed appreciation for the United States Navy and Melville's concern about the effects on morale if a British warship were captured between Britain and Ireland.

In these narrow waters, success continued to greet Allen and his command. On 12 August, the same day that the *Pelican* sailed in search of the *Argus*, the Americans sank the *Ann*. Allen next encountered a neutral Portuguese merchant vessel, and he left the prisoners from two recent captures with her. No sooner had Allen released his prisoners than his lookouts spotted two large ships and a brig. He allowed the brig to escape, but closed with the ships. Since both flew English flags and came to at the same time, they likely thought the *Argus* was a British warship. Her paint scheme had already fooled the Royal Navy officer commanding the signal station overlooking the Shannon, and Allen likely sealed the deception by flying English colors. One of the *Argus*' lieutenants took a boat across and boarded the larger of the two ships. However, the master of the merchant ship refused to leave his ship or surrender. Instead, both ships tried to escape. Allen recovered his boat and pursued. The *Argus* captured the larger ship, but the other got away. Then, at 2:00 a.m. on 13 August, the *Argus* took the *Baltic*, laden with a cargo of sugar from the West Indies. Three hours later, a sloop laden with timber fell victim to the *Argus*. The Americans threw her cargo into the ocean, and Allen sent her away with the crews of the recent prizes. Then, around 9:00 p.m. a large vessel almost collided with the *Argus*. Allen immediately sent over a boarding party, and she proved to be the *Belford*, a rich prize carrying a cargo of linen. At midnight Allen had her and her cargo set afire.[84]

Allen had thus far captured twenty-one prizes.[85] The secretary of the navy had wanted the war brought to Britain. In this, Allen had proved exceedingly adept. British newspapers ran articles such as "American Barbarity" and "Depredations of the *Argus* off the Coast of Ireland." An Edinburgh newspaper reported, "The officers of the *Argus* mentioned that their orders were to destroy every BRITISH vessel they fell in with."[86] Each prize added to the fervor in Britain and Ireland and cries about inadequate naval protection.

Though the British navy had responded slowly, one British warship was on the *Argus'* trail. The *Pelican* under Commander Maples fell in with a merchant brig on 13 August, and Maples learned that the brig had sighted a stranger that resembled a man of war. Maples pursued. As the first rays of daylight upset the darkness on 14 August, the *Pelican's* lookouts sighted the *Belford* as she burned. Nearby, they spied the *Argus*.[87]

On board the *Argus* Allen and his men had suffered from a prolonged and stressful cruise in enemy waters. As one lieutenant later put it, "They had frequently been on duty for thirty hours in succession and immediately preceding the action they had enjoyed no rest for at least twenty four hours."[88] Moreover, the *Pelican* had the weather gauge as she bore down on the *Argus*, and Maples' actions prevented Allen from weathering his opponent to gain this advantageous position. Placing the *Pelican* between the wind and the *Argus* allowed Maples freedom of maneuver. Soon the *Pelican* was close enough for the men of the *Argus* to see her British ensign. In response, Allen ordered American colors hoisted.[89]

Allen brought his portside 24-pound carronades to bear on the British warship. At approximately 6:00 a.m. Allen gave the order to fire. The *Pelican* immediately replied with her larger 32-pound carronades. One of these early rounds shattered Allen's left leg. Several minutes later, Allen, delirious and weak from the loss of blood, was taken below. Barely had Lieutenant William Henry Watson assumed command but grape shot grazed his head. Dutifully, the men carried him to the surgeon.[90]

Maples sensed a kill. His ship had survived the initial broadsides with little damage, and unlike his opponent's, the *Pelican's* leadership remained intact. In addition, the *Argus* had suffered extensive damage aloft, limiting her maneuverability and allowing Maples to bring his vessel across the stern of his opponent to deliver a raking broadside before coming up her starboard side. About 6:30 a.m. Watson, now somewhat recovered and with his head wound dressed, came back on deck in time to see that the *Pelican* had closed "within pistol shot." In desperation, Watson ordered his men to prepare to board, but "in consequence of our shattered condition were unable to effect it." Maples then positioned the *Pelican* in a raking position off his opponent's starboard bow. Damage prevented the American warship from maneuvering, and it proved nearly impossible to bring more than musketry to bear. Seeing no point in continuing what was becoming a slaughter, Watson ordered the colors struck. The fight had lasted between forty-two and forty-five minutes, leaving the *Pelican* lightly damaged with two dead and five wounded. Her fire had severely damaged the *Argus*, mortally wounding Allen, killing six of his men outright, and wounding at least eleven others.[91]

Minister Crawford later wrote to Jones, "You will no doubt have been informed of the death of Capt Allen, and of the loss of the *Argus*. I was apprehensive that they would risk an engagement with vessels greatly superior to the *Argus*."[92] This was the problem with a young, impetuous officer, but after eluding the British so many times, was it asking too much not to chance an engagement for the sake of honor?

Although the British had eliminated the *Argus*, this had only occurred after more than three weeks in British home waters. More important than actual losses inflicted on the British were the disruptive and psychological effects. Ten days before her capture, Melville declared to Secretary John Wilson Croker, who was from Ireland, "I am not surprized at *Argus* appearing in the Bristol Channel, & as long as we leave it unprotected, she will not be the only one who will approach your native land."[93] In an effort at spin control, one newspaper remarked, "The Americans wanted another proof of British superiority on the ocean. The *Pelican* has afforded it, in the capture of the *Argus*."[94] However, this statement belies the fact that the *Argus* was captured well into a mission that highlighted the vulnerability of British trade in home waters. Over the next sixteen months, the size of the Cork Squadron increased by a third, and the British did not reduce the overall size of their deployments around Britain and Ireland, even though the Napoleonic Wars ended.[95] The memory of the *Argus* certainly factored into these decisions.

After learning of the *Argus'* capture, President Madison questioned Secretary Jones: "Would it be amiss to instruct such Cruisers positively never to fight where they can avoid it, and employ themselves entirely in destroying the commerce of the Enemy[?]" Particularly about the *Argus*, the president reasoned, "Her previous success in pursuing the plan of her instructions sufficiently proves the just views which led to it."[96] Madison had bought into Jones' strategy of commerce raiding. The summer of 1813 marked a shift in American naval operations. Battles had been sought in the first months of the war. Jones, however, demanded a new concept of operations where American warships, in his words, would "cruise the Ocean *singly* and if I mistake not will make such havock among their commercial fleet, and light cruizers of the enemy as will divert him from the Petty Larceny Warfare in our Bays and Rivers to the protection of his own commerce and colonies."[97] The *President* and *Argus* had certainly wreaked havoc, and the *Congress*, though less successful, had added to the disruption. Jones had issued similar orders for the *United States*, *Macedonian*, *Chesapeake*, and *Hornet*, but the British also got a vote as they continued to adapt to the unique character of the naval war with America.

CHAPTER 7

"A Glorious Retrieval of Our Naval Reputation"

The Turning Point, 1 June 1813

C ommodore Stephen Decatur pondered a letter from Secretary Jones. Dated 22 February and addressed to several of America's senior naval officers, including Decatur, it announced that American warships would undertake long, individual cruises for the purpose of commerce destruction. The letter ended by asking the opinions of these senior officers about specific missions for their warships.[1] Decatur surely felt vindicated because this had some resemblance to the plan he had proposed to Secretary Hamilton the preceding May.[2] But that was prior to the war and the bloodying of the guns—current operations demanded Decatur's entire attention.

On 24 April Decatur reported that his frigate, the *United States*, was ready to sail from New York—yet he did not proceed to sea. The reason remains unclear, but the delay led to a significant reassessment. Originally, the *United States* had orders to sail with the *Argus*, but the latter vessel received instructions to carry Minister Crawford to France.[3] However, the former British frigate *Macedonian*, now commissioned into the United States Navy, also rode at anchor at New York. Her commander, Captain Jacob Jones, the victor of the engagement between the *Wasp* and *Frolic*, wanted to sail with Decatur's frigate, since the combined firepower of two frigates would prove beneficial in breaking through the British blockade. Moreover, the *Hornet* had arrived in New York after a successful cruise that included the capture of the *Peacock*. Secretary Jones ordered her new commander, Master Commandant James Biddle, to sail, with orders to rendezvous at sea with the *Chesapeake*. The strength of the British blockade squadrons worried Biddle, however, and he determined that a more prudent course of action would involve sailing with the *United States* and *Macedonian*.[4]

Decatur now planned to sail with the *United States*, the *Macedonian*, and the *Hornet*. Once free of British patrols, the three warships would separate. Sailing as a squadron could be advantageous in an encounter with a British squadron, but three warships concentrated risk, and Secretary Jones wanted long, disruptive cruises rather than an engagement.

For Admiral Warren, the American warships at New York posed little threat in February 1813. Intelligence indicated the presence of the *United States*, but the *Macedonian* needed repairs and the *Hornet* was still at sea. The greatest issue involved covering the two passages out of New York. Opposite the passage across the bar at Sandy Hook, Warren placed a 74-gun ship of the line. On the other passage, via Long Island Sound, Warren placed two frigates.[5] As April transitioned to May and May became June, the weather improved and the days grew longer. For the British, these factors provided heady force multipliers. Storms became less likely to disrupt operations, and the longer period of daylight allowed for a better opportunity to sight American warships; the demands placed on Warren increased during the spring, however. His government ordered him to expand the blockade to encompass the entire coast from New York to the south.[6] Moreover, the Admiralty had become increasingly disenchanted with Warren. It seemed that he only asked for more ships and brought few results. Particularly, his command proved incapable of dealing with the United States Navy. The Admiralty had begun to appreciate the advantage of America's heavy frigates, however, and had sent Warren additional ships of the line.[7] This allowed for stronger blockade squadrons, but the reinforcements came with higher expectations. Moreover, the *President* and *Congress* had sailed from Boston on the last day of April. A similar failure could not occur at New York. As a result, Warren deployed a ship of the line and a frigate opposite Sandy Hook, and placed a similar force at the entrance to Long Island Sound.[8]

Early May witnessed a tremendous gale lasting six days. Though reports later reached the Admiralty that the *United States* had used the weather to mask her escape, these proved incorrect.[9] As Decatur explained to Jones, "The last gale which promised the finest opportunity for us to get out terminated in light southerly winds which continued until the blockading ships off the Hook had resumed their stations."[10] This left both sides in a curious position, with the *United States*, *Macedonian*, and *Hornet* anchored inside the bar at Sandy Hook, and a British squadron under Captain Dudley Oliver, comprising his ship, the 74-gun *Valiant*,

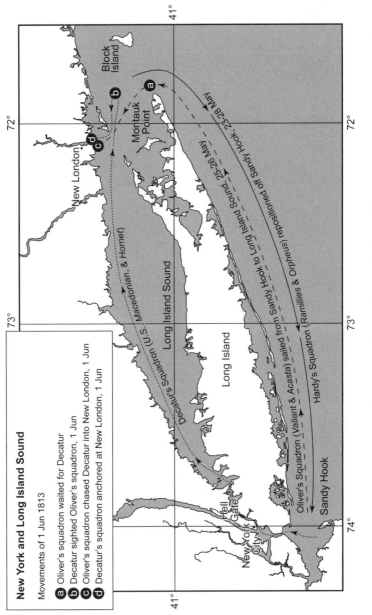

New York and Long Island Sound

Movements of 1 Jun 1813

ⓐ Oliver's squadron waited for Decatur
ⓑ Decatur sighted Oliver's squadron, 1 Jun
ⓒ Oliver's squadron chased Decatur into New London, 1 Jun
ⓓ Decatur's squadron anchored at New London, 1 Jun

Block
Island

New London

Montauk
Point

Decatur's Squadron (U.S. Macedonian, & Hornet)

Long Island Sound

Long Island

Oliver's Squadron (Valiant & Acasta) sailed from Sandy Hook to Long Island Sound, 25-26 May

Oliver's Squadron (Ramillies & Orpheus) repositioned off Sandy Hook

Hardy's Squadron (Ramillies & Orpheus) sailed from Sandy Hook to Long Island Sound, 25-26 May, 23-28 May

Hell
Gate

New York
City

Sandy Hook

Map 7.1 New York and Long Island Sound

and the frigate *Acasta*, outside the bar. Oliver, however, noted the American warships "after laying several days at Sandy Hook, and finding no chance for making their escape, *that* way returned up the North River."[11]

Decatur had concluded that the British force off Sandy Hook posed too great a threat, and he decided to sail via Long Island Sound after learning that the blockade squadron there comprised the 74-gun *Ramillies*, which "is a much duller ship than the *Valiant* which is off the Hook." The other half of the British squadron then off Sandy Hook was the *Acasta*, a 44-gun frigate, while the frigate in the Sound was much smaller, being the 36-gun *Orpheus*.[12]

Captain Oliver was only too aware of British naval weakness in Long Island Sound, and reports of Decatur's movements worried him. His information accurately recounted that the American warships were headed toward the Sound, and the *United States* had grounded at Hell Gate, though the notation in the *Valiant*'s log lamented that it occurred "unfortunately at low water [and] got off without Damage." Oliver had to consider the possibility that this was a feint to draw his squadron off. More important and unknown to Decatur, the *Valiant* and *Acasta* had but ten days of water on board. If Decatur dallied, Oliver would have to raise the blockade, but on 22 May the 18-gun British sloop *Martin* fell in with the *Valiant*.[13] Within hours she sailed for Captain Sir Thomas M. Hardy's squadron in Long Island Sound.[14] Since Oliver was senior officer, he ordered Hardy to repair immediately to Sandy Hook to relieve his squadron so he could obtain water at Block Island. Conveniently, the island lay near the mouth of Long Island Sound and placed Oliver in a position astride Decatur's expected route. One could even argue that Oliver wanted the glory of confronting Decatur, rather than Hardy, who had already gained fame for commanding Admiral Lord Nelson's flagship at Trafalgar. Although Hardy asserted, "It gives me a great uneasiness to have quitted my Station just at this moment," he dutifully left the *Orpheus* alone off the Sound and proceeded toward Sandy Hook with the *Ramillies*.[15] Leaving only a 36-gun frigate in the path of the American squadron was a risky move. Moreover, the Americans were aware of the British weakness, with Decatur learning, "The *Orpheus* has of late ventured considerably in the Sound, and it is not altogether improbable that I may fall in with her, out of the protection of the *Ramillies*."[16]

While Hardy sailed toward Sandy Hook, Oliver grew impatient and proceeded on the afternoon of 25 May toward Long Island Sound with the *Valiant* and *Acasta*. In this, he gambled that Hardy would soon be off Sandy Hook. In the meantime, though, he had left one of the entrances to New York completely uncovered. As it turned out, Decatur was in no position to take advantage of Oliver's departure, and Hardy arrived off Sandy Hook less than twenty-four hours after Oliver had left. At nearly the same time, Oliver arrived off Long Island Sound and exchanged numbers with the *Orpheus*. Immediately, she sailed to join the *Ramillies*, and Oliver watered his ships at Block Island.[17] The British had flipped their squadrons. Instead of the dull-sailing *Ramillies* and a 36-gun frigate off Long Island Sound, Decatur sailed toward an informed opponent with the more nimble *Valiant* and the more formidable *Acasta.*

These complex British movements occurred while Decatur attempted to get his squadron into Long Island Sound. The ships finally passed the difficult and swirling waters at Hell Gate on 24 May. Only hours later, the American ships encountered a severe thunderstorm. Lightning struck the mainmast of the *United States,* passed down the lightning rod, made its way into her gun deck, and continued down a hatchway and into the wardroom; next, it transited the doctor's cabin, leaving his bed smoldering. Finally, the bolt made contact with her copper and "ripped up about twenty nails at the waters edge." At the time of the strike, the *Macedonian* was about one hundred yards astern. Captain Jones "immediately hove all his topsails aback, fearing the fire might make its way to her magazine."[18] However, the damage proved far less catastrophic than Jones feared, and did not affect the operability of the American frigate.

As Decatur's squadron slowly pressed onward, area newspapers reported a significant British naval force at the mouth of Long Island Sound, estimated at as much as two ships of the line and a frigate.[19] This inflated number likely had to do with counting both Hardy and Oliver, instead of realizing they had flipped their squadrons. However, confused reporting caused Decatur to hesitate while trying to obtain a better appraisal of the strength and location of the British.[20] On board the *Hornet* a master's mate concluded that the *United States, Macedonian,* and *Hornet* "dilly dallied for several days in Long Island Sound. . . . This gave the enemy time."[21]

Decatur's movements were hardly a secret. Various newspapers published accounts of his movements only twenty-four to forty-eight hours after their correspondents had sighted the American warships. For example, on May 28 a newspaper reported that a packet boat had passed Decatur's squadron two days earlier some eighteen miles west of New London, and that the two frigates sailed in company with the *Hornet* scouting ahead. A second newspaper confirmed this position report. Another newspaper published a day-old account, indicating that Decatur's ships had anchored about ten miles west of New London.[22] A combination of avid reporting and extremely slow progress meant that Decatur had no operational security.

The British had also received reports of Decatur's progress. On 26 May a British warship in Long Island Sound had stopped a merchant ship and announced they were "waiting for Com. Decatur's squadron which was expected every moment from New-York."[23] Although Captain Oliver was aware of the approaching American warships, several foggy days added to the tension. When the fog lifted on 30 May, the *Acasta's* lookouts sighted Decatur's squadron anchored in the distance, while lookouts on board the *United States* had the *Acasta* in sight from the deck and the *Valiant* from the masthead.[24]

The next day, Oliver positioned his ships off Montauk Point, located at the northeastern end of Long Island, and his lookouts did their best to watch the American squadron.[25] Decatur kept his distance, and that afternoon he ordered all his captains to repair on board his frigate. He told them, "We had various information of the force of the Enemy off Montaug, but we were only certain of his having a line of battle ship & a frigate there."[26]

With this accurate information, the three American warships got under way at 5:00 a.m. on the morning of 1 June. Two hours later, lookouts on board the *United States* espied two warships near Montauk Point. An hour passed before lookouts on board the *United States* accurately made them out as a ship of the line and a frigate: the Americans had sighted the *Valiant* and *Acasta*. Lookouts on board the *Hornet*, however, inflated the strength of the British squadron, asserting to have sighted four large ships between Montauk Point and Block Island: one appeared to be a ship of the line, two had the appearance of frigates, and one resembled a sloop of war.[27] In response Decatur had his squadron steer toward Block Island in order to give the British warships off Montauk Point a wide berth.

The Americans had caught the British by surprise. Lookouts on board the *United States* sighted the British ships several hours before their counterparts on either the *Valiant* or *Acasta* observed Decatur's squadron. Once the British sighted the Americans, however, Oliver quickly got his warships under way.[28]

As the Americans approached Block Island, their lookouts sighted one or two large ships that had been hidden by the island. Decatur described them as warships. Captain Jones mentioned only one ship with "the appearance of a ship of the line." Likewise, Biddle described "a large Sail to the Northward apparently a Ship of the Line." This ship or these ships stood athwart the squadron's route to the sea, while the *Valiant* and *Acasta* off Montauk Point could sever the squadron's line of retreat. Facing this dual threat, Decatur ordered his ships to come about and make all sail toward the safety of New London, Connecticut.[29]

Across the water, Oliver did not consider that he had obtained assistance from warships off Block Island. The reason being—they did not exist.[30] The *Valiant* and the *Acasta* were the only large British warships in the area. What the American lookouts sighted off Block Island will forever remain a mystery. Perhaps they were merchant vessels: this was a busy body of water, and, given the stress of the escape, along with the knowledge of British warships off Montauk Point, it is not inconceivable that the Americans had simply been spooked.

Regardless of the reason, Dudley took advantage of Decatur's decision to run toward New London and ordered his ships to pursue. He had one decided advantage in the chase. His warships were sailing light, being very low on water.

Conversely, the Americans were deeply laden with everything necessary for a cruise that could stretch into the autumn. By noon the British had cut into the American lead, but Decatur was then approaching the Race, an aptly named area of racing current resulting from the channeling of tidal waters into and out of Long Island Sound, coupled with the currents associated with the discharge of the Connecticut and Thames Rivers. Oliver explained, "There was no person in either of our Ships that had ever been thro' the Race before, and it certainly is a Navigation for the great strength of the tide and other circumstances that requires some local knowledge."[31] His ships, however, safely passed the Race, and a few minutes later the *Acasta* fired her chase guns at the *United States*. The American frigate replied. The rounds proved ineffective because neither was in range. About 2:00 p.m. the Americans entered the Thames River and soon after anchored off New London. In his assessment Oliver concluded, "The *Macedonian* and *Hornet* kept a head and appeared to sail much better.—I extremely regret it was not in my power to prevent their reaching a Port."[32]

Oliver decided to stay in the offing rather than pursue the Americans into the river. On the next day, 2 June, Oliver commissioned a fishing boat to sail for Sandy Hook and fetch the *Ramillies* and the *Orpheus*. When these ships arrived on 7 June, the British blockade tightened considerably. But attacking the Americans proved difficult, and the British captains agreed that sailing up the Thames and engaging Decatur's squadron, though desirable, was not only impractical but also very risky, given the nature of the channel.[33]

In New London Decatur found few fortifications. Only Fort Trumbull had mounted ordnance and a garrison, but it was weak and inadequate. In an effort to improve defenses, Decatur coordinated with militia, used several guns from his ships to strengthen batteries, and saw to the construction of new fortifications. However, Decatur soon became irked with the available land forces and ranted, "I thank God, that our safety does not mainly depend upon them." The commodore asserted that the batteries of his ships, coupled with the difficulty of the channel, provided a formidable defense. This was particularly important because "the Enemy has declared his intention to cut us out—and where it is considered how important the destruction of these ships is to him I think if he could detach a force sufficient to secure it there is no doubt it would be attempted." Decatur added, "For although I am satisfied, that we should destroy two or three of their leading ships, there is no doubt, but the remaining force of the Enemy would be sufficient to secure the capture of our vessels or their destruction."[34]

When Secretary Jones learned that the British had forced Decatur into New London, he exclaimed, "The loss of two or three ships would not, in itself, be very serious, and could soon be repaired; but the triumph of the enemy, the food it would furnish for the gulls in England and the serpents in our own bosom, excites apprehensions in the public mind."[35] Decatur harbored similar concerns and decided to return to New York if he could not find an opportunity to proceed to sea. In his opinion, "If the Ships of the Enemy in sight maintain their present position we shall be enabled to pass up Sound without risk."[36] Secretary Jones agreed wholeheartedly: "In every point of view, it is extremely desirable that the Squadron should return to New York if practicable, as the enemy will undoubtedly guard the passage to the sea with a formidable force."[37]

Secretary Jones' summation proved correct. Captain Oliver stayed in the offing while he had soundings taken of the channel into New London. Oliver maintained this position for as long as he possibly could, thinking that Decatur would try to sail, given the fact "they are now in a situation where perhaps they can be more easily watched than in most others." The *Valiant* and *Acasta*, however, again needed water. Thus, on 12 June, Oliver was forced to transfer as many supplies as possible to the *Ramillies* and *Orpheus* and sail toward Halifax.[38] Though this severely depleted the British blockade squadron, reinforcements soon arrived. Captain Beresford, upon learning of Decatur's predicament, hastened toward New London with his ship, the 74-gun *Poictiers*. Along the way, he fell in with the 38-gun *Loire* and 14-gun *Contest*. On 23 June Decatur reported that the British had two ships of the line anchored across the mouth of the harbor.[39] This prevented the Americans from returning to New York. The noose had been secured, and the American warships were destined to remain trapped at New London, at least until the winter storms afforded a better prospect of escape.

One wonders why Decatur did not try to slip at least part of his squadron back to New York harbor before the British tightened their grip on New London. Although there was some risk in the operation, Decatur saw it as practical, and the secretary of the navy thought it desirable. The British had won a decisive victory. Oliver's actions had not only prevented three American warships from reaching the open sea, but they had placed them in a position easily blockaded by a single British squadron. This was the sort of operation that the Admiralty had long expected of Warren. For the first time in the war, the British navy had acted like the sovereign of the seas, but 1 June had the potential to be even more gratifying because of what transpired off Boston.

The road to the 1 June 1813 occurrences off Boston can be traced in large part to the employment of Captain James Lawrence. While commanding the *Hornet*, he had defeated the *Peacock*. Of this action, Secretary Jones had asserted, "Notwithstanding the rapid succession of splendid Victories which adorn the short annals of our Stripling Navy, there is in this last triumph, a distinguishing feature, which excites new interest and increased admiration."[40] Though Jones thought of appointing Lawrence to the *Constitution*, she required months of work. The secretary, therefore, gave him command of the *Chesapeake*, then in Boston undergoing minor repairs, but Lawrence asked Jones to reconsider. His wife's "health is so delicate and her *situation* at this time so very critical, that I am induced to request you for permission to remain until the *Constitution* is ready." Commodore Bainbridge dissuaded him, however, from pursuing this frigate, since she had been offered to another officer, and on 20 May Lawrence assumed command of the *Chesapeake*.[41]

Her mission involved a cruise off the coast of Nova Scotia and then into the Gulf of St. Lawrence. Jones explained, "It is impossible to conceive a naval service of a high order in a national point of view than the capture and destruction of the Enemy's Store Ships with military and Naval Stores destined for Supply of his armies in Canada and fleet on this station." Jones expected the *Chesapeake* to fall in with the *Hornet* off Cape Breton, and the two warships would then sail into the Davis Strait to prey on British whaling ships.[42]

Before Lawrence could undertake this mission, however, he had to elude a British squadron off Boston, still smarting from its inability to prevent the sailing of the *President* and *Congress*. Much of the blame for this failure rested on Captain Philip Broke of the *Shannon*. He had challenged Rodgers to bring out the *President* and the *Congress* and fight his frigate along with the *Tenedos*. But Rodgers had learned that other British warships lurked off Boston. Sensing a trap, Rodgers took advantage of British deployments designed to facilitate Broke's challenge and disappeared into the Atlantic.[43] If it became common knowledge that Broke's desire for battle had assisted in Rodgers' escape, it could be professionally catastrophic. The Admiralty did not look kindly on the sailing of the *President* and *Congress*, and the First Lord of the Admiralty later questioned British deployments off Boston prior to the sailing of the *President*. Particularly, Melville wanted to know why "the Line of Battle Ship [*La Hogue*] does not appear to have ever come within 150 miles of the Port, & to have left the strict watch to the *Shannon* & *Tenedos*."[44] Though the Admiralty voiced discontent, slow communications gave Broke a window of opportunity to avenge his failure to confront Rodgers.

On the morning of 25 May, Broke had the *Tenedos* transfer fifteen tons of water to the *Shannon*. The *Tenedos* then sailed toward Halifax, while the *Shannon* proceeded into Boston Bay to await the *Chesapeake*. Broke asserted to have done this so "that we might shew our own & more *inviting* appearance to our Enemy, now only a single frigate—of our own size—we shall do a grand service if we can get hold of him—*preventing* all the *mischief he* would do to our trade if he escapes out."[45]

Given the *Shannon*'s dwindling provisions, Broke decided to issue Lawrence a challenge. He wrote, "As the *Chesapeake* appears now ready for Sea, I request you will do me the favor to meet the *Shannon* with her, Ship to Ship, to try the fortune of our respective Flags." Broke described the exact strength of his frigate that, like the *Chesapeake*, mounted 18-pound long guns on the main deck and 32-pound carronades on the quarterdeck and forecastle. Broke asserted to have three hundred men and boys, along with thirty more from recaptures. He also took great pains to explain that he would meet Lawrence at a place of his choosing, writing "I will warn you (if sailing under this promise) should any of my Friends be too nigh, or any where in sight." Broke even went so far as to offer to sail with Lawrence "under a truce Flag, to any place you think safest from our Cruizers, hauling it down when fair to begin Hostilities." Desperate to avenge the frigate losses suffered by the Royal Navy in 1812, Broke next appealed to the American's sense of honor. "You will feel it as a compliment," wrote the British captain, "if I say the result of our meeting may be the most grateful Service I can render to my Country." Moreover, Broke explained to Lawrence, "I doubt not that you, equally confident of success, will feel convinced that it is only by continued triumphs in *even combats*, that your little Navy can hope to console your Country for the loss of that Trade, it can no longer protect." Yet, this part of his letter gave away the asymmetry of the challenge. Britain had little to lose. Another frigate loss would not be welcomed, on the one hand, but it would not be as shocking as the first. On the other hand, the Americans had not suffered such a loss, and though Lawrence could obtain greater laurels—this time in an engagement between two very similar frigates—defeat could erode some of the honor obtained in America's earlier victories. Broke needed a quick answer, given the state of his frigate's provisions and water, and he implored Lawrence: "Choose your terms, *but let us meet*."[46] Now that Broke had written the challenge, he had to deliver it. As a result, he sailed toward Boston on the morning of 1 June. The *Shannon* "came to within full view of the town, backed her topsails and displayed her colors." Such actions within sight of Boston demonstrated British naval power and goaded Lawrence to action even before Broke sent the challenge ashore.[47]

That morning the crew of the *Chesapeake* awoke unready for combat. Several bumboats were alongside waiting for the return of the women who had spent the night on board. Standing watch over this tawdry image of a seaman's life was Lieutenant George Budd. Between 8:00 and 9:00 a.m., he discovered a large ship in the offing and informed Lawrence. Moments later the captain came on deck, and Budd told him that he thought the unknown ship was a frigate. Lawrence immediately climbed aloft for a better view. Several minutes later he came down and said that she was indeed a frigate. He then mustered the crew, to whom Lawrence announced, "A Frigate was in sight; and it was his intention to go out and bring her to action." Some of the men grumbled, asserting they had yet to receive their prize money from the last cruise. Later that morning the prize money disbursements occurred, but the sour mood had already been cast. Lawrence ordered the bumboats to collect their women and depart, and "as they went the men appeared still more dissatisfied."[48]

Around noon Lawrence wrote to his brother-in-law: "An English frigate is close in with the light house, and we are now clearing the ship for action. Should I be so unfortunate as to be taken off, I leave my wife and children in your care. . . . The frigate is plain in sight from our deck and we are now getting under way."[49] Though Lawrence had not received Broke's challenge, he had decided to fight.[50]

Although the *Shannon* was rated for thirty-eight guns and the *Chesapeake* for thirty-six, both frigates carried the same number of 18-pound main deck guns.[51] The officers and men of the two frigates, however, could not be more dissimilar. Lawrence had only commanded the *Chesapeake* since 20 May. When the *Chesapeake* returned from her winter cruise, two of her lieutenants and several midshipmen had left the frigate, and the morale of the crew was something less than desired.[52] Conversely, Broke had commanded the *Shannon* for years, and though his opponent had more men and Broke counted many boys among his crew, the previous year of operations off the American coast, along with Broke's penchant for gunnery practice, had honed the nucleus of the *Shannon*'s company to a high degree of skill.

The people of Boston sensed an engagement. One newspaper recorded, "The bay was covered with craft and boats . . . from this town . . . full of passengers, and great numbers went . . . to see the expected rencontre."[53] During the afternoon they watched as the *Shannon* stood out to sea with the *Chesapeake* in pursuit. Broke accurately identified his opponent as the *Chesapeake*, and Lawrence received information from a pilot boat, as well as several small craft, that the British frigate was the *Shannon*.[54] During the afternoon, Lawrence came down to the gun deck and found the guns loaded with a single-round shot and grape. He then ordered his men to place a canister and a bar shot "to be put in besides." Such heavy charges for the main deck guns indicated that Lawrence intended to fight at close range, since the cannons could not throw so much metal a great distance. More ominous, Lieutenant Budd reported that a number of the men were intoxicated, one to the point of insensibility.[55] This should not have been surprising, though: the *Chesapeake* had been at Boston nearly two months, and the flow of alcohol on board while in port was difficult to control.

The mood on the *Shannon* could not have been more different. The crew greeted reports that the *Chesapeake* was coming out with a belief that the "weary, toilsome weeks was ended." Broke then gathered his crew and gave them a speech. One of the lieutenants later recounted that Broke mentioned American victories but blamed them on their superior force. Inciting his men, he asserted that

Americans have "said . . . that the English have forgotten the way to fight." Broke then counseled, "Don't try to dismast her. Fire into her quarters. . . . Kill the men and the ship is yours." After such provoking words, Broke ordered, "Don't cheer. Go quietly to your quarters . . . you have now the blood of hundreds of your countrymen to avenge."[56]

The *Chesapeake* closed late in the afternoon. About 5:40 p.m. she came within pistol shot, and the crew gave three cheers that could be heard on board the *Shannon*.[57] Broke ordered his men to fire as the guns bore on the *Chesapeake's* foremast. From stern to bow the British discharged a rolling broadside that the Americans did not return until "directly abreast, when the *Chesapeake* fired her whole broadside."[58] Much of the American fire apparently went high. As for the British fire, one observer, then on board the *Shannon*, described the British broadside: "A hurricane of shot, splinters, torn hammocks, cut rigging, and wreck of every kind was hurled like a cloud across the deck."[59] In the first broadsides, the *Chesapeake's* master was killed and many others fell, including Lawrence, who suffered a severe leg wound. Though it bled much, he refused to go below and have it tended to. Adding to the confusion on board the American frigate, an arms chest on her quarterdeck exploded.[60]

For most of the crew on board the *Chesapeake*, this was their first battle. Because they lacked familiarity with and respect for their officers, keeping the crew in order even under routine conditions, let alone during an engagement, was difficult. Indeed, some of the men were intoxicated when the fight began. Thus,

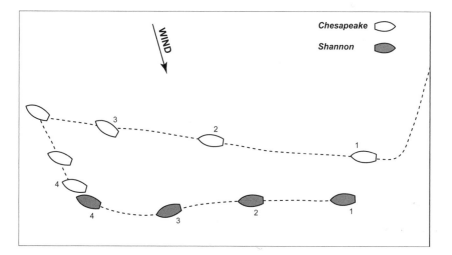

Diagram 7.1 Plan of the Engagement between the *Chesapeake* and the *Shannon* (Adapted from Mahan, *Sea Power and its Relations to the War of 1812*, 2:136–37)

when faced with the dual horrors of musketry and cannon fire, the defense of the *Chesapeake* began to unravel almost immediately.[61] Heavy casualties among the ship's officers only magnified the shock of battle and further undermined the men's ability to successfully react to the events unfolding before them. Across the water, the *Chesapeake*'s broadsides and small arms fire caused considerable damage, but most British officers survived the deadly opening volley, and the crew's experience began to tell. All of these factors caused the tide of battle to quickly shift in favor of the *Shannon*.

As the smoke cleared from the *Shannon*'s third broadside, the *Chesapeake* "appeared Unmanageable." Damage caused the American frigate to luff into the wind, making her lose all headway. In fact, the wind began to press against the front of her sails, causing her stern to drift toward the *Shannon*. During these moments, the *Shannon*'s gun crews wreaked terrible destruction, raking the American at short range. The *Chesapeake*'s stern then collided with the British frigate a bit more than a third of the way aft of her bow. Immediately, grapples flew from the deck of the *Shannon*, locking the two frigates together.[62]

Time became critical. Lawrence ordered the bugler to sound assembly for boarders, but the bugler had fled his station. When found, he "was unable, from fright to sound his horn."[63] Instead, several midshipmen received instructions to relay the order for boarders. In the meantime, Lawrence received a second wound—a musket ball through the body that proved mortal.[64] Without their leader or the sound of the bugle, the crew responded poorly: "Confusion prevailed; a greater part of the men deserted their quarters and ran below."[65] The American boarding attempt had failed before it began.

Seizing the advantage, Broke led a group of boarders onto the *Chesapeake*. As the British cleared the quarterdeck, the two frigates broke apart, trapping Broke and the boarders, which could have led to their extermination. Fortunately for the British captain and his men, the Americans were leaderless and in great confusion. When Lieutenant Budd appeared topside, he tried to rally the men, but Broke's boarding party was too strong and forced the remaining Americans down into the gun deck.[66] Before the resistance completely collapsed, however, Broke received a blow to the head, leaving it rent with a huge gash "from the top to near his mouth by the ear."[67]

Down in the *Chesapeake*'s cockpit, amidst the gore of her wounded, Lawrence lay dying. He implored the surgeon to go on deck and tell the officers "to fight the ship till she sunk."[68] It was, however, too late. The British were in possession of the quarterdeck and the forecastle. The end of the fight came grudgingly. It does not appear that the Americans struck their colors; instead, the British boarders, including George Watt, the *Shannon*'s first lieutenant, hauled them down.[69] Watt went to hoist British colors over the American one, a signal that the *Chesapeake* had become

The Wounding of Captain Philip Broke on Board the USS *Chesapeake*, 1 June 1813
(U.S. Naval Institute Photo Archive)

a British prize, but in the confusion, he placed the American colors over the British. As he and a group of men hoisted these colors the wrong way, men on board the *Shannon* took this as a sign their boarders had been overwhelmed and opened fire on Watt and his companions, killing Watt along with five to seven seamen.[70]

This moment of fratricide occurred close to the end of the encounter. The entire fight had lasted only fifteen minutes, but it had been a bloody contest. The *Shannon* had lost twenty-four killed and fifty-eight wounded.[71] American losses proved heavier, with the British asserting seventy killed and one hundred wounded. This number seems an estimate, but American losses were certainly higher than those suffered by the British.[72] A British newspaper rightfully reported, "The loss on both sides was great, considering the short period the ships were engaged."[73]

The *Shannon*, with her prize in company, made Halifax on the afternoon of 6 June. The senior officer at the port, Captain Thomas Balden Capel, wrote the Admiralty, "Under the circumstances of this important capture, . . . I have judged it proper in the absence of the commander in chief, and being ignorant of his actual position at this moment, to send a vessel to England" with a report of the battle. He ended, "I trust their Lordships will approve."[74] Capel needn't have worried, however, because this was the news the Admiralty and the British people so eagerly sought. The secretary of the Admiralty, John Wilson Croker, stood in Parliament and provided the details of the action. An Edinburgh newspaper wrote, "It is impossible to conceive a more enthusiastic effect than the statement produced." Another paper added, "We do not recollect any naval occurrence which has excited so much expression of general congratulations, as the recent capture. . . . We are obliged to regard the *Chesapeake* not as an event to have been expected with certainty, but as a glorious retrieval of our naval reputation."[75] In an era of difficult promotions, the Admiralty promoted two of the *Shannon*'s lieutenants to commander and two midshipmen to lieutenant. Broke received an offer from Melville to command a new ship "of the same class & size as the large American Frigates."[76] In addition, Warren suggested, "I should hope His Royal Highness the Prince Regent would bestow some mark of his Royal approbation upon Broke for so Heroic an action."[77] Considering the two frigates had been virtually equal in weight of metal, these marks of distinction were almost unheard of and underscored Britain's need for the victory. Warren echoed this when he congratulated Broke: "Such an Event restores the History of Ancient Times & will Do more good to the Service than it is possible to conceive."[78] A British frigate captain added, "This will prove a seasonable relief to the gloomy state, our frigate captains were reduced to."[79] Broke had indeed been correct when writing his challenge to Lawrence: "The result of our meeting may be the most grateful Service I can render to my Country."[80]

Hoping for the future, the *Times* of London entreated, "We trust that this is only the first fruits of a harvest which the whole American navy is destined to yield to our

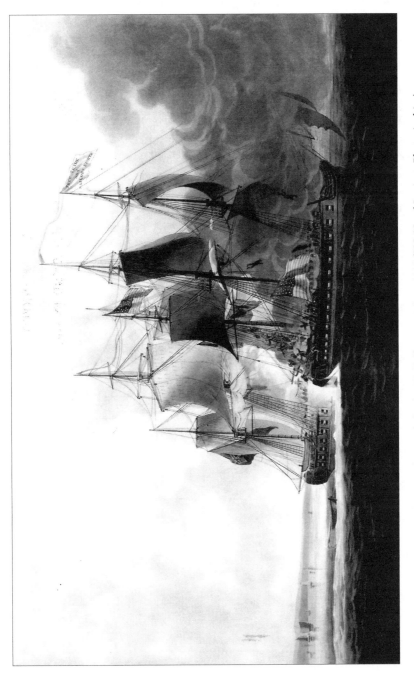

The Capture of the USS *Chesapeake* by the HMS *Shannon*, 1 June 1813 (U.S. Naval Institute Photo Archive)

brave tars."[81] A sea change occurred on 1 June. When the two sides had traded broadsides, the Americans had won six encounters, beginning with Britain's loss of the *Alert* and followed by the *Guerriere, Frolic, Macedonian, Java,* and *Peacock.* In April 1813 a British naval captain had asserted, "We have an opportunity to wipe off the disgrace which attaches to the loss of our frigates."[82] Broke and his crew did just that.

Broke's victory was not a single point of light though. The effects of 1 June extended to Long Island Sound. The encounter between Captain Oliver and Commodore Decatur proved equally important. When adding the combat loss of the *Chesapeake* to the operational loss of Decatur's squadron, at least until winter, the Royal Navy had rendered ineffective in a single day four U.S. warships, or slightly less than half of the total operational strength of America's oceanic navy.

CHAPTER 8

"More Than Ordinary Risk"

United States Frigates, Winter 1813–14

"The Nathans are tarnation mad at the capture of the *Chesapeake*," wrote one British naval officer, using a slang term for Americans.[1] A woman in Philadelphia wrote, "Tho' we had no right to expect our Ships coud always be successful, the recital of this transaction chills us with *horror*."[2] President Madison cogently asked if the *Chesapeake* was "the more decided character of an exception resulting from unpropitious circumstances, not a check to our maritime triumphs."[3] If Secretary Jones had anything to do with it, the *Chesapeake* would certainly serve as the exception. Jones wrote, "Whilst the gallant spirit and high minded character of our Naval Officers justly excites the national admiration, their zealous devotion to the cause and honour of their country must be tempered by judgment and sound policy. The glory we have acquired is too precious to commit to the wiles of an insidious foe. . . . The just and honorable contest in which we are engaged must be directed to the most effectual annoyance of the enemy, not to naval chivalry in which the numbers and force of the respective combatant, are unequal by example."[4]

The above admonition proved even more important because the United States Navy looked increasingly fragile, with few operational warships as 1813 drew to a close. Jones hoped, however, that Commodore Decatur could sail from New London with the *United States*, *Macedonian*, and *Hornet*. He also desired that Captain Charles Gordon of the *Constellation* proceed to sea from Norfolk, that Commodore Rodgers slip the *President* out of Rhode Island's Narragansett Bay, and that Captain Charles Stewart, commanding the newly refitted *Constitution*, elude the British blockade off Boston.

For the British, Admiral Warren harbored significant concern about the *Constitution* and the *President*. He concluded that their most likely course of action would involve rendezvousing at sea. They would then fall upon the British blockade squadron off New London in order to overwhelm or drive it off, so as to rescue Decatur's warships and allow their escape. To combat such a potential course of action, Warren made sure that his squadron at New London contained at least one ship of the line. However, Captain Henry Hope, who had recently arrived on the North American Station commanding the British frigate *Endymion*, assessed the American course of action differently than Warren by concluding, "They don't wish to attack your [British] ships of the line, their object is to get out of port and do your [British] Trade as much mischief as possible." This captain, moreover, provided a starkly negative assessment about the ability of the Royal Navy to prevent the escape of American commerce raiding warships, in that "they will put to sea, and you cannot prevent it during the winter. They have every advantage to favour their escape, long nights and frequent Gales of wind with thick weather."[5]

Jones could not have agreed more about commerce raiding and the advantages that winter bequeathed. Overall, his winter cruising orders demonstrated a slight reassessment from his previous instructions. Though the *Constitution, President,* and *Constellation* received orders to cruise singly, Jones took advantage of the concentration of warships in New London and ordered Decatur to keep the *United States, Macedonian,* and *Hornet* together, "so long as the public interest and means of annoying the Enemy shall appear to you to be better promoted by the combination than the separation of your force."[6] The cruises, moreover, became longer. Specifically, he wanted the *Constitution* to return at the earliest in March or April 1814, but if possible, she was to remain out until the autumn. In addition, the object of the cruises became more clearly defined, and Jones explained, "The commerce of the Enemy is the most valuable point we can attack and its destruction the main object." To reap the greatest rewards, Jones cautioned against manning prizes, because "it will be imprudent and worse than useless to attempt to send them in. The chances of recapture are excessively great." Jones, instead, ordered their destruction.[7]

Secretary Jones' strongest card rested with Decatur's squadron; getting it to sea would help erase a considerable blight on American naval operations during 1813. In mid-October Decatur received orders to sail from New London, but the British blockading squadron remained in the offing, leading the commodore to temporize: "The Enemy off here, keep a vigilant look out for us." Two months later, in early December, the British had still not withdrawn their blockade squadron as the winter storms pelted the coast. Decatur recounted that four British warships were at "anchor in the mouth of the Harbour spreading the channel about three gun shot from" the American warships, while several additional British men of war patrolled the offing.[8] Things did not look promising for the Americans, and a Royal Navy officer agreed: "How long it may be possible to keep him in God only knows. . . . We have been hitherto much favored by the weather but various are conjectures: what we may expect when violent Gales come on."[9]

As winter descended, Decatur decided to sail. "In the course of the evening two blue lights were burnt on both points at the harbor's mouth as signals to the enemy . . . There is not a doubt, but that they have, by signals and otherwise, instantaneous information of our movements," Decatur wrote. He cancelled the sailing, believing that British sympathizers had shown the lights, thus alerting the blockade squadron. An incredulous Jones exclaimed, "I . . . am truly astonished at the turpitude you have witnessed in the bosom of our own happy country."[10]

Several weeks later on board the 74-gun *Ramillies*, the commander of the British blockade squadron, Captain Sir Thomas Hardy, examined Nicholas Moran, the master of a captured merchant vessel. Also at the meeting was Captain Henry Hope, who posited the idea of a challenge between his frigate, the *Endymion*, and the *United States*. Hardy then expressed a desire that the *Macedonian* and the British frigate *Statira* could also engage in combat, but the British would not issue the challenge. Afterward, Moran obtained his release, later relating the event to Decatur at a local tavern.[11]

Interested, the American commodore wrote to Hardy, and between 17 and 20 January a series of letters tried to settle on an arrangement. Decatur seemed willing for the *United States* to engage the *Endymion* because both had a main armament of 24-pound guns. Also, the *Macedonian* could engage the *Statira*: "The force on both sides is as nearly equal as we could expect to find."[12] Hardy replied, "I have no hesitation whatever in permitting . . . the *Statira*, to meet the *Macedonian*, as they are sister ships carrying the same weight of metal." But, he refused to entertain a duel between the *Endymion* and the *United States*. Though the main armament of both consisted of 24-pound guns, Hardy maintained that the *United States* carried thirty versus twenty-six on the *Endymion*, and the *United States* carried 42-pound carronades versus the 32-pounders on the British frigate. Accordingly, Hardy explained his decision, saying, "I must consider it my duty . . . to decline the invitation."[13] Decatur then refused to allow the *Macedonian* and *Statira* to meet, on the grounds that "in my proposal for a meeting . . . I consented and I fear incautiously."[14]

Although Decatur's most recent sailing instructions, dated 13 October 1813, did not contain a statement about challenges, Jones had provided Decatur with the orders he had recently sent to Captain Stewart of the *Constitution*, with the following directive: "Should any attempt be made to allure you by challenge to single combat, I am directed by the President to prohibit strictly the acceptance either directly or indirectly."[15] Perhaps this was why Decatur declined the challenge.

In any event, Decatur did not try to hide his actions and sent Secretary Jones a copy of his correspondence with Hardy, but more than six weeks passed without a reply. Decatur questioned the silence: he thought these documents were important enough to be released to the newspapers. Period newspapers shed great light on naval operations. Important documents were routinely printed verbatim, but in this case, Jones wrote, "The documents were not published, because the President does not incline to give sanction to the principle on which the invitation was founded." Moreover, Jones explained, such naval chivalry did not benefit the United States, given "the great inequality of the Naval force of Enemy and our own." Relenting slightly, Jones admitted, "If an exception to the general principle was at all admissible, it was in your case. The rigorous blockade you have sustained, seemed to sanction more than ordinary risk."[16]

Hardy also recounted the events to his superiors, writing, "I am well aware of the responsibility I have taken upon myself in this correspondence and the strictures that may be passed on my conduct, in a case so novel." The affair shocked Admiral Warren, who replied, "I am very glad the matter terminated in the manner it did." To avoid a recurrence, he issued orders to forbid challenges. The Admiralty stood in complete agreement.[17]

The leadership of both countries wished to avoid challenges for the same basic premise—the weakness of the United States Navy and the strength of the Royal Navy. British leaders had come to the conclusion that their superiority in numbers could overwhelm their opponent, and according the Americans anything like a fair fight would forsake their material dominance. Jones, however, thought his ships were too precious to risk, and he could obtain greater strategic effects from other operations.

In the wake of the challenges, Rear Admiral George Cockburn arrived off New London and found a curious predicament. Without ground troops, the British could not eliminate Decatur's squadron; however, Cockburn described the British position as "a Capital anchorage and I have no idea of the Enemy's Ships getting out of New London whilst you keep a Squadron here, indeed it appears to me quite impossible and although I understand they threaten it yet I have no Idea that they will make the attempt."[18] A stalemate had developed that was completely acceptable to the British but not the Americans: Jones could ill-afford it. Since the ships could not escape, he transferred the precious crews of the *United States* and *Macedonian* to places of better use for the American war effort.[19]

With the sailing of Decatur's squadron thwarted, the American options narrowed. Secretary Jones, however, seemed his own worst enemy. Whether overworked or absentminded, he failed to provide Captain Gordon of the *Constellation* with cruising instructions, even though his frigate was manned and ready for sea. This led Gordon to write, on 28 December, "The Ship is waiting yr. orders *only*—The favourable opportunities which have offered of late for our escape; And particularly the present moment induces me to trouble you again." Jones quickly dispatched orders, but the moment had passed, and the weather consistently favored the blockade squadron.[20] Admiral Warren accurately concluded, "The *Constellation*, I suppose She will not easily trust herself out of Hampton Road."[21]

Even in port, her presence caused the British to incur significant costs. And in writing about the *Constellation* during March 1814, the British commander in the Chesapeake ranted, "We are here three sail of the line viz. *Marlborough Victorious & Dragon*—literally doing nothing but blocking up a Yankee Frigate." He also had a squadron of frigates operating between the Chesapeake Capes and another nearby in Lynnhaven Bay.[22]

The *Constellation* at sea could arguably have abstracted even more British naval strength, but Secretary Jones decided, "In the present state and probable continuance of the Blockade, the prospect of your getting to sea is not only hopeless but it would be temerity to make the attempt." Thus in April 1814 he canceled Gordon's cruising orders and directed him to use the *Constellation*'s men to protect Norfolk.[23]

Another option for Secretary Jones involved the *President*. Under Commodore Rodgers, she had ended her summer cruise anchored in Narragansett Bay. In the not-too-distant future, this frigate required extensive repairs, but Rodgers thought she could soon be ready for a short cruise. Manning her, however, proved problematic. Approximately seventy men elected not to reenlist upon the expiration of their term of service, and it took until mid-November to recruit replacements.[24]

While Rodgers prepared to sail, Admiral Warren strengthened his force off Narragansett Bay, but November found his command stretched. Battle, disease, and accidents thinned Warren's crews. Moreover, service on the Lakes along the border between the United States and Canada became an increasingly important theater of operations and demanded manpower. In August Warren sent the entire crew of the 18-gun *Indian* to the Lakes, but this was merely the first of several warship crews he had to transfer.[25] In addition to manning, Warren made a familiar complaint about having thirty fewer warships than the Admiralty asserted. With numerous convoys and blockading squadrons, Warren found it difficult to balance the competing demands placed on his command.[26]

Adding to British naval problems was a severe storm that ripped through the crowded harbor at Halifax, Nova Scotia, during the night of 12 November, causing ships to break free of their moorings. At anchor was the 38-gun frigate *Tenedos*. One of her crew recounted the scene. Around 7:00 p.m. "it was reported from the forecastle that a large ship was coming down upon us, right a head. Lights were accordingly shown on our bows—immediately the helm put hard to port." The ship "passed on our larboard side distant at most only twelve feet." Minutes later, an even larger ship approached the *Tenedos*, this time the 74-gun *Poictiers* cleared the frigate by a narrower margin. The same member of her crew asserted, "Could there be any thing more alarming than such a . . . ship so near to another half her size." Soon after, "a large cluster of ships came down upon us." Among the gaggle of fouled ships was the 74-gun *Victorious*. Her bowsprit hooked *Tenedos'* mizzenmast, and she became tangled in the frigate's anchor cable. On board the frigate the crew cut the cable, while others feverishly hacked down the mizzen that fell "over the stern into the water with a tremendous crash." Free, the *Tenedos* let go her spare anchor, and it held fast. "At dawn of day the sight along shore was truly distressing; nothing but shipwrecks every side."[27] Another witness concluded, "Not a ship or vessel of any kind can go to Sea for this week at least, and I do not think the harbor and dockyard will recover for it this year."[28] Though Warren reported no warships destroyed, nine had gone on shore, including two 74-gun ships and a frigate.[29]

Even with so many ships out of action, Warren deployed the 74-gun *Albion* and the 36-gun *Orpheus* off Rhode Island. In addition, he placed a second squadron, consisting of the 74-gun *Ramillies*, 40-gun *Endymion*, and 38-gun *Loire*, farther out to sea. This information did not escape Rodgers, but he sailed anyway on the evening of 4 December. Though Rodgers "expected to have [to] run the gauntlet through the enemy's squadron that was reported to be cruising . . . for the purpose of intercepting the *President* I had the good luck to avoid them."[30]

The first day of the cruise resulted in the recapture of an American merchant vessel, but danger lurked nearby in the form of several British warships.[31] Rodgers knew about the *Albion* and *Orpheus*. In addition, the *Ramillies* was close, but Rodgers could consider himself fortunate that the *Loire* and *Endymion* had chased well to the south.[32] He did not expect, however, the 74-gun *San Domingo*, flying Warren's flag, and the schooner, *Canso*. Both had sailed from Halifax on 3 December. Warren knew time was of the essence and would have sailed sooner had not both the *San Domingo* and the *Canso* been driven on shore during thhe 12 November hurricane.[33]

The events of 6 December, or the second day of the *President*'s cruise, began with her lookouts sighting a suspicious sail to the southeast. Cautiously, Rodgers observed his quarry and deemed "it imprudent to chace [sic] owing to our being in the vicinity of several of the enemies [sic] vessels and believing from his maneuvres that his object is to decoy us into the neighborhood of a superior force." In all like-lihood, the Americans had sighted the *San Domingo*. On board this ship, British lookouts had descried a strange sail along the *President's* bearing. Warren gave chase, but darkness soon enveloped both parties.[34]

Rodgers had his company shorten sail "with the intention of offering her battle in the morning, should nothing else be in sight and she not be a Ship of the line." At daylight on 7 December, poor visibility and squally conditions persisted. The *President's* lookouts sighted a single sail, but she was in the opposite direction of the previous day's sighting and quickly disappeared from view.[35]

Rodgers' caution paid handsome dividends. Warren had come very close to falling in with the *President* while the *Albion* and *Orpheus* lurked in the area. In addition, the *Ramillies* was well positioned to encounter the *President* and actually fell in with the *Albion* and *Orpheus* on 7 December.[36] Overall, Rodgers had avoided three 74-gun ships, a frigate, and a schooner through a combination of hazy condi-tions, luck, and caution, leading Warren to write, "I am sorry to say that sneaking fellow Rogers [*sic*] has got out of Rhode Island & is again at sea."[37]

Though Rodgers might have proved cunning in his escape, he failed to take a prize while crossing the Atlantic. Finally, on 25 December, just north of Madeira, lookouts sighted two large sail. Rodgers noted, "From Some particulars about their Sails, the paint of their Hulls, the Stem of their Bowsprits, and their royal poles being painted black, I thought it probable they were french [*sic*], possibly, British Indiamen and accordingly determined to keep in Sight of them during the night." Rodgers had his crew back the mizzen topsail to slow the *President*, but he mis-judged the speed of his opponents and one of the strangers got near enough to fire a shot over the American frigate. Rodgers responded by filling the sails and the chase was on. They pressed after the *President* during the night, but Rodgers kept his pursuers at bay. Sunrise showed they were nine to ten miles distant. Later that morning the pursuers disappeared in the haze.[38] Several days later, the *President* fell in with a Portuguese brig. From her, Rodgers obtained information that a day and a half earlier she had been boarded by the British troopship *Melpomene* and an unnamed consort. Rodgers pursued, but four days later he admitted, "I was again disappointed."[39]

The *Melpomene* had sailed with a convoy that had departed England on 27 November. Consisting of nearly two hundred merchantmen, the Admiralty pro-vided a heavy escort comprising the 74-gun *Queen*, 40-gun *Severn*, 20-gun *Bonne Citoyenne*, 18-gun *Columbine*, as well as *Melpomene*, under the overall charge of

Captain John, Lord Colville, of the *Queen*. Five days out the convoy encountered "a most violent tempest blowing in the squalls with the utmost fury, and a very heavy sea running." Visibility dropped and the ships fought for survival. Several days later, Colville recounted, "Since the last gale I have only been joined by 27 sail, and have not seen any of the Men of War that sailed in company with me." He hoped, however, to fall in with them at the rendezvous north of Madeira.[40] As the *Queen* approached that island on 14 December, her lookouts sighted fifty-four sail under the *Columbine's* escort. Two days later, the *Queen* fell in with approximately forty merchant vessels, as well as the *Severn* and *Bonne Citoyenne*; the *Melpomene* and some eighty merchantmen remained unaccounted for, however.[41]

The *Wanderer* was one of these vessels. After parting with the convoy during the storm, she had proceeded alone. Near Barbados on 5 January 1814, the *President* captured her. Her crew provided information about the convoy and the storm, and Rodgers realized that he could take advantage of the dispersed convoy. A convoy sailing in mass offered only a single point of contact, but a scattered convoy offered dozens. Only two days after capturing the *Wanderer*, Rodgers encountered the *Prince George*. After separating from the convoy, she had been captured by the French frigates *Nymphe* and *Meduse*. Rather than destroy her, they sent her in as a cartel with 155 prisoners from other captures. Putting the puzzle together, Rodgers concluded that these French frigates were the ones he had encountered north of Madeira on 25 December.[42]

Rodgers let the *Prince George* proceed, given her status as a cartel; she arrived at Barbados around 10 January, providing the commander of the Leeward Islands Station, Rear Admiral Sir Francis Laforey, news of the French frigates and the *President*.[43] Laforey had four frigates in his command. Two were on patrol, but the 38-gun *Rhin* and the 32-gun *Cleopatra* returned around the time the *Prince George* reached Barbados. With the arrival of the *Queen* and *Bonne Citoyenne* on 10 January, Laforey had a powerful force at his disposal, but he allowed it to languish. Only the *Cleopatra* sailed east of Barbados "for the purpose of protecting the dispersed Ships of the *Queen's* convoy."[44] Considering that her likely opponents were a pair of French frigates or the *President*, the response appears negligent, given the availability of the *Queen*, *Rhin*, and *Bonne Citoyenne*.

Rodgers remained east of Barbados searching for vessels of the scattered convoy until 16 January, but he captured just one more merchant ship. He then plied the waters of the West Indies but only encountered neutrals, until capturing a British schooner on 3 February. Rodgers then shaped a course toward the United States, arriving off Charleston on 11 February. Close to the bar, the *President*'s lookouts made out two schooners. Correctly identifying them as American warships, Rodgers made the private signal of the day but received no response. The weather made crossing the bar impossible, so he ordered the *President* out to sea.[45]

Though the United States Navy had contested the inland waterways around Charleston, its attempts did not extend very far into the offing. As a result, British warships since the autumn of 1812 had operated off the Carolina coast with near impunity. Now Rodgers could turn the tables: about sixty miles west of Charleston on the morning of 12 February, Rodgers encountered the 18-gun British ship-sloop *Morgiana*, under Commander David Scott.[46]

As the morning ticked toward afternoon, the number of sightings by lookouts on board the *President* and *Morgiana* each totaled three. In hindsight, the two warships had sighted each other and two other vessels that plied the area. Around midday, the *Morgiana* spoke with one of the strangers, a Swedish merchant vessel. From several miles off, Rodgers watched the encounter and then observed the *Morgiana* close with the *President*. The commodore correctly concluded she was probably a small frigate or a large sloop, and by mid-afternoon she was approximately four miles distant. At this point Scott realized he was closing with a frigate, and he ordered the *Morgiana* to flee. Rodgers hesitated, asserting, "On discovering the third sail, added to the maneuvre of the first and Second, I was induced to believe them part of an enemy squadron." Though Rodgers accurately identified the *Morgiana*, he never realized that one of the unknown vessels was a Swedish merchantman. For the final ship, Rodgers' masthead lookouts descried her as a "large frigate." Scott certainly did not harbor this opinion, for he was operating alone. The identity of the third sail remains a mystery, but her presence added fog to Rodgers' assessment and certainly aided in the *Morgiana*'s escape.[47]

Still believing that he had encountered a British squadron, Rodgers shortened sail. At daylight he hoped to pick off one of his opponents if they were widely scattered. Dawn found the *President* enveloped in a fog. Suddenly it parted, revealing a ship, and Rodgers closed. The line of sight opened further to reveal three additional sails. Now facing four vessels, Rodgers fled, and in several hours the *President* lost sight of them.[48] One of the unknown vessels might have been the *Morgiana*. Her log recounted the sighting of an unknown sail that morning, but Scott did not linger in the area. He pressed for Bermuda with information about the frigate. In response, the *San Domingo* sailed toward Charleston, but the *President* had already departed the area, steering north.[49]

On the morning of 17 February, the *President* arrived off the Delaware. Shrouded in fog, Rodgers groped along using soundings to measure the depth of the water. Suddenly, a large ship, "apparently a man of war," loomed out of the mist, but after a few minutes the fog enveloped the mystery ship. Rodgers then heard the boom of signal guns, and he "stood on to the northward from a belief I was near another squadron."[50] Three British warships plied the waters off the Delaware that morning: Admiral Cockburn, flying his flag in the 74-gun *Albion*, sailed in company with the frigate *Acasta* some fifty miles off the coast. Closer in, the 32-gun *Narcissus* sailed alone. This was probably the warship Rodgers encountered. Though the signal guns indicated communication between warships, meaning the *Albion* and *Acasta*, the depth of the water and location indicate it was probably the *Narcissus*.[51] Yet again, Rodgers had encountered a weaker warship and did not pursue, given the fear of other British ships in the fog. Though prudent and in keeping with Secretary Jones' intent, such risk-averse behavior had cost Rodgers the opportunity of taking the *Morgiana* and the *Narcissus*. Capturing either would likely have forced Warren to concentrate his force by strengthening his squadrons and being more careful about letting warships operate alone, thus reducing the area of sea that his already stretched command could effectively patrol. Chance, however, gave Rodgers one more opportunity to capture a British warship.

Daybreak on 18 February found the *President* near Sandy Hook. Rodgers planned to slip over the bar and enter New York harbor. This was much easier said than done, for the bar could only be crossed at high tide and Rodgers knew that large British warships patrolled the area. About 8:45 a.m. the commodore dispatched a boat to the lighthouse for a pilot. While awaiting her return, his lookouts sighted a sail, and Rodgers made her out to be a frigate. Sensing an opportunity, he ordered the colors hoisted. Over the next minutes, Rodgers altered his conclusion because he "could perceive that the enemy was something more than a frigate."[52]

About 2:45 p.m. the boat Rodgers had sent to fetch the pilot returned, but apparently without a pilot. The nature of the bar at Sandy Hook, in combination with the size of the *President*, meant that Rodgers needed the guidance of an expert. The tide, moreover, was out, and he needed to cross at high water. Rodgers was trapped outside the bar with an enemy warship in sight. Under such circumstances he decided to engage his opponent, even if she was a 74-gun ship. He spoke to the crew with "a few but impressive words," then he closed, but the unknown warship edged away. About this time, an American revenue cutter joined the *President*, and the cutter's commander and a pilot came on board, asserting that the stranger was a ship of the line. She was now "no more than a long gunshot off," and another sail had been descried on the edge of the horizon. Rodgers decided on prudence and had the pilot take his frigate over the bar. One of the *President*'s lieutenants asserted, "From the position of the two ships, for seven hours, it is evident the enemy could have compelled us to action, at any hour within that interval for he had the weather gage, and the water on the bar was too low for the *President* to get over till 5 o'clock." Rodgers added, "How to account for the Enemy's extraordinary conduct is impossible."[53]

For the British, the encounter looked quite different. Rodgers' decision to approach close to the shore had allowed the *President* to get between the British warships and Sandy Hook. Moreover, the British squadron was poorly deployed. The 74-gun *Ramillies* was off station, leaving only the 38-gun *Loire*, under Captain Thomas Brown, within sight of Sandy Hook. About 10:30 a.m. Brown had sighted the *President* and made her out to be a warship. Throughout the day he kept a wary distance, hoping that the *Ramillies* would return; however, she spent the morning chasing a schooner that turned out to be a neutral. Without assistance, Brown decided to respect the Admiralty directive dated 10 July 1813, entreating frigate commanders to avoid single combat with the largest class of American frigates.[54]

The Americans, however, tried to cast the incident in a more positive light by transforming the *Loire* into the 74-gun *Plantagenet*. Admittedly, she had been off Sandy Hook when the *President* had sailed from Narragansett Bay in early December, but on 18 February she was in the mid-Atlantic. Still, an American newspaper printed an article titled "*President* and *Plantagenet*" that asserted, "The fact that an American frigate having . . . pursued a British ship of the line, offered her battle, and lain within the power of her attack for seven hours, is a circumstance of which the occurrence is so honorable to our naval reputation, and so unfavorable to that of Britain."[55] Such an appraisal did not account for the lack of a pilot, not enough water being over the bar, or the *Loire* possessing the weather gauge, meaning the wind allowed her, and not the *President*, the advantage of maneuver.

To Secretary Jones, Rodgers related, "After contemplating the extent and nature of my late cruise, you will readily conclude that I cannot feel otherwise than disappointed; for altho I excited the enemies fears, I did not do him that injury I had anticipated."[56] However, the operating environment had changed since the summer of 1813. Merchant ships increasingly sailed under convoy, making them difficult targets. Simultaneously, British naval deployments had become ever-more expansive, and one has to consider how much of the *President*'s safe arrival at New York rested on luck. Off Barbados Rodgers profited from the poor utilization of British warships, and off Sandy Hook he profited from the positions of the *Ramillies* and *Loire*; the afternoon would likely have ended much differently had they been reversed. Overall, Rodgers seemed to be spoiling for a fight; but in actual encounters with British warships, he proved risk-averse, even when facing an inferior force, because he understood that his warship was an asset that could not be chanced lightly. Secretary Jones summed up Rodgers' cruise by asserting that it "exhibits another proof of the exaggerated power and fictitious omnipresence of the British Flag."[57]

But one wonders if the secretary was merely content with the safe return of one of his most valuable warships.

Secretary Jones expected great things of the *Constitution*. She had a tradition of victory, and had spent much of 1813 undergoing an extensive refit in Boston. Jones envisioned a six- or seven-month cruise plying the seas from the West Indies to the British Isles. If fortunate enough to capture ships carrying provisions, the secretary wanted her cruise extended to almost a year.[58]

Although Jones issued the *Constitution*'s cruising instructions on 19 September, she did not emerge from her refit until early November. Then, it took another month to complete her crew. Finally ready for sea, the mildness of the weather "permitted the enemy to hover near the port."[59] The mere concept of the British operating off Boston during the winter was novel. The previous year, Warren had thought it too dangerous without the shelter of a protected anchorage, but in late October 1813 the British determined that Provincetown Harbor near the tip of Cape Cod was "perfectly safe to ride out a Gale of Wind from any point on the Compass."[60]

The end of the year found the British taking advantage of this anchorage with the 56-gun razee *Majestic*, as well as the 38-gun frigates *Tenedos* and *Junon*, when the 18-gun *Wasp*, under Commander Thomas Everard, arrived on 28 December with news that the *Constitution* had not sailed. Over the next days, the British warships rode out a gale.[61] Meanwhile, Captain Charles Stewart steered the *Constitution* to sea on 30 December, taking advantage of favorable wind, weather, and tide.[62] Two days later, the British squadron sailed from Provincetown under Captain John Hayes of the *Majestic*. His overriding concern dealt with the *Constitution*: "We have had such repeated Gales with frost and snow, it would have been extraordinary if she had not made her escape." Hayes sent the *Junon* and *Tenedos* to patrol the northern egress from Boston, while he dispatched the *Wasp* to reconnoiter Boston harbor. Everard accomplished this task on 2 January: "I ascertained positively that the *Constitution* . . . was gone from thence, as the day was tolerably clear." He then sailed to warn Hayes. Though he arrived at the prearranged rendezvous the next day, foul weather kept him from finding the *Majestic* until 8 January, when Everard relayed the information that the *Constitution* had sailed. Hayes immediately followed his instructions, chasing the *Constitution* to the east in the direction of the Azores and Madeira.[63] Given previous U.S. naval operations and the importance of these islands as a rendezvous for scattered British convoys, this action appeared a logical choice.

Hayes arrived off the Azores on 20 January but learned nothing of the *Constitution*.[64] He then shaped a course for Madeira. Soon after daylight on 3 February, the *Majestic*'s lookouts espied three ships and a brig. Hayes soon identified two of the strangers as large frigates, but private signals went unanswered. He wrote to Warren, "Having the good fortune Sir, to be placed at the head of an excellent Set of Officers and my people being in perfect health and high Spirits, I determined on forcing them to show their colours." Hayes also realized his ship was special. The *Majestic* had once been a 74-gun ship of the line, but she had been turned into a razee by removing her poop and forecastle, leaving her with two complete gun decks. Designed to defeat America's heavy frigates, she carried an impressive armament of 28 x 32-pound long guns on her lower gun deck and 28 x 42-pound carronades on her upper deck. That afternoon the *Majestic* "commenced firing with considerable effect." A frigate was not designed to sustain hits from 32-pound shot, and the *Majestic*'s opponent, the French frigate *Terpishore*, soon struck. Her consorts escaped. Hayes reported that she had "been captured without a drop of Bloodshed, on our part."[65] The *Terpishore* was part of a group of at least thirteen French frigates that had sailed in twos and threes in late 1813, a group that included the frigates that had chased the *President*.[66]

Though Hayes had taken a French frigate, the *Constitution* was the reason for his cruise, but he had chased in the wrong direction—Captain Stewart had sailed to the West Indies. Around daybreak on 3 February, the 18-gun British sloop *Mosquito*, under Commander James Tomkinson, encountered the *Constitution* off the coast of Suriname. Squalls and rain reduced visibility, but Tomkinson still made his opponent out to be a frigate. Private signals were answered by what appeared to be Portuguese colors. Suspicious, Tomkinson fled. Stewart pursued, accurately describing the *Mosquito* as a brig of war. In the early afternoon, Tomkinson decided his only chance involved a risky run into shoal water. The *Mosquito* escaped while Stewart grudgingly ordered the *Constitution* to haul off. Disappointed but safe, Stewart sailed north toward Barbados; however, the encounter with the *Mosquito*, followed five days later by the failure to run down an English packet vessel, betrayed the *Constitution*'s presence.[67]

At Barbados, news of the *Constitution* received a far different response from the reception the *President* had garnered the previous month. The reason stemmed from the presence of a new and more aggressive station commander, Rear Admiral Philip Durham. In addition to being aggressive, Durham seemed lucky. On his passage out he had captured a pair of French frigates.[68] Then, information about the *Constitution* arrived, and he decided "that no chance should be lost for intercepting the Enemy." Durham's predecessor, Rear Admiral Laforey, was still at Barbados. Hoping to rescue something from the command he had so recently held, he hoisted his flag on board the 74-gun *Queen* and, along with the 18-gun *Columbine* and the

4-gun schooner *Balahou*, sailed in quest of the *Constitution* on 9 February. The next day, Durham sent his flagship, the 74-gun *Venerable*, accompanied by the 18-gun *Heron*, after the American frigate. He then ordered the 36-gun *Galatea* to patrol to the windward of Barbados. In less than seventy-two hours, Durham had six warships searching for the *Constitution*.[69]

Meanwhile, Stewart's lookouts sighted two sail around 11:00 p.m. on 13 February.[70] On board one of these, Midshipman George Hannaford saw the *Constitution* in the darkness. Immediately, he called all hands and personally roused his commanding officer, Lieutenant Edward Stephens. A grizzled lieutenant of nineteen years seniority, Stephens came on the deck and looked through the glass. Immediately, he had his schooner, the 14-gun *Pictou*, close with her consort, the merchant vessel *Lovely Ann*. Stephens hailed, explaining that he thought the stranger a frigate, and the *Lovely Ann* was to make all sail.[71] Now about midnight, Stephens made the night signal. There was no response from the *Constitution*, and Stephens ordered more sail. The *Pictou* rapidly left the *Lovely Ann* and the American frigate far astern.[72] But Stephens had second thoughts. He had sailed from Bermuda with Warren's direct order to see the *Lovely Ann* to Suriname.[73] Stephens decided that he could not abandon his charge, so he brought his vessel to in hopes the merchant vessel would come up. At daylight lookouts sighted the *Constitution*, and another sail, assumed to be the *Lovely Ann*, was reported even more distant. Stephens ordered all sail in an effort to escape.[74] However, the *Constitution* rapidly closed. Signal flags broke over the *Constitution*, and Midshipman Hannaford told Stephens, "The flags were not of English bunting, and he [Stephens] said he believed not." About 9:00 a.m. the *Constitution* showed American colors. Minutes later, a round from the *Constitution* did considerable damage aloft. The accuracy proved unnerving, and the following shots did even more harm. After enduring about forty-five minutes of punishment, Stephens called his company together, told them he would be forced to surrender, and that they were "to behave like Englishmen."[75] He then had the colors hauled down. When Stephens went on board the *Constitution*, he found that Stewart had captured the *Lovely Ann* in the darkness.[76]

Captain Stewart spent the day disposing of the prizes. He ordered his men to throw the *Lovely Ann*'s cargo overboard, and then used her to transport Stephens, his officers, and his men to Barbados. Later in the day he ordered the *Pictou* burned.[77] These were questionable decisions, though. The *Pictou* could have served as a tender or scout, at least until her provisions were exhausted. Though she sustained damage in the chase, her masts had not been injured.[78] More critical, the *Lovely Ann* had dried fish and flour on board that the *Constitution* needed to extend her cruise, but these items mostly went into the water. Later, Stewart would assert, "The time was not favourable to take much from that vessel."[79] Transferring cargo incurred a degree of risk with British warships in search of the *Constitution*, but the reward was a longer cruise. Finally, sending the *Lovely Ann* to nearby Barbados as a cartel further alerted the British.

Two days after parting company with the *Constitution* and 120 miles from the site of her capture, the *Lovely Ann* fell in with the *Venerable* and *Heron*. Stephens provided information of the *Constitution*. Though the *Venerable* and *Heron* immediately pursued, they sailed too far east, while the American frigate sailed toward Grenada, where Stewart took a pair of prizes between 17 and 19 February.[80]

The *Constitution* then sailed north. The morning of 23 February found her coasting along the southwestern shore of Puerto Rico toward the Mona Passage separating Puerto Rico and Hispaniola.[81] In this area Stewart encountered the 36-gun *Pique*. Her commander, Captain the Honorable Anthony Maitland, had received information from the 18-gun *Crane* and 16-gun *Bustard* that an enemy frigate was in the area. Rather than detain these vessels, Maitland allowed them to continue their mission, meaning that the *Pique* had to confront the *Constitution* alone.[82]

On board the *Constitution*, Stewart made the *Pique* out "to be a frigate with fourteen gun ports on the gun deck." Thinking that perhaps his eyes had deceived him, he ordered the private signal, "Supposing the Ship to be the United States frigate *President*." Maitland, however, showed English colors but asserted, "It was not till I saw his Broadside that I had the least idea of his size. . . . I felt it no longer my Duty (with reference to my Secret Orders) to seek an Engagement with a ship so much superior." At this point the wind deserted the *Constitution*, but a light breeze stayed with the *Pique*, allowing Maitland to escape. Stewart lost his opponent in the darkness.[83]

Maitland understood he lacked the power to engage. Though Admiralty instructions supported his decision, he lamented that the *Crane* and *Amaranthe*, two 18-gun sloops under his orders, were not in company. The other vessel in his command was the *Bustard*, but Maitland considered her "force is so trifling as to be of little consequence."[84] Later, Admiral Durham questioned why Maitland had not detained the *Crane* and *Bustard* when they had warned him of a frigate in the area. However, the Admiralty entirely approved of Maitland's decision not to engage the *Constitution* because its members understood the power of America's heavy frigates and feared a public backlash if Britain lost another frigate.[85] Stewart ranted, with good reason, that "it is our misfortune and not our fault that . . . the conscious inferiority of the Enemy's frigates has led them to avoid where they used to seek combat with us."[86]

Durham spent the next month searching for the *Constitution*. On 9 March he sent the *Ister* and *Pique*, two 36-gun frigates, on a patrol. The *Venerable* and *Heron* returned the next day, having been out for nearly a month searching for the *Constitution*. News of the American frigate would not die, and several days later

Durham ordered the 36-gun *Galatea* and two 18-gun sloops to sail off Suriname, "as it is generally believed the *Constitution* will be making her appearance in that quarter." He then ordered the first ship of the line to arrive at Barbados to sail to the windward of the island to protect trade. Another issue involved Laforey, who had sailed in quest of the *Constitution* with his flag on board the *Queen*. Durham received scant information about Laforey's progress and sent a schooner to find him on 10 March. Ten days later, he received news that Laforey had arrived off Puerto Rico, following up on the *Pique's* encounter, but this sighting was now a month old. Finally, on 23 March Durham sent another vessel after Laforey because he needed the *Queen* to escort the next homeward-bound convoy.[87]

Meanwhile, Stewart had sailed north from Puerto Rico, departing the area patrolled by Durham's command, never comprehending the disruption he had caused. Stewart faced a quandary, having discovered a contradiction in his cruising orders. Secretary Jones had written his instructions in September, thinking the *Constitution* would soon sail, but Stewart did not proceed to sea until the end of December. Jones had not amended his orders, however, which called for a cruise of six to seven months before returning "in March or April so as to revictual, and get out again before the mild season shall admit of a close Blockade of our Harbours." But as of 1 March, the *Constitution* had been at sea only two months. Did Stewart stay out, or did he dash in to obtain enough provisions to extend his cruise through the summer? Jones had given him the option of "touching off Savannah or Charleston for refreshments and intelligence," but this was with the understanding that this would occur after the *Constitution* made a full circuit of the Atlantic in the track of British convoys. Looking for an answer, Stewart referenced the following part of his order: "These instructions are given with a strong desire that they may be adhered to, unless some unforeseen want or particular information you may derive in the course of your cruise shall in your particular judgement render a deviation indispensable."[88] Considering this caveat, Stewart steered for a southern port in the United States, hoping to secure provisions.[89]

When the *Constitution* arrived off Charleston and Savannah in mid-March, Stewart found the weather thick and squally, with a gale developing, so he took his frigate out to sea.[90] Stewart again reassessed. He had food for approximately three and a half months and water for about two and a half months. This meant he needed a port in June. At that time of the year, it would prove difficult to enter Boston or New York, given the mild weather, long hours of daylight, and the British blockade. He could follow the track of Britain's homeward-bound convoys, though, putting in at a European port for provisions. Still undecided, he learned on 27 March that the *Constitution's* mainmast needed repair or perhaps replacement.[91] The cumulative effect of these various issues led Stewart to sail for Boston: "The information we obtained induced us to believe that Boston Bay was clear of the Enemy's Cruisers

The Escape of the USS *Constitution* from the HMS *Junon* and the HMS *Tenedos*, 3 April 1814 (U.S. Naval Institute Photo Archive)

and that a favorable opportunity presented for coming into Port to replace what would be required, and get out again in time to follow the Enemys [*sic*] Convoys."[92]

On the morning of 3 April the *Constitution* was approaching Boston when her lookouts observed "two square rigged vessels standing for us."[93] Stewart's intelligence had been wrong. The Americans had encountered the 38-gun British frigates *Junon* and *Tenedos*. One crewmember on board the *Tenedos* described their prey as "a beautiful large frigate, having 15 gun ports on her deck, beautifully painted, and carrying a crowd of canvas."[94] Captain Clotworthy Upton of the *Junon* added, "She was painted with a single Yellow Streak, Black Stern, and her entire line so perfectly straight, that when her hull first rose above the Horizon, I could scarcely persuade myself she was more than a Corvette." Upton wrote that she was much larger than the *Tenedos*, and "I know no other Ship which would answer the description, except *President*, that she is an American I have no doubt."[95] An engagement appeared imminent as the superior British force closed, but against such odds, Stewart pressed for safety and ordered his crew to lighten the ship in order to gain more speed. This kept the British frigates at bay until just after midday, at which time the *Constitution* made Marblehead and soon after anchored at Salem.[96]

Upton learned she was the *Constitution* from the markings on a cask of flour that had been heaved overboard during the chase. He faced a quandary, having received reports that the frigate *Congress* and the newly commissioned ship-sloop *Wasp* would soon sail from Portsmouth, New Hampshire. Given the strength of the American forces at Portsmouth and Salem, Upton asserted that he "should feel myself risking one, or both of His Majesty's Ships too much, were I to separate them." He assessed that the *Constitution* could not sail on another oceanic voyage after throwing so much into the ocean during her escape. As a result, the most likely course of action for this frigate would be to run to Boston, but Upton argued, "We *cannot*, by any Possibility prevent *Constitution* getting to Boston, and as the Ships at Portsmouth are nearly ready for sea, shall give them a preference in my Conduct." The 38-gun *Nymphe* soon reinforced Upton, but it was too late. The *Constitution* cleared Salem on 17 April and coasted into Boston the following evening.[97]

About this time, Stewart's cruise report reached Washington. As a matter of course, captains provided the secretary of the navy with descriptions of their operations. Although the length and organization of each report varied, most contained extensive detail. For example, Rodgers' report on his seventy-five-day cruise ending in February 1814 totaled more than 1,500 words. Stewart's report on his three-month cruise, however, was only one-third as long. Muddled with few dates, locations, or coordinates, it even lacked a solid chronology.[98] Upon reading the report, Secretary Jones became livid. In a scathing response, he seethed, "I do not perceive in the reasons and motives assigned a satisfactory case for the premature termination of the cruise." Jones ended by ordering, "It is due to yourself, Sir, as well as to the public that an enquiry should be made into the causes which have produced these comments."[99]

For several days in early May, a court of inquiry took place to look into Stewart's early return to Boston. The verdict stated, "The reasons assigned by Capt Stewart . . . do not appear to this court to comprise a sufficient cause for his return at the time he did. Yet the Court believes that Capt Stewart considered these reasons sufficient to justify his return; and if he has erred it is the opinion of the Court that it was an error of judgment."[100] Jones apparently decided to keep the verdict confidential, leading the *Delaware Gazette* to report, "As we are informed Capt. Stewart remains in command, and no court marshal is to be called. It is, therefore, to be presumed that the return of the ship was not premature; and that the circumstances of the case fully justified her commander."[101] Though not accurate, such a conclusion was certainly better for the country's morale and the image of the navy. Nevertheless, the inquiry detained the *Constitution* in Boston while the weather increasingly favored the British blockade. She would not sail before autumn.

Jones could not have been happy with oceanic operations during the winter of 1813–14. Stewart had come in early, though part of this stemmed from the secretary's faulty instructions; Gordon never sailed, in part owing to the secretary's delay in issuing his orders; and Decatur remained trapped in New London. Only Commodore Rodgers had come close to meeting Jones' expectations. Though prizes proved few and results appeared scant, American actions still solicited a disproportionate response from the British. The *San Domingo* sailed toward Charleston in quest of the *President*, and Hayes with the *Majestic* stretched to Madeira. Convoys had to be strengthened, such as attaching the 56-gun razee *Goliath* to a January convoy from Bermuda to England. Moreover, Warren sent the 74-gun *Plantagenet* and 18-gun *Childers* on a cruise ranging as far south as Barbados. The 40-gun *Severn* and 38-gun *Surprize* received orders to sail toward the West Indies, and the 74-gun *Sceptre* received orders from Warren to follow.[102] Admittedly, these deployments were designed to thwart both American and French frigate operations, but they still diverted substantial resources. This does not account for the turmoil the *President* and particularly the *Constitution* caused in the Leeward Islands station. Although the sailings of the American frigates caused disruption, the British deployments increased the risk for the Americans, and the Admiralty's restrictive rules of engagement, coupled with the American fear of losing a frigate, meant that the naval war had taken an increasingly favorable turn for Britain.

CHAPTER 9

"Pursuing My Own Course"

The Essex *in the Pacific, 1813–14*

Half a world away from North America, Captain David Porter, commanding the U.S. frigate *Essex*, wreaked havoc during 1813. In the process he unknowingly implemented Secretary Jones' strategy by targeting a critical vulnerability in Britain's maritime network. Sailing alone from Delaware in October 1812, the *Essex* was one of three ships assigned to Commodore Bainbridge's squadron. Porter had orders to rendezvous with his squadron commander, but poor timing and the exigencies of war prevented their meeting. By early January, Porter explained, "I was perfectly at a loss now where to find the commodore, as, . . . he had departed from his original instructions, and had already disappointed me at three rendezvous."[1] Then, off the coast of Brazil in mid-January 1813, Porter received three pieces of intelligence. First, Bainbridge had captured a British frigate; second, the British had captured an American sloop belonging to Bainbridge's squadron; and finally, the British naval force on the Brazilian coast had received reinforcements. Though only the first item of intelligence was correct, Porter had little choice but to accept each as fact. He was far from home, alone, and operating against the most powerful navy in the world. In light of these factors, he determined that "it was then necessary to decide promptly on my future proceedings." Moreover, provisions were running low, and Porter believed that "there was no port on this coast where we could procure a supply, without the certainty of capture, or blockade (which I considered as bad); to attempt to return to the United States, at a season of the year when our coast would be swarming with the enemy's cruizers, would be running too much risk." Porter reasoned, "I therefore determined to pursue that course which seemed to me best calculated to injure the enemy, and would enable me to prolong my cruize: this could only be done by going into a friendly port . . . and the first place that presented itself . . . was . . . on the coast of Chili [*sic*]."²

The depth of Porter's reasoning underscored his situation: "I was departing from the letter of my instructions, and in prosecution of a plan which might not prove successful, or meet the approbation of my commanding officer, or the navy department." With such weighty thoughts, he took his frigate toward the Pacific "pursuing *my own course*." Early in the voyage, rumors swirled among the crew about their destination. Realizing that he had committed his men to a long and dangerous mission, Porter needed to provide great rewards, so he provided the

David Porter (Navy History and Heritage Command, Photo # 80-G-K-17588)

following enticements: "The Pacific ocean [sic] affords us many friendly ports. The unprotected British commerce . . . will give you an abundant supply of wealth; and the girls of the Sandwich islands, shall reward you for your sufferings during the passage around Cape Horn."[3]

Rounding Cape Horn took the *Essex* off the beaten path. Porter concluded, "We were now groping in the dark, and entirely ignorant of what British ships were on the coast; and until we could obtain some intelligence, no plan could be adopted that would afford us hopes of success." In search of information, the *Essex* put into Valparaiso, Chile, on 15 March.[4] There, he learned from the master of an American whaling vessel that several English whalers operated around the Galapagos Islands, and others could be found off the Peruvian coast.[5] From this source and others, Porter concluded, "Our commerce has been much harassed in those seas . . . , and as I have as complete power in the Pacific as the whole British Navy can have in the Atlantic I shall be enabled to afford it that protection it now stands in need of."[6]

To make good on this promise, the *Essex* sailed north from Valparaiso. Outside of Callao—the port city for Lima, Peru—on 5 April, Porter recaptured the American whaling vessel *Barclay*. As luck would have it, several days earlier he had come across her former master, Gideon Randall, and now Porter returned the *Barclay* to him, but Randall lacked a crew. Not to be deterred, Porter made a deal. If he provided men, Randall, who was familiar with the Galapagos Islands, would accompany Porter there.[7]

On 17 April the *Essex* and *Barclay* made the Galapagos Islands in their search for British whalers. As the days passed, Porter commented, "I believe that many began to think that the information we had received respecting the practice of British vessels frequenting those islands . . . had been altogether deception." Porter, however, had risked much of his reputation sailing to the Galapagos, and he refused to abandon the venture. Still, he could not help but worry, and to his own admission he passed a sleepless night on 28–29 April.[8]

But as the day broke, lookouts on board the *Essex* sighted three whaling ships and Porter chased under the ruse of English colors. This allowed the American frigate to come up with the first vessel; her captain came across to the *Essex*. Continuing the deception, Porter masqueraded as a British naval officer. This fooled the whaling master, who identified his ship as the *Montezuma*. He then described what he knew about other whaling ships in the area. In the meantime, men from the *Essex* took possession of the *Montezuma*, and Porter steered after the other two vessels. Just before noon the wind died. Fearing that a breeze would reach his quarry first, allowing their escape, Porter ordered the boats armed and manned before dispatching them toward the two becalmed whalers. After a grueling pull, the *Essex*'s men took possession of both the *Policy* and *Georgiana* without bloodshed. Porter estimated the value of his three captures at nearly half a million dollars. More

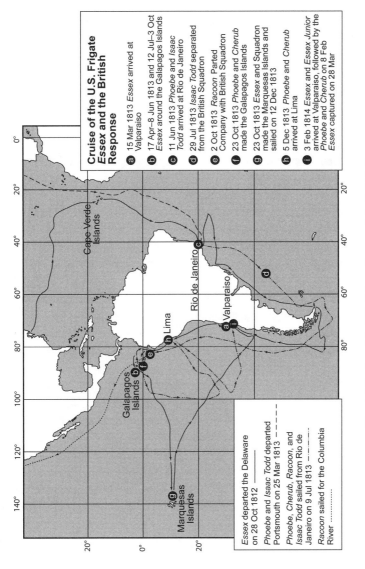

Cruise of the U.S. Frigate *Essex* and the British Response

ⓐ 15 Mar 1813 *Essex* arrived at Valparaiso

ⓑ 17 Apr–8 Jun 1813 and 12 Jul–3 Oct *Essex* around the Galapagos Islands

ⓒ 11 Jun 1813 *Phoebe* and *Isaac Todd* arrived at Rio de Janeiro

ⓓ 29 Jul 1813 *Isaac Todd* separated from the British Squadron

ⓔ 2 Oct 1813 *Racoon* Parted Company with British Squadron

ⓕ 23 Oct 1813 *Phoebe* and *Cherub* made the Galapagos Islands

ⓖ 23 Oct 1813 *Essex* and Squadron made the Marquesas Islands and sailed on 12 Dec 1813

ⓗ 5 Dec 1813 *Phoebe* and *Cherub* arrived at Lima

ⓘ 3 Feb 1814 *Essex* and *Essex Junior* arrived at Valparaiso, followed by the *Phoebe* and *Cherub* on 8 Feb *Essex* captured on 28 Mar

Essex departed the Delaware on 28 Oct 1812 ——————

Phoebe and *Isaac Todd* departed Portsmouth on 25 Mar 1813 – – – – –

Phoebe, Cherub, Racoon, and *Isaac Todd* sailed from Rio de Janeiro on 9 Jul 1813 –·–·–·–·

Racoon sailed for the Columbia River ··············

Map 9.1 Cruise of the U.S. Frigate *Essex* and the British Response

important, the whalers had items the Americans needed, including provisions, tar, cordage, and other assorted supplies for the maintenance of the *Essex*. The only thing the prizes did not provide was a sufficient quantity of water.[9]

Of his captures, Porter learned the *Georgiana* was a remarkably fast ship "apparently well calculated for a cruizer." As a result, he ordered her mounted with sixteen guns and sent her on an independent cruise with forty-two men under Lieutenant John Downes. Porter kept the *Montezuma*, *Policy*, and *Barclay* with him and sailed in quest of other whaling vessels that were reportedly around the Galapagos.[10]

Porter's choice was rewarded on the afternoon of 27 May, when lookouts sighted a strange sail on the horizon. The Americans pursued, but as darkness fell Porter realized that his opponent had too much of a lead. Unwilling to abandon the chase, he hailed the commanders of the *Montezuma* and *Barclay* and ordered them to steer in different directions for seven miles and then come to. This created a situation where the three ships were within sight at daybreak but spread out to cover a large area. At dawn the *Montezuma* signaled that she had sighted the stranger, and the *Essex* closed under English colors. Porter's deception worked yet again. In events mirroring the capture of the *Montezuma*, the Americans took possession of the whale ship *Atlantic*. While this occurred, a lookout on board the *Essex* spied another sail. Porter gave chase. Night fell, but the pursuit continued. Eventually, threats of a broadside at short range led to the surrender of the whale ship *Greenwich*.[11]

On board the *Atlantic* the Americans found nearly one hundred tons of water that Porter described as "an article of more value to us than any thing else she could have had." Now comfortably supplied with the most basic of necessities, Porter returned to the South American mainland, but this was easier said than done. Strong currents and contrary winds kept his command among the Galapagos until 8 June. Eleven days later, Porter's little squadron anchored on the southern side of the Gulf of Guayaquil, in what today is the border between Peru and Ecuador.[12]

There, Porter's men obtained additional water, as well as wood from the shore, and on 25 June the *Georgiana*, under Lieutenant Downes, arrived in the bay. After leaving the *Essex*, Downes took advantage of the *Georgiana*'s past as a British whaler. As a result, she seemed harmless when she came up on the British whalers *Catherine* and *Rose*, and both masters came over to speak with their counterpart. They did not find out their mistake until they boarded the *Georgiana*. By then, the *Catherine* and *Rose* were in American hands. Several days later, Downes fell in with another strange sail. He faced a profound disadvantage, having detached slightly more than half his crew to man the *Catherine* and *Rose*. To make matters worse, the *Georgiana* contained nearly fifty prisoners. Still, Downes pursued the strange vessel. Upon coming up with her, she refused to surrender, and Downes directed five broadsides into her that killed two men and wounded several others before she struck. She proved to be the British whale ship *Hector*. Downes now had almost seventy-five prisoners, compared to slightly more than forty of his own men scattered among four vessels. To solve this problem, he sent the dull-sailing *Rose* away with the prisoners before sailing to join Porter with his two remaining prizes.[13]

In the Gulf of Guayaquil Porter continued to prepare for the next part of his mission. He determined that the *Atlantic* and *Greenwich* were his two best prizes and decided to take advantage of their sailing qualities. As a result, he transferred the men from the *Georgiana* (a disappointing ship) to the *Atlantic*, armed her with twenty guns, and renamed her the *Essex Junior*. He also directed that the *Greenwich* be fitted as a store ship, mounting twenty guns. Between what the store ship and each vessel could carry, Porter had seven months of supplies. Porter then sailed from the coast on 30 June, because, as he wrote to Hamilton, "the Governors in Peru . . . are excessively alarmed at my appearance on the coast as my fleet now amounts to nine sail of vessels all formidable in their appe[arance]."[14]

Since the moment the *Essex* had departed the coast of Brazil in January 1813, Porter had operated within the British decision-making loop. Such a condition proved very advantageous, allowing the Americans to maintain the initiative of being able to act without the Royal Navy knowing the *Essex*'s movements or intentions. Moreover, the abrupt departure of Bainbridge's squadron from Brazilian waters (the *Constitution* and *Hornet* sailing north and the *Essex* around Cape Horn) confused Rear Admiral Manley Dixon, the British commander on the South American Station. Without reliable information about the *Constitution*, *Essex*, or *Hornet*, Dixon speculated that if any of the warships had not sailed north, "it is imagined she is gone round Cape Horn."[15]

It took until early June to confirm Dixon's suspicion when he learned that the *Essex* had made Valparaiso on 15 March and that Porter planned "to take & destroy the English Whalers on the Coast." By this time, however, the Americans had taken eight prizes without British naval interference. Dixon pleaded that he did not have warships to send after the *Essex*.[16] His position was especially acute, given the Admiralty instructions received on 29 April to dispatch one or two warships to the Pacific for the protection of British trading and whaling interests. This Admiralty order had nothing to do with the *Essex*; instead, it stemmed from the general weakness of Spanish authority in the region that had created "circumstances of great atrocity . . . on the coast of South America."[17]

Dixon's instructions to dispatch warships to the Pacific, coupled with the presence of the *Essex*, placed him in a quandary, but on 10 June the 36-gun *Phoebe*, under Captain James Hillyar, made Rio de Janeiro. Though Dixon knew the *Phoebe* had orders to continue to the Pacific, he did not know her specific mission, and Hillyar refused to provide information, since he did not consider that Dixon had a need to know. Information soon leaked that Hillyar had orders to go to the Columbia River on the border between the present states of Oregon and Washington and assert authority in the name of the British North West Company. To get there however, the *Phoebe* would have to sail through the *Essex*'s likeliest cruising ground. Not only could Hillyar protect the Columbia River settlement, but he could also potentially eliminate the *Essex*.[18]

Hillyar dallied nearly a month in Rio de Janeiro before sailing on 9 July. The reason dealt with the *Isaac Todd*, a store ship contracted to accompany the *Phoebe*. Serious discontent raged among her crew. Recruiting new men in their stead proved slow, and by the time the ships sailed, Dixon lamented, "This Expedition, with its object, I am sorry to say, appears to be, too generally known." Moreover, information about their sailing could cross the continent faster than Hillyar could round Cape Horn. As a result, Dixon reinforced Hillyar with the 20-gun *Cherub* and 18-gun *Racoon* in case Porter had augmented his command in expectation of Hillyar's arrival.[19]

Porter had indeed armed several prizes. One, the *Essex Junior* under Lieutenant Downes, escorted the *Hector*, *Catherine*, *Policy*, *Montezuma*, and *Barclay* to Valparaiso, where he had orders to bid farewell to the *Barclay* and sell the *Hector*, *Catherine*, and *Montezuma*. The *Policy*, fully laden with whale oil, received orders to slip into an American port to provide news of Porter's exploits. Downes then received orders to proceed with the *Essex Junior* to rendezvous with the *Essex* in late September or October.[20]

While Downes sailed to Valparaiso, Porter returned to the Galapagos in company with the *Greenwich* and *Georgiana*. On the afternoon of 13 July, lookouts descried three strange sail. Porter immediately chased. The *Essex* quickly captured the British whaler *Charlton*. Another of the strangers bore down on the *Greenwich* and *Georgiana*. This was the *Seringapatam*, mounting fourteen guns and having forty-one hands. Porter could only watch this encounter because it occurred far to the windward: it was impossible for him to steer the *Essex* to the *Greenwich*'s aid. Porter, however, had little to fear. The *Greenwich*'s commander, Lieutenant John Gamble of the marines, gained the initiative by raking the *Seringapatam* and causing her to strike. In the meantime, the *Essex* captured the third vessel, the whale ship *New Zealand*.[21]

Porter had his men remove the guns and stores from the *Charlton*, since she was old and sailed poorly, then he sent her off with the prisoners. Whale oil found in these captures was transferred to the *Georgiana*, and Porter dispatched her to the United States. He reasoned that she should arrive in the winter when the weather would favor eluding the British blockade.[22]

The *Essex* fell in with another strange vessel on 28 July. In a pursuit lasting well into the following day, the whaler escaped using advantageous currents and baffling winds. Porter lamented, "Nothing, perhaps, could equal our disappointment in not taking this vessel . . . this was the first enemy who had ever escaped us." Stinging from his failure, Porter decided to refit his squadron in the protected anchorage at Santiago Island in the Galapagos.[23] He decided to turn the *Seringapatam* into a vessel of war, for she was teak-built, "pierced for 22 guns, sails fast, and is well calculated for the service, she is remarkably strong."[24] Porter also "caused the *Seringapatam* to be painted exactly like the *Essex*, so that it would have been very difficult to have known them apart at a short distance. I then changed entirely the appearance of the *Essex* and gave to the *Greenwich* the appearance of a sloop of war, hoping at some future period to derive some advantage over the enemy by the deceptions."[25] Upon leaving Santiago Island, he placed a note in a bottle. In it, he lamented the death of many of his men, and wrote, "The *Essex* leaves this in a leaky state, her foremast very rotten . . . and her mainmast sprung. . . . Should any American vessel, or indeed a vessel of any nation, put in here, and meet with this note, they would be doing an act of great humanity to transmit a copy of it to America."[26] Porter hoped such ruses would serve well against the ever-looming British pursuit.

The *Essex* was not finished, however. On 14 September Porter captured the British whale ship *Sir Andrew Hammond*. Then, on 30 September the *Essex Junior* returned. While at Valparaiso Lieutenant Downes had learned that Hillyar's British squadron had sailed for the Pacific. Porter knew only one reason the British would send such a large force, and because of this he needed to be prepared, but that required a major refit. Since he needed a place where he would not be disturbed, Porter decided to visit the Marquesas Islands, some four thousand miles to the west.[27]

On 23 October the *Essex* made landfall in the Marquesas Island group after a passage of twenty-one days. Soon, Porter settled on a spot where he could refit his ships and set up a base camp. The chosen island teemed with indigenous peoples. Before long, significant trade and communication developed between the Americans and the island's inhabitants. This led the Americans to become involved in local hostilities, but overall work on the *Essex* progressed quickly. As Porter explained, "My ship as may be supposed after being near a year at sea required some repairs to put her in a state to meet them [the British] . . . on near equal terms." With four months' provisions, the *Essex* and *Essex Junior* sailed on 12 December.

Porter sent the *New Zealand*, laden with whale oil, to the United States and left the *Seringapatam*, *Greenwich*, and *Sir Andrew Hammond* behind, protected by a battery served by twenty-one volunteers under Lieutenant Gamble.[28]

The *Essex* and *Essex Junior* made Valparaiso on 3 February, but Porter learned nothing of Hillyar's squadron. He concluded that they "were supposed to be lost in endeavouring to double Cape Horn."[29] The British squadron, however, had not succumbed to the wiles of the ocean. On their run south, Hillyar had lost sight of the *Isaac Todd*, but the *Phoebe*, *Racoon*, and *Cherub* kept together, rounded the Cape, and then stretched north. Once in the Pacific, Hillyar received a letter from John McDonald, a passenger on board his frigate and a representative of the North West Company. McDonald asserted it was too late in the season for a ship as large as the *Phoebe* to enter the Columbia River, and he entreated Hillyar to send either the *Racoon* or the *Cherub* in the frigate's stead. Moreover, McDonald thought the *Phoebe* and the remaining sloop would serve a greater purpose tracking down the *Essex* and protecting British maritime interests in the South Pacific. Hillyar agreed, and he dispatched the *Racoon* to carry out the secret mission.[30] The *Phoebe* and *Cherub* sailed for the Galapagos, where their lookouts sighted land on 23 October. They spent several weeks among the islands before returning to the coast of South America.[31] At Lima, Peru, Hillyar learned that Porter had armed some of his prizes and converted another to a store ship. Other information provided disturbing news about some two hundred Americans having settled along the Columbia River. It seemed that Porter had obtained reinforcements and the *Racoon* faced stronger-than-expected opposition. Hillyar, however, could not find the American frigate, and he lacked provisions to go to the Columbia River. Given the condition of his ships, he wrote, "I propose to proceed to Valparaiso for information, previous to my repassing Cape Horn, accompanied by the *Cherub*." At his wits' end, he concluded, "I am not without hope in Providence of doing some good at Valparaiso, and this is my only present consolation for having been obliged to give up a voyage, once promising to be productive of much usefulness to my Country, interesting adventure and personal emolument."[32]

Hillyar made Valparaiso on 8 February, where to his surprise he found the *Essex* and *Essex Junior*. Fighting within the neutral waters of the port was inconsistent with diplomatic precedent, but tensions mounted as Hillyar worked his way into the harbor and brought the *Phoebe* alongside the *Essex*. It is unclear if the nature of the harbor precluded anchoring elsewhere or if Hillyar's action was an attempt at provocation. The latter seems more likely, given that the *Phoebe* was cleared for action, and she approached close enough for Porter to hail, "Sir—if you by any accident get on board of me I assure you that . . . I am prepared to receive you but shall only act on the defensive." Midshipman David Farragut, then serving on board the *Essex*, recounted, "We were all at quarters and cleared for action, waiting with breathless anxiety." The *Phoebe* came within feet of fouling the *Essex*, and Porter asserted that Hillyar afterward apologized, saying "I had not intention of coming so near you." The veracity of these details remains questionable. The *Phoebe's* log merely stated, "Spoke the United states [*sic*] Frigate *Essex*."[33] Though the Americans likely embellished the event, Hillyar did come close enough to hail the *Essex*, and this set the tone during the coming days.

On 15 February Hillyar observed the *Essex Junior* under sail, and he proceeded into the offing with the *Phoebe* and *Cherub* so as to intercept the Americans when they emerged from Chilean territorial waters. Over the next two weeks, Porter sailed out of the port on three occasions, sparring with Hillyar's ships, testing their sailing qualities, but refusing to come to action.[34] Of these encounters, Porter asserted, "I endeavoured to provoke a chalenge [*sic*] and frequently but ineffectually to bring the *Phoebe* alone to action." Furthermore, he "ascertained that I had greatly the advantage in point of sailing."[35] Given these conclusions, Porter's actions deserve critique. Other than glory, why challenge even one British warship on the far side of the world? The crews of the *Phoebe* and *Cherub* had not suffered heavy attrition. The *Phoebe* was a standard British 36-gun frigate with long 18-pounders on her gun deck, as well as a mix of long 9-pound guns and 32-pound carronades on her quarterdeck and forecastle. The *Cherub*, being a ship-sloop, added 32-pound carronades as her principal armament. To these, Porter had only 255 men on board the *Essex*. Moreover, his frigate mounted 40 x 32-pound carronades and 6 x long 12-pounders. The *Essex Junior* had but sixty men mounting 10 x 18-pound carronades and 10 x 6-pound guns.[36] Unless Porter could bring the *Phoebe* to close action, the long guns of his opponent would wreck the *Essex* before his short-range carronades could respond, while the *Essex Junior* had a weak armament and was very much undermanned. Such considerations, coupled with the superior sailing of the *Essex* and *Essex Junior*, made flight a prudent choice.

In the meantime, additional British forces closed in. Particularly, the Admiralty had reinforced the squadron at Brazil to include eleven frigates. This increase, in part, stemmed from reports about the *Essex* that led the Admiralty to order Admiral Dixon to send the 38-gun *Tagus* to the Pacific. She sailed in late February 1814, and Dixon ordered the 38-gun *Briton* to Valparaiso late the next month when he learned the *Essex* and *Essex Junior* had arrived there. Moreover, Dixon had information that the *Constitution*, *President*, and *United States* were at sea. He wrote, "One of these frigates will most likely endeavour to effect a junction with the *Essex* and her prizes."[37]

Though no American frigates were coming to Porter's aid, he did benefit from superb intelligence. The movement of information overland again proved faster than sailing around Cape Horn and led Porter to explain, "I had gained certain intelligence that the *Tagus* rated 38 and two other frigates had sailed for that sea in pursuit of me, and I had reason to expect the arrival of the *Racoon* from the NW coast of america [*sic*]." Though he inflated the force moving against him by one frigate, the basis of his intelligence was accurate, and Porter prudently decided to slip out of Valparaiso.[38]

On 28 March it "came on to blow." As the weather deteriorated, Porter realized that Hillyar had allowed the *Phoebe* and *Cherub* to be caught to the leeward. Taking advantage of this mistake, Porter weighed anchor and passed to the windward of the British, but just as he reached open water, "a heavy squall struck the ship and carried away her main Top mast."[39] Porter thought the crippled state of his ship prevented him from outrunning the British. Regaining Valparaiso proved impossible, owing to a combination of the wind and the position of Hillyar's warships. Instead, Porter anchored his frigate close in with the shore.[40] Porter hoped he would be protected by Chile's neutrality while his men repaired the damage, but "the enemy continued to approach and shewed an evident intention of attacking me regardless of the neutrality of the place where I was anchored."[41] The young Farragut added, "Well do I remember the awful feelings, produced on me at their approach, by perceiving in the face of every one as clearly as possible even to my young mind that all was hopeless."[42]

Of the British, Porter ranted, "The caution observed in their approach to the attack of the crippled *Essex* was truely ridiculous." Yet the *Essex* was trapped; Hillyar could dictate the engagement, and he understood that such an opportunity would not come again. Moreover, strong winds made the approach particularly difficult. The *Phoebe* opened a long-range cannonade about 4:00 p.m. These rounds did little damage, and after ten minutes the British ceased firing. Hillyar tried to close a second time, again without success, and he later wrote, "appearances were a little inauspicious."[43] During this time, the *Cherub* joined the fight. Being armed with short-ranged carronades forced her to come closer to the American, and she suffered accordingly. Early in the fight a splinter wounded her captain, numerous rounds sliced at her rigging, and one lucky shot killed a marine and wounded two others. After thirty minutes, the captain, bloody but refusing to go below, had his men haul off to repair damages.[44]

For the third attempt, Hillyar had both the *Phoebe* and *Cherub* approach the *Essex*'s stern. Porter explained that the British took a position "out of reach of my carronades, and where my stern Guns could not be brought to bear, he there kept up a most galling fire which it was out of my power to return." With damage and casualties mounting, Porter acted in pure desperation: "I saw no prospect of injurying him without getting underway and becoming the assailant." He decided to close with the *Phoebe* and try to board her. The cables were cut, but, Porter wrote, "the *Phoebe* from our disabled state was enabled however by edging off to choose the distance which best suited her long guns, and kept up a tremendous fire on us which mowed down my brave companions by the dozen."[45]

Following the failed boarding attempt, Porter decided to run the *Essex* ashore to keep her from falling into British hands, but his frigate refused to respond. Since it had fallen nearly calm, Porter ordered the *Essex* to anchor, hoping that the *Phoebe* would drift out of range, but this ploy failed when the anchor cable broke.[46]

At this point, the situation on board the *Essex* took a disastrous turn when a fire broke out: "The flames were bursting up each hatchway and no hopes were entertained of saving her." Men came on deck with their clothes afire. The flames approached "the magazine and the explosion of a large quantity of powder below served to increase the horrors." Though all the boats had been destroyed, she then lay only three-quarters of a mile from shore, and Porter ordered his men to swim for it. Many tried, but others, including Porter, remained on board and soon extinguished the flames. Returning to the guns, Porter beseeched his men to resist, but the few who remained could continue no longer. He then called for the opinions of his surviving officers, "but what was my surprize to find only Acting Lt. S D McKnight remaining." Porter asserted, "I was informed that the Cock pit, the steerage, the ward Room and Birth [*sic*] deck could contain no more wounded." Porter had the colors struck.[47] Later, he would argue, "She was lost . . . *honorably—very honorably*."[48]

The British warships had sustained light to moderate damage, with but eleven killed and wounded on board the *Phoebe* and four casualties on board the *Cherub*. The *Essex*, though, was a slaughterhouse: of 255 on board at the start of the action, fifty-eight died or received mortal wounds, sixty-six suffered less-severe wounds, and thirty-one could not be accounted for, for a total of 155 casualties. Later, Porter argued, "I must in justification of myself observe that . . . myself & officers applied to Paul Hamilton Esq[r]. for a greater proportion of long guns, which were refused us, and I now venture to declare, that if she had been armed in the manner I wished, she would not have been taken by the *Phoebe* and *Cherub*—With our six twelve pounders only we fought this action, our carronades were almost useless."[49] The presence of more long guns would certainly have made the engagement bloodier for the British, but the *Phoebe* and *Cherub* still had more men and greater weight of metal.

David Farragut drew a different conclusion, believing the "greatest error was in our attempting to regain the anchorage." Even after sustaining damage aloft, Farragut thought the *Essex* could have easily out-sailed the dull-sailing *Cherub*. There was also a chance she could have escaped the *Phoebe*. If not, the odds would have been better. To Farragut, a second alternative involved running the *Essex* ashore at the start of the engagement because this would have prevented raking fire, and when things became too hot, the men could have abandoned the frigate. Farragut largely attributed the outcome to the personalities of the two commanders. He explained, "Capt. P. was about 32 years of age and the Pink of Chivalry of an ardent and impetuous temperament While Capt. H, was a man of 50 [years] of age, of as cool, calculating man."[50] A final point of critique involved the *Essex Junior*. Downes surrendered her with the *Essex*, but, given her speed and the British preoccupation with Porter's frigate, the *Essex Junior* would likely have been able to escape during the engagement, forcing the British to scour the Pacific for her.

Given the location of Valparaiso and the difficulty in transporting prisoners from there, Hillyar allowed Porter and his survivors to return on parole to the United States under passports of safety on board the disarmed *Essex Junior*. Once home, the officers and men would be exchanged for a similar number of British prisoners.[51]

Fifteen days after the battle, the *Tagus* hove into sight, followed on 21 May by the *Briton*. Her commander commented, "There is I think little probability of our continuing in these Seas for a longer period than Adm[l] Dixon has mentioned in my orders." This assessment, however, proved incorrect. Though the capture of the *Essex* and the return of the *Essex Junior* under passport had cleared the Pacific, rumors circulated that a large American frigate had sailed to join her. Admiral Dixon directed the *Tagus* and *Briton* to remain on station. They did not depart from the region until March 1815, when the 44-gun *Indefatagable* relieved them.[52]

On 5 July 1814 the *Essex Junior* encountered the British blockade squadron off New York, where the *Saturn*, a 56-gun razee, detained her. A Royal Navy officer examined her papers and then let her proceed. Two hours later the *Saturn* again brought the *Essex Junior* to. Porter believed being detained a second time had violated his parole. He offered his sword to surrender, but it was refused. Still detained the next morning, Porter had a boat pull him ashore. The British chased but lost him in the thick morning fog.[53] After Porter made it safely ashore, the U.S. government concluded that the *Saturn*'s commander violated the paroles of Porter and his men. As such, they were "accordingly declared discharged from their paroles."[54] Like so many other events in the war and particularly with Porter's cruise, the British saw the event differently. The commander of the British North American Station wrote,

"I lament particularly that it should have occurred in this instance as Captain Porter is the Person above all others in the United States I should most wished to have detained."[55] Finally, in February 1815, with the war at an end, the British grudgingly admitted that because the *Saturn's* captain did not respect the parole, "the American Government had a perfect right to release Captain Porter and the Crew."[56]

CHAPTER 10

"Some Hard Knocks"

Reassessment—The United States, September 1813–March 1814

"Ten seventy-fours & 15 frigates with a number of smaller vessels are at this time or will be in a short time upon our coast—We must look out for some hard knocks—Our enemy is powerful and we can't expect he will always be asleep," wrote one Virginian to his brother in early 1813.[1] Several months later, a New York newspaper added, "The British cruisers at the eastward are committing extensive depredations among our defenceless coasters. Our eastern brethren will scarce deny that *their* rights and property, if not *their territories*, have now been invaded."[2] For Secretary Jones, however, an inequality existed between British threats and available American means. As he put it, "If we were to attempt to provide any thing like the force which the most reasonable of local demands call for . . . the resources of the Naval establishment would not accomplish it." He jested, "Complete protection is out of the question." Incredulously, Jones added, "The expence of our harbour and coasting Flotilla has been considerably more than the whole of our Oceanic force." Not only did the United States lack the financial and material wherewithal for a comprehensive coastal defense, but also, Jones argued, reducing the oceanic force in favor of coastal defense would give the British the ability to "harass without hazarding any thing." Still, something had to be done in strategically important coastal areas. The quandary, according to Jones, dealt with assessing an area's "ratio of its exposure and importance."[3]

Scoring high in both ratio and exposure was America's northeastern coast. Important naval bases existed near Boston and at Portsmouth, New Hampshire. Moreover, two ships of the line and a pair of sloops of war were being built in the region. Some of the items needed to complete the ships could only reach the dockyards by water. Thus, the United States Navy required the coasting trade. Moreover, the region depended on maritime commerce, but the war had damaged trade. Not surprisingly, antiwar sentiment ran high, necessitating attempts by the U.S. government to placate the inhabitants.

"The call for protection on that Coast was very loud," so Jones sent the *Siren* and *Enterprize* to patrol the litorrals north of Boston.[4] The early months of 1813 had found the former at New Orleans and the latter in Georgia, but maintaining warships in the southern United States proved difficult: during the first months of the war, American warships in the south had proved to be better targets than weapons. In mid-June 1813 the *Enterprize* arrived in Portsmouth, while the *Siren* made Boston. Captain Isaac Hull, the commanding officer at Portsmouth and the senior naval officer north of Boston, argued that the *Enterprize* was too weak to provide protection for the coastal trade. Hull requested the *Siren's* assistance, but she required a major overhaul.[5]

Meanwhile, the British became more aggressive. In late July the *American Advocate*, a newspaper from Hallowell, Maine, published, "The British ship *Rattler* has been for some time cruizing on the Eastern shore, and, together with two or three frigates have at times been seen within a few miles of Portland harbor." Reports placed numerous warships, including a ship of the line, in the area.[6] Most of these warships, however, were assigned to the British squadron off Boston and made only occasional appearances to the north. Only the 18-gun *Rattler*, 12-gun *Boxer*, and 4-gun *Bream*, along with several British privateers, focused their operations north of Boston.[7]

Although Hull considered the *Enterprize* too weak to confront the British threat, Jones ordered her to sail to appease the local population. After one cruise in mid-August that resulted in the capture of a British privateer, Lieutenant Commandant William Burrows assumed command. For his first mission, Hull explained to Burrows, "As the object of your cruise is to protect the coasting trade to the eastward which has been so much interrupted by small cruisers of the enemy of late, you will keep as close along the land as the safety of your vessel will admit, and by all means keep so close as not to let the large Cruisers of the Enemy get in shore of you to cut you off." Particularly, Hull implored Burrows to convoy any vessels desiring protection and maintain a close lookout for locals supplying the British.[8] Burrows proceeded to sea on 1 September. Several days later he decided to investigate reports that British privateers frequented Monhegan Island, about fifty miles east of Portland.[9]

Meanwhile, the British gun brig *Boxer*, under Commander Samuel Blyth, rode at anchor off Monhegan Island on 4 September. That morning Blyth had allowed two midshipmen, the brig's medical officer, and a passenger to visit the island. While they were gone a schooner hove into sight, and Blyth dispatched several ship's boats under First Lieutenant David McCrery to capture her. No sooner had McCrery gained possession of the schooner but an American privateer retook her. The privateer's next victims appeared to be the boats, now rowing frantically for the *Boxer*. In an effort to save his boat crews, Blyth abandoned his men ashore on Monhegan Island and made all sail. After rescuing McCrery and his men, Blyth sailed in pursuit of the privateer, but the wind died, leaving the *Boxer* becalmed ten or twelve miles from Monhegan, where those ashore spent the night.[10]

The next morning Blyth spoke with the master of a schooner and learned that the *Enterprize* was one of several sail in sight, and he gave chase. Across the water Burrows fled, while trying to ascertain the *Boxer's* force. At a distance of about three-quarters of a mile, he concluded that his opponent was a small brig.[11] Considering this a fair fight, Burrows had his vessel come about and stand for the *Boxer*. When forty yards separated the warships, Blyth ordered the helm brought up, exposing his broadside so as to rake the *Enterprize*. Burrows frustrated the attempt by bringing his vessel onto a parallel course. With the vessels only a few yards apart, they exchanged broadsides.[12] This played to the strength of each, since the primary armament of both comprised short-ranged 18-pound carronades—six for the *Boxer's* broadside to seven for the *Enterprize's*.[13]

Early in the engagement an American round shot passed through Blyth's body, leaving him a bloody pulp. At nearly the same moment, a British musket ball struck Burrows. Although mortally wounded, he refused to be carried below and reportedly demanded "*that the flag might never be struck.*"[14]

With both commanders down, the two vessels, yardarm to yardarm, exchanged seven or eight broadsides. Much of the British fire went high, but the first American broadside "nearly cleared the three foremost Guns." American fire also caused significant damage aloft, allowing the *Enterprize* to range ahead to gain a raking position. To counter, the *Boxer's* new commander, Lieutenant McCrery, brought his wounded vessel under the *Enterprize's* bow so he could rake her at close range, but one of his carronades had been dismounted and the crews of the three foremost guns had either fallen or fled—only one gun crew got off a single round.[15]

Resistance on board the *Boxer* began to collapse, and few officers remained to rally the crew. The two midshipmen ashore were sorely missed. Moreover, the absence of the medical officer surely affected the will to resist, especially since the captain's clerk, with no medical background, received orders to tend to the wounded. Not surprisingly, men abandoned their quarters in the middle of the fight.[16]

Rounds from the *Enterprize* had turned the *Boxer* into "a complete Wreck." McCrery solicited the opinion of the remaining officers, who concluded that nothing else could be gained by continuing the action. Surrender proved difficult, however, since the colors had been nailed to the mast, either to cajole the men to fight harder or make the colors less likely to be shot down. This forced McCrery to hail the *Enterprize* to state that he surrendered.[17] The *Boxer* had lost four killed and eighteen wounded of sixty-six officers, men, and boys, whereas the *Enterprize* sustained one killed and thirteen wounded, of which three were mortal, including Burrows, of 102 on board.[18]

After the engagement, the *Enterprize*, along with her prize, anchored at Portland, but this led to concerns that the British would seek revenge against the port. Captain Hull contended "that the guns of the two vessels will be sufficient to keep off any force the Enemy may send in boats, but not against Ships." Hull soon returned to Portsmouth, but on 14 September he learned that a British squadron had appeared off Portland and threatened to burn the town if demands were not met. The next day Hull received information that the British force consisted of three frigates, three brigs, and a schooner, and "the town was in great confusion and that the women and children were moving, out as fast as possible."[19]

Hull had fallen victim to a rumor made all the more credible by the presence of the *Enterprize* and *Boxer*. Instead of a large British squadron, Captain Alexander Gordon of the *Rattler* had led his ship, as well as the 18-gun *Fantome* and schooner *Shelbourne*, off Portland on 13 September. A lieutenant then went ashore under a flag of truce to deliver a letter asking for the release of the *Boxer's* survivors because Gordon asserted that he had, "during the time that I have been on this station, released and sent into Portland many American subjects, made prisoners by His Majesty's ship under my command." If this request could not be observed, he asked to communicate with the officers from "motives of humanity to the friends of the survivors." The response proved negative on both accounts, and the British sailed away.[20]

The *Enterprize* remained in Portland while Captain Hull and Secretary Jones contemplated her next mission. Since repairs continued on the *Siren*, Jones dispatched the *Rattlesnake*, a former privateer purchased into the navy and mounting fourteen guns. Captain Hull described her as a quick sailer, particularly in light seas, but her armament was poor, consisting of a mix of long guns and carronades.[21] Under the command of Master Commandant John O. Creighton, she anchored at Portsmouth in mid-September. Moreover, Lieutenant Commandant James Renshaw arrived in Portland to replace the *Enterprize's* slain commander. In late September Hull wrote to Jones, "I hope the two brigs will be able to join . . . as the Enemy's vessels generally on this sea are too heavy for these small brigs separate."[22]

The two vessels linked up in early October, and Hull immediately sent them on a cruise to show the flag, protect American commerce, and make British operations in the littoral more difficult. They returned to Portsmouth on 21 October "without having seen any of the cruisers of the Enemy."[23] Then on 31 October the *Rattlesnake* and *Enterprize* escorted twenty to thirty coastal trading vessels from Portsmouth to Boston. Little did Creighton know, but this route teemed with British warships. Off

Cape Ann lurked the 18-gun brigs *Fantome* and *Epervier*; the 56-gun razee *Majestic* and 18-gun *Wasp* also were in the area. When the American convoy reached Newburyport Lighthouse, Creighton determined that the coast was clear as far as Cape Ann, and he "concluded it most proper to leave them apprehensive that the two Brigs would draw the Enemy's attention by which we should lead the trade into difficulty—consequently I wore and returned to the northw[d]." That evening, Creighton learned that the British had intercepted the convoy.[24]

Even Portsmouth offered limited safety. On the morning of 3 November, Commander John Lawrence of the *Fantome* led his vessel and the *Epervier* close in with Portsmouth Lighthouse. At 1:00 p.m. he heard a single cannon. Closer investigation revealed two brigs under American colors.[25] Lawrence had stumbled upon the *Rattlesnake* and *Enterprize*.

Across the water, Creighton concluded that his opponents were "Brigs of the largest class." This was correct, with both British vessels rated for eighteen guns and mounting 32-pound carronades. Realizing that the *Rattlesnake* and *Enterprize* could not defeat them, Creighton obtained three gunboats as reinforcements, and they sailed to meet the British.[26]

Lawrence decided to allow the Americans to come out, but Creighton refused to engage, since he believed that a third British brig lurked in the offing. For the next few hours, the two sides kept several miles apart. As darkness fell, Lawrence ordered "a Rocket to shew the Enemy our position." A second rocket followed, and finally, around midnight, Lawrence withdrew.[27]

Captain Hull wrote to Jones, "There can be no doubt but Captain Creighton was perfectly correct in leaving to the Enemy the choice of coming to action or not, rather than to chase so far from the land as to suffer a third vessel to cut them off, as we were well informed there was one at no great distance." But, there was no third warship.[28] Even a successful engagement, however, would have resulted in the Americans sustaining damage and limiting their availability for other operations.

As 1813 drew to a close, Jones took stock of his ocean-going naval force. The two ships of the line being built at Portsmouth and Boston had estimated launch dates in July 1814, while another being built at Philadelphia had an estimated launch date of December. As for the three large frigates under construction, Jones anticipated the ones in Philadelphia and Baltimore to be launched in April 1814, and the one at the Washington Navy Yard in July; however, these were launch dates, and once in the water, it would take months to fit and man them, meaning the first of these new warships would not become operational until late 1814.[29]

Of existing warships, the *Constitution* and *President* put to sea in the winter of 1813–14, but the latter entered an extensive planned refit when she returned in February. When the *Congress* made Portsmouth in December 1813, she also needed repairs and encountered manning problems. The *United States, Macedonian,* and *Hornet* remained blockaded in New London, and the British blockade had trapped the *Constellation* in Norfolk. Given these circumstances, Jones had to rely on America's smaller warships in 1814.

Of existing vessels, the *Siren* continued to refit in Boston and the *Enterprize* operated out of Portsmouth. In addition, there was the *Adams*: she began her career as a 28-gun frigate, but during 1813 she had been rebuilt at Washington, having her hull lengthened by fifteen feet and her upper works removed, turning her into a flush-deck corvette mounting twenty-seven guns.[30]

The United States Navy also counted five vessels that Secretary Hamilton had purchased during 1812. However, the *Louisiana* at New Orleans, the *Troup* at Savannah, and the *Alert* at New York were only fit to act as guard ships.[31] The 14-gun *Nonsuch* spent much of the war patrolling off the Carolinas. Given her size and armament, Jones maintained, "A vessel of her class is much more likely to meet with disaster than render any essential service on a cruise." He directed that she sail no more than thirty miles off the coast.[32] The 14-gun *Carolina* was the final vessel that Hamilton had purchased. Though not capable of extended oceanic cruises, she proved a capable light cruiser.[33]

Jones continued his predecessor's policy of purchasing vessels. Several were designed for coastal defense, including two vessels for the Delaware.[34] More notably, he bought the *Rattlesnake* and *General Horsford* for oceanic service. Though Jones had seen the *General Horsford* being built at Philadelphia, the sagacity of the secretary's decision to purchase her was debatable. While serving as an American privateer, the British had captured her. Then the Americans had recaptured her, making her twice unlucky. Late 1813 found her in Savannah, where men and naval stores were scarce. More disturbing, an officer reported to Jones, "Her present state differs widely with that in which you saw her at Philadelphia." Undeterred, Jones had the *Carolina* escort her to Wilmington, North Carolina, but this port lacked resources to fit her out. Now renamed the *Vixen*, she sailed unarmed and unescorted for the Delaware.[35]

At daybreak on 25 December 1813, she encountered the 36-gun *Belvidera* under Captain Byron, who considered the sighting "Suspicious." By late morning, his frigate had closed within range of her bow guns. The *Vixen* pressed on with "the Enemey shot flying all round." The *Belvideria* drew closer and "grape came athwart us very thick." Gunfire wounded the *Vixen's* rigging, and one round penetrated the hull below the waterline. Hopelessly outmatched, she struck.[36]

In addition to vessels purchased for the United States Navy, 1813 found six large sloops under construction (Table 10.1). Authorized by Act of Congress dated 3 March 1813, two were complete by February 1814, and Jones expected the remainder by early spring.[37] Although the purchased vessels did not seem to worry the British, Admiral Warren wrote, "The Americans are building a very large Class of Corvette Ships of Six hundred tons, with twenty four Ports on one Deck, Some are launched, many are nearly ready. . . . I am very apprehensive of the mischief their Cruizers will do to our Trade." Although Warren overestimated the size of these new American warships by a small margin, they were superior in size and armament to the 18-gun *Cruizer*-class brigs that dominated British naval deployments.[38] In part, the Americans tried to reap some of the same advantages that their large frigates had over the British. In addition, these large sloops were designed to operate in a very hostile environment. With few friendly ports, they had to carry large quantities of provisions, be able to survive battles, and sail quickly to escape superior British forces.[39]

In choosing a strategy for his small ships, Jones still considered, "The Commerce of the enemy is the most vulnerable interest we can assail, and your main efforts should be directed to its destruction."[40] Jones argued that prizes were in all but the most unusual cases to be destroyed, and vehemently objected to reducing the crews

Table 10.1. U.S. Warships Smaller Than a Frigate Available for Oceanic Operations in 1814

Name of Vessel	Guns	Location as of 1 January 1814	Description
Enterprize	16	Portsmouth, NH	Existing
Rattlesnake	14	Portsmouth, NH	Purchased
Siren	16	Boston	Existing
Peacock	22	New York	New
Frolic	22	Boston	New
Wasp	22	Moving toward Portsmouth, NH	New
Erie	22	Baltimore	New
Ontario	22	Baltimore	New
Argus	22	Washington	New
Adams	27	The Chesapeake	Rebuilt

of American warships so as to provide prize crews. Jones believed, "Thus has a Single Cruiser, upon the destructive plan, the power perhaps, of twenty acting upon pecuniary views alone; and thus may the employment of our small force, in some degree compensate for the great inequality compared with that of the Enemy." As for British warships, Jones added, "The Character of the American Navy does not require those feats of Chivalry and your own reputation is too well established, ... Whenever you meet an equal Enemy, under fair Circumstances, I am sure you will beat him; but it is not even good policy to meet an equal; unless, under special circumstances, where a great object is to be gained, without a great sacrifice."[41] This was a bitter pill to swallow, considering the sentiment expressed in one contemporary periodical about how the navy's officers and men relished combat, and thus they "not only like it, but are educated to believe that it is their unequivocal duty to seek such, . . . to increase our naval renown."[42]

When considering available warships, the United States Navy had never looked weaker in its war with Britain. None of the small cruisers carried the prestige of a frigate. Moreover, Jones wanted the United States Navy to act like commerce-raiding privateers, albeit ones disinterested in sending prizes into port and instead bent on wreaking havoc and inflicting destruction on British trade. To one naval commander, Jones wrote, "The service you may render your country will be estimated by the extent of the injury you may inflict upon its implacable enemy; and this will be in the annoyance and destruction of his commerce, from which, no other object should be sufficient to divert your attention for a moment."[43] Although Jones knew the United States could never win the oceanic war against Britain, he thought his navy could "make him feel the war."[44]

The first of the small cruisers ready for sea were the *Rattlesnake* and *Enterprize*, but Captain Hull considered neither of them a superior instrument of war. Although the *Rattlesnake* sailed fast, she was not a purpose-built warship, and she did not have an effective armament. The *Enterprize's* armament was solid, but her sailing qualities were at best dull.[45]

On the last day of 1813, instructions from Secretary Jones arrived in Portsmouth directing Master Commandant Creighton to proceed with the *Rattlesnake* and *Enterprize* to the West Indies. Although Jones had ordered most warships to sail singly since early 1813, he explained to Crieighton, "The design of attaching the *Enterprize* to your Command, is to render you superior to any one of the Enemy's heavy Brigs of War; which are more numerous than any other of his Cruisers in those Seas."[46]

The *Rattlesnake* and *Enterprize* sailed on 10 January, running before a strong wind. Though the weather favored the Americans, they also benefitted from the *Constitution* sailing from Boston on 30 December because the British response had emasculated their blockade squadron in the area of Portsmouth. The *Majestic* had sailed in quest of the American frigate. The *Junon* and *Tenedos* had been off Portsmouth as late as 6 January, but with the *Constitution* gone, they sailed for Halifax, failing to realize that the Americans would push out small warships in the *Constitution's* wake.[47]

Creighton shaped a course toward the West Indies. On the way he encountered the Spanish brig *Isabella* on 18 January. Finding a British prize crew on board, he sent her into a U.S. port. Two days later, the Americans took possession of the Swedish ship *Sincerity*. Prize law was more nebulous in this instance, because the ship was a neutral but her cargo was English. Creighton decided to send her in, however, rationalizing that the presence of British goods made her a lawful prize. Then on 7 February Creighton destroyed a British brig laden with coffee.[48]

The next day, while in the Windward Passage, the Americans sighted a large ship. Her size, coupled with her cruising in a natural choke point, betrayed her as a warship. During the next minutes, Creighton ascertained her to be a frigate. The Americans had fallen in with the 38-gun British frigate *Leonidas*. She quickly bore down on the American warships, leading Creighton to split his command since he realized his opponent could not pursue both. The captain of the *Leonidas* decided to chase the American warship that he thought most resembled a privateer, but he lost her in the darkness.[49]

The *Rattlesnake* and *Enterprize* individually made their way toward a prearranged rendezvous off the western end of Cuba, but the 74-gun *Barham* under Captain John Spranger lay astride their passage. Only twenty-four hours after escaping the *Leonidas*, the *Rattlesnake* encountered the *Barham*, but Creighton easily outsailed her. The next morning the *Barham* fell in with the *Enterprize*. Renshaw had a more difficult time. All day Spranger tried to close, but he lost sight of his prey in the darkness. Finally, on 14 February, a relieved Creighton fell in with the *Enterprize*.[50]

Even after encountering British warships, the *Rattlesnake* and *Enterprize* had failed to cause much alarm. According to the *Barham's* log, Spranger had no clue that he had chased both American warships. In part, small warships looked at a distance like merchant vessels. On the other hand, the log of the *Leonidas* had described one of the two American warships as a privateer and, given the nature of Creighton's mission, this was almost correct. Though privateers concerned the British, they did not cause the alarm of a frigate, and American privateers already plied the Caribbean.

Another factor aided Creighton. He operated in the area of Britain's Jamaica Squadron that included the coast of Central America, the mouth of the Mississippi,

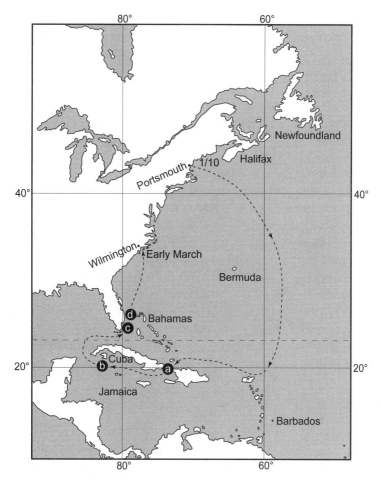

Key to Warship Movements

Departed Portsmouth on 10 Jan
ⓐ Chased by *Leonidas* on 8 Feb in Winward Passage
ⓑ Chased by *Barham* on 9 Jan and 10 Feb
ⓒ Captured *Mars* and *Eliza* on 22 Feb
ⓓ Encountered Unknown Frigate on 25 Feb
Returned to Wilmington in early March

Map 10.1 Cruise of the *Rattlesnake* and *Enterprize*: January–March 1814

the Florida Strait, and the Bahamas, as well as the supervision of convoys. The Admiralty ideally assigned the station three large frigates and fifteen small frigates and sloops of war. During the time Creighton's vessels plied the region, however, the squadron comprised one line of battle ship, one large frigate, and eleven small frigates and sloops. The lack of ships in part stemmed from the commander of the neighboring station in the Leeward Islands siphoning off ships to track down the *President* and *Constitution*. Moreover, a large homeward-bound convoy had sailed from Jamaica on 31 January under an escort of one ship of the line, two frigates, and a sloop.[51]

Creighton learned of this convoy from a neutral on 20 February and sailed in pursuit. The next day the Americans sighted a strange sail. For thirteen hours the *Rattlesnake* and the *Enterprize* doggedly closed. She turned out to be the *Rapid*, an American privateer also sailing in quest of the convoy. Her master, needless to say, was not the happiest after losing a day being chased by his own countrymen.[52]

Although Creighton did not find the convoy, he encountered three vessels on 22 February about fifteen miles northeast of Cape Florida. It was late in the day when the *Rattlesnake* and *Enterprize* closed with the first vessel. Rather than consent to be boarded, she trained her guns on the *Enterprize*. Renshaw responded with a broadside that killed two of her crew, wounded two others, and resulted in her surrender. She proved to be the *Mars*, a 14-gun privateer from the Bahamas. Her crew had mistaken Creighton's vessels for British warships, and twenty to thirty of her men had fled ashore, fearing impressment into the Royal Navy. As a result, she was but partially manned when the *Enterprize* engaged. The second of the three vessels was the *Eliza*, a British schooner laden with salt. Creighton took possession of her. He then pursued the last vessel, but she escaped.[53]

As darkness fell Creighton faced additional problems. He was near the shore, the current was strong, the wind was onshore, and his men were scattered among four vessels. Particularly, the *Eliza* worried him, since she had only a lieutenant and six men on board. Throughout the night, Creighton showed lights, fired signal rockets, and lit false fires. Although these could have alerted a British warship, he believed it more important to keep the four vessels together. At daylight, Creighton found the *Enterprize* and the *Mars* in company, but not the *Eliza*. At noon, when he plotted his position, he determined that he had drifted well to the north of where the capture had occurred, making the chance of falling in with the *Eliza* miniscule. Creighton gave up his search and hoped she would make an American port on her own.[54]

Two mornings later, on 25 February, the American lookouts sighted another sail, but it was not a merchant ship—it was a large frigate. Survival became the paramount concern. The two vessels again separated, with the frigate continuing after the *Enterprize*.[55] While relief was surely felt on board the *Rattlesnake*, the opposite was true on board her consort. Darkness harbored safety, but that was hours in the future, and the frigate was closing quickly. Renshaw used every trick he knew to keep his opponent at bay. He ordered his men to lighten the vessel. Among other things, fifteen guns went over the side. The *Enterprize* survived until nightfall, but at daylight on 26 February the frigate was still there. The chase continued and the frigate was still in sight the next morning (27 February); however, the wind had died, becalming both warships. Renshaw watched in horror as his opponent prepared for a boat attack. The British captain must have seen the guns going over the side and realized that his opponent lay virtually impotent, but at this desperate moment a light wind sprang up. Renshaw used it to get to the windward of the frigate and escape. The chase had lasted seventy grueling hours.[56]

After separating from the *Enterprize*, Creighton arrived at Wilmington, North Carolina, in early March. Several days later on 8 March, the *Enterprize* joined him. The eight-week cruise had yielded but five prizes. Though both vessels had survived, the *Enterprize* had lost her guns. This was made worse by the difficulty in obtaining new carronades in the southern United States. In his report to Secretary Jones, Creighton recounted, "The *Enterprize* is as gallant a little vessel as ever floated, at the same time one of the dullest in point of sailing. She escaped capture to be sure but altogether by good fortune and great exertions of her officers and men. I assure you sir she has caused me much anxiety & uneasiness from that particular alone."[57]

The strategic effects of the cruise were more difficult to determine. British warships had chased both warships on three occasions, but the British did not realize these were warships of the United States Navy. Instead, the British merely identified them as suspicious vessels or, at most, privateers. Compared with the cruises of America's frigates, the *Rattlesnake* and *Enterprize* did little to meet Jones' plan to disrupt British naval operation and destroy British commerce.

The *Adams* was transformed from a small frigate to a flush-deck corvette with a broadside of thirteen light 18-pounders and one long 12-pounder as a bow chaser.[58] Late 1813 witnessed her sea trials in the Chesapeake, but her commander, Captain Charles Morris, did not like what he experienced. More particularly, as he reported to Secretary Jones, his officers did "not consider her a safe cruising vessel, owing to the motion of her rudder . . . I believe myself that this continual motion . . . must materially affect the durability of the Ship." Jones answered, "The *Adams* is far from being perfect, and in her form very different from that which a skillful constructor would adopt as an original yet I cannot but think . . . she will prove a safe efficient and swift Vessel." Jones discounted the motion in the rudder, emphatically arguing,

"I can speak with some confidence having in practice and theory devoted much attention to the form, proportions and construction of Ships of all descriptions." Dismissing Morris' concerns was a sign of Jones' weakness as secretary. Though he knew a great deal about ships, he thought he knew much more than in fact he did. When his officers disagreed, he saw their comments as a challenge to his competence. As with the *General Horsford*, Jones refused to accept the opinions of his officers and ordered the *Adams* to sea.[59] Though Morris remained unconvinced of the *Adams'* effectiveness, he planned to sail with "the first Northeast snowstorm or thick weather which may happen."[60]

While the weather presented opportunities for the Americans, it added to British difficulties. In December 1813 Admiral Warren accurately reported, "The *Adams*... is Manned and in readiness with the *Constellation* to seize the first moment of putting to Sea." Two weeks later, Captain Robert Barrie, Warren's squadron commander in the Chesapeake, added, "Hitherto I have succeeded in Blockading the American Frigates *Constellation* and *Adams* . . . but the Winter has set in with so much severity and we have broken so many Anchors . . . that I fear I shall not be able to preserve the Anchorage, but I will persevere to the last moment."[61]

On 18 January the *Adams* slipped down the Chesapeake "with a strong NW. [*sic*] wind, and cloudy weather, and occasional squalls of snow." The conditions caused Morris and his pilots to become disoriented, and the *Adams* grounded, but Morris quickly found deeper water. Though worried about damage, Morris could not turn back, given the wind and the presence of the British squadron. Several hours later, the *Adams* passed "within half musket shot" of three large warships of the Royal Navy at the entrance to Chesapeake Bay but raised no alarm. Morris had slipped by the blockaders. More than two months later, Rear Admiral Cockburn confirmed, "The *Adams* I am sorry to say (as suspected by Captain Barrie) certainly went to Sea in January last."[62]

Morris shaped a course south of Bermuda, capturing a British merchantman on 29 January followed by a second prize on 9 February. Nearly a month elapsed before he took a small sloop off the African coast on 4 March. Rather than destroy her, he plundered her cargo of rice and let her go. The next week, Morris obtained his fourth prize, which was laden with ivory and palm oil. He had the ivory transferred to the *Adams* and sent her away with the prisoners.[63]

In squally weather on 24 March, Morris brought the English East India country ship *Woodbridge* to by firing several guns.[64] These were heard on board the *Albacore*, a British 18-gun sloop under Commander James Boxer. At nearly the same moment, her lookout peering through the thick weather sighted two strange vessels. Given the poor visibility, this was nothing but luck. The *Albacore* and her consort, the 74-gun *Dannemark*, exchanged signals. Captain Reginald Baker, of the latter ship, faced a decision. As senior officer he had a convoy of valuable

East India Ships to protect, but the sighting seemed suspicious, so he signaled the *Albacore* to investigate while the *Dannemark* protected the convoy. As the *Albacore* closed, Boxer saw what appeared to be a warship and her prize. Private signals went unanswered.[65] Almost simultaneously, lookouts on board the *Adams* "discovered a fleet of 25 Sail immediately to the windward of us & two ships of war standing for us—we were compelled to abandon the prize with precipitation and attend to our own safety."[66]

That evening the *Albacore* recaptured the *Woodbridge* and then pressed after the *Adams*. Half an hour later the breeze died, and Boxer reported, "The enemy not more than three miles from us, and my boats ahead towing, I have great hope of bringing the Enemy to action."[67] Daylight found the *Adams* still in sight with the *Albacore* in pursuit, but the *Adams* was too far "to Windward at too great a distance to admit any hope of the *Albacore* coming up with him." Baker signaled recall, understanding his convoy, not the *Adams*, was his primary concern.[68]

After escaping the *Dannemark* and *Albacore*, Morris headed for the United States, since his crew had nearly exhausted its provisions. Moreover, he remained unsatisfied with his command, writing, "Our Ship sails tolerably well in smooth water but in a head sea every clump we have chased has beaten us." The *Adams* made landfall near Tybee Lighthouse on 29 April. The next day the pilot got her over the bar, but she drew too much water to proceed up the river to the safety of Savannah. The anchorage at Tybee was exposed to potential British attack, so Morris needed to quickly obtain provisions and proceed to sea.[69]

For Morris, the difference between a mediocre cruise and a good one involved only the bad luck with the *Woodbridge*. Captain Baker later attested that if the *Albacore* had not reported a sail "we should otherwise have been so far to the Southward, as not to have seen them on the weather clearing."[70] In addition, the *Adams* did not stir the Admiralty. She did not need to, because the size of the British navy allowed for a level of presence that slowly restricted U.S. naval operations.

Though the *Enterprize*, *Rattlesnake*, and *Adams* failed to obtain Secretary Jones' desired effects, he held greater hope for the six new sloops. The one built in New York was named for the *Hornet*'s 1813 victory over the *Peacock*, and Jones ordered Master Commandant Lewis Warrington to command her. Though launched on 27 September 1813, it took more than four months to rig, arm, and man her, demonstrating one of America's gravest naval weaknesses—an inadequate infrastructure.

On 4 March the *Peacock* was ready to sail, but Warrington lamented, "The weather is clear & cold with a bright moon at night, which renders it improper to start untill a change, as the enemy keep a sharp look out being seldom out of sight from the highlands." Eight nights later the *Peacock* proceeded to sea in a "violent squall of hail & Snow." The next morning Warrington encountered what he thought to be a British brig of war, but after a few minutes, the brig hauled off when her commander realized that he had no chance of catching the *Peacock*. Two hours later Warrington sighted a sail that had the appearance of a frigate. He had the *Peacock* come about, but lookouts descried a larger ship, apparently a ship of the line. Both pursued the *Peacock*, but they soon gave up since Warrington conjectured that they were "fearful . . . of getting too far off Station to leeward."[71]

After breaking through the British blockade, Warrington shaped a course for St. Marys to deliver critical naval stores. The remoteness of the base and the strength of the British navy meant that Jones had to devote one of his newest and strongest instruments of war to serve as a transport.[72] The *Peacock* arrived off St. Marys in late March. After transferring the supplies to a waiting gunboat, Warrington steered south to patrol between Cape Canaveral on the Florida coast and Great Isaac Island in the Bahamas. Between 1 April and 24 April, the *Peacock* chased only three vessels, but they all escaped.[73]

The morning of 29 April found the *Peacock* off Cape Canaveral, where her lookouts sighted the 18-gun British brig of war *Epervier* escorting three merchantmen.[74] On board the *Epervier*, Commander Richard W. Wales showed the private signal, but he received a suspicious answer consisting of an English ensign and a pendant. As a result, he maneuvered his vessel between his flock of merchantmen and the *Peacock*. At that point Wales observed the stranger hoist American colors.[75]

Though the *Epervier* had been launched in 1812, her short period of active service had not been kind. Sunk at Halifax in the November 1813 hurricane, she had remained underwater for ten days before being floated. Moreover, her bowsprit and foremast were sprung at the time of her encounter with the *Peacock*, and of the 118 on board, fifteen were boys. Her master grumbled, "I never saw a worse crew in my life in every respect."[76] Not surprisingly, her second lieutenant thought the crew "appeared to be rather confused" as the *Epervier* cleared for action.[77] This compared poorly to the *Peacock*, who had about one-third more men. Though the principal armament of both vessels consisted of 32-pound carronades, the *Peacock* mounted twenty compared to her opponent's sixteen.[78] Warrington sailed into the engagement with distinct advantages, and Wales had to fight to protect his convoy.

Wales unleashed the first British broadside at very close range. To add to the destruction, his men had double-shotted the carronades. The rounds, however, went high, doing significant damage to the *Peacock*'s sails and rigging. In particular, the Americans lost use of the foresail and fore-topsail. Though the *Peacock* carried more canvas, these sails proved especially important for maneuver and prevented Warrington from using the vessel as he wished; in his opinion, "The fate of the *Epervier* would have been determined in much less time" had his ship not sustained damage to her sails.[79]

On board the *Epervier*, the recoil of the first broadside unshipped three carronades. Because unsecured cannons could prove dangerous to the crew as well as the ship, particularly as the *Epervier* rolled in the sea, the British quickly secured the guns, but several carronades continued to unship every time they were fired. For an already outnumbered and outgunned crew, this certainly added an unwanted distraction. It likely resulted from the failure to adequately test the guns or practice with live fire.[80]

Meanwhile, American broadsides dismantled the *Epervier*, and her men began deserting their stations. Several hid under the forecastle, only to be twice driven back to their quarters by the first lieutenant, who had already lost three fingers in the first broadside. Then, the lieutenant fell with a wound in the hip and had his elbow shot off. Between American fire and poor gun tackle, only one carronade continued to fire.[81]

Wales received a report of four and a half feet of water in the hold, and then watched the main topmast come down. He expected the foremast to follow at any moment. Another officer estimated the brig had taken forty-five round shot. The *Epervier* was a sinking wreck, and Wales realized that his command had fought long enough and inflicted sufficient damage on the *Peacock* for the convoy to escape, so he hauled down the colors. His vessel had lost six to eight dead and between eleven and fifteen wounded.[82]

Not a single round had hit the *Peacock*'s hull, and only two of her men had suffered wounds, all of them minor. According to Warrington, it took but fifteen minutes to ready her for another action. As for his prize, he proudly boasted, "By great exertion we got her in sailing order just as dark came on." His only regret involved the escape of the *Epervier*'s convoy, but Warrington decided not to chase after the merchantmen, given the crippled condition of his prize and particularly the need to protect the $120,000 in specie that was found on board the *Epervier*.[83]

The two vessels sailed north toward an American port. At 5:30 p.m. on the day after the engagement, lookouts sighted two warships closing fast from the north. The Americans had encountered the 56-gun *Majestic* and 18-gun *Morgiana*. Commander David Scott of the latter watched the *Peacock* and *Epervier* come within hail. John Nicolson, the *Peacock*'s first lieutenant who had taken charge of the prize, suggested they separate. Warrington agreed. The British responded with the *Morgiana* chasing the *Epervier*, while the *Majestic* bore down on the *Peacock*.[84]

With only sixteen men on board, Nicolson brought his vessel into the shallows around Amelia Island. As the *Morgiana* approached, Commander Scott sent his cutter to scout his opposition, but the boat crew mistook the *Epervier* for an American warship. Scott faced a predicament. He did not realize he confronted a prize manned by only a small crew, and he likely figured his opponent out-gunned the 16 x 24-pound carronades his ship carried. As a result, Scott decided to remain in the offing and await help; however, Nicolson used the darkness to slip away, arriving off Savannah on 2 May.[85]

Meanwhile, the *Majestic* pursued the *Peacock*, but the two ships lost sight of each other in the darkness. As dawn broke on 1 May, Warrington came about and sailed north; however, his command again fell in with the *Majestic*. She chased the *Peacock* for most of the day until her portside main topsail yard was carried away by the wind. As she reduced sail to right the damage, the *Peacock* disappeared over the horizon. As darkness fell, Warrington had his vessel steer to the north for the third time. He "saw nothing untill daylight on Tuesday morning [3 May] when a large ship (supposed to be the frigate) was again seen in chase of us." This time, Warrington's opponent was probably the *Morgiana*, but several strange vessels were in the area and Scott investigated another sighting, letting the *Peacock* reach Tybee Lighthouse on 4 May.[86]

Warrington concluded that the British "had received information . . . and was waiting to intercept us."[87] British intelligence, however, was not that effective. Instead, the encounters with the *Majestic* and *Morgiana* resulted from increased Royal Navy presence and, more specifically, a reaction to the *President*'s transit of this region in February.

From the winter of 1813 to the spring of 1814, the oceanic strategy devised by Secretary Jones failed to achieve its desired effects, and Jones became increasingly risk-averse. Much of this behavior stemmed from managing scarce manpower resources. Recruitment continued to be voluntary. This limited the size of the navy, but the hatred of British impressment practices prohibited any American attempt at forcible recruiting. In December 1813 Jones wrote, "It appears that each District must rely upon the force to be recruited within itself, for there is no excess over the actual local demand in any one District."[88] This, needless to say, made it difficult to obtain the large number of seamen necessary to man warships. Misallocation also factored in. For example, approximately one thousand seamen were blockaded at New London, whereas the *Congress* could not sail from Portsmouth for the want of about fifty men.[89]

A similar situation existed at Baltimore for the *Erie* and *Ontario*. These two warships were similar to the *Peacock* and made up one-third of the sloops ordered the previous year. Jones had hoped they could sail in the winter, but on 9 February 1814 the commander of the *Ontario* lamented, "My ship waits for nothing but men." Sending men from New London to join the *Ontario* and the *Erie* might have allowed them to sail before the British blockade became too tight. By spring only the *Erie* had sufficient men, and when Master Commandant Charles Ridgeley tried to slip her down the Chesapeake on 1 April, he encountered a ship of the line, forcing him to flee back up the bay. Later, he asserted, "I much fear Sir the Season has too far advanced, for me to attempt to get to Sea without imminent hazard."[90] Jones agreed, writing to Ridgely "that there is not the least chance of your escape, without incurring a degree of risk."[91]

Several days later Jones placed the *Erie* and *Ontario* in ordinary and sent the men to the Lakes. Then, in mid-April, he revoked the *Constellation*'s cruising orders and directed her crew to defend Norfolk. About this time, Jones also ordered the dismantling of the *United States* and *Macedonian*. The latter's crew went to the Lakes, while the crew of the *United States* manned the *President*, then undergoing repairs at New York. In early June, Jones ordered the officers and men of the *Congress* to the Lakes.[92]

Jones had signaled the importance of operations on the Lakes, while oceanic operations became ever more dangerous and yielded fewer rewards commensurate with the risk. Poor communications, manning issues, British deployments, and risk aversion had limited the success of American frigates during the winter. In the spring, Jones developed a strategy using light cruisers. Though the *Rattlesnake*, *Enterprize*, *Peacock*, and *Adams* had survived their cruises, the *Enterprize* had returned combat ineffective. Of the *Peacock*'s capture of the *Epervier*, Jones wrote, "I like these little events, they keep alive the national feeling and produce an effect infinitely beyond their intrinsic importance."[93] After many disappointments, this small success seemed even more important. Though Jones had sent men from oceanic service to the Lakes, he understood that even a few small warships on the oceans would cause the British to redouble their efforts with convoys and patrols; as a result Jones ordered the *Peacock*, *Rattlesnake*, and *Adams* to prepare to return to sea. The *Wasp* stood ready for her first cruise, whereas the *Frolic* and *Siren* had sailed in February but remained unaccounted for. Jones could only hope for better results.

CHAPTER 11

"Into Abler Hands"

Britain Turns to New Leadership, 1814

The weather closed in on the *Siren* as she cleared Boston Harbor on 29 January 1814, forcing Master Commandant George Parker to run for the safety of Salem. There, Parker complained of failing health.[1] Stress was a likely contributor, because Secretary Jones had ordered the *Siren* to operate in the Indian Ocean and even suggested circumnavigating the globe.[2] Parker had received the most expansive cruising instructions for 1814, but, given the quantity of provisions his command could carry, he needed a great deal of luck to execute the mission. Launched in 1803, the *Siren* was smaller than the new class of ship-sloops such as the *Peacock*, and mounted but 12 x 24-pound and 2 x 42-pound carronades, as well as 2 x long 9-pound guns.[3]

The *Siren* departed Salem on 24 February. Though she avoided British warships while crossing the Atlantic, Parker died southwest of the Azores on 11 March. First Lieutenant N. D. Nicholson assumed command, and one seaman related that he spoke to the crew and "told us that it should be left to our decision whether he should assume the command and continue the cruise, or return home." In response, "We gave him three hearty cheers, in token of our wish to continue."[4]

Arriving on the African coast, the *Siren* sailed into the Senegal River on the evening of 29 March. Near a British fort at its mouth, Nicholson sighted two vessels and thought that one made "signals from which circumstance, I was lead [*sic*] to believe her a British Armed Vessel, & prepared to attack her." At close range, the *Siren* received small arms fire, and Nicholson returned a broadside. Thinking he had silenced his opponent, he dispatched a boat to take possession of her, but the boat was driven off by musketry. The fort then fired on the American warship. The *Siren*'s carronades lacked the range to reply, and as night fell Nicholson withdrew out of the reach of the fort's guns. Daylight showed that the two vessels had anchored under the protection of the fort. Nicholson probed the position, but cannon fire drove off the *Siren*. Both sides drew faulty conclusions. The two vessels were a British merchantman and a harbor boat, and the British described the *Siren* as a slave ship.[5]

Shaping a course south, Nicholson sent a note to one outpost ashore asserting to be the British brig of war *Emulous*. This was a savvy ploy, since she was the former U.S. warship *Nautilus*, and Nicholson knew that she was unknown on the coast. At another place, Nicholson spoke with the occupants of a Dutch fort, anxiously enquiring about British warships, but he only learned generalities. On 25 April Nicholson approached Cape Coast Castle in present-day Ghana under the ruse of English colors. In the harbor was the British sloop *Spitfire*, under Commander John Ellis, who showed the *Siren* a private signal. Instead of answering, Nicholson came about, set a press of canvas, hoisted American colors, and fled. Though he probably showed his colors too soon, fleeing was certainly prudent: the *Spitfire* displaced about 30 percent more than the *Siren* and threw more metal. Ellis knew he had the advantage and gave chase under a cloudy sky, broken by flashes of lightning. He was gaining on the American when, just out of gunshot, the *Siren* entered a thunderstorm, and Ellis lamented, "I lost sight of him."[6] Ellis, however, could not scour the region owing to his lack of provisions; instead, he left a letter for any arriving British naval officer, accurately describing the *Siren* as an "American Brig of War of 16 Guns."[7]

After this close call, Nicholson made São Tomé, a Portuguese-controlled island just south of the Gulf of Guinea, where he learned that an English convoy had orders to form under the *Spitfire*'s protection. Nicolson decided to chance an encounter with the British warship in the hope of picking off the merchantmen assembling for the convoy. This was a fortuitous decision, for the lack of provisions had forced the *Spitfire* to depart the region.[8] Nicholson pretended that his vessel was the *Spitfire*, and his officers even donned uniforms approximating those of the British. Using this ruse, the Americans burned a merchant vessel. One seaman on board the *Siren* recounted, "It was an imposing sight, to behold the antics of the flames, leaping from rope to rope, and from spar to spar, until she looked like a fiery cloud resting on the dark surface of the water . . . what, a few hours before, was a fine, trim ship . . . lay a shapeless, charred mass." A short time later, Nicholson used the same ruse to destroy a second British merchantman.[9]

The *Siren* again steered south. This occurred just in time: the 36-gun British frigates *Creole* and *Astrea* had made Cape Coast, obtained Ellis' letter, and gone looking for the *Siren*.[10] Nicholson, however, was far to the south, having made a port in Angola. The Americans needed provisions, but sufficient quantities were not available for them to be able to continue toward the Indian Ocean. As a result,

Nicholson steered for home by way of Ascension Island, in the expectation of encountering an English East India Company ship, but hopes faded as the *Siren*'s provisions dwindled.[11]

At 5:30 a.m. on 12 July, lookouts on board the *Siren* sighted a sail. "Supposing her to be a large merchantman, we made towards her; but a nearer approach made it doubtful whether she was an Indiaman or a man of war."[12] The mystery ship was in fact the 74-gun *Medway*. Under Captain Augustus Brine, she had sailed from the Cape of Good Hope to patrol for American commerce raiders. When Brine's lookouts sighted the *Siren*, he did not need to act timidly, given the size of the *Medway*, and Brine's command rapidly overhauled the American.[13] At 5:00 p.m. the *Medway* opened fire. "Of course, fighting was out of the question," wrote one seaman on board the *Siren*. "It would be like the assault of a dog on an elephant, or a dolphin on a whale." Seeing no chance of escape, Nicholson surrendered.[14]

Five months at sea, a near escape, two prizes, and then capture. The Court of Inquiry that looked into the *Siren*'s capture determined "that no censure can be attached to Lt. N. D. Nicholson for the loss of the *Siren*; but on the contrary, that his conduct was that of a cool, vigilant, zealous, and active officer."[15] One, however, must consider Jones' intent. What disruption did the *Siren* cause the British? Though she had diverted two British frigates, the *Medway* was not looking for the *Siren*. The near global presence of the Royal Navy made American naval cruises increasingly risky; however, the Admiralty believed that operations in one region had consistently failed to meet expectations. This critical point of failure was Admiral Warren's command in the Americas. They did not wish to learn of an American warship on the coast of Africa or her capture in the South Atlantic. Instead, they wanted to prevent the likes of the *Siren* from ever leaving American waters, but all too often, it seemed, Warren's efforts had failed.

At Bermuda on 18 February 1813, Admiral Warren stepped onto the deck of the 74-gun *Marlborough*. Before him stood "the Officers with the most abject humility, the timid shrinking behind the rest for fear of being annihilated." All around, the seamen and marines stood at attention. They had just witnessed "the approach of this Demigod." Sometime later, Warren departed and "his ambition is gorged with the repetition of adulation on his return out of the ship." Or so wrote the commander of the *Marlborough*'s Royal Marine detachment. Admittedly, he thought poorly of Warren, describing the morning as "a pompous & diabolical attempt at omnipotence." Later, he would add that Warren "is ignorant of everything we want to know."[16] But he was not the only one who harbored negative feelings about

Warren. Another officer added, "The conduct of Sir John Warren, since he has commanded on this station, has been so very inexplicable that *his* reasons must be *very secret* indeed, as there is not a person able to form a conjecture on the subject; so secret are these reasons, that some people even begin to fancy he never had any."[17] More ominously, the Admiralty decided to remove him.

Prior to Warren's appointment, the North American, Leeward Islands, and Jamaica Stations had separate commanders in chief. At the outbreak of the War of 1812, Warren assumed command of all three stations. The exigencies of the war prevented him from devoting much attention to the Leeward Islands or Jamaica, however. Unlike the situation off the U.S. coast, British naval operations in the Caribbean mainly involved the maintenance of Britain's naval dominance. The only deployment directly associated with the War of 1812 involved a few ships from Jamaica Station off the Mississippi River. Warren even suggested that the Admiralty consider the commanders at the Leeward Islands and Jamaica "responsible for the common Duty of their Stations."[18] Instead of traveling to the region to work directly with his subordinate admirals, he relied on correspondence, but this resulted in delays, and Warren understood that he had to make decisions without fully understanding the operating environment in the West Indies. As a result, he suggested to the Admiralty that the commanders at the Leeward Islands and Jamaica have "the entire responsibility and governance of their own Stations, empowering me only to Command the Force under them, in the event of necessity requiring a consolidation of greater strength than either of the Districts might otherwise be able to afford."[19]

Warren's hands-off approach allowed a major problem to fester. In January 1813 Melville had advised Warren, "We have been assailed from various quarters on the defenseless state of the West Indies & yet as far as we know, the force in that quarter is very considerable & amply sufficient." The First Lord, however, admitted, "We are left in a very embarrassing state of ignorance on the subject." As a result, the Admiralty had a difficult time responding to queries from the West India Association at Liverpool.[20] When the Admiralty questioned Warren, he answered, "With respect to the West Indies it is a subject that has cost me more trouble & pain than it is easy to Describe: I mean however more particularly Jamaica: where I am sorry to say that Admiral Stirling is acting in a very unhandsome way."[21]

A short time later, additional details about Stirling's command came to light. Particularly, Warren learned, "It is roundly asserted that Ships of War could at any time be hired as Convoy to Vessels going to the Spanish Main provided a sufficient sum of Money was offered, and that it was done very frequently and without fear of Public notice." Stirling allegedly used the 18-gun *Sappho* in such a way, employing his secretary to mask his involvement, hiding the money paid within the legal purview of freight money, and keeping the *Sappho*'s commander in the dark about the nature of his mission.[22] The more information Warren received, the more he thought Stirling had gone rogue, and Warren asked the Admiralty to investigate.[23]

This led to Stirling's recall and his replacement by Rear Admiral William Brown.[24] Even though Warren had proved incapable of controlling one of his chief subordinates, largely owing to geographical separation, the Admiralty decided not to alter the size of Warren's command, given its flexibility in meeting developing threats. Croker did apprise Warren, "If you should find that you are unequal to the management of so extensive a duty it would be better, in their Lordships opinion, to have again three distinct and responsible Commanders in Chief, than to have three Officers with divided authority and mixed responsibility."[25]

This statement, written in March 1813, planted a seed for change; as summer turned to autumn, the roots took hold, as the Admiralty increasingly believed that Warren needed to go. Warren's removal, however, had to occur in such a way to avoid damaging the credibility of the Admiralty board or the government, because they had created the amalgamated command and selected Warren. Ironically, successes, including the capture of the *Chesapeake* and the failure of American frigates to make significant captures during the summer of 1813, allowed the Admiralty to recall Warren without admitting complete failure on their own part.

On 4 November the Admiralty split Warren's command into its three component parts, deciding that it was "therefore unnecessary any longer to employ you on the North American Station; I have their Lordships [sic] Commands to acquaint you therewith . . . you are being relieved by the officer who will be selected to command on the Halifax Station." Until that officer arrived, Warren continued to oversee the North America Station, but he would no longer have authority over the Leeward Islands or Jamaica commands.[26]

In an accompanying private letter, Melville told Warren, "This arrangement became unavoidable (though much against my inclination) by the repeated & well founded complaints from Jamaica of the almost total want of protection on that station. This evil was also liable to be increased by the order which Admiral Brown had received from you to send away to join your flag any vessel whose commander might happen to die . . . instead of an acting Captain being put on immediately."[27] The filling of death vacancies was another manifestation of the control issue. Traditionally, the Admiralty allowed commanders in chief on foreign stations a great deal of latitude over the appointment of officers to fill vacancies, but the Admiralty, by the late Napoleonic Wars, was maintaining tighter and tighter control of patronage. This was much to Warren's chagrin, particularly because the Admiralty had refused on more than one occasion to confirm his appointments. Vacancies owing to death, however, were special in that Warren had complete power to fill them.[28] It is no wonder he wanted ships from the West Indies to join him: this was among the last means of dispensing patronage to help his own protégés; sending warships to join him, however, had the adverse operational effect of taking a ship off a station where she was desperately needed. The Admiralty could not allow such luxuries, given the mood of the political public.

In the British press a letter to the editor printed about the time of Warren's removal commented on his appointment: "I believe [it is] an unprecedented command" and that "probably the *command* is too extensive for one *commander*."[29] Moreover, another British writer editorialized, "In the war with America, the hopes of the country have been *miserably* and *fatally* disappointed." In part, this writer blamed Warren, asserting, "I come now to speak of the *exploits* of the squadron placed under the orders of the admiral on the American station, who is about to resign it, I trust into *abler hands*." The writer, however, believed the naval failures went beyond Warren, to include "the apathy and supineness of the B[oard] of A[dmiralty]." In conclusion, he indicted the Admiralty as "novices."[30] Such comments were not new, and had appeared following the frigate losses of 1812. The cumulative effects had led the Admiralty to sacrifice their commander to quell dissent and allow time for a reassessment.

News of the change of command arrived at Bermuda in the first days of February 1814, and Warren responded to Melville, "I am extremely surprised at being recalled at this moment." With dignity, he added, "I shall therefore forbear saying any further upon the subject untill my arrival in Great Britain." According to Henry Hotham, then serving as captain of the fleet, "The change in the Command is quite agreeable to him."[31] Warren made little fuss, perhaps due to his own admission that "I have long since represented to the Lords Commissioners of the Admiralty how impracticable it was for me at this distance from Jamaica to direct the operations thereat but upon a general principle."[32] The part that caught Warren most off-guard was not the division of his command, but his recall. Melville explained, "I do not think it fair . . . to expect or direct that with your rank in the Service you should continue merely as the successor of Admiral Sawyer on the Halifax Station."[33] Warren was a full admiral; Sawyer had commanded on the North American coast as a vice admiral, but this did not account for the wartime expansion of Sawyer's prewar command.

After less than fourteen months commanding in North America, the Admiralty had removed Warren. Though he was pompous and proved a poor communicator, his war against the United States Navy had begun to bear fruit by late 1813. Of the eleven times that American frigates had sailed on major cruises in the war's first six months, all had reached open water, but Warren's command stopped four of the next six from sailing. This included the capture of the *Chesapeake*, as well as the trapping of two frigates in New London and one in Norfolk.[34] Moreover, these successes had occurred without promised resources. As one senior naval officer put it, "I must say Sir J. Warren was not justly supported; for instead of 100 he had not more than seventy sail."[35] The Admiralty at least partially proved this point, for the official letter announcing Warren's recall included the expected strength of the three stations that had formerly comprised Warren's command. In the case of the Leeward Islands and Jamaica, Warren explained, "The number of ships of each class nearly corresponds." However, the same could not be said for the North American Station. Though the ships of the line and razees on station equaled the Admiralty allotment, Warren was short three frigates and two sloops. In addition, one frigate and four sloops were unmanned largely because their crews were needed on the Lakes. In total, he lacked ten of the fifty-five warships that the Admiralty had assigned to North American waters.[36]

The Admiralty considered Vice Admiral Sir Richard Keats as Warren's successor. An audacious officer, he was best known for events on the night of 12–13 July 1801 while captain of the 74-gun *Superb*. In darkness he had engaged a Spanish 112-gun ship that caught fire and then collided with another Spanish warship of the same size. The flames quickly spread, leading to the destruction of both Spanish vessels. Later that night Keats captured a French 74-gun ship. Since then he had served with distinction, and in 1813 he had taken command of the Newfoundland Station where his orders directed him to assume command of the North American Station in case of Warren's death or incapacitation.[37] The Admiralty decided that Keats was Warren's logical successor.

To command at Newfoundland, the Admiralty decided on Vice Admiral Sir Alexander F. I. Cochrane, an officer of considerable combat experience dating back to the American Revolution. He had been second in command in the action at San Domingo on 6 February 1806 when the British had captured three French ships of the line and destroyed two others. While commanding the Leeward Islands Station, he had overseen the capture of the French Islands of Martinique (1809) and Guadeloupe (1810). About the Newfoundland command, Cochrane wrote, "Having through life been employed upon active service I know I should feel ill at ease in holding a command in time of war where so little was to be doing as on the Newfoundland Station." Cochrane related of Keats: "He is my Junior officer I confess I should not like to take a Secondary Situation." It seemed that Cochrane had thrown a wrench into the Admiralty's plan, but Keats' health was too fragile for the rigors of command on the American coast, leading the Admiralty to change its mind and instead offer the North American Station to Cochrane.[38]

Deeper consideration made Cochrane a more logical decision than Keats. In April 1812 Cochrane had written Melville about potential courses of action if war with the United States occurred. He described America's critical vulnerabilities and how he could bring victory by inciting tensions between the northern and southern states, fomenting slave unrest, and occupying New Orleans, which he saw as the gateway to the interior. Overall, he asserted, "A war with the United States ought be carried on with energy—they are an enterprising people and must be met in the same way." He added, "It . . . must be prosecuted in a very different skill than that adopted in the Revolutionary War.— We must not be so sanguine in our efforts as at that period."[39]

Cochrane's proposed concept of operations did not match British strategic priorities in 1812, but late 1813 proved different, because the threat of Napoleonic France had lessened. Britain's military and naval forces became available in ever-larger numbers, providing the means to implement Cochrane's 1812 plan. On 26 November 1813 the Admiralty met with Cochrane, but waited another month to draft his orders, then dallied yet another month before directing Cochrane to sail. Finally, on 1 February the new commander proceeded to Bermuda.[40]

These delays had significant ramifications. The boisterous weather of the winter limited British operations north of New York, whereas the winter months allowed for campaigning in the south, avoiding the oppressive summer heat as well as the "sickly" and hurricane seasons. The delays in Cochrane's appointment curtailed any thought of operations in the south during the early months of 1814, and scant time remained to prepare for operations in the north.

When Cochrane finally reached Bermuda on 7 March, he could hardly control his desires to take the war to the United States. Time was critical, yet Warren did not relinquish command and even refused to provide complete details about it. He only released information that made him look abused. For example, Warren explained to Cochrane that he had only fifteen frigates, seventeen sloops, and ten smaller vessels. Shocked, Cochrane beseeched the Admiralty for more ships. Requirements for blockade, patrols, and convoys proved far greater than the strength of the squadron would allow; moreover, the area of operations had expanded. Prior to Cochrane's appointment, the Gulf Coast of the United States and the Bahamas were assigned to the Jamaica Station. Now, everything north of the Tropic of Cancer came under Cochrane's authority. Given these considerations, Cochrane thought his command should include thirty frigates, forty sloops, and twenty smaller vessels of war. This would allow for the deployments shown in Table 11.1. Though these numbers allowed for one-third refitting and reprovisioning, the totals did not include convoy escorts.[41]

Such deployments, however, could not be executed until Warren relinquished command. Though he had learned of his replacement more than a month before Cochrane's arrival, Warren did little to prepare for his relief and even dispatched his

Table 11.1. Cochrane's Planned Deployments, Dated 8 March 1814

	Line	Razee	Frigate	Sloop	Smaller
NORTHEAST					
Gulf of St. Lawrence			1	2	1
Coast of Nova Scotia and Cape Breton			2	3	2
Bay of Fundy to Boston Bay		1	2	3	2
Boston Bay to Nantucket	2		3	3	2
Total for the Northeast	2	1	8	11	7
MID-ATLANTIC					
Rhode Island and Long Island Sound	1	1	2	3	1
New York	1	1	2	2	1
Delaware	1		3	2	1
Chesapeake	1	1	4	4	4
Total for the Mid-Atlantic	4	3	11	11	7
SOUTH OF THE CHESAPEAKE					
The Coast of North Carolina			2	2	
Charleston to Tybee		1	2	3	1
Tybee to St. Augustine			2	3	1
New Providence			2	4	2
Gulf of Mexico including New Orleans			1	4	2
Total for South of the Chesapeake	0	1	9	16	6
Grand Total	6	5	28	38	20

Source: ADM 1/505/106A.

flagship to find the *President* after her encounter with the *Morgiana* off Charleston. Though Cochrane saw this as a ploy to delay Warren's departure, Cochrane awaited the return of his flagship "before I urged him to place me in the direction of the Squadron." Warren's continued refusal to step aside brought out Cochrane's prickly side.[42] One admiral in 1801 had found him a difficult subordinate and later described him as "a crackheaded, unsafe man" as well as "wrongheaded, violent, and proud."[43] Cochrane was not above being difficult when he believed the situation warranted. With Warren, he certainly deemed it so, and a feisty correspondence developed, leading Cochrane to write, "The Commission of Commander in Chief of the Squadron on the North American Station is vested with me alone and this I ought to date from the 7th of the present month, the day on which I produced to you the Order of my Lords Commissioners of the Admiralty directing me to assume it. I know of no other Commission for this Station than the one I hold; the extensive one you possessed has been annulled." He demanded immediate command. Warren refused, and indicated Cochrane would have to wait ten days. To assuage hostility, he placed the 36-gun *Orpheus* and the armed schooner *Shelburne* under Cochrane's orders for a special mission to the Gulf Coast of Florida, under Captain Hugh Pigot of the *Orpheus*. Cochrane was to provide arms to Native Americans who were hostile to the United States and secure intelligence about New Orleans and its defenses.[44] Though Cochrane saw this area as America's critical vulnerability, he needed confirmation about the situation in the southern United States.

Daylight on 20 April found the *Orpheus* and *Shelburne* off the north coast of Cuba with a strange sail in sight. Pigot decided to investigate. The British had encountered the U.S. warship *Frolic*, under Master Commandant Joseph Bainbridge, who ordered the private signals hoisted. The *Orpheus* responded with signals that were not understood on board the American warship. Soon after, Pigot showed American colors, but Bainbridge did not fall for the ruse.[45] The incorrect response to his private signal told him differently—he had fallen in with what appeared to be a British frigate and a smaller vessel.

Bainbridge decided that his best course of action involved running toward the port of Matanzas on the Cuban coast. Throughout the morning, the British warships gained, and Bainbridge soon realized wind and current would prevent his ship from making port. Running the *Frolic* ashore was not an option: the coast appeared "bold and craggy." Caught against the shore with the frigate slightly to the leeward and the schooner to the windward, Bainbridge tacked in order to cross the bow of the *Orpheus* at a distance of about half a gunshot. While the *Frolic*'s men accomplished this maneuver, Pigot fired his frigate's chase guns, one fell short and the other overshot the *Frolic*. Bainbridge then had his men lighten the ship to get more speed. This did not help. As the *Orpheus* prepared to give the *Frolic* her broadside, Bainbridge ordered the colors struck.[46]

Cochrane's first order had the unintended consequence of leading to the capture of the *Frolic*. This contrasted sharply with the accomplishments of his predecessor. Moreover, the *Frolic* had caused little disruption. The day after sailing from Boston on 18 February, she had been chased by the 38-gun *Junon*. Her log described the *Frolic* as "apparently a Man of War."[47] Even after this encounter, no British war-ships received instructions to track her down. At sea, the *Frolic* destroyed but two merchant vessels and a privateer.[48] Admiral Durham in the Leeward Islands identi-fied the *Frolic* as a privateer. For one of America's new sloops, described by Pigot as a "remarkable fine ship of 509 Tons and the first time of her going to sea," she had not obtained the effects Secretary Jones desired.[49] Something had gone awry with his naval strategy. To be effective, the British had to react in a manner that was both costly and disruptive, but this did not happen with the *Frolic*.

Though Cochrane arrived at Bermuda on 7 March, Warren's refusal to relin-quish his command meant that the planned expedition against Portsmouth, New Hampshire, had to be canceled. This was particularly irksome because the *Congress* as well as an almost complete ship of the line were at that northern port. Moreover, if Cochrane had acted quickly, he might also have destroyed the newly constructed sloop *Wasp* before she sailed. Abandoning this expedition had significant ramifi-cations on the naval war, but Cochrane argued the "responsibility must not rest with me." He added, "I can only date the Commencement of my preparations from the day Sir John Warren thinks proper to deliver up to me the direction of the Squadron."[50]

When Cochrane finally assumed command on 1 April, he expanded the block-ade. Beginning in November 1812, the Admiralty had ordered the blockade of the Chesapeake and the Delaware. The following March, New York, Charleston, Port Royal, Savannah, and the mouth of the Mississippi were placed under blockade. In April 1813 the Admiralty directed Warren to establish a blockade anywhere neces-sary, but he was to keep permanent forces off the aforementioned areas. Deciding that he needed something more permanent, Warren amended the blockade on 16 November 1813 to place the entire coast from the Mississippi River to Long Island Sound under strict blockade.[51]

No blockade existed to the north due to the difficulty in maintaining a naval presence during the winter, but Cochrane thought this detrimental to Britain's war effort. Particularly, he wished to stop maritime commerce. At one time, maintain-ing a level of trade with the United States proved necessary, given the war with Napoleonic France and the need for American foodstuffs to support operations in the Iberian peninsula, but the end of the Napoleonic Wars in 1814 decreased Britain's reliance on America. The United States, moreover, had signaled its finan-cial weakness by prohibiting most maritime commerce through the Embargo Law of December 1813. Almost six months later Cochrane asserted that the U.S.

government, "finding themselves deceived in their expectations and failing in their loans to enable them to prosecute the war have thought proper to repeal those Laws." Writing about the expected tax revenue from repeal of the Embargo Law, Cochrane further argued, "It is obvious that this Revenue is intended to enable them to carry on the war against Canada, it must therefore be equally clear that it is the Interest of Great Britain to prevent by every possible means, those deriving that advantage, which they must do in their Ports of the Northern States are left open to the neutral Trade." Moreover, Cochrane understood that trade in neutral merchant ships was "the *only means* left [by] which a Revenue could be raised to enable them to prosecute the war that the Loans having failed and the Commerce annihilated they had no other recourse left." On 25 April Cochrane expanded the blockade to include the entire American coast. Even after protests from merchants he refused to modify the blockade, arguing, "However much it may affect the Interests of a few, [the blockade] must alternately lead to the future safety and advantage of British America at large."[52]

Between 7 March and the end of April 1814, the character of Britain's naval war with the United States had changed. First, the blockade became total. Second, Cochrane planned for amphibious raids far different from the pinpricks that had occurred the previous year. Third, the Gulf Coast became an increasingly important theater of operations. Finally, Napoleon had surrendered, which allowed the Admiralty to reinforce Cochrane. For example, during spring 1814 the commander of the Mediterranean Fleet dispatched five frigates and three sixth rates and three sloops to Bermuda.[53]

These and more were exactly what Cochrane needed, and until sufficient reinforcements arrived, he used the lack of warships to deflect criticism. For example, he wrote to the Admiralty, "The force being so much inferior to what I expected I cannot of course carry my original intentions into execution." In another letter, he responded to demands that more men be sent to the Lakes by explaining that his squadron "is not only reduced in its number of ships, but they are unusually short of men."[54] These were the same arguments Warren had repeatedly voiced to the Admiralty. Such issues were not, however, confined to North America. They affected British naval deployments on a near-global scope and were constant points of friction between commanders in chief and the Admiralty. In a moment of frank honesty, one member of the Admiralty admitted in February 1814, "Where we are to find vessels for all our convoys the devil take me if I know.—We must do our best."[55] A fleet commander more clearly explained to Melville the crux of the problem: "I can readily believe that your Lordship must find considerable difficulty in collecting squadrons sufficient for the numerous services that require them; we must all do the best we can with what can be afforded us; your Lordship must attend to the whole."[56] The Admiralty had to prioritize, and so did Cochrane. Though he wished to escalate the war, his principal task remained the blockade with the adjunct of keeping American privateers and the United States Navy contained.

For the latter objective, Cochrane developed an accurate picture of American naval deployments, demonstrating the porous nature of American information security.[57] One British naval officer offhandedly wrote in his journal, "Received stock and our daily newspaper from the shore."[58] The British learned a great deal in this manner. Rear Admiral Cockburn, writing to Cochrane, said, "I send . . . a file of American Papers for April by which you will see the wretched state of this Country and how anxious they are to have an end of this foolish mad war." Newspapers also allowed Cochrane to know when operations had been compromised, as when information about his proposed attack on Portsmouth appeared in American newspapers.[59] The shore-to-ship movement of everything from newspapers to food made the British blockade easier to sustain. As one officer put it, "Federalists pretend to be friendly to the English. They hate the war on their own account, hate the war because it prevents their making money, and like the English as a spendthrift loves an old rich wife; the sooner we are gone the better."[60]

Cochrane could exploit increased naval strength, improved intelligence, and American financial weakness, but he needed skilled leadership and an effective chain of command with an understanding of Cochrane's intent. Rear Admiral Griffith had arrived in the summer of 1813 to command at Halifax. Cochrane kept him in this position with authority over naval operations from Boston to the north. Additional flag officers arrived on station in 1814. Cochrane appointed one specifically to oversee the blockade of Boston, serving as a subordinate to Griffith, because the British squadron off that port required several ships of the line and frigates. By August, Griffith believed his "Squadron is now quite as strong as is necessary."[61] To the south, Henry Hotham, formerly Warren's captain of the fleet, was given a squadron off Long Island Sound, Sandy Hook, and the Delaware.[62] Under Warren each of these deployments had been a separate squadron under a senior captain. Having an officer responsible for multiple ports allowed for more flexibility. To the south of Hotham, Rear Admiral Cockburn commanded in the Chesapeake region.

Overall, the Admiralty appeared more content with Cochrane than with Warren. Melville reassured Cochrane in late October that complaints against him in the press and in the House of Commons did not bother the Admiralty because "you are not singular in being so distinguished."[63] Melville did, however, provide Cochrane with the following advice: "The experience of twenty years of War on an extended scale has taught the Government of this Country to have no more Irons in the fire than what we can continue to keep *red hot*."[64] Cochrane had great ambitions, and Melville could not let him become overextended.

CHAPTER 12

"Repulsed in Every Attempt"

The Culmination of the Jones' Small Cruiser Strategy, mid-1814

W illiam Jones, during his first year as secretary of the navy, failed to obtain single-ship victories equal to those of 1812. Part of this had to do with the growing British naval strength on the North American coast as well as stronger convoy escorts, but part dealt with different priorities. Jones did not desire battles with the Royal Navy; instead, he wanted long cruises with the object of commerce disruption and destruction. Although this strategy resulted in fewer spectacular moments, it worked to preserve the United States Navy. Even so, attrition gave cause for concern. Jones had few operational warships through the spring, summer, and autumn of 1814. Not until winter would additional men of war become available and the weather deteriorate so these warships could have a better chance of eluding the British blockade and casting their luck to Neptune.

One of Jones' few operational warships during the spring of 1814 was the *Rattlesnake*. After an eight-week cruise during January and February 1814, she had reached the safety of Wilmington, North Carolina. As a reward to her commander, Jones offered Master Commandant John O. Creighton the new sloop *Argus*, then being fitted out in Washington. Creighton accepted: "The *Rattlesnake* is of that class of vessels only calculated for the destruction of the Enemy's commerce, and I freely give her up for the command of a ship on board of which I shall not always be obliged to fly before the foe." With Creighton's decision, a command vacancy occurred, and Jones selected the commander of the *Enterprize*, James Renshaw.[1]

Under Renshaw, the *Rattlesnake* reached the open sea on 2 May 1814 and steered toward the Azores. Though Renshaw stopped five merchantmen during this period, one was a prize to an American privateer, and four sailed under neutral or American colors.[2] It seemed that British merchant shipping had disappeared. In part this disappearance resulted from the strict British convoy system, but the ease of changing or hiding a merchant vessel's nationality contributed to the failure to capture British merchantmen on the high seas.

Just after daylight on 31 May, the *Rattlesnake's* lookouts sighted a frigate, and Renshaw ordered his crew to make all sail. The frigate chased, and Renshaw tried the private signal hoping in vain that she was the *Constitution*, but the frigate hoisted French colors. In near-gale conditions, the frigate overhauled the *Rattlesnake*. The frigate then opened fire, but her shot fell slightly short. Renshaw, in consultation with his officers, decided to lighten the ship by heaving four guns overboard. The frigate still gained, and her shot now passed over the *Rattlesnake*. In desperation, all but two of the remaining guns went into the deep. In hindsight, this occurred prematurely. Almost as soon as the last gun went over the side, the wind began to die. The weather now favored the *Rattlesnake*, and within thirty minutes, she had sailed out of range. Renshaw last saw his pursuer at 10:00 p.m., when the darkness finally enveloped the frigate. The chase had lasted seventeen hours.[3]

The identity of the frigate remains in question.[4] She sailed under a French flag, and Renshaw's report asserted that she remained under such colors throughout the chase. This was important, because custom should have prevented her from firing under French colors if her captain used them as a ruse. She was probably French, but this encounter occurred two months after Napoleon's abdication, and the cessation of hostilities between Britain and France at sea occurred on 23 April, more than a month before this encounter. The French, however, had pushed numerous frigates to sea in the last months of Napoleon's Empire, and even in late May not all had returned to port.[5] Regardless of the frigate's identity, the pursuit had rendered the *Rattlesnake* virtually impotent, and Renshaw decided to obtain new ordnance at a French port. But one day from Lorient, the *Rattlesnake* encountered a Swedish vessel that carried news of Napoleon's abdication and the end of the war in Europe. To Renshaw, these were "events so unpropitious to our views in entering a port that I did not conceive myself authorized under any circumstances to attempt it at this time." With no friendly port, most of his armament in the ocean, and half his command's victuals consumed, Renshaw decided to return to the United States.[6]

On 9 June in the Bay of Biscay, Renshaw learned about a nearby British convoy from a pair of neutral merchantmen. The next day he fell in with an English merchant vessel and scuttled her. Several hours later, the *Rattlesnake's* lookouts

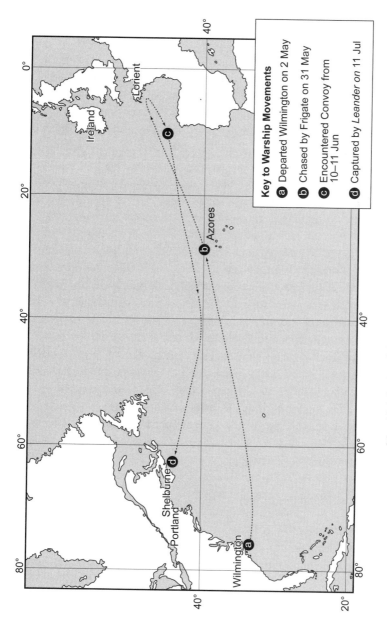

Map 12.1 Cruise of the *Rattlesnake*: 2 May– 11 July 1814

sighted the convoy. Renshaw explained, "I did not succeed in capturing any of them being chased off as often as we attempted to close and on the evening of the 11th gave up the pursuit." Renshaw overstated his actions. Neither British convoy escort recounted an interloper in their logbooks.[7]

Renshaw then shaped an indirect course for the United States.[8] Although Renshaw described his vessel as "harmless," he still planned to disrupt English commerce, and on 23 June he captured a British merchant vessel laden with fish. The *Rattlesnake* then attempted to make a northern port in the United States, but the weather remained hazy, precluding accurate observations. Sailing by dead reckoning, her officers thought they were near Portland, Maine, on the morning of 11 July when daylight revealed a strange sail. Being cautious, Renshaw had his vessel edge away, but the stranger gave chase.[9]

About this time the *Rattlesnake's* lookouts sighted land, and about half an hour later they observed a lighthouse. Hoping against hope that this was Portland Light, Renshaw pressed onward. He also showed the private signal in case his pursuer was American. However, this merely betrayed the *Rattlesnake* as a man-of-war because the stranger was the *Leander*, a new British frigate built especially to counter the largest class of American frigates. Captain Sir George Collier, the veteran commander of the *Leander*, knew his opponent had made a poor decision. Renshaw realized this only minutes later when the *Rattlesnake* passed within hail of a fishing boat. In the exchange, he learned that, rather than Portland Light, it was Shelburne Light on the coast of Nova Scotia. Not only did the *Rattlesnake* have to out sail the *Leander*, but she also had lost precious sea room and now had to clear the land.[10]

Soon the *Leander* had closed within range, and Collier hoisted English colors. Renshaw responded with the same. The ploy did not work, and ten minutes later, Renshaw raised the American ensign. Desperate, he ordered the *Rattlesnake* lightened. The men worked quickly, pushed on by a spent round that struck her stern. These efforts proved in vain, and just as the *Leander* was about to fire her broadside, Renshaw ordered the colors struck.[11]

Collier later asserted, "The *Rattlesnake* is reputed one of the fastest sailing cruizers from the American States, and appears to have been chased by eight different British Men of War during her present cruize."[12] This was stretching the truth. In reality, the *Rattlesnake* was far from an effective instrument of war and Renshaw had proved even less effective as a commander. The inquiry into the loss of the *Rattlesnake* acquitted him of negligence but damned him for poor navigation and decision-making.[13] This decision highlighted a concern that Jones lamented: "With the rapid increase of our naval force, the promotion of young officers has been *necessarily very rapid*; and those whose experience and talents that have exalted our flag are comparatively few in number."[14]

Rapid promotion also applied to Captain Morris of the *Adams*. The first lieutenant of the *Constitution* at the capture of the *Guerriere*, he was advanced directly to captain, bypassing the rank of master commandant.[15] His first cruise had lasted slightly more than three months and concluded when the *Adams* arrived off Tybee Lighthouse outside Savannah on 29 April. Though the tone of Morris' writing made it seem like he languished at Tybee for weeks, he sailed on 8 May, a mere ten days after his arrival, using provisions that the Americans had captured on board the *Epervier*. At sea Morris steered for Cape Canaveral, even though this was the same position that the *Peacock* had occupied during much of April when she had captured the *Epervier*. For Morris, two weeks elapsed before he learned from a neutral vessel that a Jamaica convoy had passed during the night. He pursued.[16]

The information about the convoy was accurate. On the last day of April, the convoy had sailed from Jamaica with a powerful escort under the overall authority of Captain John Spranger of the 74-gun *Barham* with the additional escorts of the 38-gun *Statira*, 20-gun *Bonne Citoyenne*, and 18-gun *Forester*.[17] On 24 May the lookouts on both the *Barham* and *Statira* espied the *Adams*, and the two warships investigated. Morris' only option involved a hasty retreat. The British warships soon abandoned their pursuit lest they become separated from their flock of merchantmen. The next day Morris made a second attempt to cut up the convoy. About 6:30 a.m. the *Barham*'s lookouts sighted a strange sail, but, rather than chase, Spranger dispatched the *Statira*. Meanwhile, the *Barham* signaled the other escorts—"Enemy in the NW." Morris had obtained a poor position, having approached from the leeward. This allowed his opponents to bear down on him while he found it difficult to close with the convoy. Not surprisingly, Morris again fled, and Spranger signaled the *Statira*'s recall.[18] Though engaging a commerce raider was important, the more-valuable object was the convoy's protection.

After two failures Morris dared not venture a third attempt, because "they kept in very close order and their convoying force [was] too strong for us to injure them." Next, Morris shaped a northeasterly course toward the Grand Banks. But again he was thwarted—this time by a combination of fog and icebergs. With limited visibility, the chance of striking an iceberg proved too great, so Morris steered to the southeast. Finally, on 24 June, after more than six weeks at sea, he captured a British merchant vessel. Four days later, Morris captured another. Nearly two months into her cruise, the *Adams* made landfall on the west coast of Ireland, but a strong wind turned the coast into a dangerous lee shore. Though the *Adams* remained in the area for nearly a week in early July, "The weather was so thick that we saw not a single vessel."[19]

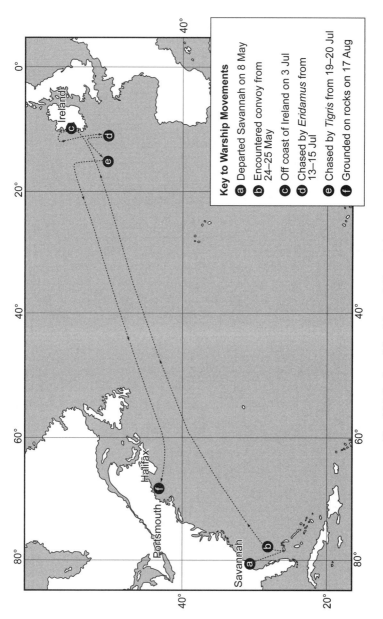

Map 12.2 Cruise of the *Adams*: 8 May–18 August 1814

Key to Warship Movements

- ⓐ Departed Savannah on 8 May
- ⓑ Encountered convoy from 24–25 May
- ⓒ Off coast of Ireland on 3 Jul
- ⓓ Chased by *Eridamus* from 13–15 Jul
- ⓔ Chased by *Tigris* from 19–20 Jul
- ⓕ Grounded on rocks on 17 Aug

Daylight on 13 July found the *Adams* about two hundred miles south of Ireland when her lookouts spied a strange sail. Morris chased, thinking she had the appearance of a large merchant ship. While closing the hunter became the hunted when the 36-gun *Eridanus* under Captain Henry Prescott bore down on the *Adams*. Though chased by a frigate, the encounter could have ended much worse for Morris and his crew. The first ship sighted that morning was not a merchantman but the *Orestes*, a 16-gun British brig-of-war. Moreover, a second British frigate, the 36-gun *Tigris*, had the *Eridanus* in sight that morning. The logs of both the *Tigris* and *Orestes* noted other vessels in sight, one of which was undoubtedly the *Adams*, but neither chased because distance and sea conditions prevented accurate observations. Only Captain Prescott thought the *Adams* suspicious, but he did not signal this to either the *Tigris* or *Orestes*. As a result, the three British warships separated with only the *Eridanus* in chase of the *Adams*.[20]

Prescott had the faster ship, and by sunset he nearly had the *Adams* in range. About this time it fell calm, and Prescott ordered out two boats to tow the *Eridanus* onward. Morris came to a similar decision but had more experience, for he had been instrumental in using boats during the *Constitution's* escape from Broke's British squadron nearly two years before. This time, however, there was no bottom, meaning he could not use anchors to warp the *Adams* forward. By massive exertion, daylight found the *Adams* five or six miles ahead; throughout that day, her advantage extended to nearly eight miles. Moreover, the weather increasingly favored the *Adams*. It started to rain and by nightfall became squally. A short time later, Morris dowsed all the lights and altered course. As dawn broke on 15 July, or what would have been the third day of the chase, Morris found an empty sea.[21]

Four mornings later, in what could almost be seen as déjà vu, Morris made out a frigate in chase of the *Adams*. His lookouts soon sighted a second warship also in pursuit.[22] The latter was the *Tigris* under Captain Robert Henderson. Hazy conditions caused Morris to lose sight of the first frigate about noon, but the *Tigris* remained approximately four miles astern. The wind soon carried away Henderson's foretopgallant mast, and it took an hour and a half to jury rig new one. Only an hour later, the *Tigris* suffered more damage aloft. This slowed the frigate, and her lookouts lost sight of the *Adams* around 9:40 p.m. Five hours later, however, they again found the *Adams*, and Captain Henderson continued the chase. Henderson had a problem: he needed to set more sail to close with the *Adams*, but every time he did the wind did more damage to his frigate. Henderson never determined a solution to this quandary before the *Adams* disappeared from view at 9:45 p.m. on 20 July. The chase had covered four hundred miles, and Henderson had accurately identified his opponent as the *Adams*.[23]

After two and a half months at sea, the *Adams* had few remaining provisions. Moreover, scurvy had made its appearance. The stress of the mission and the lack of fresh provisions certainly made the crew susceptible, and the warship had been at sea for all but ten days since 18 January. Morris lamented, "So many of the men were now affected with it and their number so rapidly increasing as to render our immediate return to Port indispensable." Thus, he brought his command west along the sea-lanes between Newfoundland and Europe and then shaped a course toward Portsmouth, New Hampshire. This track led to the capture of three British merchant vessels between 28 July and 16 August.[24]

On the day of the last capture, Morris recounted, "Foggy weather had prevented accurate observations for latitude or longitude during the last two or three days." As a result, he had to rely on soundings and reckoning. Though he placed the *Adams* about sixty miles from Cape Ann at 2:00 a.m. on 17 August, two hours later the forward lookouts sighted breakers. Only seconds passed before the *Adams* ran onto a rock. Morris decided to wait for daylight to assess the damage. At dawn "the fog dispersed for a few minutes, showing us a perpendicular rocky cliff about a hundred yards from our bows." Though refusing to give up, Morris took the precaution of transferring the sick and the prisoners ashore. Since it was almost low tide when the *Adams* struck the rock, he decided to pull his ship off as the tide rose. In the meantime, Morris set two anchors to prevent her from drifting the last few feet onto the rocky shore.[25] "After some heavy strains," Morris explained, "at 1/2 past 10 the surf lifted her off." There was now a dim chance of escape, but the dangers had increased. She rode at anchor only half a ship length from the shore, but Morris edged down the coast using the *Adams* sails and anchors to keep her off the rocks. For more than three-quarters of a mile, she continued this torturous path until she "passed but 50 yd. to the windward of the Rocks and reefs" at 4:00 p.m.[26]

The next morning the Americans saw land. Although Morris expected to see Portsmouth, the *Adams* had made landfall well to the north, near Mount Desert Island and Penobscot Bay. At about 8:00 a.m. lookouts descried a warship to the windward, but the stranger's course prevented Morris from determining her size. Considering the damage the *Adams* had sustained and the number of sick put ashore, any sort of a fight appeared too risky. At a distance of two miles, the stranger showed her broadside. She was the 18-gun *Peruvian*. Since the *Adams* was a much larger vessel, Morris decided to use his size advantage and pretended to give chase. Not realizing the crippled state of the *Adams*, the commander of the *Peruvian* edged away. Her log noted, "The stranger appeared to be a Frigate and Suspicious." Once Morris gained the entrance to the Penobscot, he abandoned his pursuit and steered into the bay, bringing her well inland to Hampden. This was the prudent choice, for the *Peruvian* was not alone. Only a few miles distant, the 18-gun brigs *Rifleman* and *Wolverine*, as well as the 14-gun schooner *Alban*, prowled.[27]

The increased British presence off the Penobscot resulted from an order Lieutenant General Sir John Sherbrooke, the lieutenant governor of Nova Scotia, had received to use recently arrived soldiers "in such manner as he might judge most effective toward making the Enemy feel the pressure of the War." In consultation with Rear Admiral Griffith, the senior naval officer at Halifax, they decided to attack Maine in an attempt to influence antiwar feelings in northern New England and potentially occupy the region. Given the small size of the available force, however, Griffith explained, "I have given it as my opinion that he could not attempt any place to the Southward and Westward of the Penobscot." But, Griffin admitted, "We have no Information of the Penobscot on wh[ich] we can depend, and it may have been made too strong for our force—However there is no harm in going to *look at* it."[28]

Griffith and Sherbrooke sailed from Halifax on 26 August with an expeditionary force comprising the 74-gun *Dragon*, two frigates, a sloop, and ten transports carrying approximately 2,400 soldiers. Arriving off the Penobscot on 31 August, they joined several warships, including the *Rifleman*. From her commander, Griffith learned that the *Adams* had put into the Penobscot and then proceeded to Hampden. The expedition met only token resistance in the bay, and Griffith dispatched a force under Captain Robert Barrie of the *Dragon* to attack the *Adams*. With significant experience commanding light forces in the Chesapeake, Barrie immediately assembled two 18-gun brigs, the *Dragon*'s tender, and a transport to convey some six hundred soldiers and marines. On 2 September the force sailed up the Penobscot River through "a most intricate channel, of which we were perfectly ignorant." Moreover, Barrie learned that the Americans had decided to defend the *Adams*.[29]

At Hampden Morris had his men remove the *Adams*' guns; he had his men position some on a wharf to command the river channel and others atop a nearby hill. For the defense, he counted his crew as well as twenty-eight regular soldiers and some 370 men of the local militia, though many of the latter lacked arms and ammunition.[30]

Late in the afternoon of 2 September, Barrie's command reached a point three miles below the *Adams* where his force spent a miserable night pelted by torrential rain. The next morning the British attacked. Armed barges and a boat carrying Congreve Rockets advanced up the river while the brigs and tender remained in reserve. Simultaneously, the soldiers and marines moved overland in an attempt to envelop the American position. Barrie wrote, "So soon as the boats got within Gunshot, the Enemy opened his fire upon them from the Hill & Wharf which was warmly returned." Then, the rockets under Barrie's personal direction "threw the enemy into confusion. Meantime our troops stormed the Hill with the utmost gallantry." The American defense disintegrated. Morris asserted, "We had no alternative but precipitate retreat or captivity—Our rear and flanks entirely exposed." In the next confused minutes, Morris ordered the *Adams* burned and the guns spiked.[31]

Morris then extracted his crew, losing only a pair of men to capture. Two weeks later, he and his arrived in Portsmouth, and Morris exalted their conduct. Not only had his men endured a long mission at sea, survived a near-catastrophic wreck, and prepared to repel a British assault, but they had abandoned all their personal belongings and then marched two hundred miles without one desertion.[32]

For the British, Barrie's expedition led to the capture of a dozen vessels as well as destruction of others, including the *Adams*. He obtained these results for the cost of one seaman dead, eight soldiers wounded, and one missing.[33] The British then occupied the area around the Penobscot. One British naval officer related, "So far from making them feel the pressure of the war by this expedition, we are making them much easier and in a better situation than ever, and it is the intention of the General and Admiral to grant them trade to Nova Scotia and to fish on their own coast." This assisted merchants in Canada who were heavily dependent on trade with New England, while it also led to the extensive smuggling of American goods through the Penobscot.[34] The British had found a weakness in the American system, and a mere Royal Navy lieutenant recounted, "All these people exceedingly discontented with the war and all join in abusing the government. Self, the great ruling principle, more powerful with Yankees than any people I ever saw."[35] The effect of occupying the Penobscot and blockading those areas under American control led one British naval officer to chart out a developing British endgame: "I am perfectly of opinion that in a very short time if the Blockade is strictly persevered in and no Licenses granted to trade even with Nova Scotia, and the inhabitants be made still to feel the pressures of the war; that they will be ready to separate themselves from the southern states and will accept of any terms offered."[36]

British operations were certainly aimed at causing support for the U.S. government to collapse. During the same period as the Penobscot operation, the British raid on Washington occurred, resulting in the destruction of the new frigate *Columbia* and the new ship-sloop *Argus*. The head of the British government opined, "The capture of Washington cannot fail to make a lasting impression upon the American People, & I trust its first effect will be to induce them to withdraw their confidence from a Government who have wantonly embarked them in this unnatural war & who have now so clearly manifested their imbecility in conducting it."[37] One British newspaper presented a counterargument by asserting, "Many people here think that the public edifices at Washington which were not devoted to the purposes of war, ought to have been spared; and some consider the system of burning as altogether of doubtful policy. If it really weakens the enemy, it must be efficacious; but if it does little else but irritate, as some contend, it is unquestionably an erroneous course."[38] Were such British actions "an erroneous course," or would they cause the Americans "to withdraw their confidence from a Government"? The strategic effects remained in question.

⊷

The British executed several amphibious operations in 1814, including the attacks on Washington, Baltimore, and the Penobscot region of Maine, but Admiral Cochrane canceled an attack on Portsmouth, New Hampshire, even though the naval base appeared a vulnerable and lucrative target. Instead, he extended the blockade to include Boston, Portsmouth, and areas to the north, and instructed Admiral Griffith on 2 May to maintain a strong naval presence in the region, but the *Wasp* had sailed from Portsmouth the previous afternoon under Johnston Blakeley, formerly of the *Enterprize* and recently promoted to master commandant.[39]

The *Wasp* was the sister ship of the *Frolic* and *Peacock*. In comparison to the *Adams*, *Siren*, and *Rattlesnake*, she was the superior instrument of war, stoutly built and quick, with a powerful armament. As a result, the Americans expected great things of her, but she passed her first month at sea without a prize. Then her luck changed, and she took five British merchant vessels between 2 and 26 June.[40]

About three hundred miles south of Ireland on the morning of 28 June, lookouts sighted a pair of vessels; several minutes later, they descried a third. Blakeley closed with the latter. His prey, however, had claws of her own. She was the British sloop *Reindeer* under Commander William Manners. When the *Wasp* failed to answer his private signal, Manners also closed.[41]

Manners watched the stranger hoist three American ensigns. This was the moment of decision, for he had "made her out to be a large Corvette, mounting 22 guns." Did he fight or flee? Though technically the *Reindeer* was a *Cruizer*-class brig, she mounted 16 x 24-pound carronades instead of the class standard 32-pound weapons. Built in 1804 of fir, her soft wood construction adversely affected her durability, and the *Reindeer* was by 1814 the only remaining operational vessel among her five fir-built sisters. Moreover, she was short a lieutenant and seven men, and of the 118 on board, nineteen were boys. Taking this vessel against the *Wasp* appeared long odds, but Manners decided to fight.[42]

As the two vessels closed, Blakeley maneuvered, trying to prevent his opponent from having the weather gauge, but Manners had his men man the sweeps, transforming the *Reindeer* into a galley of sorts; by strong rowing Manners gained a position about sixty yards astern of the *Wasp*. Manners personally attended the 12-pound carronade mounted on the forecastle and fired the opening shot of the

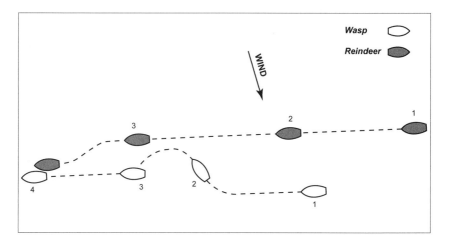

Diagram 12.1 Plan of the Engagement between the *Wasp* and the *Reindeer*
(Adapted from Mahan, *Sea Power and its Relations to the War of 1812*, 2:254–55)

engagement a few minutes after 3:00 p.m. During the next minutes, the gun crew got off five rounds. Rather than continue to get sniped at without being able to bring a gun to bear, Blakeley ordered the helm brought up, exposing his broadside. On Blakelely's order fire spewed from the *Wasp*'s 32-pound carronades. According to one officer on the *Reindeer*, the rounds "mowed down our men like grass."[43] Manners, however, took advantage of Blakeley's maneuver and sailed under his opponent's bow. As each of the *Reindeer*'s guns bore, she raked the American at very close range. Manners then "laid her onboard, our small bower anchor hooking her larboard Quarter." The two warships came to rest with the bow of the *Reindeer* within a few feet of the *Wasp*'s stern.[44]

Around this time part of Manner's calf was torn off by a cannon round and he suffered other wounds in both thighs, but he refused to go below. Instead, he decided his only chance of victory involved carrying the *Wasp* by board-ing, given "the immense superiority of our opponent, and our men falling fast." Manners, though badly wounded, led the boarders onward but "two balls from the *Wasp*'s tops penetrated the top of his skull and came out beneath his chin . . . he exclaimed—'My God!' and dropped lifeless on his own deck." By this point in the action, the master had sustained severe wounds in the arm and thigh. The purser had fallen with multiple wounds. Thomas Chambers, the senior lieutenant, had received a wound in the hip. Though he remained on deck, he fainted from the loss of blood. Within minutes, every officer was a casualty.[45] According to Midshipman David Geisinger on board the *Wasp*, "The Execution from our musketry at this time was terrible every man without exception was either shot down or killed as they Showed their heads." Meanwhile, the *Wasp*'s carronades spewed round after round, pounding the fir-built *Reindeer* to splinters.[46]

Boarding had been the *Reindeer*'s only real chance, but the British were "repulsed in every attempt." On board the *Reindeer*, the wounded master decided nothing more could be done, and as the senior surviving officer on deck, he had the colors struck just as the *Wasp*'s boarders spilled across.[47]

Geisinger described the scene, "Her deck presented an awfull and shocking spectacle." Twenty-six lay dead and forty were wounded out of a crew of only 118. "The *Reindeer* was literally cut to pieces," and Blakeley ordered her burned on the evening after the engagement. The *Wasp* had not escaped lightly, with the Americans having lost five dead and twenty-one wounded, four mortally—or one-seventh of her crew. Moreover, she had sustained significant damage to her masts and rigging with one 24-pound round shot passing through the center of her foremast. Considering that only nineteen minutes had elapsed between the firing of the first American gun and the *Reindeer*'s surrender, this was a particularly brutal action.[48]

The battle left the *Wasp* in need of repair, overcrowded with prisoners, and full of both British and American wounded. On the morning of 1 July, Blakeley brought to a Portuguese brig and transferred into her thirty-two officers and men from the *Reindeer*, including her surgeon and the most severely wounded.[49] However, Blakeley still needed to see to his wounded and repair his foremast. As a result, he steered for Lorient, on France's Atlantic coast. On the way the *Wasp* destroyed another pair of British merchant vessels, giving her a record of seven merchantmen and a warship.[50] Though Napoleon had abdicated and hostilities no longer existed between France and Britain, the French played the role of the neutral, allowing the *Wasp* to refit in Lorient.[51]

Meanwhile, news arrived at Cork, Ireland, that the *Wasp* had been operating in the mouth of the English Channel. Though correct, the report described the American as a privateer. In response, the British dispatched the 18-gun *Castilian* and the 10-gun *Protector* to find and eliminate the *Wasp*. Then, the Portuguese brig with the *Reindeer*'s survivors arrived at Plymouth. While the wounded went to the hospital, the British sent the *Cruiser*-class brigs *Avon* and *Scylla* in search of the American warship.[52] The Admiralty informed Admiral Lord Keith, commander of the Channel Fleet, about the *Wasp*, correctly describing her armament and complement.[53] Keith, however, never realized she had made a port in his command's area of operations.

At Lorient repairs progressed slowly. After six weeks, on 27 August, the *Wasp* finally proceeded to sea, but the delay had rendered a large part of Blakeley's instructions invalid.[54] As a result, he followed his own course, and this bore fruit. In the approaches to the English Channel, Blakeley captured a pair of British merchantmen. Then at 8:45 a.m. on 1 September, within a hundred miles of where the action

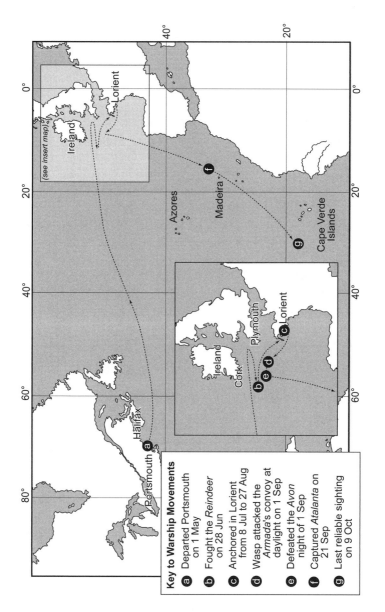

Map 12.3 Cruise of the *Wasp*: 1814

Key to Warship Movements

a Departed Portsmouth on 1 May

b Fought the *Reindeer* on 28 Jun

c Anchored in Lorient from 8 Jul to 27 Aug

d Wasp attacked the *Armada*'s convoy at daylight on 1 Sep

e Defeated the *Avon* night of 1 Sep

f Captured *Atalanta* on 21 Sep

g Last reliable sighting on 9 Oct

with the *Reindeer* had occurred, the *Wasp*'s lookouts sighted a convoy. Several factors assisted Blakeley in attacking the convoy. Thick, hazy weather masked his approach. Moreover, the convoy was scattered in three groups with the 74-gun *Armada* having taken a merchantman in tow; the *Strombolo*, bomb-vessel, having ten merchant vessels clustered about her; and eight or nine miles to the southeast, the merchant ship *Prince* having taken the merchant brig *Mary* in tow.[55]

The *Wasp* closed with the latter vessels, and Blakeley ordered the colors hoisted and a broadside fired into the *Prince*. In an act of self-preservation, her master ordered the towrope cut and made all sail to escape, while the *Wasp* "continued our fire upon the Ship as long as the guns would reach." The *Mary* surrendered. Blakeley found her laden with military stores from Gibraltar, and he received from her crew accurate information about the convoy.[56]

Captain Charles Grant of the *Armada* had heard the firing but ascribed it to the *Strombolo* policing wayward merchantmen. When the weather cleared he saw the *Mary* and a ship lying to. He mistook the *Wasp* for the *Prince*, but changed his opinion as the *Mary* began to burn. He immediately severed his own towrope and gave chase to the *Wasp*, but Blakeley escaped.[57]

Only a few hours after the *Armada* gave up her pursuit, the *Wasp*'s lookouts sighted in a space of fifteen minutes three sail to the leeward and a single sail to the windward. Given their position, they did not belong to the convoy. A quarter of an hour passed before Blakeley realized the sail to windward was a brig-of-war. He "called all hands to quarters and prepared for action."[58]

The *Wasp* had encountered the *Avon*. Under Commander James Arbuthnot, she had sailed from Cork on 13 August in company with another *Cruizer* class brig, the *Castilian*, commanded by Lieutenant George Lloyd, who had assumed temporary command of her the previous day. Arbuthnot and Lloyd had orders to seek out American commerce raiders. Until 1 September, their cruise had been uneventful, but that morning they chanced upon a British convoy escorted by the 18-gun *Kangaroo*.[59] The *Avon*'s lookouts sighted an American schooner privateer in the rear of the convoy, and Arbuthnot ordered chase. The privateer fled from the convoy so as to escape the *Avon* and *Castillian*. Moreover, the 20-gun *Tartarus* under Captain John Pasco joined the pursuit. The *Tartarus*, however, could not carry a full press of canvas owing to damaged masts, and she quickly fell behind the more nimble sloops.[60]

The chase continued through the day. The *Castilian* gained on the privateer, but the *Avon* could not keep up. About 4:00 p.m. the *Avon*'s lookouts discovered the *Wasp*. Arbuthnot prudently signaled the *Castilian*; however, "the weather being hazy, she did not see my recall, nor did they hear the report of the many Guns I fired." Arbuthnot then edged away from the *Wasp*, hoping to buy enough time so that the *Castilian* or even the *Tartarus* could join him.[61]

As the *Wasp* bore down on the *Avon*, Blakeley "hoisted an American jack at the fore, and pendant at the main." Darkness, however, prevented them from being distinguished. Around 9:00 p.m. the two ships came within hail, and a voice from the *Avon* demanded, "What ship is that?" Blakeley countered with "What brig is that?" The reply came, "His Majesty's brig . . . " but the remainder was drowned out by the sound of the wind. A voice from the *Avon* again hailed, demanding the identity of the *Wasp*. In response came an order telling the *Avon* "to heave to and he would be informed." The banter continued with neither commander willing to betray his warship's name. Finally, Blakeley sent a shot over the *Avon* to emphasize his point.[62] Arbuthnot responded with a broadside, and "the action then became general . . . , and within Pistol shot." The two ships battered each other at very close range, constantly maneuvering to rake the other or avoid being raked.[63]

When Blakeley sensed the incoming fire slacken and then stop, he ordered his "men to cease firing, and hailed the enemy to know if he had surrendered." In response, the *Avon*'s carronades belched their iron. Neither Arbuthnot nor his second lieutenant mentioned the surrender summons, though this was hardly surprising, given the din of the battle. Blakeley had his men resume fire, systematically pounding the *Avon* to splinters. As in her engagement with the *Reindeer*, the *Wasp* had a significant advantage in size, but this time Blakeley kept his distance. According to British reports, the action continued for about two hours after the *Avon* fired her first broadside, but Blakeley asserted it lasted approximately forty-five minutes. Regardless, the effects were the same. The *Wasp* wrecked the *Avon*. She was dismasted with six to seven feet of water in the hold. The magazine had flooded and five guns were dismounted. Estimating forty killed and wounded, Arbuthnot ordered the colors struck.[64]

To the southwest, the *Castilian* continued in pursuit of the privateer first sighted among the *Kangaroo*'s convoy that morning. While gaining on the privateer, Lloyd lost sight of the slower *Avon*. After it became dark, however, Lloyd "saw the flashes of Guns and heard a very heavy firing in the NNE."[65] He immediately gave up chasing the privateer and steered toward the guns under a full press of canvas, firing rockets and burning a blue light to signal his approach "as I considered the *Avon* to be engaged." The *Castilian* reached the *Avon* about a quarter hour after Arbuthnot surrendered. Lloyd trembled at the sight, writing, "I had the mortification to observe the *Avon* a totally dismasted and ungovernable wreck."[66]

On board the *Wasp*, lookouts saw the *Castilian* emerge from the darkness. Since the *Avon* was obviously shattered, Blakeley turned his attention on the interloper, but just before he issued orders to close with the *Castilian*, which he accurately described as a brig-of-war, Blakeley made out two other vessels with the *Castilian*.[67] Blakeley was deceived, however. The *Castilian* was alone, but Lieutenant Lloyd had acted audaciously, brashly closing and gaining the weather gauge. When a hundred yards separated his sloop from the *Wasp*, Lloyd opened fire. But "the *Avon's* situation became most alarming;—she commenced firing minute Guns and making every other signal of distress and of being in want of *immediate* assistance." Lloyd reluctantly ordered the *Castilian* to disengage with the *Wasp* and sail to the *Avon's* rescue. Five minutes after taking off her last man, she slipped under the sea. The Admiralty later agreed with Lloyd's decision, saying, "There could be no doubt that their first duty was to give their assistance" to the *Avon*.[68]

On board the *Wasp*, Blakeley correctly maintained that the *Castilian* "could have engaged us if he thought proper, . . . but . . . immediately returned to his companion."[69] Blakeley continued to believe, however, that two other vessels accompanied the *Castilian*, but another person on board the *Wasp* drew a different conclusion. He was the master of a previously captured British merchant vessel who asserted that the *Wasp* was "obliged to sheer off herself on account of another British ship heaving in sight." He made no mention of the *Castilian's* two ghostly consorts.[70] The best explanation involved Blakeley being spooked by Lloyd's audaciousness after a confused engagement in the dark. Indicative of the action's nature, Blakeley never ascertained the *Avon's* name, and at the time the *Castilian* appeared, he was uncertain of the actual damage his command had suffered. Blakeley's decision to flee was likely the prudent choice. Even if the *Castilian* was alone, fleeing allowed Blakeley to continue his mission.

When the British tried to make sense of the engagement, they also drew a spurious conclusion. Initially, they believed, "After the broadside from the *Castilian*, she [the *Wasp*] was observed water-logged, and was not afterwards seen." The First Lord of the Admiralty added, "I should hope from the account respecting the *Avon* & *Wasp*, that though the latter has not been captured, she is gone to the bottom." It took several weeks to debunk this wishful rumor.[71]

The *Wasp* had sustained only four round shot in the hull and lost two dead and one wounded, but she had suffered significantly aloft.[72] After making repairs at sea, the *Wasp* sailed south. Off Cape St. Vincent, Blakeley captured two British merchant vessels in mid-September and then shaped a course for Madeira, where on 21 September he captured the British merchant vessel *Atalanta*, richly laden with wine, brandy, and silks.[73] Blakeley questioned the ownership of her cargo and "did not feel authorized to destroy [the] vessel." Another factor differentiated her from previous captures: she was formerly the American schooner *Siro*. Rather than scuttle a vessel that had once been American property, Blakeley dispatched her to the United States under Midshipman Geisinger, who had distinguished himself as the first American to board the *Reindeer*.[74]

The *Atalanta* arrived in Savannah on 4 November, bringing with it the last official report from Blakeley as well as a letter from one of the *Wasp's* officers explaining that "ages average only 23 years—the greatest part so *green*, that is, so unaccustomed to the sea, that they were sea-sick for a week. In time however she has destroyed twelve British merchant vessels and their cargoes, . . . the thirteenth merchantman we are now dispatching for the United States. . . . Besides these merchant vessels, we have whipped two of his Britannic Majesty's sloops of war." Although boastfully worded, the contents of the letter were true, as was the final word—"Adieu."[75] The last confirmed sighting of the *Wasp* occurred on 9 October about three hundred miles northwest of the Cape Verde Islands.[76] The next spring, an American newspaper printed, "There is something in the mystery hanging over the fate of" the *Wasp*, for she had disappeared in the vastness of the Atlantic.[77]

⁓

Of all the small cruisers that Jones had sent out in 1814, only the *Peacock* under Master Commandant Lewis Warrington remained operational. After sailing from New York in early March, she captured the *Epervier* on 29 April before anchoring off Tybee Lighthouse outside Savannah, where Warrington disposed of his prize, collected provisions, and repaired his ship. After completing these duties around 20 May, he waited for new instructions from Secretary Jones, thinking the fall of Napoleon would necessitate changes to his orders. Ten days later nothing had arrived from Jones because no orders had been sent. From earlier correspondence, Jones thought that before any revised instructions reached Warrington, the *Peacock* would proceed to sea because of the exposed nature of the anchorage and the presence of British warships. The latter was certainly a concern, for the 56-gun *Majestic* and 18-gun *Morgiana* briefly appeared off Tybee on 10 May; ten days later these two warships returned accompanied by the 18-gun *Dotterel*, but the British noted nothing of the *Peacock*.[78] Fearing the British, Warrington sailed on 4 June without Jones' orders, and early the next morning his lookouts sighted two large sail. Assuming they were the British warships, Warrington edged away.[79] They could not have been the squadron previously seen off Tybee, however. That morning found the *Morgiana* and *Dotterel* near the border between North and South Carolina while the *Majestic* operated off Great Abaco in the Bahamas.[80]

Warrington snapped up his first prize in the mid-Atlantic followed by his second off the Azores. The *Peacock* then steered north, arriving off Ireland in late July. This was the same region where the *Wasp* had captured the *Reindeer* at the end of the previous month. Little did Warrington know the *Peacock*'s sister was nearby at Lorient completing repairs. After taking three prizes off the south coast of Ireland, Warrington shaped a course north, taking another three prizes off the west and northwestern coasts of Ireland between 1 and 3 August. This was the same area the *Adams* had trolled in early July. Passing north of Ireland, Warrington shaped a

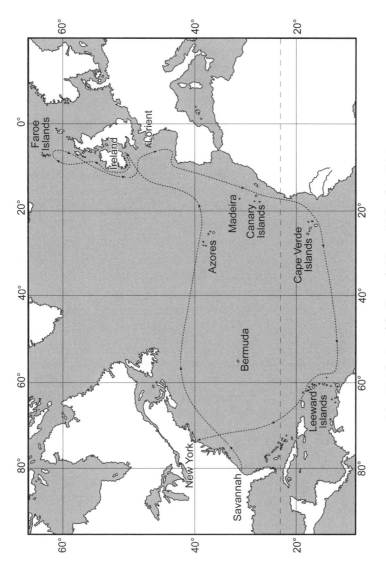

Faroe
Islands

Ireland

L'Orient

Azores

Madeira

Canary
Islands

Cape Verde
Islands

Bermuda

Leeward
Islands

New York

Savannah

Map 12.4 Cruise of the *Peacock*: 4 June–29 October 1814

course for the Orkney Islands, then the Faroe Islands. Finding nothing, he brought the *Peacock* south. Warrington blamed the lack of prizes on "uncommonly severe weather."[81]

Though the stormy weather limited Warrington's effectiveness, it also had obscured him from the prying eyes of the Royal Navy, meaning the *Peacock*'s movements attracted little direct attention. The 18-gun *Pelican* had cruised off Cape Clear, Ireland, between 28 July and 4 August in search of an American privateer; several days later she sailed north of Ireland for a patrol. Both cruises took the sloop near the *Peacock*; although the *Pelican* had captured the *Argus* a year before, her new opponent was much more formidable. On 13 August Vice Admiral Herbert Sawyer, now commanding at Cork, received a report indicating that an unknown frigate had been sighted in the same region. This was the *Peacock*, who after leaving the Faroe Islands had shaped a course back down the west coast of Ireland. Describing the *Peacock* as a frigate was a logical mistake. Like frigates, she had three masts and displaced far more than the average British sloop. As a result, Sawyer sent a 38-gun frigate in quest of her.[82] However, Warrington eluded Sawyer's net, captured a pair of prizes, and then pressed south across the Bay of Biscay toward the coast of Portugal where he made two more captures.[83]

The *Peacock* next headed for Madeira and then the Canaries. Though this was the track of the outward convoys to the West Indies and one sailed from Britain on 11 August, Warrington failed to encounter it.[84] By September procuring water had become more important than prizes, and Warrington watered in the Cape Verde Islands. He then shaped a course for home, crossing the Atlantic in the vain hope of falling in with a convoy. In early October Warrington made the northeastern coast of South America and sailed north through the Leeward Islands and then toward the United States. Since leaving the Portuguese coast, he had taken but two prizes.[85]

On 22 October Warrington gave chase to an unknown sail. He brought her to after an eighteen-hour pursuit, but she was an American privateer. Thinking the *Peacock* British, the commander of the privateer had his men throw two guns over the side and had sprung his vessel's mainmast in a futile effort to escape. Feeling guilty and also needing intelligence, Warrington worked out a trade. The *Peacock* provided spare stores in exchange for some newspapers. Using this information to help avoid the British blockade, Warrington slipped into New York harbor on 29 October.[86]

Warrington had taken fourteen prizes with an estimated value of nearly $500,000.[87] Merely returning to port without major damage put her in a category to herself, yet her cruise did not yield the strategic effects Jones had expected. All her prizes were running ships, meaning they were not attached to convoys. Moreover, with the exception of the British naval commander in Ireland dispatching a frigate to find the *Peacock*, the Royal Navy's leadership failed to send warships specifically after the *Peacock*. It was not that reports of her actions did not reach the British: rather, it was the timing of the reports. The 36-gun British frigate *Ethalion* fell in with a Russian merchant ship on 26 August and from her crew learned that she had encountered the *Peacock* off Cape Finisterre three days before. This news, however, only reached the Admiralty on 9 September.[88] By then it was completely out of date, and there was nothing to do but hope British naval patrols swept up the *Peacock*. The time lag grew worse as Warrington operated farther from London. Two reports that she had been seen in September off the Canaries reached the Admiralty about the time the *Peacock* anchored at New York.[89]

Warrington had incurred considerable costs on British trade, but he had not directly disrupted their flow of commerce. Moreover, in his June to October cruise Warrington had failed to inflict damage such as he visited earlier in the year against the *Epervier* or Blakeley obtained in his actions with the *Reindeer* and *Avon*. The *Peacock* had in fact mimicked a privateer, but privateers merely reinforced the continued need for British naval deployments—they did not solicit any specific costly British naval reaction. In June 1814 the British Admiralty had reassessed, concluding that if frigates could "cruise singly attaching a good brig to each of them, perhaps they would cover more ground & as from all accounts the American frigates are laid up there is no chance of them meeting a superior force."[90] By relying on small warships during the spring and summer of 1814, Jones had at least temporarily removed one of America's greatest naval advantages—its heavy frigates.

Though several factors beyond Secretary Jones' control forced him to rely on smaller warships in 1814, there were in fact other flaws in his strategy. For it to be successful, American warships had to hunt in such a way as to force the British to react. This could occur by defeating a British warship or savaging a convoy or commerce at a specific point. Such actions, however, increased the risk to American warships, but Jones' strategy aimed at minimizing risk. Other defects in Jones' strategy related to poor resource allocation. The *Erie*, *Ontario*, and *Argus*, all new large sloops like the *Peacock* and *Wasp*, could not reach open sea owing to a combination of manning and procurement issues coupled with the British blockade. In addition, Jones could not use the frigates trapped at Portsmouth, New London, and Norfolk. Finally, the inability to make the newly built ships of the line and frigates operational in a timely manner meant that only a minority of the United States Navy confronted the Royal Navy in 1814.

CHAPTER 13

"The Current Demands of the Service"

An Appraisal of British Naval Operations,
1813–14

B y late 1814 the British navy had minimized the damage the United States
Navy could inflict at sea. Still, this had taken longer than expected and
continued to cost more than anticipated. In part, this was a result of
how Britain assessed competing threats. Until the spring of 1814, the war against
Napoleon raged. Though the 1812 Russian and the 1813 German campaigns had
weakened France, Napoleon continued to be a legitimate threat, necessitating large
British naval deployments to the Mediterranean, Baltic, and North Seas, as well as
the Bay of Biscay. These European deployments far outnumbered the warships off
North America and in the West Indies.[1] Britain faced an existential threat in France,
and the Americans had taken advantage of Britain's divided attention and then the
Americans had stretched British deployments on a near-global scale. As a rule, vessels smaller than a frigate were sufficient to combat American privateers, but the
United States Navy fielded a small but well-designed and well-manned group of
warships. Operations by a few American men-of-war forced the British to expend
disproportionate resources by deploying frigates and even ships of the line, often
in squadron strength, to areas where smaller vessels would normally have sufficed.

A comparison of the British and American navies provides a stark contrast. The
United States Navy at best sent ten warships simultaneously to sea, and that
occurred only briefly, in 1812. Constructing new men-of-war took longer than

expected, and fitting and manning them took months. In comparison to the American navy, the Royal Navy in mid-1812 deployed slightly more than five hundred warships in operational commands.[2] Managing such a force required a complex infrastructure including administrators, dockyard personnel, and suppliers capable of functioning on a near-global basis.[3] Even with effective management, however, various sources of friction limited British naval effectiveness.

Manpower topped this list. Britain's long wars of the eighteenth century had continually highlighted the role of attrition among its skilled seamen, and the War of 1812 came at the end of the longest such conflict. In September 1813 Melville wrote, "Not less than 6 sail of the line and 16 frigates with a great number of sloops and smaller vessels are at this moment ready to receive men, and are lying useless because men cannot be supplied to them." Bleakly, Melville lamented, "The supply of seamen is so inadequate to the current demands of the service."[4] The termination of the war with France in April 1814 did little to reduce manning troubles. This might appear chimerical, but in an effort to ease discontent, seamen who had served continuously since 1 January 1804 were discharged from the service.[5] This led one British naval officer to chide the Admiralty for having "turned adrift all our old men-of-war's men, of eleven years standing." He cited the effect on the British brig *Reindeer* at the time the *Wasp* defeated her: "This policy deprived us of nine of our best men, all petty officers, and well affected to the service."[6] The result of the discharge policy for seamen led Melville to caution Cochrane in August 1814 that the navy had "very scanty means to supply any considerable demand."[7]

Moreover, the Royal Navy devoured men. For example, between March 1812 and January 1814 the 38-gun *Junon*, while operating principally off the North American coast, lost nearly one hundred men out of an established complement of 315. Only five died in action and one was invalided for wounds sustained in combat. Sixty-two were discharged or died "principally arising from infirmity alone." Another twenty-nine deserted. Replacements arrived slowly, and the *Junon*'s commander asserted being thirty-five short of full strength in January 1814, with three more at a hospital and not expected to return to duty, as well as five on light duty "who are only fit subjects to be invalided."[8] This had both an operational and a psychological impact on the British navy. A lieutenant on board the 38-gun *Nymphe* learned that the complement of the American frigate *Congress* approached four hundred men. He correctly asserted, "The *Congress* and *Nymphe* are nearly of a size, but the allowed establishment of the *Nymphe* is 315 souls, of which she has 300 (on paper only) . . . yet the Admiralty appear not to take the slightest trouble to man those frigates opposed to so superior a force . . . people perhaps may cease to wonder at Americans having captured so many of our ships."[9] In November 1814 Rear Admiral Hotham echoed the above concern: "Our ships are very much in want of men; & are not manned equal to those of the enemy."[10] More effective manning, however, meant fewer ships on station, creating a difficult trade-off for the British; both the Admiralty and their commanders in chief grudgingly chose more ships over better manning. This allowed for greater presence but resulted in British warships operating at a disadvantage. Only in late 1814, with the Napoleonic Wars at an end and with American ships of the line about to become operational, did the Admiralty advocate laying ships up so as to use their crews to bring Britain's larger warships up to proper manpower levels.[11]

Though manning proved problematic, the Royal Navy by the War of 1812 possessed approximately half the world's warship tonnage.[12] This was both unprecedented and misleading: Just because a country had warships did not mean that the warships could be deployed or were of the most effective type for their assigned missions. In some respects Britain's warships were an embarrassment of riches. First, the Royal Navy lacked enough manpower to make all its warships operational; however, extra ships and transferring personnel between ships allowed some warships to undergo repairs without further impairing the size of the navy. Second, the War of 1812 found Britain without the most effective navy to confront the United States. For twenty years, British naval leadership had procured a navy to fight France, but the geography of the war and the size and employment of American warships demanded a different set of ships. One reason for British naval problems during the war's first year dealt with making do with the navy they possessed rather than the one needed.

The ship of the line served as the centerpiece of the navies of France, Spain, and several other European states.[13] To defeat or minimize the threat posed by navies built around ships of the line required Britain to maintain its own fleet of such warships, either to fight a Trafalgar-like battle or to blockade its opponent's ships of the line in naval bases like Toulon. When the Napoleonic Wars came to an end, a tremendous reconfiguration of the Royal Navy occurred. The number of British ships of the line in deployed commands declined precipitously. More especially, first and second rates (ships with ninety or more guns) disappeared from active service because they were manpower intensive and extraordinarily expensive to operate. Though third rates (principally 74-gun ships) had a purpose in the War of 1812 serving as command ships, supporting amphibious operations, or acting as the centerpiece of squadrons detailed to escort large convoys or to blockade the northern ports in the United States, the end of the war against France allowed Britain to reduce the number of deployed third rates by 60 percent.

Whereas the ship of the line served as the key instrument of war against France, frigates were crucial to the naval war against the United States by serving as the most effective platforms for hunting American warships, blockading American ports, and protecting convoys, given their ratio of endurance and firepower to economies of manning as well as procurement and operating cost. The frigate, however, served as a perfect example of Britain having to fight with the available navy instead of the one needed. In 1812 the standard British frigate was rated for either thirty-six or thirty-eight guns. Only one month prior to the outbreak of hostilities with the United States, British naval leaders decided to augment their aging frigate force by ordering six 36-gun frigates. Before the end of 1812, the order had been increased to 10 x 36-gun and 8 x 38-gun frigates.[14]

The loss of the 38-gun frigates *Guerriere* and *Macedonian* showed that standard British frigates were too small to defeat the largest class of American frigates even though numerous ships of this size were then under construction. Frigate losses led to cries "that ships capable of carrying heavier metal, be ordered immediately to be built, with every possible expedition."[15] The Admiralty responded by ordering five 40-gun frigates between December 1812 and January 1813.[16] The loss of the 38-gun *Java* contributed to the decision to order two very large frigates, eventually named the *Leander* and *Newcastle*, "of the same class & size as the large American Frigates."[17] Melville, however, refused to build more: "I am unwilling at present to introduce a new & cumbersome description of Ships into our Navy to any considerable extent, merely because the Americans have three of them; we may more easily supply Line of Battle Ships."[18] Moreover, the Admiralty on 10 July 1813 directed its frigate commanders to avoid single combat with the large American frigates, and it became common practice for 36- and 38-gun frigates to operate in pairs. Although the number of frigates fell from 101 in mid-1813 to 81 in late 1814, the average size of the remaining frigates became larger with the smallest frigates (those of thirty-two guns) declining from eighteen in deployed commands to four.[19]

The British naval establishment found vessels smaller than a frigate both essential and effective. The lack of seamen made smaller vessels a necessity: the manpower needed for one 38-gun frigate could provide for two and a half *Cruizer* class brigs. Moreover, small vessels were less expensive than frigates. Manpower and financial costs spurred the Admiralty to deploy this type of vessel in great numbers to support Britain's geographically extensive commitments. In addition, the widespread use of the carronade enhanced the lethality of small vessels by increasing the weight of metal the vessels could throw in a broadside.

During the War of 1812, three factors defined British decision-making regarding smaller warships. First, they became larger as a rule, with Britain ordering twenty-eight sixth rates (or those rated from twenty to twenty-eight guns). This increased the number in deployed commands by approximately 20 percent between mid-1813 and late 1814.[20] Broadly similar in size to U.S. warships such as the *Peacock* and *Frolic*, the procurement of these ships was at least in part an attempt to negate the size advantage of America's large sloops.[21] The second factor defining British decision-making involved gun brigs designed for work in the littorals. Ever-present around the British Isles, in the North Sea, and in the Baltic, such

Table 13.1. Deployed Ships of the Royal Navy, July 1812, July 1813, December 1814

	First & Second Rates	Third Rates	Razees	50-gun Two-Decked Ships	50-gun Frigates	44-gun Two-Decked Ships	40-gun Frigates	38-gun Frigates	36-gun Frigates	32-gun Frigates	Sixth Rates	Sloops	Gun Brigs	Bombs	Cutters	Schooner	Totals
Jul 1812	13	84	0	2	0	2	3	41	39	18	32	171	62	5	9	34	515
Jul 1813	12	79	1	2	0	2	4	37	37	15	33	170	61	8	15	28	504
Dec 1814	0	31	2	1	2	2	7	36	32	4	40	129	29	5	5	24	349

Source: Ships in Sea Pay, 1 Jul 1812, 1813, ADM 8/100; Admiralty Board Minutes, Late 1814, ADM 7/266.

Note: These figures do not include ships of the Lakes, unappropriated warships (that often lacked full complements), or certain types of ships such as troopships, receiving ships, guard ships, and prison ships.

vessels were of limited use in the War of 1812 due to their small operating radius. A few were employed in the defense of the maritime regions of Canada, the Bay of Fundy and the coast of Maine, but the loss of the *Boxer* showcased their vulnerability. It should not be surprising, therefore, that the end of the Napoleonic Wars saw the Admiralty decrease the number of gun brigs in commission by one-half (see Table 13.1).[22] The third factor relating to smaller warships and the War of 1812 were their overall numbers. Between mid-1813 and late 1814, warships smaller than sixth rates had declined by about one-third. This was a greater decline than frigates, but much less a reduction than line of battle ships.

Even sanguine decisions relating to manpower and procurement meant little if British naval leadership deployed their warships ineffectively. This was undoubtedly the toughest part of the balancing act, particularly as long as Britain had to fight both France and the United States. One year into the War of 1812, Melville wrote, "The naval means of this country great as they are have great and extended claims upon them." This necessitated Melville's admonition: "I must scramble on as well as I can with the means in my power." One admiral added, "The Admiralty with all their exertions can scarcely find ships for the numberless duties which require them." Fighting both Napoleonic France and the United States unbalanced British naval deployments and resulted in the juggling of warships. Fighting two wars simultaneously proved difficult for fleet commanders, leading one to complain, "This perpetual changing of ships gives me a great deal of trouble and makes my service very unsatisfactory. I never know who I am to have with me; and what I arrange one day I am obliged to alter the next."[23]

The fluidity in deployments served as the symptom to an underlying issue: the character of Britain's naval war changed in 1812. Many contemporary observers, particularly in the press, failed to draw this conclusion. Even the Admiralty was slow to grasp the difference. In December 1812 Melville explained his assessment of the script Britain had used to minimize the threat posed by the French navy in the Revolutionary and Napoleonic Wars. He rationalized that the British navy had made the sailing of French warships such "a hazardous enterprize" that French ships of the line and frigates hardly ever attempted to sail "& that their exertions by Sea are chiefly confined to small privateers in the Channel."[24] Melville then tried to apply this script to the United States, but he failed to account for differences in geography, winds, currents, and the nature of the naval threat. It took at least through the first year of the War of 1812 for the British to realize that the United States was a distinct enemy and the script used against Napoleonic France did not necessarily apply.

The Americans lacked a fleet of line of battle ships. With the exception of Rodgers' cruise during the first months of the war, there was never a large American squadron at sea with the wherewithal to fight a squadron-sized engagement. Particularly after Jones became secretary of the navy, the United States Navy conducted privateering-type cruises with warships. American leadership did not decide it would be too expensive, too dangerous, counterproductive, or impossible to contest the sea; instead, the Americans set different victory conditions. They could not defeat the entire British navy, but they could make the war costly for Britain by forcing expensive deployments in anticipation of expected threats and in reaction to developing threats.

One way for the Americans to make the war costly involved creating size advantages over the most numerous classes of British frigates and sloops. The larger size of America's warships contributed to a series of ship-on-ship victories. Though losses were small in comparison to the number of warships in the British navy, both its leadership and population recoiled against naval defeats unknown for more than a generation. Three times, British 38-gun frigates lost against their distant American cousins, and *Cruizer*-class brigs posted the eventual record of one victory in seven engagements.[25] A Royal Navy officer explained that warship procurement decisions led the British to "risk our national reputation, and undermine the prestige of our power at sea, by risking a collision with the larger vessels of a like rate of other nations." Particularly, the above officer thought British brigs "would be but a morsel for any of brother Jonathan's brig sloops." Brother Jonathan, a slang term for the Americans, generally had larger warships, and this proved particularly important since the side with the larger warship and the heavier broadside won in nearly every battle during the war.[26]

America's new ships of the line, expected to become operational in 1815, posed a similar problem, leading the Admiralty to dispatch a circular letter in November 1814 explaining that "the account their Lordships have received of the size and armament of the American Line of Battle Ships, which you will perceive, render them equal in force to three-deckers [second rates], although the Enemy is reported to have assigned to them only the nominal rating of 74 gun ships." As a result, the circular went on, "it is not expected . . . that a seventy four of the British class should attempt to engage single-handed a ship of such very superior force as those of the Enemy."[27] This circular constrained the utility of British 74-gun ships to operate alone, and resembled the circular of 10 July 1813 that directed British frigate captains not to seek single combat with America's large frigates. In addition, the Admiralty directed the commissioning of the *Boyne*, a 98-gun second rate, and ordered that large warships operating off North America be better manned, even at the expense of laying up ships so as to obtain personnel to redistribute among the remaining warships.[28] These were costly decisions that limited the amount of water existing warships could patrol and necessitated the deployment of more warships.

A second way for the Americans to make the naval war more costly for Britain involved stretching the battle-space by capturing English merchant ships. Trade was vulnerable, and Melville wrote, "It is nonsense to talk of complete security in any other mode than by convoys."[29] A September 1814 report from Lloyd's, the maritime insurer, added, "Adequate security to our commerce can only be found in keeping it under convoy."[30] At least with the West India convoys, the merchant ships Britain lost were those that had separated from their convoys. The Admiralty also understood that "if any particular portion of the seas were to be exempted from the operation of the Convoy Act, the only consequence would be, that the Americans would flock thither."[31] The report from Lloyd's voiced particular concern about the area of sea from the Canary Islands to the British Isles, citing 172 captures in this area between 3 May and 16 September 1814, of which the "most numerous class of Vessels captured, is those that sail without convoy altogether." Lloyd's called for "preventative measures," particularly on routes from the Azores, Madeira, or Spain to England to stop "the injurious effects of the numerous captures lately made." The same document cited insurance premiums for British ships without convoy as anywhere from three to ten times the premiums for neutrals on the same voyage.[32] Though insurance costs for certain routes at certain times could be prohibitively expensive, high insurance costs were not pervasive and merchants paid lower insurance rates for ships under convoy. This created an incentive to sail in convoy and led the Admiralty to increase the number of convoys and limit licenses allowing ships to sail alone.[33]

Although convoys could potentially act like a magnet, forcing the Americans to make risky attacks on well-protected merchant ships, the American naval officers generally pressed their attacks home only when the weather proved favorable or the convoy escorts were poorly deployed. Instead, the Americans focused on ships sailing without convoy and merchant vessels that had separated from convoys. On the one hand, when U.S. warships did encounter properly escorted convoys on the high sea, as was the case with the *Adams* in May 1814, the Americans failed to penetrate the escort screen. On the other hand, the British could not pursue fleeing American warships lest they abandon the convoys they were charged to protect. Thus, convoys did little to eliminate the threat posed by America's commerce raiding, and merely minimized the damage commerce raiders could inflict.

Convoys, however, did limit naval demobilization by requiring large numbers of escorts. For the West Indies service alone, the Admiralty estimated an escort requirement of ten ships of the line, ten frigates, and twenty to thirty sloops so that each convoy had a line of battle ship, a frigate, and at least two sloops in attendance. Secretary Croker explained, "Each convoy therefore equaled in force the

Table 13.2. British Deployments in Late 1814

	Totals	First and Second Rates	Third Rates	Razees	50-gun Two-Decked Ship	50-gun Frigates	44-gun 2-Decked Ships	40-gun Frigates	38-gun Frigates	36-gun Frigates	32-gun Frigates	Sixth Rates	Sloops	Gun Brigs	Bombs	Cutters	Schooner
Gibraltar	18	0	1	0	0	0	0	0	2	3	1	4	7	0	0	0	0
Leith	14	0	0	0	0	0	0	0	0	1	0	3	7	3	0	0	0
Nore	11	0	1	0	0	0	0	0	0	0	0	0	4	4	0	1	1
Portsmouth	10	0	0	0	0	0	0	0	0	0	0	0	7	0	0	2	1
Plymouth	30	0	0	0	0	0	0	1	2	3	1	4	10	4	0	2	3
Cork	24	0	0	0	0	0	0	0	2	2	0	5	12	3	0	0	0
Mediterranean	13	4	0	0	0	0	0	1	2	0	0	0	5	0	0	0	1
North America	106	1	11	2	0	2	0	4	15	6	2	6	27	12	5	0	13
Newfoundland	12	0	1	0	0	0	0	0	1	2	0	3	4	0	0	0	1
East Indies	18	0	1	0	0	0	0	0	3	6	0	3	5	0	0	0	0
Leeward Islands	29	0	3	0	0	0	0	0	2	4	0	0	16	2	0	0	2

Jamaica	25	0	3	0	0	0	0	0	4	0	3	13	1	0	0	1
Convoy	4	0	0	1	0	0	0	0	0	0	1	2	0	0	0	0
Cruising	8	0	0	0	0	1	0	1	0	0	4	2	0	0	0	0
Africa	3	0	0	0	0	1	0	0	0	0	1	1	0	0	0	0
Misc. Duties	7	0	2	0	0	0	0	0	0	0	1	3	0	0	0	1
Cape of Good Hope	8	0	2	0	0	0	0	1	2	0	1	2	0	0	0	0
South America	9	0	1	0	0	0	1	3	1	0	1	2	0	0	0	0
Totals	349	5	26	1	2	2	7	32	36	4	40	129	29	5	5	24

Source: Admiralty Board Minutes, late 1814, ADM 7/266.

whole American navy; the consequence of which was, that not a single merchant-ship had been taken which sailed under convoy, and that no convoy had been at all disturbed, except by weather."[34] To protect the sea-lanes from the British Isles stretching south, the Admiralty in late 1814 maintained stations at Gibraltar, Cork in Ireland, and Plymouth. Together, these stations contained one ship of the line, seventeen frigates, thirteen sixth rates, twenty-nine sloops, and twelve smaller ves-sels (see Table 13.2). This list does not include twenty-one additional vessels of war in the English Channel and fourteen off Scotland and waters to the north. The strength of the commands surrounding Britain and Ireland accounted for roughly 30 percent of the entire Royal Navy.[35] The high concentration of warships around Britain and Ireland highlighted both the level of traffic and the vulnerability of British commerce in home waters. The cruise of the American brig *Argus* in 1813 demonstrated what could be done even against convoys as they fragmented near their arrival ports in the British Isles. In the end, one member of the Admiralty wrote, "I think we have taken every step for the protection of both the outward & homeward bound trade that we possibly can, but as to having ships on every point where an enemy may go in the present extensive state of our trade it is totally impossible and all we can do is to make the best distribution we can, trusting that we shall be more fortunate than we have hitherto been in falling in with them [U.S. warships]."[36]

There were certainly limits to what the British could do, given the size of their navy. One way to reduce costs involved suspending convoys after the fall of Napoleon. Given the reach of American warships and privateers, the Admiralty only thought it prudent to suspend convoys in the Mediterranean and the Baltic, but merchants trading in the latter region demanded the continuance of convoys in order to reduce insurance premiums.[37]

The cost of the War of 1812 increased significantly for Britain owing to the inter-active effect of victories by the United States Navy in single-ship encounters and the vulnerability of merchant British commerce. Whereas strongly escorted convoys protected merchant ships and large deployments largely insulated British warships from single-ship losses, neither convoys nor larger deployments cured the source of the problem. The Admiralty, however, thought that deployments on the American coast coupled with declared blockades would create the conditions for the elim-ination of America's naval war fighting capability. Such assertions were made in late 1812 and particularly in 1813, but tremendous tension developed between Admiral Warren and the Admiralty over the implementation of the plan. The crux of the issue was, in Warren's opinion, an inadequate number of warships, but the Admiralty wanted greater results with limited means. In reality, the Admiralty did not have enough warships to obtain the objectives desired of Warren's command.[38] This changed in 1814 with the defeat of Napoleonic France. Reinforcements became

Table 13.3. Strength of the North American Station (excluding Jamaica and Leeward Islands)

	Total ships	80-gun ships	74-gun ships	64-gun ships	Razees	50-gun frigates	40-gun frigates	38-gun frigates	36-gun frigates	32-gun frigates	Sixth rates	Sloops	Smaller vessels	Troop ships
Mid-1812	23	0	0	1	0	0	0	3	1	1	1	10	6	0
Early 1813	40	0	6	0	0	0	1	5	2	4	3	15	4	0
Mid-1813	57	0	10	0	1	0	2	7	3	4	2	18	10	0
Late 1813	72	0	11	0	1	0	4	10	2	2	0	31	9	2
Mid-1814	101	1	11	0	3	2	5	15	6	1	5	28	16	8
Late 1814	120	1	11	0	2	2	4	15	6	2	6	27	30	14

Source: Ships in Sea Pay, 1 July 1812, 1 January 1813, 1 July 1813, ADM 8/100; Admiralty Board Minutes, late 1813, early 1814, late 1814, ADM 7/264, 265, 266.

available, allowing Cochrane to better interdict American and neutral commerce that was attempting to use ports in the United States.[39] This had significant effects, given the importance of customs duties as a source of American revenue. Blockades also restricted the safe arrival of prizes and made the sailing of warships and privateers more difficult.

The British slowly came to the conclusion that the size of the U.S. coastline and weather conditions precluded a total blockade. In May 1814 Secretary Croker opined, "During half the year, it was impossible to blockade the American ports; and during the other half, the blockade was necessarily very imperfect."[40] This led Cochrane to implement the blockade in a different manner from Warren. First, he extended the blockade to include the entire coast. Though he continued Warren's practice of keeping powerful squadrons with ships of the line, razees, and frigates off ports frequented by American warships and privateers, he more effectively centralized leadership off major ports that had the infrastructure to sustain large American warships.[41] Moreover, Cochrane received significant reinforcements allowing for a more robust littoral war fighting capability than Warren possessed (Table 13.3). This led to the deployment of small vessels to intercept American coastal trade and larger forces for amphibious raids. Overall, the Admiralty concluded, "If this Blockade should be thus executed the Coast would be kept in a continual state of alarm—and the Distress it would occasion would be inconceivably great."[42]

Escorting convoys and maintaining extensive global deployments with a particular emphasis on powerful squadrons off the U.S. coast were the costs paid by Britain as the dominant maritime state during the War of 1812. It took time, however, for the Royal Navy to effectively apply convoys and blockades to account for the unique character of the American war, and eventually British deployments became one factor that prevented the United States Navy from reaping the rewards from single-ship victories on the scale similar to the war's first six months. Though the British continued to lose merchant vessels, well-escorted convoys minimized the losses in most areas. Such deployments, however, proved expensive. The Admiralty deployed approximately five hundred warships on active assignments during the last two years of Napoleon's First Empire. The fall of Napoleon in the spring of 1814 should have resulted in a major drawdown of British naval forces, but in the last nine months of 1814 the strength of the Royal Navy fell by only 30 percent (see Table 13.1). By late 1814 British deployments totaled approximately 350 warships. To be sure, the British maintained squadrons in places that had little or nothing to do with the War of 1812 such as the Mediterranean, but operations relating to the war against the United States easily accounted for more than half of its 350 deployed warships.

"A Wreath of Laurels . . . a Crown of Thorns"

The Last Naval Campaign, 1815

William Jones had created conditions to make the naval war costly for Britain, but he rightly concluded in late 1814, "Though all is well and my reputation high I feel as if I was standing upon Gun Powder with a slow match near it."[1] Jones understood that his strategy could only delay American naval defeat, given the lack of financial resources to extend the fight indefinitely. Even if funds were available, the strength of the Royal Navy worked to slowly attrite American naval power. The second key reason that Jones believed he was on a keg of gunpowder dealt with personal financial ruin. Between 1808 and 1812 he had suffered significant losses due to trade restrictions and the ongoing European war.[2] In April 1814 Jones had warned President Madison of his impending decision to resign. He felt it was not proper "to serve her [the United States] under the irresistible embarrassments of my private affairs." However, he asserted, "I shall endeavour to remain at my post if possible until the next meeting of Congress unless it shall accord with your convenience and views sooner to appoint a Successor." In September Jones set 1 December as the last date possible for his resignation.[3] Jones explained to his wife that after this date, "I shall be free." In the meantime, "the ensuing two months will be the largest and most irksome of my life."[4]

"The fact is," Jones related, "that I am wholly absorbed in the pressing duties which the very short time I have to remain will scarcely permit me to execute." First, he worked to reorganize the Navy Department. Second, he provided detailed instructions to his naval officers for operations in 1815. Finally, he provided "a long and laborious communication to the President on the subject of our prospects in the ensuing campaign." This document focused on the problems in creating an adequate naval force on Lake Ontario, but the underlying theme developed his more general thoughts on naval strategy and operational planning. He believed that the document was well received by the president and asserted that Madison called it "in the highest degree able and interesting that many of the views were to him entirely new . . . and commuted some erroneous impressions he had entertained."[5]

To Jones, funding and manning were the United States Navy's critical vulnerabilities: "With respect to money the Department is truly in the most untoward situation. . . . I am destitute of money in all quarters. Seamen remain unpaid and the recruiting service is at a stand. I have none for the most urgent contingent purposes." The ability to conduct maritime operations, which were incredibly expensive, would be limited during the foreseeable future unless the United States obtained more tax revenue or reasonable creditworthiness. In relation to manning, Jones went on, "It is remarkable that we invariably look to our capacity to build ships and vessels and lose sight of our resources in volunteer seamen and our means of procuring them." As long as the United States Navy relied on volunteers, Jones asserted that the navy had a manpower ceiling of twelve thousand men, but he found this number too few to contest the Lakes, defend the oceanic coasts, and conduct the war at sea. Coastal defense took the most men. Given the extensive nature of the seaboard, any number of seamen would be too little; however, appeals from various interest groups forced him to assign a large proportion of the navy to such duties. In addition, Jones explained, "The difference between the Lake and Sea service is that in the former we are compelled to fight them at least man to man and gun to gun whilst on the Ocean five British frigates cannot counteract the depredations of one Sloop of War." Even so, Jones had to dismantle warships assigned to oceanic operations to send their crews to the Lakes. In his opinion this was not the best use of manpower, but he found it necessary to confront British warships under construction on the Lakes. Though Jones hoped for twelve thousand men, the navy was then about 1,400 short of that target. He argued, "With this distribution of force out of an aggregate of 10617. Officers [*sic*] and men we have 450 on the Ocean!—3250—on the Lakes—and 6512. [*sic*] employed in harbour defence." But these numbers were misleading. The harbor defense numbers included the crews of the *Constitution, Constellation, Guerriere, President,* and *Hornet.* These ships were ready or nearly ready to sail.[6]

The first move required the *Hornet,* under Master Commandant Biddle, to slip out of New London, sail up Long Island Sound, and make New York. Biddle hoped that the season of "blustering weather which will favour our eluding the Enemy in this vicinity, is approaching." Jones agreed but advised Biddle to be careful and stealthy. On the night of 18 November, Biddle got the *Hornet* out of New London under threatening skies. The British blockade squadron had other things to worry about and did not notice as the *Hornet* slipped through its grasp. Then, Biddle coasted up Long Island Sound toward New York, where she joined the *President* and the recently arrived *Peacock*.[7]

Even though Jones knew his last day in office would be 1 December, he issued detailed instructions for cruises that would occur after his departure. Most had a dreamlike quality, given the financial and manpower status of the navy, but the directives to Commodore Decatur and Captain Stewart came to fruition. After much thought and ink, Decatur received orders to take the *President*, now under his personal command, as well as the *Peacock, Hornet,* and two fast sailing store ships filled with provisions, and sail to the Indian Ocean. Jones hoped that "a great blow might have been, and still in all probability, may be struck, by the Capture of the whole China fleet." This referred to the deeply laden merchant vessels that conducted British trade in that region. Jones provided Stewart, commanding the *Constitution*, with cruising instructions to operate in the track of Britain's East and West India convoys. Jones believed that the "grievous complaints of the merchants of Great Britain sufficiently attest the efficacy of the system."[8]

In early November the outgoing secretary wrote to his wife, telling her that he spoke with Madison "of several persons as my successor but no one is yet Solicited, and he will have great difficulty." He jested, "Much joy to my successor whoever he may be—I hope he may acquire honor for himself and fame for his country but instead of a wreath of laurels he has a much greater chance of acquiring a crown of thorns."[9] On 24 November Madison offered the position to Commodore Rodgers. Rodgers grudgingly agreed, with several conditions, including that it must be of a short duration and "I must beg leave to stipulate [that it] is not to be done at the expence of interfering with rank or further pretentions as an officer of the Navy." Madison could not accept the last condition and instead appointed Benjamin W. Crowninshield of Salem, Massachusetts.[10] In mid-1814 one British officer wrote, "The Crowninshields indeed have made money by privateering, but they also have now lost their vessels. They are violent Democrats, although the Federalist party have the majority in the town."[11] The new secretary, however, did not take his post for six weeks, leaving the navy to function during the last stage of the war under the directions Jones had provided prior to his resignation.

For the British navy, the continuance of the blockade and expansive operations in the American south marked the last months of the war. Even before the declaration of war in 1812, Admiral Cochrane had described New Orleans as a critical vulnerability of the United States. His first action in command of the North American

Station involved sending the *Orpheus* and *Shelbourne* to the Gulf Coast of Florida to make contacts with the Native Americans. Moreover, Cochrane had the support of the Admiralty; significant discussion occurred in mid-1814 about the practicality and timing of an attack on New Orleans.[12] In reference to this operation, Melville, the First Lord of the Admiralty, wrote to Cochrane, "The arrangements you mention for your further operations appear to be perfectly proper."[13] By November Cochrane had arrived in the West Indies, temporarily assuming command in the region as he attempted to route ships and soldiers from the British Isles, the West Indies, and the eastern coast of the United States toward New Orleans.[14] Cochrane explained to Melville that the attack on New Orleans would draw American soldiers, particularly those from the Western States, away from Canada. Then, he wished to reinforce Admiral Cockburn, who had orders to attack the coast of Georgia. By the combination of attacking Georgia and New Orleans, Cochrane believed that Madison "will find himself awkwardly situated."[15]

Although amphibious operations focused on the southern United States during the winter of 1814–15, British blockade squadrons prepared to face grueling winter storms off America's northern ports. The Admiralty provided specific instructions if ships of the United States Navy sailed. First, each blockade squadron was to be strong enough "as may ensure your being able to meet the enemy upon equal terms."[16] Compared with previous years, the Admiralty admitted that the British blockade would not be entirely effective, and some American warships would elude the blockade. As a result, the Admiralty provided pursuit instructions: "In all events of the Enemy's escape, whether the senior officer shall have any information as to their destination or not, he is to use every possible exertion to communicate as widely and publikly as he can the fact of the Enemy being at Sea."[17]

In Boston, Captain Stewart had the *Constitution* ready for sea. Since arriving from her previous cruise on 4 April 1814, the months had proved difficult for Stewart. First, he had to answer questions about returning early. Jones demanded a court of inquiry. Though the verdict was less than damning and Stewart remained in command, the inquiry had raised questions about his ability. Subsequently, the summer months had witnessed an increasingly vigilant British blockade, and only with the onset of the tempestuous winter weather did the *Constitution* have a chance to sail.

On 12 December Lord George Stuart, commander of the British squadron off Boston, obtained reliable intelligence detailing the imminent departure of the *Constitution*. In order to avoid being blown off the coast by a storm, Stuart's ship, the 50-gun *Newcastle*, anchored in Cape Cod Bay and was soon joined by the 44-gun *Acasta* and 18-gun *Arab*. Though a gale kept Stuart's ships in the bay, he received news from ashore that the *Constitution* had sailed on 17 December. Not until 22 December did the weather moderate enough to dispatch the *Arab* to confirm the report. About the same time Stuart received information that the *Congress* had sailed from Portsmouth, New Hampshire, and had joined with the *Constitution*. "Since that the *Congress* was ready for Sea," Stuart deduced, "I have every reason to suppose this Intelligence is correct." Added to this, he also learned from people ashore that the *President* was out, and "knowing for a *certainty*" that the *Hornet* had sailed from New London, Stuart believed "the Enemy would concentrate their force."[18]

Before Stuart could decide on a course of action, the 50-gun *Leander* under Captain Sir George Collier fell in with the *Newcastle*. Since Collier was senior to Stuart and had orders to assume command of the blockade squadron, the decision on how to confront the Americans now rested with him. Collier's orders stated, "In the event of *the Constitution* escaping to Sea *two* Frigates should proceed . . . in quest of her."[19] Collier believed, however, he needed three frigates to have a chance against the *Constitution* as well as the *Congress*, and possibly against the *President* and *Hornet*. Sailing in quest of the Americans with all three frigates would leave Boston unblockaded, however. Raising the blockade of Boston was particularly problematic because the American ship of the line *Independence* was nearly ready for sea from that port. Still, Collier assessed the ships at sea to be the more immediate threat and pursued with the *Leander*, *Newcastle*, and *Acasta*.[20]

Though several pieces of intelligence that Collier had obtained were wrong, one critical piece proved correct: the *Constitution* had sailed. At sea the *Constitution* encountered a schooner under English colors on the morning of 24 December. One of the Americans described her: "She proved to be a perfect slop ship and grocery store." This was especially important because the lack of funds had forced the Americans to sail with little beyond the standard rations such as salt beef and salt pork. Moreover, the schooner proffered critical intelligence that she had become separated from a convoy that had sailed from St. John's, Newfoundland, on 1 December, escorted by the 20-gun *Medina*. Stewart immediately went in search of the convoy, but it was more than a thousand miles to the south.[21]

Not far away from the *Constitution*, Collier with the *Leander*, *Newcastle*, and *Acasta* continued their search. However, Stewart's decision to look for the convoy meant that the *Constitution* had dallied in the central Atlantic while the British squadron continued toward the Azores. By 28 December Collier was already to the

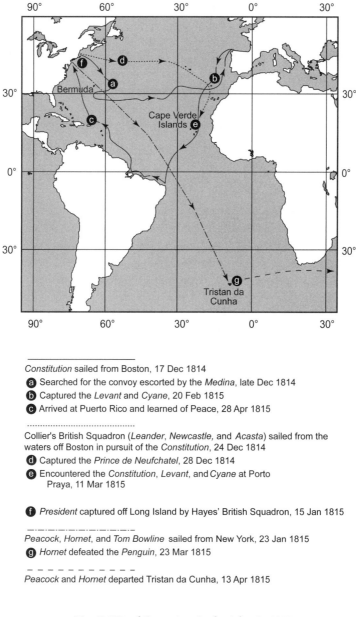

Constitution sailed from Boston, 17 Dec 1814

a Searched for the convoy escorted by the *Medina*, late Dec 1814

b Captured the *Levant* and *Cyane*, 20 Feb 1815

c Arrived at Puerto Rico and learned of Peace, 28 Apr 1815

Collier's British Squadron (*Leander*, *Newcastle,* and *Acasta*) sailed from the waters off Boston in pursuit of the *Constitution*, 24 Dec 1814

d Captured the *Prince de Neufchatel*, 28 Dec 1814

e Encountered the *Constitution*, *Levant*, and *Cyane* at Porto Praya, 11 Mar 1815

f *President* captured off Long Island by Hayes' British Squadron, 15 Jan 1815

Peacock, *Hornet*, and *Tom Bowline* sailed from New York, 23 Jan 1815

g *Hornet* defeated the *Penguin*, 23 Mar 1815

Peacock and *Hornet* departed Tristan da Cunha, 13 Apr 1815

Map E.1 Naval Operations in the Atlantic, 1815

east of the *Constitution* when his squadron captured the American privateer *Prince de Neufchatel*, with eighteen guns and 130 men.[22] Since Collier thought he was treading on thin ice for having taken the entire blockade squadron away from Boston, he sent the prize to England with a private letter to Melville, beseeching him, "What I am most anxious for is that your Lordship may approve of my conduct." Collier explained to the First Lord that his instructions only covered the escape of a single American warship, but various information "has enabled me to satisfy myself with the correctness of several points of intelligence, . . . and I consider there is no doubt but the two Ships of War [*Constitution* and *Congress*] formed a junction, & were to be joined, *if possible*, by a third [*President*], if not a fourth [*Hornet*], on some secret rendezvous!"[23]

At Halifax, Admiral Griffith became aware in early January that Collier had taken the squadron toward the Azores, but he also learned that the *Congress* remained in Portsmouth "and that she was *not ready for sea*." This contradicted a key component of the intelligence Collier had acted upon, and Griffith lamented, "It is therefore to be regretted, that Sir George Collier should upon such vague information, have taken so large a force off the Station, thereby depriving me of the means of keeping up even the semblance of a Blockade of the Enemy's Ports."[24]

With the *Constitution* at sea and Cochrane operating against New Orleans, the United States and the United Kingdom signed a treaty of peace at Ghent on 24 December. The Admiralty, however, declared, "Until which Ratifications shall have been exchanged hostilities are still to continue." Both the Prince Regent, who ruled for the mentally unstable George III, and the U.S. Senate had to ratify the proceedings. Until that occurred, Melville explained, "We shall continue sending our fleets under convoy as usual & shall make no alterations till we hear again from America that the Peace is final."[25]

The Prince Regent quickly ratified the treaty.[26] The British government had not officially sought war with the United States. By 1814 peace had returned to Europe; Britain, after fighting more than two decades against Revolutionary and Napoleonic France, desired peace rather than the continued sacrifices of war. Particularly, British debt and taxation had mushroomed during its wars against Revolutionary and Napoleonic France, and fighting the United States proved costly. Britain had to defend Canada, the navy had to remain on war footing, and merchant vessels had to continue the practice of sailing in convoys. For Britain, peace seemed the best option, and the British government hoped their American counterparts thought the same.

War with America was costlier to Britain than many might realize. Demobilization orders for the British navy give some indication. On 30 December the Admiralty sent Cochrane orders, contingent upon ratification by the United States, to hand over command to Griffith and retain only a single ship of the line, four frigates, and six sloops on the North American Station. This was a far cry from the 120 warships then under Cochrane's orders. Even as far away as the East Indies, peace with America allowed the Admiralty to order a force reduction from two to one ships of the line, from nine to four frigates, and from six to two smaller warships.[27] Downsizing would occur months in the future, however, given the sluggishness of communications, the necessary requirement of American ratification, and the continuance of the war at sea.

Around 24 January, a full month after the signing of the treaty at Ghent, the Admiralty received information that the *Constitution* and *Congress* had sailed and the *President* and *Hornet* might also be at sea. Such news proved particularly unwelcome because the Admiralty had allowed six East Indiamen to sail from England on 15 January without an escort. Moreover, a convoy escorted by the 74-gun *Cornwallis* had proceeded toward the East Indies on 18 January without information that the Americans were at sea. To counter the threat to such valuable commerce, the Admiralty immediately directed a 74-gun ship, a pair of frigates, and a sloop to steer for the Cape of Good Hope. More unwelcome news followed when Lloyd's reported that weather had scattered a homeward-bound West India convoy. The Admiralty dispatched two 74-gun ships and a sloop to the Azores with orders to join a frigate already on that station. Since these islands served as a rendezvous for scattered convoys, the Admiralty hoped these warships could police the fragments of the convoy and keep the Americans at bay.[28] Several days later, the Admiralty received information that Collier, with the *Leander*, *Newcastle*, and *Acasta*, had sailed toward the Azores in pursuit of the Americans. Though Collier had worried about raising the blockade of Boston, the Admiralty, seeing the larger picture, approved.[29] Britain's naval leadership, however, had reacted to false information, and even when correct details about the *Constitution* operating alone emerged, other fallacious information continued to influence British decision makers. For example, the commander at Bermuda obtained intelligence at the end of January that the *Constitution* was nearby, and in response he dispatched a pair of frigates.[30] The American frigate was, however, more than a thousand miles to the east. By the end of January 1815, now former-secretary Jones had for the first time since the summer of 1813 forced the Royal Navy to devote significant forces against a single American warship. Yet,

one factor must temper this positive appraisal of Jones' strategy—in most cases the British did not believe they faced a single warship; instead, they thought they faced a naval squadron containing the heart of the United States Navy.

At sea, Captain Stewart learned on 8 February from two separate neutral merchantmen of the treaty of peace. Without official news of its ratification, however, Stewart continued with his mission.[31]

Twelve days later in the early afternoon of 20 February while sailing northeast of Madeira, the *Constitution*'s lookouts spied a sail. As the *Constitution* closed, her lookouts made out a second. About 3:00 p.m. one of the strangers displayed signal flags, betraying her as a vessel of war. Stewart had gained enough by 5:00 p.m. to try his chase guns, but the rounds fell short. About forty minutes later, the two strange vessels "closed, passed within hail of each other, shortened sail, hauled up their courses, and appeared to be making preparations to receive us."[32]

The *Constitution* had encountered the *Levant* and the *Cyane*. On board the former, Captain the Honorable George Douglas surveyed his options. His ship was but a sixth rate, as was her consort commanded by Captain Gordon Falcon. Time became critical as the *Constitution* neared. Falcon hailed Douglas and explained that he thought the stranger "an American frigate, but that I had not been able to ascertain her force as she had kept nearly always end on to us." In response, Douglas proclaimed "his intention to engage her."[33]

In preparation for battle, the *Cyane* took a position about one hundred yards astern of the *Levant*. Douglas attempted to gain the weather gauge, but Stewart frustrated the attempt and continued to close. In response, the two British warships again came within hail.[34] Douglas explained that it was his "intention if possible of forcing a night action." This was, however, not to be. The *Constitution* came up too quickly. When within gunshot, Stewart finally betrayed his force. Douglas accurately descried her as "a Frigate of the largest class."[35]

The *Constitution*'s position to the windward and the superior sailing of the American frigate left Douglas little choice but to fight, but the odds were steep. The *Levant* mounted 18 x 32-pound carronades and 2 x long 9-pounders; and the *Cyane* mounted 22 x 32-pound and 10 x 18-pound carronades, and 2 x long 9-pounders. The *Constitution* had a larger crew than the two British warships combined, however, and mounted a combination of 24-pound long guns and 32-pound carronades.[36] Particularly, the former had much greater range and hitting power than the carronade-dominated armaments of the British warships.

At 6:05 p.m. the *Constitution* commenced the action with the *Levant* opposite her bow, while the *Cyane* was a bit aft of the American's beam. Accounts differ as to the range, with Stewart asserting three hundred yards and British officers between four hundred and six hundred yards. Falcon, on board the *Cyane*, watched a number of rounds from his short-ranged carronades fall short, so the British estimate was probably more accurate, though in the failing light, range, accuracy, and visibility were all questionable.[37]

Fifteen minutes into the action, Stewart noticed the *Cyane*'s fire slacken, and he ordered his men to cease firing so the smoke could dissipate. In this time, the *Constitution* had drifted forward and "finding ourselves abreast of the headmost ship gave her our broadside." After pounding on the *Levant*, Stewart backed the *Constitution*'s sails, allowing his broadside to again bear on the *Cyane*.[38] On board the *Cyane*, Falcon found the fight turning against his ship because the *Constitution*'s "fire being greatly superior, and ours rather slacker in consequence of four of the Guns being disabled."[39]

On board the *Levant*, Douglas received reports that his warship had not escaped lightly and "that the whole of the running rigging, and greater part of the standing rigging were shot away, and the masts and yards considerably injured." Douglas put the *Levant* before the wind and tried to distance himself from the *Constitution* in order to gain a respite and allow his crew to make repairs.[40] On board the *Cyane* Falcon saw the *Levant* get before the wind and tried to follow, but damage prevented this maneuver.[41] The *Constitution* remained battle-worthy, and Stewart, thinking the *Levant* was attempting to escape, "filled our after sails, shot ahead, and gave her two broadsides into her stern." Seeing this, Falcon nursed enough steerage from the *Cyane* to again bring his guns to bear on the *Constitution* "for the purpose of covering the *Levant*." Now receiving fire from the *Cyane*, the American frigate returned to finish her off. Falcon consulted with his officers, and they agreed that their only recourse was to surrender to avoid futile bloodshed, "imagining the *Levant* to be at such a distance as to insure her escape."[42]

Across the water, Douglas pressed his crew to complete hasty repairs. Given that darkness had now descended, he explained, "I could not discover whether the Colours of the *Cyane* were still flying or not." About that time, he received reports of "the *Levant* being again ready for action . . . tacked to close with the enemy." The almost suicidal decision to renew the action against such unfavorable odds was questionable, but Douglas was senior British officer, and he did not know the fate of the *Cyane*. For almost the next hour the two warships closed, with Douglas attempting to obtain the weather gauge, but "it was out of my power to weather him, passed close under his lee, and gave him our starboard broadside, as long as the Guns would bear, receiving at the same time, a most heavy and destructive fire from the enemy." Given the disparity in force, the *Levant* could not long sustain such a battering. Moreover, Douglas concluded, "The *Cyane* had undoubtedly been obliged to strike her Colours, the *Levant* was again put before the wind, with the hope of saving the ship." As the *Levant* tried to escape, the Americans put several raking broadsides into her stern, but Douglas refused to surrender. This forced Stewart to order chase, and a running fight developed. Douglas received damage

The Capture of the HMS *Levant* and HMS *Cyane* by the USS *Constitution*, 20 February 1815 (U.S. Naval Institute Photo Archive)

reports. Though all his masts stood, they had been wounded, and his ship had been severely mauled. As the *Constitution* was about to unleash another broadside, Douglas consulted with his officers and then ordered the colors struck.[43]

Even if the *Levant* and *Cyane* were taken together, the number of their crews and the hitting power of their broadsides did not equal the *Constitution*. However, fighting two warships simultaneously with most of the action occurring at night was quite a feat, perhaps enough to avenge the savaging that Stewart's reputation had taken after his winter cruise of 1813–14. For the British, Douglas related, "Although I was aware of the superiority of the enemy's force, I nevertheless conceived it was my duty to bring him to action, with the hopes of at least disabling him, and prevent his intercepting two valuable convoys which sailed from Gibraltar on the same day with the *Levant*, which I knew to be in our neighbourhood."[44] A closer analysis of the details leads to a different conclusion. The *Levant* and the *Cyane* had sailed from Gibraltar on 16 February. On that same day a convoy had sailed to England, escorted by the 18-gun *Snake* and the armed naval storeship *Sir Francis Drake*. The track of this convoy took them away from the *Constitution*, and at the time of the action they were approximately 350 miles to the northeast. The second convoy that sailed from Gibraltar on 16 February was slightly closer to the action, but it was very small, comprising the 32-gun *Castor* and two merchant ships.[45] Rather than both convoys being at risk as Douglas wrote, neither had a particularly large chance of encountering the *Constitution*; however, Douglas had a vested interest in inflating the risk to the convoys because he had chanced an engagement with a superior foe and lost both the *Levant* and the *Cyane*.

Other British warships continued to search for the *Constitution*. Closest in pursuit was Collier's squadron consisting of the *Leander*, *Newcastle*, and *Acasta*. They narrowly missed the *Constitution* around the time of the *Levant* and *Cyane*'s capture. The next weeks took Collier south toward the Portuguese-controlled Cape Verde Islands, but poor visibility, the result of blowing sand, prevented accurate lunar observations between 8 and 10 March. Dead reckoning led Collier to try to make Porto Praya in the Cape Verde Islands. Just before noon on 11 March the British lookouts sighted land, but Collier lamented, "I was disappointed in observing . . . that we were to leeward of Porto Praya."[46]

At that time the *Constitution*, *Levant*, and *Cyane* were at anchor in Porto Praya trying to dispose of the prisoners and obtain fresh provisions. About noon the *Constitution*'s lookouts "discovered a large ship through the fog standing in for Port Praya." Several minutes later, the number had grown to three. Stewart thought they had the appearance of warships, "and from the little respect hitherto paid by them to neutral waters I deemed it most prudent to put to Sea." The *Constitution* and her prizes bent their sails, cut their cables, and pressed for open water with the *Constitution* in the lead.[47]

Across the water Collier signaled "chase" and then "prepare for battle." Any thought that his opponents were British warships was dashed when they did not answer the private signals. As the pursuit continued, the *Newcastle* became the lead ship with the *Leander* about two miles astern and the *Acasta* about a mile to the windward. Collier lamented that the Americans were "going with a more favorable Wind from off the land."[48] But Stewart came to a different conclusion: that the British were gaining on his two prizes. Particularly, Stewart saw the "*Cyane* dropping fast astern and to leeward and the frigate gaining on her fast." He had two choices—bring the *Constitution* around and fight, or detach the *Cyane* and hope this "would detach one of the Enemy's ships in pursuit of her." Stewart chose the latter and signaled the *Cyane*. She tacked, making sail toward Porto Praya; however, Stewart declared, "They all continued in full chase of the *Levant* and this ship." Though the *Constitution* kept her distance, the British now came up on the *Levant*. This forced Stewart to signal the *Levant*. After receiving his signal she tacked, also making her way back toward Porto Praya. Incredulously, Stewart watched as "the whole of the Enemy's squadron tacked in pursuit of the *Levant* and gave over the pursuit of this ship." Stewart later explained, "The sacrifice of the *Levant* became necessary for the preservation of the *Constitution*."[49] Collier saw things differently and thought he had no chance of catching the *Constitution* for she "out sailed all the Squadron & . . . was all but out of sight." Moreover, the hazy conditions led him to mistake the *Levant* for the *Congress* and he decided to cut her off, salvaging something from the encounter.[50]

Bringing his squadron onto their new course placed the *Leander* closest to the *Levant*, and Collier ordered his chase guns to fire. On board the *Levant*, Lieutenant Henry Ballard explained, "At 3 30, finding it impossible to escape . . . it was determined to bear up for the harbor, . . . the neutrality of which we were all under the strongest belief the enemy would not violate." As the *Leander* neared the port, Collier found his ship too close to the rocks and gave over the pursuit to the *Acasta*. She soon unmasked her broadside. Now receiving the *Acasta's* fire, the *Levant* struck her colors in four fathoms of water, only 150 yards from the shore.[51]

In hindsight, Collier wrote, "I shall endeavour to explain the circumstance of my having been led perhaps to infringe in some degree upon the Rights of Neutrality." This was an understatement. The *Acasta* had fired within the roadstead, while one American on board the *Levant* asserted that both the *Newcastle* and particularly the *Leander* also had fired at the *Levant* within neutral waters. Collier argued that Stewart had sailed from the port thinking his squadron to be three East

India ships. Sailing from a neutral port to attack British merchant ships negated the port's neutral status, but he could not have drawn this conclusion until after capturing the *Levant* in neutral waters. Collier also asserted that "the fire was opened at some miles distance from the land," and, given the rate of sailing and the nature of the pursuit, it was impossible not to continue the pursuit to its conclusion. More honestly, he declared, "I hope . . . to convince you that I acted throughout from the best intentions."[52]

Regardless, the *Levant* was retaken, and the Portuguese official at Porto Praya did not complain too loudly. The *Constitution* escaped, but what of the *Cyane*? After receiving the signal from the *Constitution* to separate, she steered away from the other ships. At extreme range, one of the British warships fired upon her without effect. She soon lost sight of the British squadron and disappeared in the confusion.[53]

The British had reacted with vigor to the sailing of the *Constitution*; however, their response was predicated on faulty assumptions. Incorrect reports had placed the *Congress* with her, and initial information also indicated that the *President* under Commodore Decatur had sailed from New York to join the *Constitution*. But Rear Admiral Henry Hotham, commanding British ships off New York, knew better: he had received accurate reports that the *President*, as well as the *Peacock* and *Hornet*, remained at New York. To keep them blockaded, Hotham commanded the squadron in Long Island Sound and deployed a second squadron off Sandy Hook. Of the American warships, Hotham had received accurate reports that they planned to sail to the East Indies, but he worried, "I have no ships which can follow them that distance."[54]

As a result, it was critical to intercept Decatur's squadron when it emerged from port, but would Decatur sail from Sandy Hook or through Long Island Sound? Decatur's failure on 1 June 1813 demonstrated the difficulty of using the Sound, and, given the strength of Hotham's squadron, Decatur faced even longer odds in January 1815. Thus, Hotham believed that Decatur's ships would sail via Sandy Hook, and he placed a powerful squadron under Captain John Hayes with orders to maintain a close blockade.[55] Hayes, however, disagreed with Hotham over the deployment of his squadron by arguing that boisterous weather rendered a close blockade ineffective. Instead, Hayes thought that a more distant blockade would "be more effectual in keeping the Enemy in Port than if we were able to hold a station constantly, for in that case he could from observing our situation at close of day in blowing weather come out in the early part of the night and easily avoid us."[56]

Though Hayes had his ideas, he implemented Hotham's plan by keeping a close watch of Sandy Hook where, on 13 January, the 38-gun frigate *Tenedos* arrived and exchanged numbers with the 58-gun razee the *Majestic*; the 40-gun *Endymion*; and the 38-gun *Pomone*. Though "piercing cold," her captain immediately repaired on board the *Majestic* to speak with Captain Hayes. That night a storm came up that blew the squadron off the coast.[57]

This was exactly the information Decatur wanted to hear. Given the difficulty in getting over the bar at Sandy Hook with a deeply laden frigate, three factors needed to converge: wind, tide, and the absence of the British. The evening hours of 14 January promised all three; however, one of his two supply ships, the *Tom Bowline*, had run aground and would not be ready to sail that night. As a result Decatur divided his force, ordering the *Peacock* and *Hornet* to delay their departure until the *Tom Bowline* was ready; he would sail that night with the store ship *Macedonian*. Several gunboats marked the passage across Sandy Hook bar with lanterns at their mastheads, and at about 8:00 p.m. the *President* and *Macedonian* started to thread their way through the channel, but Decatur's frigate grounded on the bar.[58]

The *President* "remained thumping" and "beat heavily."[59] Given the strong westerly wind, Decatur had but one option—force his frigate over the bar. He did not have long to work. If the tide fell, the *President* would be stranded and vulnerable to the British. After an hour and a half, the frigate crossed the bar, but Decatur determined that his ship had sustained "material injury as to render her return into port desirable." Then, just before daylight on 15 January, lookouts sighted three ships ahead.[60]

The strangers were the *Majestic*, *Endymion*, and *Pomone*, the *Tenedos* having drifted several miles to the leeward. As Decatur had expected, the storm had blown them away from Sandy Hook on the night of 13–14 January. Captain Hayes realized the weather favored Decatur, and "I had no doubt but he would attempt his escape that night; it was impossible from the direction of the wind to get in with the Hook."[61] The weather gave Hayes no other choice but to implement his more distant blockade rather than Hotham's close blockade. Moreover, he could take solace in knowing that he was viewed by his contemporaries as one of the great seamen of his age. His efforts in 1812 to save the 74-gun *Magnificent* off a lee shore had led others to refer to him as "Magnificent" Hayes.[62] Off Sandy Hook, Hayes certainly lived up to this name by using his knowledge of the wind and current to sail away from Sandy Hook "till the Squadron reached the supposed track of the Enemy." Though a gamble, "what is a little singular," Hayes related, "at the very instant of arriving at that point, an hour before day light . . . we were made happy by the sight of a Ship and Brig standing to the Southward and Eastward, and not more than two miles on the *Majestic*'s weather Bow." Hayes signaled chase. At daylight the *Majestic* was leading, followed by the *Endymion*, *Pomone*, and *Tenedos*.[63]

The Engagement between the HMS *Endymion* and the USS *President*, 15 January 1815 (U.S. Naval Institute Photo Archive)

Decatur fled, and by noon "we had increased our distance from the Razee, but the next Ship astern, which was also a large Ship, had closed & continued to gain upon us considerably." This was the *Endymion*, under Captain Henry Hope. Decatur had his crew jettison nonessential items in a gambit to lighten his frigate. In another effort to obtain more speed, he had his men wet the sails. The *President* had proved a fast ship in previous encounters, but her damage allowed the *Endymion* to come within range about mid-afternoon. The *President* opened the engagement with her stern guns, and about half an hour later, the *Endymion* returned fire.[64] The *Endymion* continued to close, and after trading shots for two hours Captain Hope brought his frigate "within half point blank shot" of the *President*'s starboard quarter. Decatur lamented that his guns would not bear, and, "I remained with her in this position for half an hour in the hope that she would close with us on our Broadside, in which case I had prepared my crew to board, but . . . it became evident that to close was not his intention."[65] Decatur assembled his crew and told them he intended to take the *Endymion* by boarding. Decatur even told his men if they captured her intact, then he would abandon the *President* and continue the cruise in the *Endymion*. After three cheers the men returned to their quarters, and Decatur had his frigate close with the British frigate. However, Captain Hope frustrated the attempt by bringing the *Endymion* onto a parallel course. Both frigates then ran before the wind, trading broadsides at a distance of a quarter mile.[66]

Though the *President* boasted a larger crew and displacement, the *Endymion* was much more formidable than the *Macedonian*, which Decatur had captured in 1812. Launched in 1797, the *Endymion*, like the *President*, carried 24-pound guns on her gun deck, though the *President*'s broadside numbered two more guns. The *President* also carried 20 x 42-pound carronades to a similar number of 32-pound carronades on the *Endymion*.[67] The *President* was the more powerful ship, but between the grounding and the damage already inflicted by the *Endymion*, the field had been leveled.

Captain Hope frustrated all Decatur's attempts to close. In exasperation, Decatur ordered his men to concentrate on the *Endymion*'s spars. According to one of his midshipmen, this was "an order which the Commodore afterwards regretted having given." Though Decatur asserted, "We completely succeeded in dismantling her," this was not his object, since he wanted to capture this frigate with her sails, masts, and rigging intact. The damage the Americans had inflicted slowed the *Endymion* and allowed the *President* to sail away. This exposed her stern to the British frigate but the *President* did not receive a raking broadside. Decatur concluded that he had silenced his opponent. However, Hope asserted that he had ceased fire because he saw that the Americans had hoisted a light and thought it a sign of surrender.[68]

Both Decatur and Hope were wrong. The *Endymion* had suffered far less than Decatur described, and the *President* had not struck like Hope had concluded. In fact, the Americans claim to have hoisted the light some two hours after leaving the *Endymion*.[69] One point, however, proved inescapable: the American frigate had suffered considerable damage, slowing her enough so that the *Pomone* and *Tenedos* came up with the American frigate just before midnight. Decatur decided "to receive the fire of the nearest ship & Surrender for it was Vain to Contend with the whole Squadron."[70] The *Pomone* gave the *President* a broadside "which she never returned; *Pomone* again fired a few guns; no return from the enemy." The *Tenedos* then hailed, asking if she surrendered. Decatur replied in the affirmative.[71]

Captain Hope later attested, "When it is considered that we were for two hours and a half in close action our loss of 11 killed and 14 wounded is very small." This compared very favorably against the thirty-five killed and seventy wounded on board the *President*. As close to boasting as Hope came was when he admitted, "My Brother officers all regret that we had not met single handed." Hope, as well as other British officers, realized that the Americans would claim that it had taken a squadron to defeat the *President*. Whereas the British believed that the *Endymion* could have won without the assistance of others. Perhaps, but the battle had left Hope's frigate in need of major repair that Bermuda could not provide. Still, Hotham believed Hope's victory had "done him infinite honor and the service much credit."[72] The Royal Navy had at last captured a heavy frigate of the United States Navy, albeit a warship crippled by grounding and chased by a British squadron, and the British had captured her after the signing of the peace treaty. Still, ratification had not occurred, so both countries remained at war and only one ship of the British squadron had been heavily engaged.

In company with the *President* during her failed escape was the *Macedonian*, store ship. After watching the *President* engage the *Endymion*, darkness fell, and her crew watched the flashes of gunfire. Between 11:45 p.m. and midnight, a last flurry lit up the horizon. The master concluded that the British squadron had overwhelmed Decatur. When day broke and no ships were in sight, he made sail toward the East Indies to inform the *Peacock* under Captain Warrington and the *Hornet* under Captain Biddle.[73]

Warrington and Biddle, however, were still at New York, oblivious to the *President*'s fate, prepared only to follow Decatur's instructions, directing their warships and the store ship *Tom Bowline* to proceed to a rendezvous with the *President* in the South Atlantic. On 23 January the *Peacock*, *Hornet*, and *Tom Bowline* sailed,

The Capture of the USS *President* by Captain Hayes' British Squadron, 15 January 1815 (U.S. Naval Institute Photo Archive)

quietly slipping through the British blockade.[74] When the British realized they had sailed, Admiral Hotham wrote, "I have no information on which I can rely as to their destination; but always understood they were intended to accompany the *President*; and they may possibly proceed to a given Rendezvous for meeting her." However, he lamented, "I have no Ships or Vessels which I can detach in pursuit, or with information of them."[75]

Only three days out the *Hornet* lost sight of the *Peacock* and efforts to reunite proved futile. Both then individually made their way toward a rendezvous at the Island of Tristan da Cunha. Situated 1,750 miles from South Africa and nearly 2,100 miles from South America, it was a perfect location for the United States Navy to rendezvous. It was remote, and, given prevailing winds and currents, it was on the outward-bound track of ships destined for the Indian Ocean. On 23 March Biddle gained a position off the north end of the island where his lookouts sighted a sail. Immediately, he went to investigate.[76]

The stranger was the *Penguin*, a British *Cruizer*-class brig, under Commander James Dickinson, that had been patrolling in the vicinity of the island. "At 1.40 P.M. nearly within musket shot distance, she hauled her wind . . . hoisted English colours, and fired a gun," Biddle wrote, adding, "We immediately luffed too, hoisted our Ensign and gave the enemy a broadside." The *Penguin* then approached the *Hornet* "to within Pistol Shot when the Action became Warm and Brisk." Dickinson decided "to lay her on board." Biddle made out his opponent's intentions and directed his men to repel boarders. As his men assembled, Biddle recounted that they "eagerly pressed me to permit them to board the enemy." He understood, however, that boarding would be bloody and perhaps risk the outcome of the engagement, adding, "This I would not permit, as it was evident from the commencement of the action, that our fire was greatly superior both in quickness and effect." Biddle was correct. The *Penguin* had sustained significant damage. Then Dickinson fell, mortally wounded.[77]

Lieutenant James McDonald assumed command. Noticing the masts were tottering and expecting them soon to fall, he decided to follow through with Dickinson's last order, realizing the *Penguin*'s only chance involved boarding before his brig became an unmanageable wreck. Moments later the *Penguin*'s bowsprit fouled the *Hornet* near her stern. The fighting became intense. The area of the *Hornet* near the location where the *Penguin*'s bowsprit fouled her witnessed all but one of the American casualties, including the only man killed in the action, a Marine who had "the top of his scull taken off by a ball." Rather than the two warships remaining locked together, a swell lifted the *Hornet* ahead of the *Penguin*, and at nearly this instant, the *Penguin*'s bowsprit and foremast went into the sea.[78]

McDonald decided that continued resistance was futile, so he hailed that he surrendered, but Biddle later asserted that he was severely wounded in his neck

The Capture of the HMS *Penguin* by the USS *Hornet*, 23 March 1815 (U.S. Naval Institute Photo Archive)

after receiving the surrender plea, and so ordered another broadside. Afterwards, a voice from the *Penguin* again asked for surrender. According to Biddle, "It was with difficulty I could restrain my crew from firing into him again, as he had certainly fired into us after having surrendered."[79] McDonald never reported any such confusion.

Before the engagement Dickinson "generally observed that if he fell in with an Enemy's Vessel, he would Engage him muzzle to muzzle." Biddle, however, had kept his distance until he crippled the *Penguin*. The British admitted forty-three killed and wounded out of 132 on board, though Biddle later asserted that he had received information "that the number of Killed was certainly greater." The *Hornet* lost one killed and twelve wounded, though Lieutenant McDonald maintained that he "learnt from their wounded they had hove from 10 to 15 overboard." McDonald went on, "The *Hornet* is in a leaky state from our shot which I trust will shorten her Cruise." Biddle, however, maintained, "This ship did not receive a single round shot in her hull." These allegations highlight how each side cast the encounter in a better light. In reality, the *Hornet* had 18 x 32-pound carronades to his opponent's sixteen similar weapons, a slightly larger crew, and three masts instead of two, giving the *Hornet* greater redundancy aloft. In conclusion, the British had taken enough of a pounding that Biddle had to order his prize scuttled, but the British did not inflict enough damage to force Biddle to curtail his mission.[80]

Two days after the action, the *Peacock* and *Tom Bowline* joined the *Hornet*. As senior officer, Warrington decided to remain at Tristan da Cunha for twenty days to await the arrival of Decatur, but he had an idea that waiting would be fruitless: the *Macedonian* store ship had previously visited the island, leaving a report detailing the *President*'s capture. During the twenty-day wait, Warrington removed all the stores he could from the *Tom Bowline* and sent her to Brazil with the *Penguin*'s survivors. When the *President* did not arrive, Warrington decided "to prosecute the cruise although aware of our great deficiency in point of force."[81]

On the coast of North America, at Bermuda, and in the West Indies news slowly trickled in about the peace treaty signed at Ghent. Rear Admiral Hotham responded, "I shall be careful not to cease hostilities till I have full authority; and not allow the enemy here to take any advantage of the present situation of affairs."[82] For in reality the treaty was powerless, and the war continued until it had been ratified by both sides. Both the bloody British repulse at New Orleans and the capture of the *President* occurred between the signing of the treaty and its ratification. Though the British quickly ratified the treaty, its leaders did not assume the Americans would follow suit. Captain Hope of the *Endymion* concluded that the British failure at New Orleans had the potential to lead Madison to demand better terms, but the American people "are all heartily tired of war." Moreover, an American officer on board the *Constitution* unequivocally stated, "I observe the terms of the treaty . . . are very favorable to us."[83] While waiting to hear of the treaty's ratification, Admiral Griffith in Halifax prepared for operations during 1815, writing, "There have by one means or the other, *slipped* from under my Orders, no less than *one* ship of the line, *five* frigates, and six or seven sloops of war . . . before the month of April I shall want a reinforcement."[84] Particularly, he explained, "I have left myself without a disposable frigate, and the Ports of Massachusetts and New Hampshire with only one ship of the line and two frigates for their blockade; and in those Ports the Enemy have two ships of the line and one frigate."[85]

The British concerns proved unwarranted, however. The U.S. Senate gave the treaty its unanimous approval on 17 February and Madison quickly signed it into law, but the maritime war did not come to an immediate end. If it had, the *Constitution*'s action with the *Levant* and *Cyane* on 20 February and the *Hornet*'s engagement with the *Penguin* on 23 March would have to be viewed in a different light. According to Article II, the naval war would continue for twelve days after ratification on the coast of the United States, thirty days in the Atlantic north of the equator, and either sixty or ninety days in the Atlantic south of the equator, with the location of the *Hornet*'s action with the *Penguin* in the ninety-day region. In the Indian and Pacific Oceans, the war would continue for 120 days.[86] The reason for this delayed ending of the hostilities dealt with the slowness of communications. This meant that prizes taken, even four months after the ratification, would still be considered legitimate. In response, Admiral Griffith lamented, "Our Commissioners at Ghent seem to have been outwitted," meaning that the Americans would be able to continue their war on distant seas for several months. Because the war had terminated on the American coast, they would be able to send their prizes into American ports, and the British navy could not stop them.[87]

To prevent this eventuality, the British wished to get the warships of the United States Navy home as soon as possible. Cochrane, as a result, dispatched another squadron to find the *Constitution* and "acquaint her of the cessation of Hostilities."[88] This squadron failed in its mission, but the American frigate fell in with a British ship of the line on 26 April "and concluded from her manoeuvres there was peace." Immediately, Captain Stewart went into a harbor in Puerto Rico for confirmation "and there learned for the first time the ratification of the treaty." Stewart then shaped a course for home, arriving off Sandy Hook in mid-May. The *Cyane* had beaten him home by more than a month.[89] Only the *Peacock* and *Hornet* remained at sea.

The Escape of the USS *Hornet* from the HMS *Cornwallis*, 28–30 April 1815 (U.S. Naval Institute Photo Archive)

Unaware of the peace treaty, the *Peacock* and *Hornet* pressed east from Tristan da Cunha. On 27 April the American warships chased a strange sail. Throughout the day, the American warships closed; Midshipman William Rodgers, then serving on board the *Peacock*, related that she was "a very large ship—probably a *fat* East India Man . . . a good recompense for all our lost time." The next morning, the chase continued, with the *Peacock* ranging well ahead of the slower *Hornet*. About 2:30 p.m. the *Peacock* had closed to within four miles, and Rodgers exclaimed incredulously, "Made her out to be to all intents & purposes an English *Line of Battle Ship*." Warrington signaled to the *Hornet* "superior force," then he signaled "Line of Battle Ship," followed fifteen minutes later "that the Strange sail was English."[90]

The stranger was in fact the 74-gun *Cornwallis*, conveying Rear Admiral Sir George Burlton to his new command in the East Indies. Burlton knew of the peace treaty but not the ratification. From Collier's squadron off Madeira, he had obtained information that American warships "might very probably be bound to the Coast of Brazil, or the East Indies."[91] Though lookouts on board the *Cornwallis* sighted the *Peacock* and *Hornet* on 27 April, Burlton continued on his course, likely under the correct impression that the treaty had been ratified and the war was over. As day broke on 28 April, the Americans continued to close, and finally the captain of the *Cornwallis* ordered his ship to come about and make all sail in chase.[92]

On board the *Hornet*, a master's mate asserted, "The *Peacock* . . . took herself off like a grey hound. The poor *Hornet* was left a prey as the big ship who on perceiving our distress and the improbability of capturing both took after us and let the *Peacock* go her way." On board the *Peacock*, Midshipman Rodgers also thought the *Cornwallis* had the advantage and "tis probable she will capture her as she sails much faster than the *Hornet*."[93]

Around 9:00 p.m. Biddle concluded, "The Enemy was gaining upon us, as there was every appearance that she would be enabled to keep sight of us during the night, I considered it necessary to lighten this Ship." Twelve tons of ballast went into the deep followed by shot, extra spars, an anchor, and cable, but the *Cornwallis* continued to gain throughout the night, and at daylight she opened fire. Biddle again ordered the *Hornet* lightened, this time to include most of her guns. Biddle explained, "The Enemy fir'd about thirty shot, not one of which took effect, tho' most of them passed over us. While he was firing, I had the satisfaction to perceive that we slowly dropt him."[94] Squally conditions persisted throughout the day, and the commander of the *Cornwallis* toyed with the *Hornet*, being unwilling to set a full press of sail for fear of damage. Even so, the *Cornwallis* again closed to about three-quarters of a mile around midday.[95] Biddle called the crew together: "He told

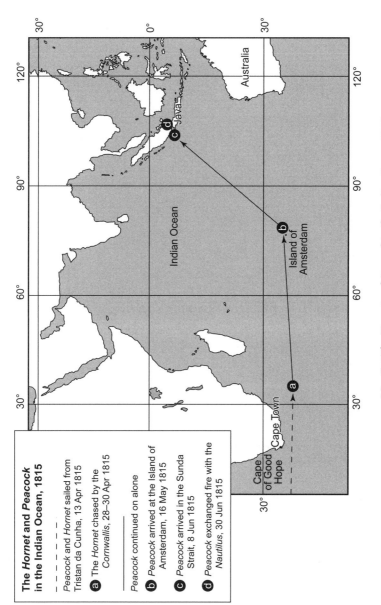

**The *Hornet* and *Peacock*
in the Indian Ocean, 1815**

- - - - - *Peacock* and *Hornet* sailed from
Tristan da Cunha, 13 Apr 1815

ⓐ The *Hornet* chased by the
Cornwallis, 28–30 Apr 1815

———— *Peacock* continued on alone

ⓑ *Peacock* arrived at the Island of
Amsterdam, 16 May 1815

ⓒ *Peacock* arrived in the Sunda
Strait, 8 Jun 1815

ⓓ *Peacock* exchanged fire with the
Nautilus, 30 Jun 1815

Indian Ocean

Australia

Java

Island of
Amsterdam

Cape Town

Cape
of Good
Hope

30° 60° 90° 120° 30°

30° 0° 30°

120°

Map E.2 The *Hornet* and *Peacock* in the Indian Ocean, 1815

them it was likely we should very soon be captured, and if that should be our lot, he would stand by them. If they were confined in the Black Hole at Calcutta for twenty years, he would stay with them, and he hoped they would continue to behave as well as they had done. They appeared to be very much gratified, and could hear it murmured among them 'Let's hold on.' "[96] Biddle then ordered all but one of his remaining guns overboard. Across the water on board the *Cornwallis* firing her cannons seemed to "deaden his wind," slowing the ship and allowing the *Hornet* to survive. As night fell the weather turned boisterous, and Biddle gambled, keeping a great deal of his sails set. He gained on his more conservative opponent, and soon after daybreak the *Cornwallis* abandoned the pursuit. The chase had left the *Hornet* with a single gun; in the confusion of lightening the ship, though, all its ammunition had gone into the deep. Impotent, Biddle shaped a course for home. Along the way, he learned of the peace.[97] Only the *Peacock* remained in quest of the British.

On board the *Peacock*, Warrington could only suppose the fate of the *Hornet* while he sailed eastward to the second rendezvous about halfway between Africa and Australia at the Island of Amsterdam. The *Peacock* made landfall on the morning of 16 May. On the island the crew found a bottle with a letter inside from the commander of the *Macedonian* store ship describing the probable loss of the *President*. That afternoon the *Peacock*'s lookouts espied a sail, and Warrington ordered chase. They soon lost sight of her, but a severe gale and a strong current prevented the *Peacock*'s return to Amsterdam Island, and Warrington shaped a course for Java, where he arrived on 8 June.[98]

Operating off that island and in the Sunda Strait, the *Peacock* made three captures. Warrington had two burnt and sent the prisoners off in the other. Two of the prizes had information about the peace treaty. One even had specifics about its terms and that the Prince Regent had ratified it, but there was no news about U.S. ratification. Midshipman Rodgers wrote in his journal, "I think [U.S. ratification] never will or never ought to be the case." However, "if such is the case, we are the last ship East of the Cape & so will make the most our time."[99]

On 30 June the *Peacock* made the port of Anyer in the Sunda Strait. Several ships were there and upon seeing the *Peacock*, the *Nautilus*—an armed East India Company vessel of fourteen guns—stood out for the American sloop. Warrington had English colors hoisted. This fooled the commander of the *Nautilus*, who sent over a boat with two officers, and the Englishman serving as deputy master attendant of the port came off shore. All were detained upon boarding the *Peacock*. The British later asserted that the master attendant told the *Peacock*'s first lieutenant and purser of the treaty's ratification, and the British later concluded, "It is hardly therefore to be supposed, that Captain Warrington could be unacquainted with the fact." Warrington contradicted this statement, maintaining that the master attendant "very improperly omitted mentioning that Peace existed."[100]

Only a short time after detaining the officers, the *Nautilus* came within hail and "her Commander . . . asked if I knew that there was a Peace." Warrington "replied in the negative, directing him at the same time to haul his colours down, if it were the case in token of it adding, that if he did not I should fire into him."[101] When the *Nautilus* did not lower her colors, Warrington fired a gun into her. The round wounded her commander, who ordered his men to return fire. When Warrington received her broadside, "our broadside was discharged and his colours struck." Damage to the *Peacock* was trifling, while the *Nautilus* had six killed and seven wounded. Warrington then allowed the master attendant to go ashore and obtain proof of the peace. He soon returned with documentation. However, Warrington did not consider this documentation official. Even so, his men patched up the *Nautilus* and handed her back to her East India Company officers.[102] The next day, Warrington shaped a course for home.

As was the case many times in Anglo-American naval relations during the first years of the nineteenth century, both sides saw the action differently. To the British, Warrington needlessly inflicted bloodshed after obtaining evidence of the peace.[103] Warrington's report voiced another concern: "I am aware that I may be blamed for ceasing hostilities without more authoritative evidence that Peace had been concluded but I trust Sir where our distance from home with the little chance we had of receiving such evidence are taken into consideration I shall not be thought to have decided prematurely."[104] This engagement ended the War of 1812 at sea. Considering that the conflict was precipitated by misperception, poor documentation, arrogance, and an unwillingness of compromise, the final clash served as a fitting end.

Abbreviations

A	Attachment
AC	U.S. Congress, *Annals of Congress*, collected in *The Debates and Proceedings of the Congress of the United States*
ADM	Admiralty Papers, the National Archives, Kew, Richmond, United Kingdom
Barbary	*Naval Documents Related to the United States Wars with the Barbary Powers*, ed. Knox
Castlereagh	*Correspondence, Despatches, and Other Papers of Viscount Castlereagh*, ed. Charles W. Vane, Marquess of Londonderry
CI	Court of inquiry
CLS	Confidential Letters sent by the Sec. of the Navy, NA, RG45
CM	Court martial
CO	Colonial Office Papers, the National Archives, Kew, Richmond, United Kingdom
CP	Cochrane Papers, National Library of Scotland
DNB	*Oxford Dictionary of National Biography*
DNI	*Daily National Intelligencer*, Washington, DC
Duke	Duke University, Durham, North Carolina. Rare Book, Manuscript, and Special Collection Department, William R. Perkins Library
HC	House of Commons Debates in *Parliamentary Debates. From the Year 1803 to the present Time*
HL	House of Lords Debates in *Parliamentary Debates. From the Year 1803 to the present Time*
HMC *Home*	Historical Manuscript Commission, *Report on the Manuscripts of Colonel David Milne Home of Wedderburn Castle*

HSP	Historical Society of Pennsylvania, Philadelphia, Pennsylvania
HUL	Hull History Centre (Hull University Archives), Hull, United Kingdom
JMP	James Madison Papers, Library of Congress
JQA	*Writings of John Quincy Adams*, ed. Worthington C. Ford
LC	Library of Congress, Washington, DC
M124	Miscellaneous Letters Received by the Sec. of the Navy, NA, RG45
M125	Letters Received by the Sec. of the Navy from Captains, NA, RG 45
M147	Letters Received by the Sec. of the Navy from Commanders, NA, RG45
M148	Letters Received by the Sec. of the Navy from Officers below the Rank of Commander, NA, RG45
M149	Letters Sent by the Sec. of the Navy to Officers, NA, RG45
M273	Records of U.S. Navy Courts of Inquiry and Courts Martial, NA, RG45
M441	Letters Sent by the Sec. of the Navy to Commandants and Navy Agents, NA, RG45
MS	Manuscript
NA	National Archives and Record Administration, Washington, DC
NAS	National Archives of Scotland, Edinburgh, United Kingdom
NASP Naval	*The New American State Papers, Naval Affairs*, ed. K. Jack Bauer
NLS	National Library of Scotland, Edinburgh, United Kingdom
NMM	National Maritime Museum, Greenwich, United Kingdom
NW1812	*Naval War of 1812: A Documentary History*, eds. W. S. Dudley, M. J. Crawford, et al.
PWJ	Papers of William Jones, Historical Society of Pennsylvania
R	Microfilm reel
RG24	Logbooks of U.S. Navy Ships, NA
RG45	Naval Records Collection of the Office of Naval Records and Library, NA
RFP	Rodgers Family Papers, LC
SDW	Arthur Wellesley, Duke of Wellington, *Supplementary Despatches, Correspondence*
Ser.	Series
SRO	Suffolk Record Office, Ipswich, United Kingdom
TJ	*The Writings of Thomas Jefferson*, ed. Paul L. Ford
USC	University of South Carolina, Library, Columbia, South Carolina
USNA	United States Naval Academy, Archives, Annapolis, Maryland

Notes

Note: All emphases are as found in original documents, unless indicated.

Preface

1. Lavery, *Nelson's Navy*, 40, 81–83; James, *Naval Occurrences*, 11–12; Chapelle, *American Sailing Navy*, 132.

Chapter 1. "Every Appearance of Hastening the Crisis": The Royal Navy, the United States Navy, and the Background to War

1. Bingham to Sawyer, 21 May, Rodgers to Hamilton, 23 May 1811, *NW1812*, 1:41–49. Officially, the *Little Belt* was named the *Lille Belt*, but both Bingham and the Americans used the spelling *Little Belt*.

2. John Quincy Adams to William Eustis, 24 Aug 1811, *JQA*, 4:187–91.

3. Glete, *Navies and Nations*, 2:376; British Ships Lost, 1811, James, *Naval History*, 5:447–48.

4. To the Editor, signed Naval Patriot, May 1813, *Naval Chronicle*, 29:466–69.

5. David Milne to George Home, 1 Dec 1811, HMC, *Home*, 150–51; George Collier to Croker, 1 Jun 1814 , Thomas Staines to Croker, 23 Jan 1812, Duke, Croker Papers, Boxes 1, 3.

6. Baugh, "The Eighteenth-Century Navy," 133.

7. Rodger, *Command of the Ocean*, 497–501; Rodger, *Wooden World*, 164; McCranie, "'Why Don't You Raise More Men?'"; Lewis, *A Social History*, 92; Baugh, *British Naval Administration*, 147.

8. Melville to Wellington, 28 Jul 1813, *SDW*, 8:144–47; Ships in Sea Pay, Jul 1809–Jul 1813, ADM 8/98–100; Rodger, *Command of the Ocean*, 499. The formula for arriving at these figures is as follows: The authorized complements of all deployed warships were totaled. The complements for noncombat and stationary ships such as receiving and hospital ships were not included. Ships in ordinary and ships that had yet to be deployed were also not counted because the manning of such ships was haphazard. Also, troopships were not counted, given incomplete statistics.

9. William Domett to Lord Keith, 31 May 1814, NMM, KEI 37/9.

10. Gardiner, *Frigates*, 38; James, *Naval History*, 5:426 (quote).

11. Schroeder, *Commodore Rodgers*, 114; Long, *Nothing too Daring*, 62. Much of the mistake seems to come from an incorrect reading of tables in the Annual Abstracts in the back of James' *Naval History*, Vols. 5–6.

12. Ships in Sea Pay, 1810–13, ADM 8/99–100; Glete, *Navies and Nations*, 2:377. At two points in the first half of July 1812, ten warships were at sea. Around 9 July the *Wasp, Constitution, Essex, President, Congress, United States, Hornet, Argus, Siren,* and *Viper* were at sea; on 15–16 July the *Wasp* had returned to port but the *Nautilus* had sailed.

13. Glete describes this point in nuanced detail. See *Navies and Nations*, 2:383–84.

14. Ships in Sea Pay, 1 Jul 1812, ADM 8/100; Lyon, *Sailing Navy List*. The ages for both ships of the line and frigates were compiled by averaging the year of launch for all of Britain's deployed warships.

15. Webb, "Construction, Repair," 206–19; Morriss, *Royal Dockyards*.

16. Gardiner, *Warships*, 13, 17. In 1796 first and second rates in sea service totaled twenty-two, but in 1811 they totaled only thirteen.

17. Lavery, *Nelson's Navy*, 46–47.

18. Ibid., 36, 49; Gardiner, *Warships*, 48; Lyon, *Sailing Navy List*.

19. Gardiner, *Naval War of 1812*, 88–90; Winfield, *British Warships*, 282.

20. Lavery, *Nelson's Navy*, 54–55; Gardiner, *Naval War of 1812*, 78–80; Woodman, *Victory of Seapower*, 48–49.

21. Gardiner, *Naval War of 1812*, 88–90; Lavery, *Nelson's Navy*, 82–83: Winfield, *British Warships*, 282–83. *Cruizer*-class brigs retained a pair of 6-pound weapons in the bow.

22. James, *Naval History*, 6:76–77.

23. Glete, *Navies and Nations*, 2:378; Corbett, *Some Principles*, 233–304, 337.

24. Ships in Sea Pay, 1807, 1813, ADM 8/93, 100.

25. Keith to Durham, 7 Jul 1813, ADM 1/154 (quote); Ships in Sea Pay, 1812–13, ADM 8/100; Glover, "The French Fleet," 233–52.

26. Hope to Keith, 17 Jun 1812, NMM, KEI/37/9.

27. Ryan, "British Trade with the Baltic"; Horward, "British Seapower and the Peninsular War"; Hall, *Wellington's Navy*.

28. Kennedy, *Rise and Fall of British Naval Mastery*, 145.

29. Rodger, *Command of the Ocean*, 559.

30. Henry Veitch (Consul Madeira) to Croker, 2 Oct 1813, ADM 1/3845; Laforey to Croker, 10 Jan 1813, ADM 1/334/24; Log *Queen*, 24 Dec 1813, ADM 51/2719; Crowhurst, *Defence of British Trade*, 105; Rodger, "Weather, Geography and Naval Power," 190–91.

31. Croker to Gladstone, 12 Jan 1813, ADM 2/1376/1–6; British navy in North America, 1810–13, *Castlereagh*, 8:286–87; Rodger, "Weather, Geography and Naval Power," 191.

32. Warren to Stirling, 16 Sep 1812, 2 Jun 1813, NMM, WAR/54; Warren to Croker, 21 Feb 1813, ADM 1/4359/185 Annex C; Rodger, "Weather, Geography and Naval Power," 191.

33. British navy in North America, 1810–13, *Castlereagh*, 8:287.

34. Winter Deployments, 1812–13, NMM, WAR/30/10–12; Crowhurst, *Defence of British Trade*, 171.

35. Ships in Sea Pay, 1 Jan, 1 Jul 1812, ADM 8/100.

36. The Admiralty to Robinson, 10 Jul 1812, ADM 2/1107/19; Log *Tenedos*, Sep–Oct 1812, ADM 51/2909; Crowhurst, *Defence of British Trade*, 109, 114.

37. Ships in Sea Pay, 1 Jul 1812, ADM 8/100. The only battle force around the British Isles that included ships of the line was at Portsmouth for the purpose of watching Cherbourg.

38. "Maritime Forces," *Naval Chronicle*, 29:32–36; Glete, *Navies and Nations*, 2:376–77.

39. Ships in Sea Pay, Jul 1810–Jul 1813, ADM 8/98–100; Melville to Croker, 1 Oct 1813, Duke, Croker Papers, Box 2; Lohnes, "British Naval Problems," 318.

40. Pitkin, *Statistical View*, 35; Perkins, *Prologue to War*, 29; Albion, *Sea Lanes in Wartime*, 70, 93–94.

41. Palmer, *Stoddert's War*.

42. F. Lambert, *Barbary Wars*.

43. Foster to Monroe, 1 Jun 1812, ADM 1/4222.

44. Observations on Monroe to Foster, 8 Jun 1812, ADM 1/4222.

45. St. Vincent to Erskine, 13 Mar 1801, *Letters of St. Vincent*, ed. D. Smith, 1:290–1 (quote); Lloyd, *The British Seaman*, 215.

46. Montagu to Markham, 16 Dec 1806, *Correspondence of Markham*, 391–2.

47. Hattendorf, "American Navy," 11–14.

48. Perkins, *Prologue to War*, 69–70; Gates, *Napoleonic Wars*, 155–57.

49. Jefferson to James Maury, 25 Apr 1812, *TJ*, 9:348–51.

50. William Blackledge (Rep. NC), 12 Jan 1812, AC, 12th Cong., 1st Sess., 925.

51. Rodgers to Capel, Capel to Rodgers, 17 Jul 1805, Rodgers to Capel, 18 Jul 1805, *Barbary*, 6:187–88.

52. John Shaw to John Gavino (U.S. Consul Gibraltar), 19 Jun 1805, *Barbary*, 6:126.

53. Humphries to Barron, Barron to Humphries, 22 Jun 1807, Barron to Sec. of the Navy, 23 Jun 1807, *Barbary*, 6:535–38 (all quotes); Tucker, *Injured Honor*.

54. Jefferson to Henry Dearborn, 7 Jul (first quote), to James Bowdoin (Minister to Spain), 10 Jul (second quote), to Barnabas Bidwell, 11 Jul 1807 (third quote), *TJ*, 9:101, 104–107.

55. Greig, ed., *Farington Diary*, ed. Greig, 7 Dec 1807, 4:231.

56. Taggart to John Taylor, 21 Mar 1808, "Letters of Taggart," ed. Haynes, 310–311; Castlereagh to Chatham, 31 Dec 1807, *Castlereagh*, 8:104–107; Perkins, *Prologue to War*, 190–197.

57. Jefferson to John Armstrong, 2 May 1808, *TJ*, 9:193–94.

58. Gates, *Napoleonic Wars*, 157; Tucker, *Injured Honor*, 136.

59. Jones to Madison, 25 Apr 1814, JMP, LC, Ser. 1, R16.

60. Circular from the Sec. of War to Governors, 17 Jan 1809, *TJ*, 9:237–38; J. Smith, *Borderland Smuggling*, 51–65.

61. Hickey, *War of 1812*, 21–22.

62. Adams to William Eustis, 24 Aug 1811, *JQA*, 4:187–91.

63. Poindexter to Hamilton, 30 Jun 1810, Trippe to Hamilton, 30 Jun, JMP, LC, Ser. 1, R12.

64. Jefferson to Thomas Paine, 6 Sep 1807, *TJ*, 9:136–37.

65. Jefferson to Madison, 30 May 1812, *TJ*, 9:353–54.

66. Sec. of the Navy to Macon (Speaker of the House) 28 Jan 1806, *Barbary*, 6:357–58.

67. Hamilton to Navy Department Agents, 22 Mar 1810, LC, JMP, Ser. 1, R12.

68. Hamilton to Madison, 7 Nov, 9 Nov 1809, 23 May, Aug, 1 Nov 1810, 24 Jul 1811, LC, JMP, Ser. 1, R11–13.

69. Monroe to John Taylor, 10 Sep 1810, *Writings of Monroe*, ed. Hamilton, 5:128.

70. Symonds, *Navalists and Antinavalists*, 150.

71. Hamilton to [Morton A.] Waring, 4 Nov 1811, USC, Hamilton Papers.

72. Cheves to Hamilton, 19 Nov 1811, *NASP Naval*, 1:70.

73. Hamilton to Cheves, 3 Dec 1811, *NASP Naval*, 1:70–71.

74. William Lowndes (Rep. SC, House), AC, 12th Cong., 1st Sess., 886; Symonds, *Navalists and Antinavalists*, 152.

75. John Rhea (Rep. TN, House), AC, 12th Cong., 1st Sess., 910.

76. Votes, House, AC, 12th Cong., 1st Sess., 909, 999, 1003; Symonds, *Navalists and Antinavalists*, 167.

77. Note following Hamilton to Cheves, 3 Dec 1811, *NASP Naval*, 1:72.

78. Hamilton to Cheves, 30 Jun 1812, *NW1812*, 1:176–79.

79. Tingey to Hamilton, 15 Jun 1812, M125, R24/31.

80. Rodgers to Hamilton, 8 Feb, Hull to Hamilton, 23 Feb, Decatur to Hamilton, 24 Mar, Bainbridge to Hamilton, 13 Apr 1812, M125, R23/33, 50, 86, 119; Hamilton to Cheves, 3 Dec 1811, *NASP Naval*, 1:72.

81. Rodgers to Hamilton, 8 Feb, Rodgers to Hamilton, 10 Jun, 13 Jun 1812, M125, R23/33, R24/25, 29.

82. Hull to Hamilton, 27 Jun, 1 Jul 1812, M125, R24/66, 80.

83. Secret Admiralty Order, 10 Jul 1813, ADM 2/1377/154–55 (first quote); Table attached to Hamilton to Cheves, 3 Dec 1811, *NASP Naval*, 1:71; Roosevelt, *Naval War*, 60 (second quote).

84. See Table 1.5 for more specifics.

85. Upton to Griffith, 4 Apr 1814, ADM 1/506/208A; Chapelle, *American Sailing Navy*, 127, 132; Lavery, *Nelson's Navy*, 36.

86. Chapelle, *American Sailing Navy*, 128, 132. Though this author indicates they were re-rated 38-gun frigates during construction, American documents before and during the war of 1812 call them 36-gun frigates. See Hamilton to Cheves, 3 Dec 1811, Jones to Senate, 22 Feb 1814, *NASP Naval*, 1:72, 4:198–201.

87. Winfield, *British Warships*, 188–89; Canney, *Sailing Warships*, 50–51.

88. Lavery, *Nelson's Navy*, 73; Silverstone, *Sailing Navy*, 46–47, 50–51.

89. Jones to Senate, 22 Feb 1814, *NASP Naval*, 4:198–201; Jones to Madison, 26 Oct 1814, LC, JMP, Ser. 1, R16; *New England Blockaded*, ed. Whitehill, 11 May 1814, 12–13; Daughan, *If by sea*, 286.

90. Board Minutes, 1812, ADM 7/262; Ships of the U.S. Navy, 1798–99, *NASP Naval*, 1:77.

91. Adams to Abigail Adams, 1 Jan, Adams to John Adams, 13 Jul 1812, *JQA*, 4:284–86, 369–72.

92. Latimer, *War with America*, 34; Hickey, *War of 1812*, 24–27, 47.

93. Madison to Congress, 1 Jun 1812, U.S. Congress, *American State Papers, Foreign*, 3:405–407.

94. Seiken, "To Strike a Blow, 132"; Maloney, "What Role," 46–47; Kastor, "Toward 'the Maritime War,'" 473–79.

95. Hamilton to Rodgers, to Decatur, 21 May 1812, M149, R10/41–42.

96. Decatur to Hamilton, 8 Jun 1812, M125, R24/18.

97. Rodgers to Hamilton, 3 Jun 1812, M125, R23/56.

Chapter 2. " 'A Little Bit of a Dust' With an English Frigate": The Opening Naval Campaign, June to September 1812

1. Hamilton to Rodgers, 18 Jun 1812, M149, R10/61. On use of the Navy, see Seiken, "To Strike a Blow"; Maloney, "What Role"; Kastor, "Toward 'the Maritime War.'"

2. Gallatin to Madison, 20 Jun 1812, LC, JMP, Ser. 1, R14; Hamilton to Rodgers, 22 Jun 1812, M125, R23/56.

3. Rodgers to Hamilton, 21 Jun 1812, M125, R24/47.

4. Ibid., R24/48.

5. Rodgers' Journal, 23 Jun 1812, M125, R25/2A.

6. Proceedings of the *Belvidera*, 23 Jun 1812, M125, R24/210A.

7. Proceedings of the *Belvidera*, 23 Jun, Rodgers' Journal, 23 Jun 1812, M125, R24/210A, R25/2A; Log *Hornet*, 24 Jun 1812, RG24.

8. Byron to Sawyer, 27 Jun 1812, ADM 1/502/45A.

9. Rodgers, Journal, 23 Jun 1812, M125, R25/2A.

10. Log *Belvidera*, 23 Jun 1812, ADM 51/2018.

11. Rodgers, Journal, 23 Jun 1812, M125, R25/2A.

12. Ibid.

13. Log *Belvidera*, 23 Jun 1812, ADM 51/2018; Log *Congress*, 24 Jun 1812, RG24; Perry's Journal on board the *President*, 24 Jun 1812, RFP, Pt III:34.

14. Rodgers, Journal, 23 Jun 1812, M125, R25/2A. For descriptions of the encounter, see James, *Naval Occurrences*, 37–39; Forester, *Age of Fighting Sail*, 29–33; Roosevelt, *Naval War*, 73–77.

15. Byron to Sawyer, 27 Jun 1812, ADM 1/502/45A.

16. Broke to Wife, 2 Jul 1812, SRO, HA 93/9/105 (quote); Maloney, "What Role," 52.

17. Sawyer to Croker, 5 Jul 1812, ADM 1/502/45; Broke to Wife, 2 Jul 1812, SRO, HA 93/9/105.

18. Ships in Sea Pay, 1 Jul 1812, ADM 8/100.

19. Sawyer to Croker, 5 Jul 1812, ADM 1/502/45.

20. Sawyer to Broke, 4 Jul 1812, ADM 1/1553/351A.

21. Broke to Sawyer, 12 Jul (first quote), 14 Jul 1812 (all other quotes), SRO, HA 93/6/2/8, Nos. 2, 4.

22. Hamilton to Morton A. Waring, 25 Jul 1812, USC, Hamilton Papers.

23. Hamilton to Rodgers, 10 Jul 1812 (second quote), Hamilton to Crane, 10 Jul, 11 Jul 1812, Hamilton to Ridgely, 20 Jul 1812 (first quote), M149, R10/91–93, 109–10.

24. Testimony Fitz Henry Babbet (Lt.), CI *Nautilus*, 30 Sep 1812, M273, R5/119; Crane to Hamilton, 29 Jul 1812, M148, R10/114.

25. Testimony Babbet, CI *Nautilus*, 30 Sep 1812, M273, R5/119; Crane to Hamilton, 29 Jul 1812, M148, R10/114.

26. Crane to Hamilton, 29 Jul 1812, M148, R10/114; Broke to Sawyer, 28 Jul 1812, ADM 1/1553/351A; "Fate of War," *Connecticut Herald*, 28 Jul 1812 sword; "Bad News," *New-England Palladium*, 28 Jul 1812.

27. Logs *Shannon, Africa*, 16 Jul 1812, ADM 51/2861, 2092; Hull to Hamilton, 21 Jul 1812, M125, R24/127.

28. Hamilton to Hull, 18 Jun, 3 Jul 1812, M149, R10/61, 86; Hull to Hamilton, 7 Jul 1812, M125, R24/94.

29. Hull to Hamilton, 21 Jul 1812, M125, R24/127. A number of sources indicate that the *Constitution* sighted the British ships on the 17 July when in fact it was the afternoon of 16 July. The source of the confusion deals with the manner in which Hull calculated the date. Hull used a system favored by the United States Navy that saw the day advance at noon versus midnight. As a result, what Hull considered to be 2:00 pm on 17 July was in reality 2:00 p.m. on 16 July. For the *Constitution's* encounter, see Forester, *Age of Fighting Sail*, 48–56; Toll, *Six Frigates*, 339–45; and particularly Maloney, *Hull*, 171–77, who correctly notes the dates.

30. Hull to Hamilton, 21 Jul 1812, M125, R24/127; Morris, *Autobiography*, 56.

31. Hull to Hamilton, 21 Jul 1812, M125, R24/127.

32. Byron to Broke, 20 Jul 1812, SRO, HA 93/6/2/41.

33. Log *Belvidera*, 16–17 Jul 1812, ADM 51/2018; Byron to Broke, 20 Jul 1812, SRO, HA 93/6/2/41.

34. Byron to Broke, 20 Jul 1812, SRO, HA 93/6/2/41; Log *Aeolus*, 17 Jul 1812, ADM 51/2106.

35. Hull to Hamilton, 21 Jul 1812, M125, Roll 24/127; Logs *Africa, Belvidera*, 17 Jul 1812, ADM 51/2092, 2018. Hull called this the morning of 18 July, but was off by one day according to all British sources and the chronology following their capture of the *Nautilus*.

36. Log *Aeolus*, 17 Jul 1812, ADM 51/2106.

37. Hull to Hamilton, 21 Jul 1812, M125, R24/127 (quote); *Shannon's* Journal, 17 Jul 1812, SRO, HA 93/6/2/112.

38. Hull to Hamilton, 21 Jul 1812, M125, R24/127.

39. Morris, *Autobiography*, 59; *Shannon's* Journal, 17 Jul 1812, SRO, HA 93/6/2/112.

40. Hull to Hamilton, 21 Jul 1812, M125, R24/127 (quote); Log *Shannon*, 17 Jul 1812, ADM 51/2861.

41. Evans' Journal, 19 Jul 1812, LC (first quote); Broke to Croker, 30 Jul 1812, ADM 1/1553/351 (second quote). For details of the chase, see Martin, *Fortunate Ship*, 145–51.

42. Broke to Sawyer, 14 Jul 1812, entry 21 Jul, SRO, HA 93/6/2/8, No. 4; Broke to Croker, 30 Jul 1812, ADM 1/1553/351 (all quotes).

43. Log *Aeolus*, 29 Jul 1812, ADM 51/2106.

44. Stirling to Croker, 13 Jul 1812, ADM 1/263/138; Byam to Croker, 24 Aug 1812, ADM 1/1553/359; Log *Garland*, 1–2 Jul, 11–12 Jul 1812, ADM 53/572.

45. Broke to Croker, 30 Jul 1812, ADM 1/1553/351.

46. Rodgers to Hamilton, 1 Sep 1812, M125, R25/2; Sawyer to Croker, 21 Jul 1812, ADM 1/502/68; Vashon to Stirling, 8 Jun 1812, ADM 1/263/124A.

47. Rodgers to Hamilton, 1 Sep 1812, M125, R25/2; Log *Hornet*, 2 Jul 1812, RG24; Log *Thalia*, 27 Jun 1812, ADM 51/2077.

48. Rodgers to Hamilton, 1 Sep 1812, M125, R25/2; Log *Thalia*, 8 Jul 1812, ADM 51/2077. For Rodgers' cruise, see Schroeder, *Commodore Rodgers*, 114–18.

49. William Belt to H. W. Harrington, 12 Jul 1812, "The Harrington Letters," ed. Wagstaff, 13:36.

50. Broke to Sawyer, 14 Jul 1812, entry 30 Jul, SRO, HA 93/6/2/8, No. 4; Log *Thetis*, 6 Aug 1812, ADM 51/2874.

51. Byam to Croker, 24 Aug 1812, ADM 1/1553/359.

52. Broke to Sawyer, 7 Aug 1812, SRO, HA 93/6/2/8, No. 11; Broke to Wife, 9 Aug 1812, SRO, HA 93/9/109 (quote).

53. Sawyer to Croker, 25 Aug 1812, ADM 1/502/83.

54. Logs *Hornet, United States, Congress*, 26–27 Aug 1812, RG24; Log *Statira*, 27 Aug 1812, ADM 51/2814.

55. Sawyer to Croker, 9 Sep 1812, ADM 1/502/92 (quote); Rodgers to Hamilton, 1 Sep 1812, M125, R25/2; Log *Statira*, 28 Aug 1812, ADM 51/2814.

56. Rodgers to Hamilton, 4 Sep 1812, RFP, Letter & Order Book 1811–12, Pt. III:38.

57. Log *Aeolus*, 29–31 Aug 1812, ADM 51/2106; *Shannon's* Journal, 28 Aug 1812, SRO, HA 93/6/2/112.

58. Rodgers to Hamilton, 4 Sep 1812, RFP, Letter & Order Book 1811–12, Pt. III:38.

59. Rodgers to Hamilton, 31 Aug (first and second quotes), 1 Sep 1812 (third and fourth quotes), M125, R24/222, R25/2. Seiken describes the Rodgers' cruise as "a blatant act of insubordination." See "To Strike a Blow," 133.

60. Hamilton to Rodgers, 8 Sep 1812, M149, R10/143–44.

61. "Interesting Letter from Newport, 26 Jul 1812," in *Portsmouth Oracle*, 1 Aug 1812.

62. Rodgers to Hamilton, 10 Jun, 13 Jun 1812, M125, R24/25, 29.

63. Hamilton to Porter, 24 Jun 1812, M149, R10/73–74.

64. Porter to Hamilton, 3 Jul 1812, M125, R24/81.

65. Porter, *Journal*, 11 Jul 1812, & List of Prisoners, M125, R24/133a; Log *Minerva*, 11 Jul 1812, ADM 51/2585.

66. Porter, *Journal*, 11 Jul 1812, M125, R24/133a.

67. Porter to Hamilton, 12 Jul 1812, M125, R24/104; Sawyer to Croker, 5 Jul, 21 Jul, 9 Sep 1812, ADM 1/502/45, 68, 92.

68. Porter to Hamilton, 3 Sep (including list of prizes), 7 Sep 1812, M125, R25/12 (first quote), 25; Broke to Sawyer, 14 Jul 1812, entry 1 Aug, SRO, HA 93/6/2/8, No. 4 (second quote).

69. Porter to Hamilton, 3 Sep 1812 (includes list of prizes), M125, R25/12.

70. Laugharne to Duckworth, 30 Aug 1812, Comments of Laugharne, CM *Alert*, ADM 1/5431 (quote); Winfield, *British Warships*. 271; Canney, *Sailing Warships*, 50. Laugharne asserted the *Essex* had 4 x 12-pound guns.

71. Porter to Hamilton, 3 Sep 1812, M125, Roll 25/12.

72. Laugharne to Duckworth, 30 Aug 1812, Comments of Laugharne, CM *Alert*, ADM 1/5431.

73. Laugharne to Duckworth, 30 Aug 1812, Testimonies William Haggerty (Purser) and Philip Nind (Lt.), CM *Alert*, ADM 1/5431.

74. Porter to Hamilton, 3 Sep 1812, M125, R25/12; Duckworth to Croker, 23 Jul 1812, ADM 1/477/60.

75. Duckworth to Croker, 23 Jul, 20 Aug, 31 Aug 1812, ADM 1/477/56, 59, 60.

76. Porter to Hamilton, 5 Sep 1812, M125, R25/18.

77. Log *Shannon*, 4 Sep 1812, ADM 51/2861; Porter to Hamilton and sketch, 5 Sep 1812, M125 (quote), R25/18.

78. Porter to Hamilton, 5 Sep 1812, M125, R25/18.

79. Broke to Wife, 30 Aug 1812, entry 6 Sep, SRO, HA 93/9/111. For Porter's cruise, see Long, *Nothing too Daring*, 64–69; James, *Naval Occurrences*, 40–45.

80. "Arrival of the *Wasp*," *Columbian Phenix*, 18 Jul 1812.

81. Hamilton to Jones, 4 Aug 1812, M149, R10/121; Jones to Hamilton, 8 Aug 1812, M147, R4/86.

82. Jones to Hamilton, 5 Aug 1812, M147, R4/85.

83. Jones to Hamilton, 11 Sep 1812, M147, R4/92.

84. Jones to Hamilton, 25 Aug 1812, M147, R4/90; *Shannon's* Journal, 24 Aug 1812, SRO, HA 93/6/2/112; Sawyer to Croker, 25 Aug 1812, ADM 1/502/83; Log *Statira*, 26 Aug 1812, ADM 51/2814.

85. Jones to Hamilton, 11 Sep 1812, M147, R4/92; Log *Statira*, 27 Aug 1812, ADM 51/2814.

86. Hamilton to Jones, 15 Sep 1812, M149, R10/153–54.

87. Hamilton to Hull, 3 Jul 1812, M149, R10/86; Hull to Hamilton, 2 Aug 1812, M125, R24/155.

88. Hull to Hamilton, 2 Aug 1812, M125, R24/155.

89. Hamilton to Hull, 28 Jul 1812, M149, R10/116; Bainbridge to Hamilton, 4 Aug 1812, M125, R24/158; Morris, *Autobiography*, 61; McKee, *Gentlemanly and Honorable*, 469–71; Maloney, *Hull*, 180–83; Long, *Ready to Hazard*, 135.

90. Log *Constitution*, 15 Aug 1812, RG24; Evans' Journal, 15 Aug 1812, LC.

91. Hull to Hamilton, 28 Aug 1812, M125, R24/210; Log *Constitution*, 18 Aug 1812, RG24.

92. Hull to Hamilton, 30 Aug 1812, M125, R24/219.

93. Narrative, Bartholomew Kent (Lt.), CM *Guerriere*, ADM 1/5431/7; Log *Constitution*, 20 Aug 1812, RG24.

94. Hull to Hamilton, 28 Aug 1812, *NW1812*, 1:240 (quote); Log *Constitution*, 20 Aug 1812, RG24.

95. Dacres to Sawyer, 7 Sep 1812, ADM 1/502/89A; Hull to Hamilton, 28 Aug 1812, *NW1812* (quote), 1:240; Henry Gilliam to William Jones, 7 Sep 1812, "Letters of Henry Gilliam, 1809–1817," ed. Hawes, 60.

96. Testimony Kent, CM *Guerriere*, ADM 1/5431/9.

97. Hull to Hamilton, 28 Aug 1812, *NW1812*, 1:240.

98. Dacres to Sawyer, 7 Sep 1812, ADM 1/502/89A.

99. Evans' Journal, 19 Aug 1812, LC (quote); Morris, *Autobiography*, 62–63.

100. Testimony Kent, CM *Guerriere*, ADM 1/5431/12; Dacres to Sawyer, 7 Sep 1812, ADM 1/502/89A.

101. Hull to Hamilton, 28 Aug 1812, *NW1812*, 1:240.

102. Dacres to Sawyer, 7 Sep 1812, ADM 1/502/89A (first and third quotes); Testimony Kent, CM *Guerriere*, ADM 1/5431/11 (second quote).

103. Hull to Hamilton, 28 Aug 1812, *NW1812*, 1:240. For the action see James, *Naval History*, 5:372–82; Mahan, *Sea Power*, 1: 330–35; Forester, *Age of Fighting Sail*, 59–68; Gardiner, *Naval War of 1812*, 40–43; Maloney, *Hull*, 186–91.

104. Gilliam to Jones, 7 Sep 1812, "Letters of Henry Gilliam," ed. Hawes, 61.

105. Dacres to Sawyer, 7 Sep 1812, ADM 1/502/89A; Evans' Journal, 19 Aug 1812, LC.

106. Hull to Hamilton, 28 Aug 1812, *NW1812*, 1:240.

107. Evans' Journal, 20 Aug 1812, LC.

108. Denison, ed., *Old Ironsides*, 10.

109. Hamilton to Rodgers, 22 Jun 1812, M149, R10/69–70.

110. Broke to Wife, 30 Jul 1812, SRO, HA 93/9/107.

111. Sawyer to Croker, 21 Jul 1812, ADM 1/502/68; Log *Spartan*, 9 Jul–17 Aug 1812, ADM 51/2812.

Chapter 3. "It Is a Thing I Could Not Have Expected": The Second Round, September 1812–March 1813

1. "Assassination of Spencer Perceval," *Edinburgh Advertiser*, 15 May 1812.

2. William Hamilton to Augustus Foster, 11 May 1812, *Instructions*, ed. Mayo, 379; Muir, *Britain and the Defeat of Napoleon*, 196; Latimer, *War with America*, 33–4.

3. Sainty, *Admiralty Officials*, 26–27; "Henry Dundas, first Viscount Melville," *DNB*.

4. Broke to Wife, 2 Jul 1812, SRO, HA 93/9/105.

5. Sainty *Admiralty Officials*, 27; Lavery, *Nelson's Navy*, 22

6. Melville to Keith, 11 Jun 1812, NMM, KEI/37/9.

7. Castlereagh to Foster, 17 Jun, 25 Jun 1812, *Instructions*, ed. Mayo, 381, 83; J. Jones, *Britain and the World*, 311.

8. Croker to E. Coote, 21 Jul 1812, ADM 2/1375/16–17; British navy in North America, 1810–13, *Castlereagh*, 8:288.

9. John Bennett to Croker, 20 Jul 1812, ADM 1/3993.

10. Croker to Sawyer, 29 Jul 1812, ADM 2/1375/28–29; *Morning Chronicle*, 28 Jul 1812.

11. Croker to William Hamilton, 3 Aug 1812, ADM 2/1375/33–34.

12. Hotham, *Pages and Portraits*, 2:113; "Sir John Borlase Warren," *DNB*; LeFevre, "Sir John Borlase Warren," *British Admirals*, eds. LeFevre and Harding, 219–44.

13. Warren to Melville, 8 Aug 1812, NMM, LBK/2; British navy in North America, 1810–13, *Castlereagh*, 8:289.

14. Lord Radstock to Son, 4 Aug 1812, NMM, WDG/11/13/27.

15. Warren to Stirling, 20 Aug, to Laforey, 16 Sep 1812, NMM, WAR/54, 55. The instructions in both letters were nearly identical.

16. Broke to Wife, 22 Sep 1812, entry 27 Sep, SRO, HA 93/9/114.

17. Warren to Johnstone Hope, 7 Oct 1812, NMM, MEL/101; Warren to Croker, 18 Oct 1812, ADM 1/502/111.

18. For a more negative interpretation of Sawyer, see Lohnes, "British Naval Problems," 317–24.

19. Broke to Wife, 13 Oct 1812, SRO, HA 93/9/118.

20. Warren to Croker, 5 Oct 1812, ADM 1/502/98A.

21. Broke to Wife, 22 Sep 1812, entry 28 Sep, SRO, HA 93/9/114.

22. Hamilton to Hull, 28 Jul 1812, M149, Roll 10/116; Bainbridge to Hamilton, 2 Sep, 14 Sep, Hull to Hamilton, 14 Sep, Rodgers to Hamilton, 7 Sep 1812, M125, R25/6, 26, 44, 45.

23. Hamilton to Decatur, 9 Sep 1812, M149, R10/144–45.

24. Ibid.

25. Bainbridge to Hamilton, 14 Sep, 16 Sep (second quote), Bainbridge to Decatur, 15 Sep 1812 (first quote), M125, R25/45, 52 & A.

26. Hamilton to Decatur, 26 Sep 1812, M149, R10/162–63.

27. Hamilton to Rodgers, Bainbridge, and Decatur, 2 Oct 1812, M149, R10/167.

28. Rodgers to Hamilton, 3 Oct 1812, RFP, Letter & Order Book, 1811–12, Pt III:38; Sinclair to Hamilton, 2 Jan 1812 [misdated; should be 1813], M147, R5/1.

29. Logs *Belvidera, Aeolus*, Sep–Oct 1812, ADM 51/2018, 2106; Sawyer to Croker, 25 Aug, 9 Sep 1812, ADM 1/502/83, 92.

30. "Our Little Squadron," *New-York Gazette*, 13 Oct 1812.

31. *President's* Journal, 11 Oct 1812, RFP, Pt III:34; Log *Nymphe*, 10 Oct 1812, ADM 51/2590.

32. Rodgers to Smith, 12 Oct 1812 [never sent], RFP, Letter & Order Book, 1811–12, Pt III:38; Rodgers to Hamilton, 4 Sep 1812, M125, R25/16; Log *Congress*, 13 Oct 1812, RG24.

33. *Shannon's* Journal, 3 Oct 1812, SRO, HA 93/6/2/112; Broke to Wife, 29 Sep 1812, entry 3 Oct, SRO, HA 93/9/115.

34. Warren to John Bastard (Capt. *Africa*), 4 Oct, Warren to Beresford, 10 Oct 1812, NMM, HUL/1, Nos. 1–2.

35. Logs *Acasta, Spartan*, early Oct 1812, ADM 51/2102, 2812; Warren to Broke, 14 Oct 1812, NMM, HUL/1, No. 3.

36. Log *Belvidera*, 11–12 Oct 1812, ADM 51/2018; *Shannon's* Journal, 12 Oct 1812, SRO, HA 93/6/2/112.

37. Warren to Croker, 18 Oct 1812, ADM 1/502/111.

38. Broke to Wife, 22 Sep 1812, SRO, HA 93/9/113; CM *Guerriere*, 2 Oct 1812, ADM 1/5131.

39. Milne to George Hume, 15 Oct 1812, HMC, *Home*, 156.

40. Letter to the Editor, signed Albion, 10 Nov 1812, *Naval Chronicle*, 28:386.

41. W. Jones, ed., "A British View," 485.

42. *Times* (London), 7 Oct, 10 Oct 1812.

43. Letter to the Editor, signed Albion, 10 Nov 1812, *Naval Chronicle*, 28:386–87.

44. Melville to Croker, 6 Oct 1812, Duke, Croker Papers, Box 2.

45. *Times* (London), 29 Oct 1812.

46. Carden, *Curtail'd Memoir*, 258; Leech, *Voice*, 70–71.

47. Henry Veitch (Consul Madeira) to Croker, 2 Oct 1813, ADM 1/3845.

48. Midshipman's letter on board the *U.S.*, 3 Dec 1812, in *American Watchman*, 12 Dec 1812; Testimony John Wilson (Marine Lt.), CM *Macedonian*, ADM 1/5436.

49. Testimony James Walker (Master), CM *Macedonian*, ADM 1/5436; Letter from Midshipman, 3 Dec 1812, in *American Watchman*, 12 Dec 1812.

50. Testimony David Hope (1st Lt.), CM *Macedonian*, ADM 1/5436; Letter from Officer on board *U.S.* to Father, 16 Dec 1812, in *Columbian*, 11 Jan 1813.

51. Leech, *Voice*, 73.

52. Ibid., 74–76.

53. Narrative of Carden, CM *Macedonian*, ADM 1/5436.

54. Carden to Croker, 28 Oct 1812, CM *Macedonian*, ADM 1/5436; Letter from Officer to Father, 16 Dec 1812, in *Columbian*, 11 Jan 1813. For the action, see DeKay, *Chronicles*, 66–88.

55. Carden to Croker, 28 Oct 1812, CM *Macedonian*, ADM 1/5436; Details for *Macedonian*, ADM 7/556; Decatur to Hamilton, 30 Oct 1812, M125, R25/154; Letter from Midshipman, 3 Dec 1812, in *American Watchman*, 12 Dec 1812; Letter from Officer to Father, 16 Dec 1812, in *Columbian*, 11 Jan 1813 (quote).

56. Decatur to Rodgers, [early 1813], RFP, Pt II:3; Decatur to Hamilton, 30 Oct 1812, M125, R25/154.

57. Barrie to George Clayton, 14 Jan 1813, Duke, Barrie Papers, Box 5 (first quote); Verdict, CM *Macedonian*, ADM 1/5436 (second quote).

58. Melville to Warren, 30 Dec 1812, NMM, WAR/82/29–31.

59. Decatur to Hamilton, 4 Dec 1812, M125, R25/207.

60. Rodgers to Hamilton, 17 Oct 1812, M125, R25/132.

61. Log *Congress*, 31 Oct 1812, RG24; *Jackson's Oxford Journal*, 21 Nov 1812.

62. Log *Congress*, 31 Oct–1 Nov 1812, RG24; Log *Galatea*, 31 Oct 1812, ADM 53/582; Rodgers to Hamilton, 31 Dec 1812, M125, R25/220; *President's* Journal, 1 Nov 1812, RFP, Pt III:34.

63. Croker to Warren, 18 Nov 1812, ADM 2/1375/252–59; Melville to Croker, 15 Nov 1812, Duke, Croker Papers, Box 7 (quote).

64. Winter Deployments, 1812–13, NMM, WAR/30/10–12.

65. Broke to Wife, 15 Oct 1812, SRO, HA 93/9/117; Rodgers to Hamilton, 31 Dec 1812, M125, R25/228.

66. Sinclair to Hamilton, 2 Jan 1812 [misdated; should be 1813], M147, R5/1.

67. Sinclair's Journal, 15 Dec 1812, M147, R5/1A.

68. Warren to Croker, 28 Dec 1812, ADM 1/503/16; Log *San Domingo*, 15 Dec 1812, ADM 51/2834.

69. Warren to Broke, 27 Nov 1812, NMM, HUL/1; Warren to Croker, 20 Feb 1813, ADM 1/503/33a.

70. Log *Junon*, 15 Dec 1812, ADM 53/740.

71. Sinclair's Journal, 15–16 Dec 1812, M147, R5/1A; Log *San Domingo*, 16 Dec 1812, ADM 51/2834.

72. Log *San Domingo*, 16 Dec 1812, ADM 51/2834; Log *Congress*, 16 Dec 1812, RG24; "Com. Rodgers' Squadron," *Boston Patriot*, 2 Jan 1813.

73. Sinclair's Journal, 16 Dec 1812, M147, R5/1A.

74. Log *Congress*, 17 Dec 1812, RG24; "Com. Rodgers' Squadron," *Boston Patriot*, 2 Jan 1813.

75. Perry's Journal on board the *President*, 17 Dec 1812, RFP, Pt III:34; Chapelle, *American Sailing Navy*, 184; M. Crawford, "Navy's Campaign," 169.

76. Sinclair's Journal, 16–17 Dec 1812, M147, R5/1A.

77. Sinclair's Journal, 17 Dec 1812, M147, R5/1A; Log *Congress*, 17 Dec 1812, RG24.

78. Log *San Domingo*, 16 Dec 1812, ADM 51/2834; Warren to Croker, 20 Feb 1813, ADM 1/503/33a.

79. Sinclair's Journal, 17 Dec 1812, M147, R5/1A.

80. Ibid. (all quotes); Log *San Domingo*, 17 Dec 1812, ADM 51/2834. Warren later took credit for forcing Sinclair to have lightened the *Argus*. See Warren to Croker, 25 Jan 1813, *NW1812*, 2:15–16.

81. Sinclair's Journal, 18 Dec 1812, M147, R5/1A (all quotes); Logs *Wanderer*, *Junon*, 17 Dec 1812, ADM 51/2971, ADM 53/740.

82. Sinclair to Hamilton, 2 Jan [1813]; Sinclair's Journal, 18 Dec 1812, M147, R5/1 & A.

83. Warren to Croker, 28 Dec 1812, ADM 1/503/16.

84. Sinclair to Hamilton, 2 Jan [1813], Sinclair's Journal, 18 Dec 1812, M147, R5/1 & A.

85. Rodgers to Hamilton, 31 Dec 1812, 2 Jan 1813, M125, R25/228, R26/4; Schroeder, *Commodore Rodgers*, 118–20.

86. Rodgers to Hamilton, 17 Sep 1812, M125, R25/53. Cruising instructions for the *Wasp* can be found in Rodgers' Letter & Order Book for 1811–12, but this copy omits all coordinates and place names. All that can be extrapolated from this incomplete document is that Rodgers gave the commander of the *Wasp* substantial flexibility in choosing cruising grounds and alternative courses of action if he failed to find Rodgers. See Rodgers to Jones, 26 Sep 1812, RFP, Pt III:38.

87. Officer of *Wasp* to a Friend, 31 Oct 1812, in *American Watchman*, 2 Dec 1812.

88. Jones to Hamilton, 24 Nov 1812, M147, R5/118.

89. Ships in Sea Pay, 1 Jan 1812, ADM 8/100; Testimony John Collins (Purser), CM *Frolic*, ADM 1/5434; Whinyates to Warren, 23 Oct 1812, ADM 1/502/117A (quote).

90. Testimonies Broughton Wintle (Lt.) (first quote) and Collins, CM *Frolic*, ADM 1/5434; Jones to Hamilton, 24 Nov 1812, M147, R5/118; Whinyates to Warren, 23 Oct 1812, ADM 1/502/117A (second and third quotes); Officer of *Wasp* to a Friend, 31 Oct 1812, in *American Watchman*, 2 Dec 1812.

91. Whinyates to Warren, 23 Oct 1812, ADM 1/502/117A; Jones to Hamilton, 24 Nov 1812, M147, R51/118.

92. Testimony Collins, CM *Frolic*, ADM 1/5434.

93. Jones to Hamilton, 24 Nov 1812, M147, R5/118; Testimonies Wintle (second quote), John Beresford (Captain *Poictiers*), CM *Frolic*, ADM 1/5434; Biddle to Father, 21 Oct 1812 (first quote), in *New-York Spectator*, 4 Nov 1812.

94. Narrative of Jones, CI *Wasp*, M273, Roll 6/121; Letter from an officer of the *Wasp*, 25 Oct 1812, in *Columbian Centinel*, 28 Nov 1812.

95. Evans' Journal, 27 Oct 1812, LC; Porter, *Journal*, 10.

96. Logs *Africa*, 26 Oct, *Shannon*, 27 Oct 1812, ADM 51/2092, 2861; Warren to Byron, 20 Oct 1812, NMM, HUL/1, No. 4; Warren to Croker, 5 Oct, 5 Nov 1812, ADM 1/502/98, 131.

97. Bainbridge to Jones, 5 Oct, Jones to Bainbridge, 11 Oct 1812, *NW1812*, 1:510–15.

98. Bainbridge to Porter, 13 Oct 1812, M125, R26/6 1/2; Porter, *Journal*, 28.

99. Porter to Bainbridge, 23 Mar 1813, M125, R29/139A.

100. Porter, *Journal*, 51–53 (quote); Long, *Nothing too Daring*, 76–78.

101. Porter to Bainbridge, 23 Mar 1813, M125, Roll 29/139A; Porter, *Journal*, 52, 56.

102. Evans' Journal, 13–14 Dec, 18 Dec 1812, LC; Bainbridge to Lawrence, 13 Dec 1812, Response of Henry Hill, n.d., M125, R26/7 1/2, 8; Ships in Sea Pay, 1 Jan 1813, ADM 8/100.

103. Bainbridge to Lawrence, 19 Dec 1812, M125, R26/7 1/2.

104. Evans' Journal, 23–26 Dec 1812 (quote), LC; Log *Hornet*, 25 Dec 1812, RG24.

105. Bainbridge to Hill, 26 Dec 1812, M125, R26/8A.

106. Hill to the British Consul, 28 Dec 1812, M125, R26/10A; Details for *Bonne Citoyenne*, ADM 7/556; Frederick Wright to [the Admiralty], 26 Mar 1813, ADM 1/503/88A.

107. Extract, from Greene in Hill to Lawrence, 29 Dec 1812 (first quote), Bainbridge to Hamilton, n.d., M125, R26/10 (second and third quotes); Long, *Ready to Hazard*, 147.

108. Bainbridge's Journal, 29–30 Dec 1812, M125, R26/81/2; Chads, *Memoir of Admiral Chads*, 12–13.

109. Details of Action, CM *Java*, ADM 1/5435.

110. Evans' Journal, 29 Dec 1812, LC; Bainbridge's Journal, 29 Dec 1812, M125, R26/8 1/2.

111. Bainbridge's Journal, 30 Dec 1812, M125, R26/8 1/2; Chads to Croker, 31 December 1812, CM *Java*, ADM 1/5435.

112. Detail of Action, and Testimony James Humble (Boatswain), CM *Java*, ADM 1/5435. Bainbridge recorded that after the first broadside his opponent hoisted her colors "and then immediately returned our fire." See Bainbridge's Journal, 30 Dec 1812, M125, R26/8 1/2.

113. Testimony James Saunders (Lt.), Detail of the Action, CM *Java*, ADM 1/5435.

114. Bainbridge's Journal, 30 Dec 1812, M125, R26/8 1/2.

115. Details of Action and Map, CM *Java*, ADM 1/5435.

116. Details of Action, CM *Java*, ADM 1/5435.

117. Details of Action (quote), Testimonies Saunders, Humble, John Marshall (Commander), Robert Mercer (Lt. Marines), Christopher Speedy (Capt. of the Forecastle), and Map, CM *Java*, ADM 1/5435.

118. Chads to Croker, 31 Dec 1812 and Map, CM *Java*, ADM 1/5435.

119. Details of Action, CM *Java*, ADM 1/5435.

120. Bainbridge's Journal, 30 Dec 1812, M125, R26/8 1/2; Testimony Marshal, CM *Java* (quote), ADM 1/5435.

121. Bainbridge's Journal, 30 Dec 1812, M125, R26/8 1/2.

122. Chads to Croker, 31 Dec 1812, CM *Java*, ADM 1/5435.

123. Details of Action, CM *Java*, ADM 1/5435.

124. Clarification by Chads, CM *Java*, ADM 1/5435; Bainbridge's Journal, 30 Dec 1812, M125, R26/8 1/2. For the action, see Long, *Ready to Hazard*, 149–59.

125. Bainbridge's Journal, 30 Dec 1812, M125, R26/8 1/2; Details of Action, CM *Java*, ADM 1/5435; Evans' Journal, 29–31 Dec 1812, LC.

126. Evans' Journal, 1 Jan 1813, LC: Bainbridge to Lawrence, 5 Jan 1813 (quote), Bainbridge to Hamilton, 25 Jan 1813, M125, R26/7 1/2 & 54.

127. Evans' Journal, 6 Feb 1813, LC; Log *Dotterel*, 6–8 Feb 1813, ADM 51/2294.

128. Logs *Ramillies, Acasta, Shannon*, 6–9 Feb 1813, ADM 51/2027, 2102, 2861.

129. Bainbridge to Hamilton, 15 Feb 1813, M125, R26/74.

130. Bainbridge to Lawrence, 5 Jan 1812, M125, R26/7 1/2.

131. Dixon to Croker, 14 Jan 1813, Frederick Lindeman to Dixon, 19 Dec 1812, ADM 1/20/25 & A.

132. Log *Hornet*, 24 Jan 1813, RG24; Log *Montagu*, 23–24 Jan 1813, ADM 51/2555.

133. Log *Hornet*, 23–24 Feb 1813, RG24; Lawrence to Jones, 19 Mar 1813, M125, R27/61.

134. Examination of the *Espiegle*, 1 Jun 1813, ADM 1/334/51A.

135. Lawrence to Jones, 19 Mar 1813, M125, R27/61; Narrative of four survivors, ADM 1/334/32A (both quotes).

136. Testimonies Wright and Mr. Aberdeen (gunner), CM *Peacock*, ADM 1/5436.

137. Details for *Peacock*, ADM 7/556; Wright to [the Admiralty], 26 Mar 1813, ADM 1/503/88A.

138. Wright to [the Admiralty], 26 Mar 1813, ADM 1/503/88A (all quotes); Keene, "Notes," 73.

139. Narrative of four survivors, ADM 1/334/32A; Wright to [the Admiralty], 26 Mar 1813, ADM 1/503/88A.

140. Narrative of four survivors, ADM 1/334/32A; Lawrence to Jones, 19 Mar 1813, M125, R27/61.

141. Lawrence to Jones, 19 Mar 1813, M125, R27/61; Examination of the *Espiegle*, 1 Jun 1813, ADM 1/334/51A.

142. Lawrence to Jones, 19 Mar 1813, M125, R27/61.

143. Croker to Warren, 2 Dec 1812, ADM 2/1107/346–51.

144. Broke to Wife, 14 Dec 1812, entry 18 Dec, SRO HA 93/9/128.

145. "Commodore Rodgers, 1 Jan," *New Hampshire Patriot*, 5 Jan 1813.

146. "American Squadron, Boston 10 Oct," *Constitutionalist and Weekly Magazine*, 13 Oct 1812.

147. Broke to Wife, 4 Feb 1813, SRO, HA/9/134; *Times* (London), 21 Oct 1812; Black, *War of 1812*, 129.

148. *Trewman's Exeter Flying Post*, 6 Aug 1812. The list missed the *Wasp* and *Viper*.

149. Foster to Sawyer, 15 Jun 1812, ADM 1/502/44A.

150. Dillon, *Narrative*, 2:182.

151. Cochrane to William Domett (on the Admiralty Board), 25 Jan 1813, CP, MS 2574/35–36.

152. Dillon, *Narrative*, 2:277–78.

Chapter 4. "If We Could Take One or Two of These D—d Frigates": Reassessment of Britain's Naval Objectives, 1812–13

1. John Ingles to Croker, 9 Oct 1812, NLS, CP, 2340/3; Comparative Insurance Premiums, 1812 and 1813, NAS, GD 51/2/882/4.

2. Croker to Warren, 18 Nov 1812, ADM 2/1375/252–59.

3. British navy in North America, 1810–13, *Castlereagh*, 8:290.

4. Croker to Warren, 18 Nov 1812, ADM 2/1375/252–59. Several sources outline problems between the Admiralty and Warren. See Goldenberg, "Royal Navy's Blockade," 427–29; Wade Dudley, *Splintering*, Ch. 6; Lohnes, "British Naval Problems," 324–25.

5. Bathurst to Admiralty, 21 Nov 1812, Admiralty to Warren, 27 Nov 1812, NLS, CP, MS 2340, 19, 25–26.

6. Melville to Warren, 3 Dec 1812, NMM, WAR/82/18–22.

7. Warren to Melville, 19 Feb 1813, NMM, WAR/82/22-24.

8. Melville to Warren, 9 Jan 1813, NMM, WAR/82/41–45; Warren to Melville, 18 Nov 1812 [received mid-February], NMM, Warren Papers, LBK/2.

9. Melville to Warren, 9 Jan 1813, NMM, WAR/82/41–45; Warren to Melville, 18 Nov 1812 [received mid-February], NMM, Warren Papers, LBK/2.

10. Melville to Warren, 9 Jan 1813, NMM, WAR/82/41–45.

11. Warren to Croker, 20 Feb, 21 Feb 1813, ADM 1/503/33a, 36a.

12. Warren to Croker, 5 Nov 1812 [received 29 Dec], ADM 1/502/131.

13. Broke to Wife, 10 Jan 1813, SRO, HA 93/9/133.

14. *Morning Chronicle*, 28 Dec 1812, 6 Jan 1813; *Times* (London), 29 Dec 1812.

15. Melville to Warren. 9 Jan 1813, NMM, WAR/82/41–45.

16. Croker to Warren, 9 Jan 1813, NLS, CP, MS 2340/37–42.

17. Warren to Melville, 12 Aug 1812, 25 Feb 1813 (quote), NMM, LBK/2; Melville to Warren, 9 Jan 1813, NMM, WAR/82/41–45; Lavery, *Nelson's Navy*, 252; Wade Dudley, *Splintering*, 80–81.

18. Melville to Warren, 3 Dec 1812 (first quote), 23 Mar 1813 (second quote), NMM, WAR/82/18–22, 56–64.

19. Beresford to Warren, 13 Apr 1813, NMM, WAR/69/145a-f.

20. Melville to Hotham, 6 Jan 1813, Hotham Papers, HUL U DDHO/x1/7/37.

21. Wellington to Beresford, 6 Feb 1813, Wellington, *Dispatches of Wellington*, 10:91–92.

22. Statement Baring, 18 Feb 1813, HC, 24:622; Muir, *Britain and the Defeat of Napoleon*, 236–37; Black, *War of 1812*, 129.

23. Statement Canning, 18 Feb 1813, HC, 24:642–43.

24. Thompson, *Earl Bathurst*, 52; Muir, *Britain and the Defeat of Napoleon*, 197.

25. Statements Bathurst, Marquis Wellesley, 18 Feb 1813, HL, 24:576–77, 584.

26. Statements Melville, Liverpool, 18 Feb 1813, HL, 24:583–86.

27. British navy in North America, 1810–13, *Castlereagh*, 8:286–92.

28. Warren to Croker, 29 Dec 1812, ADM 1/503/18.

29. Hope to Keith, 12 Jan 1813, NMM, KEI/37/9.

30. Croker to Warren, 10 Feb 1813, ADM 2/1376/73–87. Croker asserted a total of ninety-seven warships but the numbers he provided add up to ninety-eight.

31. Letter signed Oceanus, 1 Dec 1812, signed Æolus, 16 Jan 1813, *Naval Chronicle*, 29:12–13, 113–14.

32. Croker to Warren, 10 Feb 1813, Croker to Warren and Stirling, 16 Feb 1813, ADM 2/1376/73–87, 108–09.

33. Warren to Croker, 20 Feb, 25 Feb 1813, ADM 1/503/33a, 48.

34. ATT C: Proposed Division of Ships & Their Stations, 21 Feb 1813, ADM 1/4359/183–84.

35. Melville to Warren, 23 Mar 1813, NMM, WAR/82/56–64.

36. *Examiner*, 21 Mar 1813.

37. R. Dundas to Thomas Cochrane, 2 Apr 1813, NLS, MS 2265, 5–6.

38. Croker to Warren, 20 Mar 1813, ADM 2/1376/341–67.

39. Admiralty to Warren, 26 Mar 1813, NLS, CP, MS 2340/49; Melville to Warren, 26 Mar 1813, NMM, WAR/82/68–70 (quote); Kert, "Fortune of War"; Dudley, *Splintering*, Ch 6.

40. Black, *War of 1812*, 133–34; Wade Dudley, *Splintering*, 26–28.

41. Warren to Melville, 19 Apr 1813, NMM, LBK/2; Black, *War of 1812*, 131; McCranie, *Admiral Lord Keith*, 149–66.

42. Croker to Warren, 28 Apr 1813, ADM 2/1376/320–22.

43. Warren to Melville, 19 Apr 1813, NMM, LBK/2.

44. Broke to Wife, 14 Feb 1813, entry 17th (first quote), and 20 Mar 1813 (second quote), SRO, HA 93/9/135–36.

45. Broke to Wife, 10 Jan 1813, entry 20th (second quote), and 9 May 1813 (first quote), SRO, HA 93/9/132, 140.

Chapter 5. "Cast Away . . . or Taken": American Naval Failure and Reassessment, June 1812–Early 1813

1. Blakeley to Hamilton, 16 Apr 1812, M148 R9/191.

2. Hamilton to Blakeley, 19 May 1812, M149, R10/41.

3. David McCrery to Alexander Gordon, 6 Sep 1813, ADM 1/504/194A; Yeo to Stirling, 22 Nov 1812, ADM 1/264/17A; Shaw to Hamilton, 3 Feb 1812, M125, R23/28A. American naval deployments in the southern United States were exclusive of gunboats.

4. Hamilton to Shaw, Campbell, Dent, and Gautier, 19 Jun 1812, M149, R10/63.

5. Shaw to Hamilton, 11 Jul 1812, M125, R24/101.

6. Shaw to Henley, 16 Jun 1812, LC, Shaw Papers, Container 3, Letter Book; "Repertory Ship News," *Repertory & General Advertiser*, 7 Aug 1812; *Western Star*, 12 Sep 1812.

7. Shaw to Officer commanding the Balize Division, 9 Jul 1812, LC, Shaw Papers, Container 3, Letter Book; *Enquirer*, 22 Sep 1812.

8. Shaw to Dexter, 10 Jul 1812, LC, Shaw Papers, Container 3, Letter Book; Shaw to Hamilton, 4 Aug 1812, M125, R24/156 (quote).

9. Dexter to Shaw, 10 Aug 1812, RG45, Dexter Letter Book, 14; Winfield, *British Warships*, 252.

10. Shaw to Hamilton, 17 Aug 1812, M125, R24/171; Stirling to Warren, 30 Nov 1812, ADM 1/264/18A; Ships in Sea Pay, 1 Jul 1812, ADM 8/100. The Admiralty list placed twenty-three operational warships at Stirling's disposal, but at least three had sailed to England with convoys.

11. Shaw to Blakeley, 27 Jul, 17 Aug 1812 (quote), LC, Shaw Papers, Container 3, Letter Book.

12. Shaw to Hamilton, 23 Aug 1812, M125, R24/194; Log *Brazen*, 17–18 Aug 1812, ADM 51/2013.

13. Shaw to Hamilton, 23 Aug 1812, M125, R24/194; "Hurricane," *Enquirer*, 29 Sep 1812 (both quotes); "Extract from the *New Orleans Trumpeter* of 21 Aug," in *Newport Mercury*, 26 Sep 1812.

14. Log *Enterprize*, 19–20 Aug 1812, RG24; Shaw to Hamilton, 23 Aug 1812, M125, R24/194.

15. "Extract of a letter from New Orleans, 24 Aug," *Federal Republican & Commercial Gazette*, 25 Sep 1812.

16. Log *Brazen*, 19–20 Aug, 5–12 Sep 1812, ADM 51/2013; Log *Arethusa*, 18–20 Aug, 5 Sep 1812, ADM 51/2122; Murdoch, "British Report," 40–41.

17. *American Watchman*, 14 Oct 1812; *Newburyport Herald*, 25 Sep 1812.

18. Melville to Warren, 21 Oct 1812, NMM, WAR/82/16–18.

19. Stirling to Warren, 30 Nov 1812, ADM 1/264/18A.

20. Bainbridge to Hamilton, 5 Dec (first quote), Officers of *Siren* to Bainbridge, 6 Nov 1812, M148, R10/201 & A (second quote).

21. Blakeley to Hamilton, 3 Aug 1812, M148, R10/134.

22. Hamilton to Blakeley, 30 Aug 1812, M149, R10/137; Blakeley to Hamilton, 29 Nov 1812, M148, R10/191.

23. Shaw to Hamilton, 27 Oct 1812, M125, R25/147.

24. Shaw to Hamilton, 17 Aug 1812, M125, R24/179; Hamilton to Shaw, 12 Oct 1812, M149, R10/174; Wilkinson to Shaw, 7 Aug 1812, *NW1812*, 1:396–97.

25. Shaw to Wilkerson, 22 Dec 1812, LC, Shaw Papers, Letter Book, Container 3.

26. Dexter to Goldsborough, 28 Dec 1812, RG45, Dexter Letter Book, 44–45.

27. Henley to Hamilton, 25 Nov 1812 (quote), 1 Feb 1813, M148, R10/182, 11/30.

28. Henley to Hamilton, 1 Feb 1813, M148, R11/30.

29. Narrative of Henley & Testimonies Henley (quote), Humphrey Magrath, CI *Viper*, M273, R6/136; Log *Narcissus*, 17 Jan 1813, ADM 51/2609.

30. Blakeley to Hamilton, 23 Jan 1813, M124, R53/49.

31. Campbell to Hamilton, 4 Jul 1812, M125, R24/89; Gadsden to Hamilton, 4 Jul 1812, M148, R10/74 1/2.

32. Campbell to Hamilton, 15 Aug 1812, M125, R24/175.

33. Campbell to Hamilton, 5 Sep 1812, M125, R25/17; *City Gazette and Daily Advertiser*, 17 Aug 1812.

34. Dent to Hamilton, 27 Aug, Campbell to Hamilton, 5 Sep 1812, M125, R24/204, 25/17.

35. Logs *Moselle*, *Variable*, 14–20 Oct 1812, ADM 51/2572, 2938; Ships in Sea Pay, 1 Jul 1812, ADM 8/100; Dent to Hamilton, 14 Oct 1812, M125, R25/118; "Ship News, Nassau, 25 Oct," *City Gazette and Daily Advertiser*, 2 Nov 1812.

36. Hamilton to Waring, 26 Oct 1812, USC, Hamilton Papers (first and third quotes); Hamilton to Porter, 22 Oct 1812, M149, R10/183, 85; Hamilton to Bainbridge, 23 Oct 1812, M149, R10/183, 85 (second quote).

37. Campbell to Hamilton, 29 Oct 1812, M125, R25/151.

38. Reed to Hamilton, n.d., M124, R55/95; Testimonies Edwin Satterwhite, Glen Drayton (Lt.) (quote), CI *Vixen*, M273, R6/139; *Narrative of the Capture of the Vixen*, 3–4; Ships in Sea Pay, 1 Jul 1812, ADM 8/100; Winfield, *British Warships*, 189.

39. Drayton to Hamilton, 8 Feb 1813, M148, R11/46; *Narrative of the Capture of the Vixen*, 5 (quote). The cursory British official report can be found at Yeo to Stirling, 22 Nov 1812, ADM 1/264/17A.

40. Yeo's Narrative, dated 13 Feb 1813, CM *Southampton*, ADM 1/5434.

41. *Narrative of the Capture of the Vixen*, 7–8; Drayton to Hamilton, 8 Feb 1813, M148, R11/46.

42. Yeo to Stirling, 11 Dec 1812, *NW1812*, 1:595; Drayton to Hamilton, 8 Feb 1813, M148, R11/46.

43. Campbell to Hamilton, 8 Jan 1813, M125, R26/14.

44. Hamilton to Evans, 28 Nov 1812, M149, R10/214; Leiner, "Squadron Commander's Share," 71.

45. Log *Chesapeake*, 18 Dec 1812, SRO, 93/6/2/258; Evans to Jones, 10 Apr 1813, M125, R27/166.

46. Winter Deployments, 1812–13, NMM, WAR/30/10–12.

47. Nichols' Journal, 1 Jan 1813, Du Pont Winterthur Museum, Doc 781; Sawyer to Andrew Allen (British Consul in Massachusetts), 5 Aug, Circular by Sawyer, 4 Aug 1812, Extract of Journal, attached to Evans to Hamilton, 12 Jan 1813, M125, R26/2A, 16 (all quotes); Statement Bathurst, Address Respecting the War with America, 18 Feb 1813, HL, 24:576–77. For more details on the issue of licenses, see Hickey, *War of 1812*, 117–23; Watson, "United States and the Peninsular War"; Galpin, "American Grain Trade"; M. Crawford, "Navy's Campaign."

48. Thomas Blodget to Hamilton, 4 Feb 1813, M148, R11/34.

49. Evans to Hamilton, 12 Jan, Evans to Decatur, 10 Apr 1813, M125, R26/16, R27/166A.

50. Blodget to Hamilton, 4 Feb 1813, M148, R11/34.

51. Evans to Decatur, 10 Apr 1813, M125, R27/166A; Logs *Shannon, Inconstant, Colossus*, and *Elephant*, 1 Jan 1813, ADM 51/2861, 2487, 2210, 2344.

52. Nichols' Journal, 12 Jan 1813, Du Pont Winterthur Museum, Doc 781; Tucker to Dixon, 7 Feb 1813, ADM 1/21/48A (both quotes); Evans to Hamilton, 12 Jan 1813, M125, R26/16; Leiner, "Squadron Commander's Share," 69–71.

53. Log *Cherub*, 12 Jan 1813, ADM 51/2205.

54. Evans to Decatur, 10 Apr 1813, M125, R27/166A; Yarnall to Hamilton, 20 Feb 1813, M148, R11/73.

55. Evans to Decatur, 10 Apr 1813, M125, R27/166A.

56. Evans to Decatur, 10 Apr 1813, M125, R27/166A; Laforey to Croker, 16 Mar, 12 Apr 1813, ADM 1/334/32, 41.

57. "British Frigates," *Essex Register*, 14 Apr 1813; Warren to Broke, 3 Mar 1813, Warren to Oliver, 10 Mar 1813, NMM, HUL/1.

58. Journal of the *Tenedos*, 2 Apr 1813, HSP; *Shannon's* Journal, 2–6 Apr 1813, HA 93/6/2/112–13; Capel to Warren, 25 Apr 1813, NMM, WAR/69/165–66 (quote).

59. Evans to Decatur, 10 Apr 1813, M125, R27/166A; Log *Chesapeake*, 10 Apr 1812, SRO 93/6/2/258.

60. Journal of the *Tenedos*, 11 Apr 1813, HSP.

61. President's Annual Message, 4 Nov 1812, AC, 12th Cong., 2nd Sess., 13.

62. Burwell Bassett (Chairman, Naval Committee, House) to the House of Representatives, 27 Nov 1812, *NASP Naval*, 1:73.

63. Hamilton to Bassett, 13 Nov 1812, *NASP Naval*, 1:73–74; Symonds, *Navalists and Antinavalists*, 174–76.

64. Samuel Mitchell's Address (Rep NY, House), 16 Dec 1812, AC, 12th Cong., 2nd Sess., 413.

65. Hamilton to Bassett, 13 Nov 1812, *NASP Naval*, 1:74.

66. Stewart to Hamilton, 12 Nov 1812, *NASP Naval*, 1:76.

67. Warren to Croker, 25 Feb 1812, ADM 1/503/37 & A.

68. Senate, 14–15 Dec, House, 16 Dec 1812, AC, 12th Cong., 2nd Sess., 32–33, 404. For this and the subsequent debate, see Symonds, *Navalists and Antinavalists*, 176–84.

69. Potter's Address (House), 23 Dec 1812, AC, 12th Cong., 2nd Sess., 444–45.

70. Sawyer's Address (House), 16 Dec 1812, AC, 12th Cong., 2nd Sess., 405, 409.

71. Melville to Warren, 4 Jun 1813, NMM, WAR/82/73–77; Winfield, *British Warships*, 122–23.

72. Croker to Warren, 9 Jan 1813, NLS, CP, MS 2340/37–42; Croker to Warren, 10 Feb 1813, ADM 2/1376/73–87; Winfield, *British Warships*, 110.

73. Adam Seybert (Rep PA, House), Widgery's Address (House), Bassett's Address, Silas Stow's Address (Rep NY, House) (quote), 17 Dec, Vote, 23 Dec 1812, AC, 12th Cong., 2nd Sess., 414, 418, 423, 427–28, 449–50.

74. *City Gazette and Daily Advertiser*, 25 Dec 1812; Samuel Taggart to John Taylor, 8 Dec 1812, "Letters of Taggart," ed. Haynes, 412 (quote).

75. Porter to Samuel Hambleton, 4 Oct 1812, LC, Porter Papers, Box 2.

76. Charles Goldsborough to Madison, 7 Jan 1813, LC, JMP, Ser. 1, R14 (quote); McKee, *Gentlemanly and Honorable*, 10–11; Stagg, *Madison's War*, 289–90.

77. Hickey, *War of 1812*, 100–107.

78. Roberts to Jones, 28 Dec 1812, HSP, PWJ.

79. *City Gazette and Daily Advertiser*, 25 Dec 1812. For information about Jones, see McKee, *Gentlemanly and Honorable*, 11–13; Eckert, *The Navy Department*.

80. Roberts to Jones, 28 Dec 1812, HSP PWJ; Jefferson to Jones, 16 May, Jones to Jefferson, 20 May 1801, LC, Thomas Jefferson Papers, Ser. 1.

81. *The Evening Post*, 11 Jan 1813.

82. Bainbridge to Jones, 1 Mar 1813, HSP, PWJ.

83. Jones to Madison, 25 Apr 1814, LC, JMP, Ser. 1, R16.

84. "Paul Hamilton," *The Statesman*, 11 Jan 1813.

85. Letter from Washington, 8 Jan, *City Gazette and Daily Advertiser*, 18 Jan 1813.

86. Jones to Eleanor Jones (Wife), 23 Jan 1813, HSP, PWJ.

87. Jones to Lloyd Jones (Brother), 27 Feb 1813, HSP, PWJ.

88. Bainbridge to Jones, 1 Mar 1813, HSP, PWJ.

89. Jones to Bassett, 2 Feb 1813, Letters to Congress, RG45, Vol. 2/147–48.

90. Bassett, 5 Feb, Vote to Increase the Navy, 15 Feb 1813, 12th Cong., 2nd Sess., 1011, 1161; Symonds, *Navalists and Antinavalists*, 186–87.

91. Senate, 15–16 Feb 1813, AC, 12th Cong., 2nd Sess., 85, 87; Jones to Smith, 22 Feb 1813, Letters to Congress, RG45, Vol. 2/162–63.

92. Senate, 2 Mar, An act supplementary to the act for increasing the Navy, 3 Mar 1813, AC, 12th Cong., 2nd Sess., 116–117, 1352.

93. Jones to Evans, 19 Apr 1812, M149, R10/356–57.

Chapter 6. "Creating a Powerful Diversion": Secretary Jones and the Naval Campaign of 1813

1. Jones to Rodgers, Decatur, Bainbridge, Stewart, Morris, 22 Feb 1813, M149, R10/266, 77.

2. Melville to Warren, 9 Jan 1813, NMM, WAR/82/41–45.

3. Warren to Melville, 29 Mar, 5 Jun 1813, NMM, LBK/2.

4. Melville to Warren, 4 Jun 1813, NMM, WAR/82/73–77.

5. Broke to Wife, 14 Apr 1813, SRO, HA 93/9/138 (quote); Capel to Warren, 25 Apr 1813, NMM, WAR/69/165–66; Broke to Lawrence, Jun 1813, M125, R29/12a.

6. Robert Rose to Littleton Tazewell, 22 Apr 1813, Indiana University, War of 1812 Man. (quote); Rodgers to Jones, 5 Apr 1813, RFP, Letter & Order Book 1812–15, Pt III:38.

7. Rose to Tazewell, 22 Apr 1813, Indiana University, War of 1812 Man.; *Shannon's* Journal, 22 Apr 1813, SRO, HA 93/6/2/113.

8. Capel to Warren, 25 Apr 1813, NMM, WAR/69/165–66.

9. Broke to Lawrence, Jun 1813, M125, R29/12a.

10. Log *Curlew*, 2 May 1813, ADM 51/2223; *President's* Journal, 3 May 1813, RFP, Pt III:34. Rodgers did not mention chasing the *Curlew* in his cruise report; instead, he asserted three sail in sight being the *La Hogue, Nymphe*, and a merchant brig. See Rodgers to Jones, 27 Sep 1813, M125, R31/100.

11. Logs *La Hogue, Nymphe*, 2 May 1813, ADM 51/2527, 2590. The logbook of the *Nymphe* mentions that two strange ships were sighted just before dark.

12. Broke to His Wife, 5 May 1813, SRO, HA 93/9/139; Journal of the *Tenedos*, 3–4 May 1813, HSP.

13. Capel to Warren, 11 May 1813, ADM 1/504/170A.

14. Broke to His Wife, 9 May 1813, SRO, HA 93/9/140.

15. Capel to Warren, 11 May 1813, ADM 1/504/170A; Broke to His Wife, 9 May 1813, SRO, HA 93/9/140.

16. Rodgers to Jones, 27 Sep 1813 and list of prizes, M125, R31/100. In the letter, Rodgers indicates four prizes from 9 to 13 June, but the prize list contains five prizes for this period.

17. Warren to Melville, 1 Jun 1813, NMM, LBK/2.

18. Capel to Croker, 2 Jun, 11 Jun 1813, ADM 1/504/170A, 1/4359/203.

19. Croker to John Spranger, 16 Jun, Croker to Warren, 19 Jun 1813, ADM 2/1377/83, 88.

20. *Edinburgh Advertiser*, 29 Jun 1813.

21. Croker to Sir Richard Godwin Keats, 9 Jul, Admiralty to Charles Paget (second quote), Croker to Keith (first quote), to Warren, to George Martin, 10 Jul 1813, ADM 2/1377/142–49, 154.

22. Melville to Warren, 23 Mar 1813, NMM, WAR/82/56–64.

23. Croker to the Several Commanders in Chief . . . , 10 Jul 1813, ADM 2/1377/154–56.

24. Croker to Young, 11 Jul (quote), Admiralty to Lord Amelius Beauclerk, Croker to Keats, 12 Jul 1813, ADM 2/1377/159–65, 168–71, 176–77.

25. John Spratt Rainer to Young, 28 Aug 1813, ADM 1/573/375A.

26. Letter from on board the *Norge*, n.d., *Times* (London), 25 Aug 1813.

27. Young to Croker, 18 Jul 1813, Duke, Croker Papers, Box 3.

28. Rodgers to Jones, 27 Sep 1813, M125, R31/100; *President's* Journal, 19–20 Jul 1813, RFP, Pt III:34.

29. Proceedings of the *Precedent* [sic], 18 to 24 Jul 1813 by Mr. Gales, Master and Mr. Harrison Mate of the *Daphne* off the North Cape, ADM 1/696/221A.

30. Log *Spitfire*, 19 Jul 1813, ADM 51/2809.

31. *President's* Journal, 20 Jul 1813, RFP, Pt III:34; Logs *Alexandria*, *Spitfire*, 20 Jul 1813, ADM 51/2098, 2809.

32. *President's* Journal, 21–22 Jul 1813, RFP, Pt III:34; Logs *Alexandria*, *Spitfire*, 21 Jul 1813, ADM 51/2098, 2809.

33. Proceedings of the *Precedent* [sic], 18 to 24 Jul 1813 by Mr. Gales, Master and Mr. Harrison Mate of the *Daphne* off the North Cape, ADM 1/696/221A.

34. *President's* Journal, 22–23 Jul 1813, RFP, Pt III:34; Log *Spitfire*, 22 Jul 1813, ADM 51/2809.

35. *President's* Journal, 23 Jul 1813, RFP, Pt III:34; Log *Alexandria*, 23 Jul 1813, ADM 51/2098.

36. Cathcart to William Otway, 10 Aug 1813, ADM 1/696/221A; James, *Naval Occurrences*, 125–27.

37. Croker to Otway, 13 Aug 1813, ADM 2/1377/264–67.

38. Croker to Otway, 13 Aug 1813, ADM 2/1377/264–67.

39. Statement by George Shand to Otway, ADM 1/696/229A.

40. Rodgers to Jones, 27 Sep 1813, M125, R31/100; *President's* Journal, 31 Jul–2 Aug, 4–5, 9 Sep 1813, RFP, Pt III:34; Map Beauclerk's Movements, ADM 1/3232/6; Logs *Tenedos*, 4–5 Sep, *Bellerophon*, 8–9 Sep, *Poictiers*, 26 Aug–14 Sep 1813, *Dryad*, Aug–Sep 1813, ADM 51/2909, 2024, 2694, 2270; Warren to Croker, 4 Sep 1813, NMM, WAR/49/194; Broke to His Wife, 22 Sep 1813, SRO, HA 93/9/158.

41. Proceedings of the *Precedent* [sic], 18 to 24 Jul 1813 by Mr. Gales, Master and Mr. Harrison Mate of the *Daphne* taken off the North Cape, ADM 1/696/221A.

42. Warren had the *La Hogue* (74 guns) and *Tenedos* (38) on the edge of the Banks of Newfoundland. The *Poictiers* (74) and *Maidstone* (36) were off Cape Sable, Nova Scotia. The *Ramillies* (74) and *Loire* (40) comprised the offshore squadron at Boston. Inshore, Warren had deployed the *Nymphe* (38) (being replaced by the *Junon* [38]), *Majestic* (58), and *Wasp* (18). The *Orpheus* (36) and *Loup-Cervier* (18) were off Rhode Island (however, the *Orpheus* had sprung a mast and sailed for Halifax). The *Valiant* (74), *Acasta* (44), *Atalante* (18), and *Borer* (12) patrolled from Block Island to Long Island, including the port of New London. The *Plantagenet* (74) was off Sandy Hook at the mouth of New York harbor. The *Belvidera* (36), *Statira* (38), and *Morgiana* (18) sailed off the Delaware, while the Chesapeake Squadron consisted of the *Dragon* (74), *Lacedemonian* (38), *Armide* (38), *Doterel* (18), and *Mohawk* (12). See Warren to Croker, 16 Oct 1813, ADM 1/504/223.

43. Narrative of Capture, CM *Highflyer*, ADM 1/5441; Warren to Croker, 16 Oct 1813, ADM 1/504/113; Rodgers to Jones, 29 Sep 1813, M125, R31/105.

44. Logs *Loup-Cervier*, *Orpheus*, 13–24 Sep 1813, ADM 51/2528, 2615; Warren to Croker, 16 Oct 1813, ADM 1/504/223; Oliver to Warren, 13 Sep 1813, NMM, WAR/70/193 (quote).

45. *Morning Chronicle*, 13 Nov 1813.

46. Rodgers to Jones, 27 Sep 1813, M125, R31/100. Several sources draw a very bleak conclusion of Rodgers' cruise, and do not account for its intent or outcome. See Adams, *War of*

1812, 150; Forester, *Age of Fighting Sail*, 168–69; Daughan, *If By Sea*, 437; Mahan, *Sea Power*, 2:128–29. The disruptive element comes out in Schroeder, *Commodore Rodgers*, 121–24.

47. Log *Congress*, 8 May, 20 May, 22 May 1813, RG24; Log *Congress*, 23 May 1813, in *Baltimore Patriot & Evening Advertiser*, 23 Dec 1813.

48. Log *Congress*, 13–19 Jun 1813, RG24.

49. Dixon to Croker, 20 Aug 1813, ADM 1/21/83; Dixon to Croker, 9–11 Jun 1813, Heywood to Dixon, 23 Jun 1813, Bowles to Croker, 5 Sep 1813, *South America*, ed. Graham and Humphreys, 90, 92–93, 95, 105.

50. John Halliday to Croker, 7 Nov 1813, ADM 1/1948/434; Laforey to Croker, 15 Oct 1813, ADM 1/334/92; Log *Rhin*, 13 Aug 1813, ADM 51/2743; Letter from an officer of the *Congress*, 12 Dec 1813, *Repertory & General Advertiser*, 16 Dec 1813 (quote); Log *Congress*, 13 Aug 1813, RG24.

51. Dixon to Croker, 20 Aug 1813, ADM 1/21/83; Bowles to Croker, 28 Jul 1813, *South America*, ed. Graham and Humphreys, 102–103; Logs *Montagu*, *Indefatigable*, 1–24 Aug 1813, ADM 51/4100, 2463.

52. Log *Indefatigable*, 12–18 Aug 1813, ADM 51/2463; Log *Congress*, 17–18 Aug, 24 Aug, 5 Sep 1813, RG24.

53. Dixon to Croker, 20 Aug 1813, ADM 1/21/83; Laforey to Croker, 15 Oct 1813, ADM 1/334/92; Log *Inconstant*, 19 Aug–16 Sep 1813, Log *Rhin*, 28 Aug 1813, ADM 51/2487, 2743.

54. Logs *Rhin*, *Pique*, *Mosquito*, Sep–Oct 1813, ADM 51/2743, 2696, 2537.

55. Dixon to Croker, 6 Jan (quote), 16 Jan 1814, ADM 1/22/9, 17a.

56. Log *Congress*, 26 Oct 1813, RG24; Log *Congress*, 25 Oct 1813, in *Baltimore Patriot & Evening Advertiser*, 23 Dec 1813.

57. Admiralty to Charles Paget, 10 Jul 1813, ADM 2/1377/145–48; Log *Superb*, 22 Oct 1813, ADM 51/2051; Particulars of the cruise of the *Congress*, *Boston Daily Advertiser*, 20 Dec 1813.

58. Log *Congress*, 5 Dec, 14 Dec, RG24; Hayes to Warren, 8 Jan 1814, ADM 1/505/62A.

59. Particulars of the cruise of the *Congress*, *Boston Daily Advertiser*, 20 Dec 1813; Letter from an officer of the *Congress*, 12 Dec 1813, *Repertory & General Advertiser*, 16 Dec 1813 (quote).

60. Smith to Jones, 14 Dec, 20 Dec, 31 Dec 1813 (quote), M125, R33/49, 75, 122.

61. Jones to Allen, 8 Jun 1813, CLS, 29–31.

62. W. Crawford, "Journal," 19 Jun, 26 Jun, 30 Jun 1813, 15–18.

63. Domett to Keith, 10 Feb 1813, NMM, KEI/37/9; Keith to Croker, 28 Jun 1813, ADM 1/154/385; McCranie, *Admiral Lord Keith*, 149–66.

64. Keith to Croker, 15 Jul 1813, ADM 1/154/544.

65. W. Crawford, "Journal," 10–11 Jul 1813, 21. The identities of the two strangers remain uncertain. The 36-gun *Hotspur* was off Lorient on this day and encountered a privateer from Guernsey in the Channel Islands. However, the *Hotspur*'s log makes no mention of the *Argus*, and there is no extant report from the privateer to confirm the encounter. See Log *Hotspur*, 10 Jul 1813, ADM 51/2444.

66. Crawford to Jones, 2 Sep 1813, HSP, PWJ.

67. Keith to Croker, 14 Jul, 14 Aug, Bremer to Durham, 16 Jul 1813, ADM 154/394, 446 & A.

68. Woollcombe to Keith, 25 Jul 1813, ADM 1/154/414A; Inderwick, *Journal*, 24 Jul 1813 (quote), 16.

69. Woolridge to Croker, 26 Jul 1813, *Keith Papers*, ed. Lloyd, 3:242; Keith to Croker, 26 Jul 1813; Intelligence from William Brown, ADM 1/154/414 & A.

70. Inderwick, *Journal*, 27–28 Jul 1813, 16–17. The identities of Allen's opponents remain uncertain.

71. Fricker to Thornborough, 1 Aug 1813, ADM 1/625/557A; Inderwick, *Journal*, 1 Aug 1813, 17.

72. Thornborough to Croker, 3 Aug, 4 Aug 1813, ADM 1/625/557, 561; Winfield, *British Warships*, 259, 262.

73. Inderwick, *Journal*, 2–8 Aug 1813, 17–18; Log *Jalouse*, 8 Aug 1813, ADM 51/2500.

74. Inderwick, *Journal*, 9 Aug 1813, 18; "Depredations of the Argus off the Coast of Ireland," *Times* (London), 18 Aug 1813.

75. Inderwick, *Journal*, 10 Aug 1813, 19; Thornborough to Croker, 11 Aug 1813, ADM 1/625/581.

76. Dashwood to Croker, 6 Aug, 14 Aug 1813, ADM 1/1735/295; Log *Cressy*, 9 Aug 1813, ADM 51/2216; Winfield, *British Warships*, 221.

77. Inderwick, *Journal*, 10 Aug 1813, 19 (all quotes); Log *Coquette*, 10 Aug 1813, ADM 51/2044; Thornborough to Croker, 11 Aug 1813, ADM 1/625/581.

78. Inderwick, *Journal*, 11 Aug 1813, 19.

79. "American Barbarity," *Edinburgh Advertiser*, 27 Aug 1813, reprinted from the *Waterford Mirror*.

80. Hire's report, in Martin to Croker, 14 Aug 1813, ADM 1/833/900A; Log *Leonidas*, 12 Aug 1813, ADM 51/2522.

81. Thornborough to Croker, 11 Aug 1813, ADM 1/625/581; Thornborough's Journal, 12 Aug 1813, ADM 50/70.

82. Martin to Croker, 13 Aug (first quote), 14 Aug (second quote) 1813, ADM 1/833/893, 900.

83. Melville to Croker, 15 Aug 1813, Duke, Croker II, Box 2.

84. Inderwick, *Journal*, 12–13 Aug 1813, 20.

85. Testimony Watson, CI *Argus*, 18 Apr 1815, M273, R8/203.

86. "Naval Intelligence: Capture of the *Argus*," 24 Aug 1813, "American Barbarity," *Edinburgh Advertiser*, 27 Aug 1813; "Depredations of the *Argus* off the Coast of Ireland," *Times* (London), 18 Aug 1813.

87. Maples to Thornborough, 14 Aug 1813, *NW1812*, 2:223; Log *Pelican*, 14 Aug 1813, ADM 51/2660.

88. Testimony Watson, CI *Argus*, 18 Apr 1815, M273, R8/203.

89. Watson to Crowninshield, 2 Mar 1815, M148, R14/10.

90. Ibid.; Inderwick, *Journal*, 15 Aug 1813, 21.

91. Watson to Crowninshield, 2 Mar 1815, M148, R14/10 (both quotes); Maples to Thornborough, 14 Aug 1813, *NW1812*, 2:223; Inderwick, *Journal*, 15 Aug 1813, 20–22; Log *Pelican*, 14 Aug 1813, ADM 51/2660. For the cruise, see Dye, *Fatal Cruise*.

92. Crawford to Jones, 1 Oct 1813, HSP, PWJ.

93. Melville to Croker, 4 Aug 1813, Duke, Croker Papers, Box 2.

94. *Times* (London), 24 Aug 1813.

95. Ships in Sea Pay, 1 Jul 1813, ADM 8/100; Board Minutes, late 1814, ADM 7/266.

96. Madison to Jones, 15 Oct 1813, HSP, PWJ.

97. Jones to [unknown], 5 Apr 1813, HSP, PWJ.

Chapter 7. "A Glorious Retrieval of Our Naval Reputation": The Turning Point, 1 June 1813

1. Jones to Rodgers, Decatur, Bainbridge, Stewart, Morris, 22 Feb 1813, M149, R10/266 & 277.

2. Decatur to Hamilton, 8 Jun 1812, M125, R24/18.

3. Decatur to Jones, 24 Apr 1813, M125, R28/50; Jones to Decatur, 10 May 1813, CLS, 24.

4. Captain Jacob Jones to William Jones (no relation), 27 Mar 1813, M125, R27/97; Jones to Lawrence, 30 Mar 1813, M149, R10/328; Jones to Bainbridge, 7 May 1813, M441, R1/408–9; Biddle to Jones, 2 Jun 1813, M147, R5/67.

5. Coast of America: Proposed Division of Ships & Their Stations, Ships of the Enemy at Sea and Ready for Service, ADM 1/4359/183, 187.

6. Admiralty to Warren, 26 Mar 1813, NLS, CP, MS 2340/49.

7. Croker to Warren, 20 Mar 1813, ADM 2/1376/341–67.

8. Logs *Valiant, Ramillies*, 20 May 1813, ADM 51/2941, 2027.

9. Bennett to Croker, 18 Jun 1813, ADM 1/3994.

10. Decatur to Jones, 22 May 1813, M125, R28/170.

11. Oliver to Warren, 13 Jun 1813, ADM 1/504/176A; *Boston Gazette*, 17 May 1813.

12. Decatur to Jones, 22 May 1813, M125, R28/170.

13. Oliver to Warren, 13 Jun 1813, ADM 1/503/176A; Log *Valiant*, 20 May, 22 May 1813, ADM 51/2941.

14. Log *Ramillies*, 23 May 1813, ADM 51/2027.

15. Hardy to Warren. 29 May 1813, ADM 1/503/109.

16. Decatur to Jones, 22 May 1813, M125, R28/170.

17. Logs *Ramillies, Orpheus, Valiant, Acasta*, 25–27 May 1813, ADM 51/2027, 2615, 2941, 2102.

18. Log *United States*, 24 May 1813, RG24; *The Evening Post*, 27 May 1813 (quote).

19. *The Evening Post*, 27 May 1813; *Commercial Advertiser*, 28 May 1813.

20. Decatur to Jones, Jun 1813, M125, R29/3.

21. Skiddy, "Ups and Downs," 1:53, Mystic Collection 304.

22. *Columbian*, 28 May 1813; *Columbian Centinel*, 29 May 1813; *The Evening Post*, 29 May 1813 (published the day-old account).

23. *Boston Daily Advertiser*, 31 May 1813.

24. Oliver to Warren, 13 Jun 1813, ADM 1/504/176A; Log *Acasta*, 30 May 1813, ADM 51/2102; Log *United States*, 30 May 1813, RG24.

25. Log *Acasta*, 31 May 1813, ADM 51/2102.

26. Log *Hornet*, 31 May 1813, RG24; Decatur to Jones, Jun 1813, M125, R29/3 (quote).

27. Logs *United States, Hornet*, 1 Jun 1813, RG24.

28. Logs *Valiant, Acasta*, 1 Jun 1813, ADM 51/2941, 2102.

29. Decatur to Jones, Jun 1813, J. Jones to Jones, 2 Jun 1813, M125, R29/3, 9; Biddle to Jones, 2 Jun 1813, M147, R5/67.

30. Logs *Valiant, Acasta*, 1 Jun 1813, ADM 51/2941, 2102; Dunne, "The Inglorious First of June," 201–202, 216.

31. Oliver to Warren, 13 Jun 1813, ADM 1/504/176A.

32. Ibid. For the attempted sailing, see Mahan, *Sea Power*, 2:148; Tucker, *Decatur*, 123–27; Dunne, "The Inglorious First of June."

33. Oliver to Warren, 13 Jun 1813, ADM 1/504/176A.

34. Decatur to Jones, Jun, , 6 Jun (third quote), 14 Jun, 23 Jun 1813 (first and second quotes), M125, R29/3, 21, 61, 108.

35. Jones to Decatur, 9 Jul 1813, M149, R11/12.

36. Decatur to Jones, 6 Jun 1813, M125, R29/21.

37. Jones to Decatur, 9 Jun 1813, M149, R10/459.

38. Oliver to Warren, 13 Jun 1813, ADM 1/504/176A.

39. Beresford to Warren, 19 Jun 1813, NMM, WAR 70/43–44; Decatur to Jones, 23 Jun 1813, M125, R29/108.

40. Jones to Lawrence, 30 Mar 1813, SRO, HA 93/6/255.

41. Jones to Lawrence, 6 May 1813, CLS, 22–23; Lawrence to Jones, 18 May (quote), 20 May 1813, M125, R28/149, 160.

42. Jones to Evans, 6 May 1813, CLS, 19–22. By Jones to Lawrence, 6 May 1813, Lawrence was ordered to take command of the *Chesapeake* and follow the orders issued to her previous commander. See CLS, 22–23.

43. Broke to Lawrence, Jun 1813, M125, R29/12a.

44. Melville to Croker, 7 Aug 1813, Duke, Croker II, Box 2 55:A–B. See also Croker to Griffith, 9 Jul 1813, ADM 2/1377/140–42.

45. Log *Shannon*, 25 May 1813, ADM 51/2861; Journal of the *Tenedos*, 25 May 1813, HSP; Broke to Wife, 28 May 1813, SRO, HA 93/9/141.

46. Broke to Lawrence, Jun 1813, M125, R29/12a.

47. "*Chesapeake* and *Shannon*," *Columbian Centinel*, 2 Jun 1813 (quote); "Naval Engagement," *Essex Register*, 2 Jun 1813.

48. Testimony of Budd, CI *Chesapeake*, M273, R6/158.

49. Lawrence to James Montaudevert, 1 Jun 1813, LC, Lawrence Papers.

50. Jones to Madison, 8 Jun 1813, LC, JMP, Ser. 1, R15. Jones stated that the challenge was post-marked the day after the battle.

51. Details for *Shannon*, ADM 7/556; Valle, "Navy's Battle Doctrine," 172; Winfield, *British Warships*, 188. The British would rate the *Chesapeake* a 38-gun frigate.

52. Evans to Jones, 26 Apr 1813, M125, R28/53; Lawrence to Jones, 20 May 1813, M125, R28/160.

53. "*Chesapeake* and *Shannon*," *Columbian Centinel*, 2 Jun 1813.

54. Log *Shannon*, 1 Jun 1813, ADM 51/2861; Budd to Jones, 15 Jun 1813, M148, R11/138.

55. Testimony Budd, CI *Chesapeake*, M273, R6/158.

56. Brighton, *Admiral Wallis*, 59, 61.

57. Log *Shannon*, 1 Jun 1813, ADM 51/2861.

58. "Halifax Papers," *Times* (London), 10 Jul 1813.

59. Brighton, *Admiral Wallis*, 64.

60. Budd to Jones, 15 Jun 1813, M148, R11/138; "Extract of a Letter, dated New Bedford, 19 Jun," *Newburyport Herald*, 25 Aug 1813.

61. Testimony William Cox (Lt.), CI *Chesapeake*, M273, R6/158.

62. Log *Shannon*, 1 Jun 1813 (quote), ADM 51/2861; Testimony Budd, CI *Chesapeake*, M273, R6/158; Brighton, *Admiral Wallis*, 67.

63. Verdict, CI *Chesapeake*, M273, R6/158.

64. Testimony James Forrest (Mid), CI *Chesapeake*, M273, R6/158; "Letter from the Surgeon of the *Chesapeake*," *Columbian*, 23 Jun 1813.

65. Verdict, CI *Chesapeake*, M273, R6/158.

66. Testimonies William Randolph (Mid), Budd, CI *Chesapeake*, M273, R6/158; Brighton, *Admiral Wallis*, 125.

67. Log *Shannon*, 1 Jun 1813, ADM 51/2861; "Halifax Papers," *Times* (London), 10 Jul 1813; "Extract of a Letter, dated New Bedford, 19 Jun," *Newburyport Herald*, 25 Aug 1813. The wound might have come while Broke tried to shield several Americans from the fury of his own men. Stories indicate one American he was attempting to save picked up a weapon and brought it down on Broke's head.

68. Testimony Richard Edgar, CI *Chesapeake*, M273, R6/158.

69. Testimonies Budd, Edward Russell (Mid.), CI *Chesapeake*, M273, R6/158.

70. *Times* (London), 13 Jul 1813; *Edinburgh Advertiser*, 13 Jul 1813. For the action, see Padfield, *Broke and Shannon*, 233; and Dennis, "Shannon and the Chesapeake," 36–46.

71. Broke to Capel, 6 Jun 1813, ADM 1/503/116A; Budd to Jones, 15 Jun 1813, M148, R11/138. The *Shannon* lost her first lieutenant, purser, and clerk as well as twenty-three seamen and marines killed. The wounded included Broke, a midshipman, and fifty-six seamen and marines.

72. *Shannon*'s Journal, SRO 93/6/2/113; Broke to Capel, 6 Jun 1814, ADM 1/503/116A; Padfield, *Broke and Shannon*, 233. The difficulty in determining the number of American casualties resulted from confusion about the number of men on board the *Chesapeake* during the engagement. Her muster book listed 389. However, the British asserted, "Some men joined on the day they sailed & were not in the list [muster book]." The British estimated her real complement at 443. Fifty-four men joining on the day of battle seems excessive, however. Using the more conservative number of 389 found in the American muster book and subtracting the 333 prisoners the British sent ashore at Halifax, the difference of fifty-six comprises the killed and mortally wounded. See *Shannon*'s Journal, SRO 93/6/2/113. If approximately twice as many received lesser wounds, total casualties would still be more than 150.

73. *Times* (London), 9 Jul 1813.

74. Capel to Croker, 11 Jun 1813, ADM 1/4359/203; Log *Shannon*, 6 Jun, ADM 51/2861.

75. *Edinburgh Advertiser*, 13 Jul 1813; *Liverpool Mercury*, 16 Jul 1813.

76. Barrow to Warren, 9 Jul 1813, Melville to Broke, 23 Aug 1813, SRO, HA 93/6/2/59, 65.

77. Warren to Melville, 22 Jul 1813, NMM, LBK/2.

78. Warren to Broke, 6 Jul 1813, SRO, HA 93/6/2/58.

79. Collier to Wellington, 14 Mar [should read Jul] 1813, University of Southampton, Wellington Papers, 1/372, Folder 2.

80. Broke to Lawrence, Jun 1813, M125, R29/12a.

81. *Times* (London), 8 Jul 1813.

82. Barrie to Mrs. George Clayton, 5 Apr 1813, Clements Library, Barrie Papers.

Chapter 8. "More Than Ordinary Risk": United States Frigates, Winter 1813–14

1. Barrie to Mrs. George Clayton, 27 Jun 1813, Clements Library, Barrie Papers.

2. Jane Clarke to Mrs. Jones, 23 Jun 1813, HSP, PWJ.

3. Madison to Jones, 16 Sep 1813, HSP, PWJ.

4. Jones to Editors of *DNI*, 9 Jun 1813, M125, R29/12 1/2.

5. Hope to Sir Alexander Hope, 12 Dec 1813, NAS, GD 364/1/1253/26/1–3.

6. Jones to Decatur, 13 Oct 1813, CLS, 75–76.

7. Jones to Stewart, 19 Sep 1813, *NASP Naval*, 4:182–85.

8. Jones to Decatur, 13 Oct 1813, CLS, 75–76; Decatur to Jones, 6 Oct, 6 Dec 1813, M125, R31/130, R33/20.

9. Oliver to Warren, 15 Dec 1813, NMM, WAR/71/164–65.

10. Decatur to Jones, 20 Dec 1813, in *Niles' Weekly Register*, 1 Jan 1814, 5:302; Jones to Decatur, 29 Dec 1813, M149, R11/180; Goldenberg, "Blue Lights," 388.

11. Decatur to Hardy, 17 Jan 1814, M125, R34/49; *Niles' Weekly Register*, 10 Feb 1814, 5:416.

12. Decatur to Hardy, 17 Jan 1814, M125, R34/49.

13. Hardy to Decatur, 18 Jan 1814, M125, R34/48 also in ADM 1/505/64A. The word "sister" is omitted from the M125 version.

14. Decatur to Hardy, 19 Jan 1814, M125, R34/50 also in ADM 1/505/64A; Goldenberg, "Blue Lights," 391; DeKay, *Chronicles*, 114–21.

15. Jones to Decatur, 13 Oct 1813, CLS, 75–76; Jones to Stewart, 19 Sep 1813 (quote), *NASP Naval*, 4:182–85.

16. Jones to Decatur, 12 Mar 1814, M149, R11/240–41.

17. Hardy to Warren, 20 Jan [1814], Warren to Croker, 27 Jan 1814, ADM 1/505/64, A & Adm Response.

18. Cockburn to Warren, 26 Jan 1814, LC, Cockburn Papers, R6, Container 9, 358–67.

19. Jones to Decatur, 12 Mar 1814, M149, R11/240–41.

20. Gordon to Jones, 28 Dec 1813, 11 Feb 1814, M125, R33/111, R34/106; Jones to Gordon, 5 Jan 1814, *NASP Naval*, 4:192–94.

21. Warren to Barrie, 19 Jan 1814, Duke, Sir Robert Barrie Papers, Box 5.

22. Barrie to Eliza Clayton, 14 Mar 1814, *NW1812*, 3:18–19.

23. Jones to Gordon, 15 April 1814, M149, R11/278 (quote); Calderhead, "Constellation."

24. Rodgers to Jones, 28 Sep, 23 Oct, 5 Nov, 22 Nov 1813, M125, R28/62, R32/38, 81, 115.

25. Warren to Melville, 22 Jul, 24 Aug 1813, NMM, LBK/2; Cochrane to Croker, 2 Apr 1814, ADM 1/506/141; Lohnes, "British Naval Problems," 326.

26. Warren to Melville, 27 Sep, 26 Oct 1813, NMM, LBK/2.

27. Journal of the *Tenedos*, 12–13 Nov 1813, HSP.

28. Hotham to Broke, 13 Nov 1813, SRO, HA 93/9/177.

29. Warren to Croker, 13 Nov 1814, ADM 1/504/277; Kert, *Prize and Prejudice*, 116–17.

30. Logs *Albion, Ramillies, Endymion, Loire,* and *Orpheus,* 1–2 Dec 1813, ADM 51/2104, 2027, 2324, 2516, 2615; Rodgers to Jones, 22 Nov, 2 Dec 1813, 19 Feb 1814 (quote), M125, R32/114, R33/2, R34/125; O.H. Perry to Rodgers' Wife, 5 Dec 1813, RFP, Pt II:4.

31. *President's* Journal, 5–6 Dec 1813, RFP, Pt III:34.

32. Logs *Endymion, Loire,* and *Ramillies,* 7 Dec 1813, ADM 51/2324, 2516, 2027.

33. Warren to Croker, 13 Nov 1813, ADM 1/504/277; Log *Canso,* 2–3 Dec 1813, ADM 51/2217.

34. *President's* Journal, 6–7 Dec 1813, RFP, Pt III:34 (quote); Log *Canso,* 6 Dec 1813, ADM 51/2217.

35. Rodgers to Jones, 19 Feb 1814, M125, R34/125 (quote); *President's* Journal, 7 Dec 1813, RFP, Pt III:34.

36. Logs *Albion, Ramillies,* and *Orpheus,* 7 Dec 1813, ADM 2104, 2027, 2615.

37. Warren to Barrie, 21 Dec 1813, Duke, Sir Robert Barrie Papers, Box 5.

38. Rodgers to Jones, 19 Feb 1814, M125, R34/125; *President's* Journal, 26 Dec 1813, RFP, Pt III:34.

39. Rodgers to Jones, 19 Feb 1814, M125, R34/125.

40. Log *Queen,* 27–28 Nov, 2 Dec 1813 (first quote), ADM 51/2719; Colville to Croker, 7 Dec 1813 (second quote), ADM 1/1665/493.

41. Log *Queen,* 14 Dec, 16 Dec 1813, ADM 51/2719. The remainder of the passage proved uneventful. The *Severn* parted with nine merchantmen destined for North America on 24 December, nine other vessels sailed toward South America escorted by the *Columbine,* and Colville arrived at Barbados with 102 sail on 10 January. See Log *Queen,* 24 Dec 1813, 5 Jan, 10 Jan 1814, ADM 51/2719.

42. Rodgers to Jones, 19 Feb 1814, M125, R34/125.

43. "Extract from a file of Nassau (New Providence) papers received at the E. C. House, per *Rusa* from Havana," dated Barbados, 10 Jan, *The Evening Post,* 1 Apr 1814.

44. Laforey to Croker, 19 Jun 1814, ADM 1/335/76.

45. *President's* Journal, 4 Feb 1814, RFP, Pt III:34; Rodgers to Jones, 19 Feb, Dent to Jones, 14 Feb 1814, M125, R34/114, 125.

46. *President's* Journal, 12 Feb 1814, RFP, Pt III:34; Master's Log *Morgiana,* 12 Feb 1814, ADM 52/4190.

47. Master's Log *Morgiana,* 12 Feb 1814, ADM 52/4190; *President's* Journal, 12–13 Feb 1813 (second quote), RFP, Pt III:34; Rodgers to Jones, 19 Feb 1814, M125 (first quote), R34/125.

48. Rodgers to Jones, 19 Feb 1814, M125, R34/125; *President's* Journal, 13 Feb 1814, RFP, Pt III:34.

49. Master's Log *Morgiana,* 12 Feb 1814, ADM 52/4190; Warren to Croker, 25 Feb 1814, ADM 1/505/86.

50. Rodgers to Jones, 19 Feb 1814, M125, R34/125.

51. Logs *Acasta, Narcissus*, 15–17 Feb 1814, ADM 51/2102, 2609; *President's* Journal, 17 Feb 1814, RFP, Pt III:34. The *President's* Journal noted eighteen fathoms of water and the *Narcissus'* Log noted twenty-three to twenty-five.

52. *President's* Journal, 19 Feb 1814, RFP, Pt III:34 (quote); Extract, Log *President*, 18 Feb, *Columbian*, 9 Mar 1814.

53. *President's* Journal, 19 Feb 1814, RFP, Pt III:34 (fourth quote); Remarks from a lieutenant on board the *President* (second and third quotes), Extract, letter by an officer of the *President*, 22 Feb, *Columbian*, 9 Mar 1814 (first quote).

54. Logs *Loire, Ramillies*, 18 Feb 1814, ADM 51/2516, 2027; Croker to the Several Commanders in Chief . . . , 10 Jul 1813, ADM 2/1377/154–56.

55. Log *Plantagenet*, 6 Dec 1813, 18 Feb 1814, ADM 51/2714; "*President* and *Plantagenet*," *Columbian*, 9 Mar 1814.

56. Rodgers to Jones, 5 Mar 1814, M125, R35/17.

57. Jones to Rodgers, 26 Feb 1814, M149, R11/226. For the cruise, see Schroeder, *Commodore Rodgers*, 124.

58. Jones to Stewart, 19 Sep 1813, *NASP Naval*, 4:182–85.

59. Testimony Ballard (Lt.), CI Conduct of Capt. Stewart, M273, R7/163.

60. Hayes to Warren, 25 Oct 1813, ADM 1/504/282A.

61. Log *Wasp*, 27–28 Dec 1813, USNA, MS 157; Logs *Majestic, Tenedos*, 28–31 Dec 1813, ADM 51/2543, 2909.

62. Bainbridge to Jones, 30 Dec 1813, M125, R33/114.

63. Warren to Croker, 19 Nov 1813, ADM 1/504/282; Everard to Griffith, 7 Jan (quote), Hayes to Warren, 8 Jan 1814, ADM 1/505/37A, 62A; Logs *Tenedos*, 1–7 Jan, *Majestic*, 8 Jan 1814, ADM 51/2909, 2543.

64. Hayes to Croker, 30 Jan 1814, ADM 1/1949/103.

65. Hayes to Warren, 5 Feb 1814, ADM 1/505/99A (all quotes); Details for the *Majestic*, ADM 7/556.

66. Croker to Dixon and Tyler, 14 Feb 1814, ADM 2/1379/210–11.

67. Log *Mosquito*, 3 Feb 1814, ADM 51/2537; Log *Constitution*, 3–4 Feb, 9 Feb 1814, RG24. The *Constitution's* log contains a penciled entry that the packet was the 18-gun *Columbine*, but this is incorrect. See Durham to Croker, 10 Feb 1814, ADM 1/335/25.

68. Admiral's Journal, Durham, 9 Feb 1814, ADM 50/77; Durham to Croker, 16, 20 Jan 1814, ADM 1/335/11, 12. The French frigates were the *L'Alcmène* and *L'Iphigénie*.

69. Admiral's Journal, Durham, 9–11 Feb 1814, ADM 50/77; Durham to Croker, 10 Feb 1814 (2 letters), ADM 1/335/24–25.

70. Log *Constitution*, 14 Feb 1814, RG24.

71. Testimony Hannaford, CM *Pictou*, ADM 1/5434.

72. Log *Constitution*, 14 Feb 1814, RG24; Stephens to Warren, 17 Feb 1814, ADM 1/505/134A.

73. Stephens to Durham, 17 Feb, Warren to Stephens, 25 Jan 1814, ADM 1/335/38 & A.

74. Stephens to Warren, 17 Feb 1814, ADM 1/505/134A.

75. Testimony of Hannaford, CM *Pictou*, ADM 1/5434.

76. Stephens to Durham, 17 Feb 1814, ADM 1/335/38A.

77. Log *Constitution*, 14–15 Feb 1814, RG24.

78. According to Hannaford, the damage aloft had been confined to the sails and rigging. See CM *Pictou*, ADM 1/5434.

79. Log *Constitution* 14 Feb 1814, RG24; Stewart's Narrative, CI Conduct of Capt. Stewart, M273, R7/163.

80. Log *Venerable*, 16–19 Feb 1814, ADM 51/2958; Log *Constitution*, 18–19 Feb 1814, RG24.

81. Log *Constitution*, 23 Feb 1813, RG24.

82. Log *Pique*, 20 Feb 1814, ADM 51/2696; Admiral's Journal, Durham, 10 Feb 1814, ADM 50/77.

83. Log *Constitution*, 24 Feb 1814, RG24 (first and second quotes); Maitland to Durham, 24 Feb 1814 and attached log for 23 Feb, ADM 1/335/43A (third quote); James, *Naval History*, 6:198–99.

84. Maitland to Durham, 24 Feb 1814, ADM 1/335/43A.

85. Durham to Croker, 14 Mar 1814 and Admiralty Response, ADM 1/335/43.

86. Statement of Stewart, CI Conduct of Capt. Stewart, M273, R7/163.

87. Admiral's Journal, Durham, 16–17 Mar, 23 Mar 1814, ADM 50/77; Durham to Croker, 19 Mar (quote), Durham to Cramer, 9 Mar 1814, ADM 1/335/47 & A.

88. Jones to Stewart, 19 Sep 1813, *NASP Naval*, 4:182–85.

89. Narrative by Stewart, CI Conduct of Capt. Stewart, M273, R7/163.

90. Stewart to Jones, 4 Apr 1814, M125, R35/117; Log *Constitution*, 16 Mar 1814, RG24.

91. Narrative of Stewart, Verdict, CI Conduct of Capt. Stewart, M273, R7/163.

92. Stewart to Jones, 29 Apr 1814, M125, R35/199.

93. Log *Constitution*, 3 Apr 1814, RG24.

94. Journal of *Tenedos*, 3 Apr 1814, HSP.

95. Upton to Griffith, 4 Apr 1814, ADM 1/506/208A.

96. Log *Constitution*, 3 Apr 1814, RG24; Berube and Rodgaard, *Call to the Sea*, 76–82.

97. Griffith to Croker, 30 Apr, Upton to Griffith, 7 Apr 1814, ADM 1/506/208 & A; Stewart to Jones, 18 Apr 1814, M125, R35/152.

98. Rodgers to Jones, 19 Feb, Stewart to Jones, 4 Apr 1814, M125, R34/125, R35/117.

99. Jones to Stewart, 19 Apr 1814, M149, R11/292–93.

100. Verdict, CI Conduct of Capt. Stewart, M273, R7/163. Arguments have been made that the decision to have Commodore Bainbridge head the inquiry was detrimental to Stewart, given tensions stemming from as far back as the Barbary Wars. See Berube and Rodgaard, *Call to the Sea*, 82–83.

101. "Naval Inquiry, Boston, 30 May," *Delaware Gazette and Peninsula Advertiser*, 6 Jun 1814.

102. Warren to Croker, 12 Jan, 27 Jan 1814, ADM 1/505/52, 61; Memorandum and Observations attached to Warren to Croker, 29 Apr 1814, ADM 1/506/176.

Chapter 9. "Pursuing My Own Course": The *Essex* in the Pacific, 1813–14

1. Porter, *Journal*, 73. The other two ships of Bainbridge's squadron were the *Constitution* and *Hornet*. For their cruise, see Chapter 3.

2. Porter to Bainbridge, 23 Mar 1813, M125, R29/139; Porter, *Journal*, 72–73 (all quotes). On Porter's cruise, see Long, *Nothing too Daring*, 71–158.

3. Porter to Bainbridge, 20 Jan, Porter to His Crew, 3 Feb 1813, Porter, *Journal*, 76 (second quote), 82 (third quote), 88 (first quote).

4. Porter to Bainbridge, 23 Mar 1813, M125, R29/139; Porter, *Journal*, 112–13 (quote).

5. Porter, *Journal*, 125–26.

6. Porter to Bainbridge, 23 Mar 1813, M125, R29/139.

7. Porter to Hamilton, 2 Jul 1813, M125, R29, 139; Porter, *Journal*, 140–41.

8. Journal of Feltus, 17 Apr 1813, HSP; Porter, *Journal*, 172–73 (quote).

9. Journal of Feltus, 29 Apr 1813, HSP; Porter to Hamilton, 2 Jul 1813, M125, R29/139; Porter, *Journal*, 173–75, 181.

10. Porter to Hamilton, 2 Jul 1813, M125, R29/139; Porter, *Journal*, 177, 181.

11. Journal of Feltus, 28 May 1813, HSP; Porter, *Journal*, 197–200; Farragut, *Life*, 25.

12. Porter, *Journal*, 202, 205, 214, 219.

13. Journal of Feltus, 25 Jun 1813, HSP; Farragut, *Life*, 25; Porter, *Journal*, 227–28.

14. Journal of Feltus, 30 Jun 1813, HSP; Porter to Hamilton, 2 Jul 1813, M125, R29/139.

15. Dixon to Croker, 10 Mar, 30 Apr 1813, (quote) ADM 1/21/33, 49.

16. Dixon to Croker, 9 Jun, Letter from Valparaiso, 8 Apr 1813, ADM 21/58 & A.

17. Croker to Hamilton (Foreign Office), 10 Dec 1812 (quote), ADM 2/1375/309–10; Croker to Dixon, 12 Feb 1813, ADM 2/1376/91–92; Dixon to Croker, 30 Apr 1813, ADM 1/21/37.

18. Dixon to Croker, 11, 21 Jun 1813, ADM 1/21/60, 65.

19. Dixon to Croker, 12 Jul, Dixon to Hillyar, 1 Jul 1813 (quote), ADM 1/21/77 & A.

20. Journal of Feltus, 9 Jul 1813, HSP; Porter to Downes, 1 Jul 1813, Porter, *Journal*, 230–31. The *Policy* was taken on her return by the British frigate *Loire*.

21. Montgomery to Gamble, 15 Jul, Porter to Sec. Navy, 23 Jul 1813, *Memorial of Gamble*, 4–5; Porter, *Journal*, 231–32.

22. Porter to Hamilton, 22 Jul 1813, *NW1812*, 2:702; Porter, *Journal*, 236–37. The *Georgiana* was captured by the British frigate *Barrosa* on her approach to the United States.

23. Porter, *Journal*, 237–41.

24. Porter to Hamilton, 22 Jul 1813, *NW1812*, 2:702.

25. Porter, *Journal*, 243.

26. "Note Left By Porter," Porter, *Journal*, 253–54.

27. Porter to Jones, 3 Jul 1814, M125, R39/127; Porter, *Journal*, 266–67, 271.

28. Porter to Jones, 3 Jul 1814, M125 (quote), R39/127; Porter, *Journal*, 272–73, 283, 443. The *New Zealand* was captured by the British frigate *Belvidera*. On time spent in the Marquesas Islands, see Porter, *Journal*, 286–446; Long, *Nothing too Daring*, 109–41.

29. Porter to Jones, 3 Jul 1814, M125, R39/127; Porter, *Journal*, 473.

30. Hillyar to Croker, 14 Oct, John McDonald to Hillyar, 26 Aug 1813, ADM 1/1948/371A; Logs *Racoon, Phoebe,* 2 Oct 1813, ADM 51/2765, 2675; Gough, *Fortune's River,* 306–14.

31. Log *Phoebe,* 23 Oct–5 Dec 1813, ADM 51/2675.

32. Hillyar to Croker, 24 Jan 1814, ADM 1/1949/186.

33. Porter to Jones, 13 Jul 1813, M125, R37/183 (first and third quotes); Log *Phoebe,* 8 Feb 1814, ADM 51/2675 (fourth quote); Farragut, *Life,* 33 (second quote).

34. Log *Phoebe,* 15 Feb 1814, ADM 51/2675; Hillyar to Croker, 28 Feb 1814, ADM 1/1950/263.

35. Porter to Jones, 3 Jul 1814, M125, R37/127.

36. Questions exist over the armaments of the *Cherub* and *Phoebe.* See Porter to Jones, 3 Jul 1814, M125, R37/127; Details for the *Phoebe and Cherub,* ADM 7/556; James, *Naval Occurrences,* 155; Winfield, *British Warships,* 146–47, 259–60. Particularly, Porter seems to have inflated the weight of metal and manning of both his opponents.

37. Board Minutes, Strength South America, early 1814, ADM 7/265; Dixon to Philip Pipon, 12 Feb, Instructions to Thomas Staines (*Briton*), 25 Mar 1814, *South America,* ed. Graham and Humphreys, 128–29, 135–37 (quote).

38. Porter to Jones, 3 Jul 1814, M125, R37/127.

39. Porter to Jones, 3 Jul 1814, M125, R37/127.

40. Log *Essex,* in *Evening Post,* 8 Jul 1814.

41. Porter to Jones, 3 Jul 1814, M125, R37/127.

42. Farragut's Memoir, *NW1812,* 3:750.

43. Porter to Jones, 3 Jul 1814, M125, R37/127; Hillyar to Croker, 30 Mar 1814, ADM 1/1950/264.

44. Log *Cherub,* 28 Mar 1814, ADM 51/2206.

45. Hillyar to Croker, 30 Mar 1814, ADM 1/1950/264; Porter to Jones, 3 Jul 1814, M125, R37/127.

46. Porter to Jones, 3 Jul 1814, M125, R37/127; Farragut Memoirs, *NW1812,* 3:751.

47. Porter to Jones, 3 Jul 1814, M125, R37/127; Farragut Memoirs, *NW1812,* 3:751 (all quotes).

48. Porter to Hambleton, 26 Jul 1814, LC, Porter Papers, Box 2.

49. Log *Phoebe,* 28 Mar 1814, ADM 51/2675; Porter to Jones, 3 Jul 1813, M125, R37/127.

50. Farragut Memoirs, *NW1812,* 3:751–52. Hillyar was in fact forty-four years old.

51. Hillyar to Porter, 4 Apr 1814, ADM 1/1950/273.

52. Staines to Croker, 28 May 1814, Duke, Croker Papers, Box 1 (quote); Log *Tagus,* 13 Apr 1814, ADM 51/2873; Dixon to Croker, 10 Jun, 8 Sep, 25 Nov 1814, ADM 1/22/56, 147, 11; Dixon to Croker, 28 Apr 1815, *South America,* ed. Graham and Humphreys, 153–54.

53. Porter to Jones, 9 Jul 1814, M125, R37/147; Log *Saturn,* 5–6 Jul 1814, ADM 51/2789.

54. John Mason (Commissary General) to Jones, 10 Aug 1814, M149, R11/401.

55. Cochrane to Croker, 2 Sep 1814, ADM 1/507/281.

56. Cochrane to Mason, Feb 1815, NLS, CP, MS 2349/258.

Chapter 10. "Some Hard Knocks": Reassessment—The United States, September 1813–March 1814

1. John Campbell to David Campbell, 5 Feb 1813, Duke, Campbell Family Papers, Box 2.

2. *Columbian*, 31 May 1813.

3. Jones to [unknown], 5 Apr 1813, HSP, PWJ.

4. Jones to Hull, 5 Jul 1813, M441, R1/528.

5. Hull to Jones, 14 Jun 1813, M125, R31/172; Joseph Bainbridge to Jones, 15 [Jun 1813], M147, R5/73; Maloney, *Hull*, 231. See Chapter 5 for the operations of the *Enterprize* and *Siren* in the southern U.S.

6. *American Advocate*, 24 Jul 1813. Reports from the following newspapers added to the discontent: *Eastern Argus*, 27 May, 3 Jun 1813; *Portland Gazette, and Maine Advertiser*, 12 Jul, 19 Jul, 9 Aug 1813; *War Journal*, 23 Jul 1813; *Portsmouth Oracle*, 24 Jul 1813.

7. Logs *Nymphe, Tenedos, La Hogue, Rattler*, Jul 1813, ADM 51/2590, 2909, 2527, 2775.

8. Jones to Hull, 5 Jul 1813, M441, R1/545; Hull to Burrows, 22 Aug, 28 Aug 1813 (quote), New York Hist. Soc., Hull Letter Book; *American Advocate*, 28 Aug 1813; "Extract of a letter from Newburyport, Aug 21," *Portland Gazette and Maine Advertiser*, 30 Aug 1813; Duffy, *Captain Blakeley*, 95–97.

9. McCall to Hull, 7 Sep 1813, M125, R31/19A.

10. McCrery to Gordon, 6 Sep 1813, ADM 1/504/194A; Disposition John A. Allen (Lt. British Army), *NW1812*, 2:238–39; Testimonies McCrery and John Read (Master), CM *Boxer*, ADM 1/5440.

11. McCall to Hull, 7 Sep 1813, M125, Roll 31/19A; Testimony Read, CM *Boxer*, ADM 1/5440.

12. Testimonies Read and McCrery, CM *Boxer*, ADM 1/5440.

13. McCall to Hull, 24 Sep 1813, M125, R31/98A; Testimony McCrery, CM *Boxer*, ADM 1/5440.

14. Narrative by McCrery, CM *Boxer*, ADM 1/5440; McCall to Hull, 7 Sep 1813, M125, R31/19A; Letter from unnamed officer, *Constitutionalist and Weekly Magazine*, 14 Sep 1813 (quote).

15. Testimonies Read and McCrery, CM *Boxer*, ADM 1/5440.

16. Testimonies McCrery, Read, and Ambrose Ford (Carpenter's Mate), CM *Boxer*, ADM 1/5440.

17. McCrery to Gordon, 6 Sep 1813, ADM 1/504/194A (quote); Testimony Read, CM *Boxer*, ADM 1/5440; McCall to Hull, 7 Sep 1813, M125, R31/19A. For the action, see James, *Naval History*, 6: 75–78; Forester, *Age of Fighting Sail*, 191–93.

18. McCrery to Gordon, 6 Sep 1813, ADM 1/504/194A; List of Killed and Wounded, signed by McCall, M125, R31/19A.

19. Hull to Jones, 14 Sep, 15 Sep 1813 (quote), M125, R31/50, 55.

20. Logs *Rattler, Shelbourne, Fantome*, 13 Sep 1813, ADM 51/2775, 2335, 2295; Gordon's Letter, 13 Sep (both quotes), Col. J. D. Learned to Gordon, 13 Sep, *War Journal*, 24 Sep 1813.

21. Hull to Jones, 11 Oct 1813, M125, R32/7; Chapelle, *American Sailing Navy*, 551.

22. Hull to Jones, 11 Sep, 25 Sep 1813, M125, R31/39, 98; Jones to Hull, 16 Sep 1813, M441, R1/496–97.

23. Hull to Jones, 11 Oct, 22 Oct 1813, M125, R32/7, 28.

24. Creighton to Hull, 1 Nov 1813, M125, R32/74A; Log *Fantome*, 30–31 Oct 1813, ADM 51/2295.

25. Log *Fantome*, 3 Nov 1813, ADM 51/2295.

26. Creighton to Hull, 4 Nov 1813, M125, R32/79A; Winfield, *British Warships*, 304, 320.

27. Logs *Epervier*, *Fantome* (quote), 3 Nov 1814, ADM 51/2409, 2295.

28. Hull to Jones, 5 Nov 1813, M125, R32/79; Logs *Epervier*, *Fantome*, 3 Nov 1814, ADM 51/2409, 2295.

29. Jones, Report on the State of the Navy, 22 Feb 1814, *NASP Naval*, 4:198–201.

30. Chapelle, *American Sailing Navy*, 282, 531.

31. "List of the Naval Forces of the U. States," 8 Jun 1814, *Long-Island Star*; Chapelle, *American Sailing Navy*, 531, 545, 555. The first two were former merchant ships while the *Alert* was a British prize.

32. Jones to Dent, 23 Jun 1814, M149, R11/350.

33. Read to Jones, 22 Nov 1813, M148, R12/112.

34. Jones to Biddle, 25 Apr 1813, *NW1812*, 2:84–85. Jones directed that each of these two vessels—the *Buffaloe* and *Camel*—mount 2 x 18-pound long guns and 2 x 24-pound carronades.

35. Read to Jones (quote) and note by Jones, 16 Oct 1813, M148, R12/37; Jones to Read, 28 Sep, 29 Nov 1813, M149, R11/99, 156.

36. Log *Belvidera*, 25 Dec 1813 (first quote), ADM 51/2018; Sailing Master Hall to Jones, 20 Jan (second quote), Midshipman McChesney to Jones, 20 Jan 1814 (third quote), M148, R13/30, 31.

37. Jones, Report on the State of the Navy, 22 Feb 1814, *NASP Naval*, 4:198–201.

38. Warren to Croker, 30 Dec 1813, ADM 1/505/10; Chapelle, *American Sailing Navy*, 256, 260, 557; Winfield, *British Warships*, 282.

39. Forester, *Age of Fighting Sail*, 213; Duffy, *Captain Blakeley*, 102.

40. Jones to Charles Gordon (*Constellation*), 5 Jan 1814, *NASP Naval*, 4:192–94.

41. Jones to George Parker (*Siren*), 8 Dec 1813, *NASP Naval*, 4:187–89.

42. *Niles' Weekly Register*, 26 Feb 1814, 5:432.

43. Jones to Warrington, 26 Feb 1814, CLS, 102–105.

44. Jones to [unknown], 5 Apr 1813, HSP, PWJ.

45. Hull to Jones, 11 Oct, 22 Oct 1813, M125, R32/7, 28.

46. Creighton to Jones, 31 Dec 1813, M147, R5/199; Jones to Creighton, 22 Dec 1813, *NASP Naval*, 4:191–92.

47. Hayes to Warren, 8 Jan 1814, ADM 1/505/62A; Log *Tenedos*, 6–9 Jan 1814, ADM 51/2909; Bainbridge to Jones, 30 Dec 1813, Hull to Jones, 17 Jan 1814, M125, R33/114, R34/41; "Naval and Marine Memoranda," *The War*, 18 Jan 1814.

48. Creighton to Jones, 9 Mar 1814, M147, R5/79.

49. Ibid.; Log *Leonidas*, 8 Feb 1814, ADM 51/2522.

50. Creighton to Jones, 9 Mar 1814, M147, R5/79; Log *Barham*, 9–10 Feb 1814, ADM 51/2185.

51. Croker to Warren, 4 Nov 1813, ADM 2/1378/146–51; Brown to Croker, 13 Feb 1814 (two letters this date), ADM 1/265/25–26.

52. Creighton to Jones, 21 Feb, 9 Mar 1814, M147, R5/62, 79.

53. Creighton to Jones, 9 Mar 1814, M147, R5/79.

54. Ibid.

55. Ibid.

56. Renshaw to Creighton, 7 Mar 1814, M147, R5/79A. The identity of the British warship remains unclear.

57. Creighton to Jones, 9 Mar 1814, M147, R5/79. For the cruise, see Mahan, *Sea Power*, 2:231– 33. Roosevelt did not include the *Rattlesnake* in his description of the cruise. See *Naval War*, 216–17.

58. Chapelle, *American Sailing Navy*, 282. The weapon was something between a long gun and a carronade.

59. Morris to Jones, 31 Dec 1813, M125, R33/120; Jones to Morris, 6 Jan 1814, CLS, 88–89.

60. Morris to Jones, 31 Dec 1813, 16 Jan 1814, M125, R33/120, R34/38.

61. Warren to Croker, 30 Dec 1813, ADM 1/505/10; Barrie to Croker, 12 Jan 1814, ADM 1/1556/63.

62. Morris, *Autobiography*, 72 (first quote); Letter from an officer on board the *Adams*, 30 Apr (second quote), *American Watchman*, 14 May 1814; Cockburn to Warren, 26 Mar 1814, *NW1812*, 3:40, 42–3 (third quote).

63. Morris to Jones, 29 Apr 1814, M125, R35/198; Letter from an officer on board the *Adams*, 30 Apr, *American Watchman*, 14 May 1814.

64. Morris to Jones, 29 Apr 1814, M125, R35/198.

65. Baker to Croker, 26 Mar, Boxer to Baker, 24 Mar 1814, ADM 1/1557/243 & A; Log *Albacore*, 24 Mar 1814, ADM 51/2100.

66. Morris to Jones, 29 Apr 1814, M125, R35/198.

67. Boxer to Baker, 24 Mar 1814, ADM 1/1557/243A (quote); Log *Dannemark*, 25 Mar 1814, ADM 51/2302.

68. Baker to Croker, 26 Mar 1814, ADM 1/1557/243 (quote); Log *Albacore*, 25 Mar 1814, ADM 51/2100.

69. Morris to Jones, 29 Apr (quote), 30 Apr 1814, M125, R35/198, 202; Morris, *Autobiography*, 73. For details of the cruise, see Roosevelt, *Naval War*, 334–35.

70. Baker to Croker, 26 Mar 1814, ADM 1/1557/243.

71. Warrington to Jones, 4 Mar (first quote), 12 Mar, 29 Mar 1814 (second and third quotes), M147, R5/72, 82, 94. The identity of the British warships remains questionable. The weather and distance of the sightings made accurate identifications impossible. The Americans might very well have inflated the British opposition, while the *Peacock* looked to the British like any other unidentified sail. On 13 March, the storm had forced all British warships away from Sandy Hook. The *Belvidera*, *Nimrod*, and *Sylph* were together about 85 miles southeast of Montauk Point while the *Rattler* was about 63 miles southeast of Sandy Hook. See Logs *Rattler*, *Belvidera*, ADM 51/2775, 2018.

72. Warrington to Jones, 30 Sep 1813, M147, R5/133; Jones to Warrington, 26 Feb 1814, CLS, 102– 105.

73. Campbell to Jones, 2 Apr 1814, M125, R35/110; Warrington to Jones, 31 Mar, 4 May 1814, M147, R5/95, 119.

74. Warrington to Jones, 29 Apr 1814, M147, R5/114; Journal of Rodgers, 29 Apr 1814, LC.

75. Narrative of Wales, CM *Epervier*, ADM 1/5447.

76. Testimonies Wales, John Hacket (Lt.), David Genlan (Master) (quote), Narrative of Wales, CM *Epervier*, ADM 1/5447. Warrington's report later asserted 128 men on board. See M147, R5/114.

77. Testimony Lt. John Harvey, CM *Epervier*, ADM 1/5447.

78. Wales to Cochrane, 8 May 1814, NLS, CP, 2339/22–23. Warrington's report asserted 18 x 32-pound carronades, but this is too much for a *Cruizer*-class brig. See M147, R5/114.

79. Testimonies Hacket and Harvey, CM *Epervier*, ADM 1/5447; Warrington to Jones, 29 Apr 1814, M147, R5/114.

80. Narrative of Wales, Testimony Hacket, CM *Epervier*, ADM 1/5447.

81. Ibid.

82. Narrative of Wales, Testimonies Harvey, Genlan, CM *Epervier*, ADM 1/5447. The low number for the *Epervier*'s casualties comes from Wales to Cochrane, 8 May 1814, NLS, CP, 2339/22–23 while the high number from Warrington to Jones, 29 Apr 1814, M147, R5/114. For the action, see James, *Naval History*, 6:158–61; Gardner, *Naval War of 1812*, 91–92; Roosevelt, *Naval War*, 311–15.

83. Warrington to Jones, 29 Apr 1814, M147, R5/114.

84. Warrington to Jones, 4 May 1814, M147, R5/119; Master's Log *Morgiana*, 30 Apr 1814, ADM 52/4190; Log *Majestic*, 30 Apr 1814, ADM 51/2543.

85. Journal of Rodgers, 29 Apr 1814, LC; Master's Log *Morgiana*, 1 May 1814, ADM 52/4190; Details for the *Morgiana*, ADM 7/556; Morris to Jones, 2 May 1814, M125, R36/8.

86. Log *Majestic*, 1 May 1814 ADM 51/2543; Master's Log *Morgiana*, 2 May 1814, ADM 52/4190; Warrington to Jones, 4 May 1814, M147, R5/119.

87. Warrington to Jones, 4 May 1814, M147, R5/119.

88. Jones to [unknown], 5 Apr 1813, HSP, PWJ; Jones to Campbell, 6 Dec 1813, M149, R11/160–61 (quote).

89. Smith to Jones, 19 May 1814, M125, R36/155.

90. Spence to Jones, 9 Feb, Ridgeley to Jones, 27 Mar, 2 Apr 1814, M147, R5/49, 91, 98.

91. Jones to Ridgely, 4 Apr 1814, M149, R11/263–64.

92. Jones to Spence, 4 Apr 1814, *NW1812*, 3:23; Jones to Ridgely, 4 Apr, to Decatur, 4 Apr, to Jacob Jones, 6 Apr, to Gordon, 15 Apr 1814, M149, R11/263–67, 278; Smith to Jones, 9 Jun 1814, M125, R37/42.

93. Jones to Madison, 10 May 1814, LC, JMP, Ser. 1, R16.

Chapter 11. "Into Abler Hands": Britain Turns to New Leadership, 1814

1. Parker to Jones, 29 Jan, 1 Feb 1814, M147, R5/33 1/2, 38; *Connecticut Gazette*, 2 Mar 1814.

2. Jones to Parker, 8 Dec 1813, *NW1812*, 2:294–96.

3. Brine to Tyler, 12 Jul 1814, ADM 1/66/56A; Chapelle, *American Sailing Navy*, 555.

4. Nicholson to Sec. of the Navy, 22 Aug 1815, M148, R15/111; *Connecticut Gazette*, 2 Mar 1814; Leech, *Voice*, 104 (quote).

5. Nicholson to Sec. of the Navy, 22 Aug 1815 (quote), M148, R15/111; C. Marfurth, to Bathurst, 10 Apr 1814, CO 267/38/22; Leech, *Voice*, 106.

6. Ellis to Croker, 7 Jul 1814 (first quote), Ellis to Any Royal Navy Ship that might arrive, 25 Apr 1814 (second quote), ADM 1/1771/51 & A; Log *Spitfire*, 25 Apr 1814, ADM 51/2809; Nicholson to Sec. of the Navy, 22 Aug 1815, M148, R15/111; Brine to Tyler, 12 Jul 1814, ADM 1/66/56A. The *Spitfire* mounted 20 x 24-pound carronades, 8 x 12-pound carronades, and 2 x long 9-pound guns, See Details for the *Spitfire*, ADM 7/556. Modifications had occurred to the *Spitfire*'s armament not reflected in Winfield, *British Warships*.

7. Ellis to Captains of any HMS on the Cape Coast, 25 Apr 1814, ADM 1/1771/51A.

8. Nicholson to Sec. of the Navy, 22 Aug 1815, M148, R15/111; Ellis to Croker, 7 Jul 1814, ADM 1/1771/51.

9. Nicholson to Sec. of the Navy, 22 Aug 1815, M148, R15/111; Leech, *Voice*, 106–7 (quote).

10. Admiralty Board Minutes, 8 Sep 1814, ADM 7/266.

11. Nicholson to Sec. of the Navy, 22 Aug 1815, M148, R15/111.

12. Nicholson to Sec. of the Navy, 22 Aug 1815, M148, R15/111; Leech, *Voice*, 110 (quote).

13. Tyler to Croker, 30 Jun 1814, ADM 1/66/47; Log *Medway*, 12 Jul 1814, ADM 51/2579.

14. Nicholson to Sec. of the Navy, 22 Aug 1815, M148, R15/111; Testimony Lewis Gordon (Lt.), CI *Siren*, M273, R8/220; Leech, *Voice*, 111 (quote).

15. Opinion of Court, 2 Sept 1815, CI *Siren*, M273, R8/220.

16. Log *Marlborough*, 18 Feb 1813, ADM 51/2570; *Sea Soldier*, ed. Petrides, 18 Feb (all quotes), 3 Mar 1813, 168–69.

17. *New England Blockaded*, ed. Whitehill, 13 Mar 1814, 3.

18. Warren to Croker, 20 Feb 1813, ADM 1/4359/205–207.

19. Warren to Croker, 26 Feb 1813, NMM, WAR/49/91.

20. Melville to Warren, 9 Jan 1813 NMM, WAR/82/41–45; Croker to John Gladstone, Chairman of the West India Association at Liverpool, Croker to Warren, 12 Jan 1813, ADM 2/1376/1–8.

21. Warren to Melville, 25 Feb 1813, NMM, LBK/2.

22. Commissioner Wolley to Warren, 20 Feb 1813, CM Stirling, ADM 1/5442. The term "freight money" refers to the movement of specie, principally gold, in British warships. In return for the security of transporting the specie, British naval regulations allowed a commission to be charged, payable to the captain, with a third going the commander in chief of his station. See Rodgers, *Wooden World*, 258, 317.

23. Warren to Melville, 25 Feb 1813, NMM, LBK/2.

24. Melville to Warren, 23 Mar 1813, NMM, WAR/82/56–64. In May 1814 a court martial was held to enquire into the conduct of Vice Admiral Stirling. The verdict stated, "The Court is of opinion that the Charge has been in part proved." The court placed Stirling on the half-pay list with the express directive that he "not be included in any future Promotion." See CM Stirling, ADM 1/5442.

25. Croker to Warren, 20 Mar 1813, ADM 2/1376/354–58.

26. Croker to Warren, 4 Nov 1813, ADM 2/1378/146–51.

27. Melville to Warren, 24 Nov 1813, NMM, WAR 82/96–98.

28. Melville to Warren. 4 Aug 1812, 7 Jan (2 letters), 26 Feb 1813, NMM, WAR 82/5–6, 34–35, 38, 52; McCranie, "The Curse of the Service," 227; Rodgers, *Wooden World*, 282–86; Lavery, *Nelson's Navy*, 97.

29. Letter to the Editor, signed Mercator, *Morning Chronicle*, 13 Nov 1813.

30. Letter to the Editor, dated 16 Dec 1813 and signed Albion, *Naval Chronicle*, 31:118–20.

31. Warren to Melville, 3 Feb 1814, NMM, LBK/2; Hotham to Broke, 8 Mar 1814, SRO, HA 93/9/179.

32. Warren to Brown, 18 Jan 1814, NMM, WAR/54.

33. Melville to Warren, 24 Nov 1813, NMM, WAR 82/96–98.

34. This does not include short cruises of 1812 such as when the *Constitution* sailed in July. The long cruises of 1812 included the following: the *President*, *Congress*, and *United States* sailed in June; *Essex* sailed in July; the *Constitution* sailed in August; the *President*, *Congress*, *United States*, *Essex*, and *Constitution* sailed in October; and the *Chesapeake* sailed in December. The 1813 sailings were as follows: the *Constellation* in February (forced into Norfolk); the *President* and *Congress* in April (to sea); the *United States* and *Macedonian* in June (driven into New London); and the *Chesapeake* in June (captured).

35. E. C[odrington] to Mrs. C[odrington], 16 Jul 1814, *Memoir of Codrington*, ed. Bourchier, 1:311.

36. Warren to Croker, 28 Jan 1814, ADM 1/505/96; Croker to Warren, 4 Nov 1813, ADM 2/1378/146–51.

37. Admiralty to Keats, 8 Apr 1813, ADM 2/1376/235; "Sir Richard Goodwin Keats," *DNB*.

38. Cochrane to Melville, 3 Nov 1813, NLS, CP, MS 2574/77–78; "Sir Alexander F.I. Cochrane," "Sir Richard Goodwin Keats," *DNB*.

39. Cochrane to Melville, 27 Apr 1812, NLS, CP, MS 2574/1–6; Bartlett and Smith, "Species," 186–87.

40. Admiral's Journal, Cochrane, 27 Dec 1813, 25 Jan, 1 Feb 1814, ADM 50/122; Private Correspondence, dated 26 Nov 1813, in *Caledonian Mercury*, 29 Nov 1813.

41. Cochrane to Croker, 8 Mar, 31 Mar 1814, ADM 1/505/106 & A, 139; Admiral's Journal, Cochrane, 22 Jan 1814, ADM 50/122.

42. Cochrane to Melville, 25 Mar 1814, Indiana University, War of 1812 Man.

43. Keith to Markham, 23 Feb 1804, *Correspondence of Markham*, 153–54.

44. Cochrane to Warren, 23 Mar 1814, ADM 1/505/139A; Cochrane to Pigot, 25 Mar 1814, Questions about New Orleans, NLS, CP, MS 2346/1, 3–4. For Cochrane and Native Americans, see Owsley, "Role of the South," 26–27; Mahon, "British Strategy."

45. Log *Shelburne*, 20 Apr 1814, ADM 51/2335; Testimonies Benjamin Waine (Master), Armstrong (Mid.), CI *Frolic*, M273, R8/205.

46. Testimony Robinson (Master's Mate), CI *Frolic*, M273, R8/205; Bainbridge to Jones, 3 Jun 1814, M147, R5/139; Waine to Bainbridge, 14 May 1814, "Account of the Capture of the *Frolic*," 278; James, *Naval Occurrences*, 166–69; Roosevelt, *Naval War*, 311.

47. Log *Junon*, 19 Feb 1814, ADM 51/2465.

48. Bainbridge to Jones, 3 Jun 1814, M147, R5/139.

49. Durham to Croker, 28 Mar 1814, ADM 1/335/49; Pigot to Cochrane, 25 Apr 1814, NLS, CP, MS 2339/8.

50. Cochrane to Croker, 31 Mar 1814, ADM 1/505/139.

51. Admiral's Journal, Cochrane, 1 Apr 1814, ADM 50/122; Admiralty to Warren, 27 Nov 1812, 26 Mar 1813, Croker to Warren, 28 Apr 1813, NLS, CP, MS 2340/25–26, 49, 71–72; Proclamation of Blockade, 16 Nov 1813, ADM 1/504/252A.

52. Cochrane to Melville, 17 Jul 1814, Indiana University, War of 1812 Man. (third quote); Cochrane to Croker, 7 Mar 1814, ADM 1/505/105; Proclamation of Blockade, 25 Apr 1814, ADM 1/506/159A; Cochrane to Sherbrooke, 30 May 1814, NLS, CP, MS 2349/68–70 (first, second, and fourth quotes).

53. Croker to Pellew, 15 Apr 1814, ADM 2/1380/25–27.

54. Cochrane to Croker, 20 Jun 1814, ADM 1/506/218a; Cochrane to Prevost, 3 May 1814, NLS, CP, MS 2349/42.

55. Hope to Keith, 14 Feb 1814, NMM, KEI/37/9.

56. William Young to Melville, 10 Aug 1812, NAS, GD 51/2/1084/4.

57. Paget to Cochrane, 24 Jun, 26 Jul 1814. NLS, CP, MS 2327, 32–33, 52B-53; Griffith to Croker, 9 Jul 1814, ADM 1/506/210.

58. *New England Blockaded*, ed. Whitehill, 12 Jun 1814, 25.

59. Cockburn to Cochrane, 10 May 1814, NLS, CP, MS 2574, 103–109.

60. *New England Blockaded*, ed. Whitehill, 9 Jun 1814, 23.

61. Griffith to Cochrane, 16 Aug 1814 (quote), NLS, CP, MS 2327/66–69; Abstract of Griffith's Command, NLS, CP, MS 2335/65; Milne to Home, 6 Sep 1814, HMC, *Home*, 165.

62. Hotham to Cochrane, 26 Aug, 24 Oct 1814, NLS, CP, MS 2327/82–84, 89–91.

63. Melville to Cochrane, 25 Oct 1814, NLS, CP, MS 2574/203–204.

64. Melville to Cochrane, 10 Aug 1814, NLS, CP, MS 2574, 171–72.

Chapter 12. "Repulsed in Every Attempt": The Culmination of the Jones' Small Cruiser Strategy, mid-1814

1. Creighton to Jones, 26 Apr 1814, M147, R5/97.

2. Renshaw to Jones, 2 May, 18 Jul 1814, Vessels Captured and Boarded by the *Rattlesnake*, M148, R13/22, 49, 127.

3. Renshaw to Jones, 18 Jul 1814, M148, R13/22; Testimony Mid. W.C. Pearey and Mid. W. Armstrong, CI *Rattlesnake*, M273, R8/204.

4. It was stated in the American press that the stranger was the 38-gun *Madagascar*, but she was in Plymouth Sound on that day. See her log ADM 51/2551; "Capture of the Rattlesnake," *New-England Palladium*, 29 Jul 1814.

5. French Ships at Sea 1814, NMM, KEI/40/4; Memorial of Ship Captains, 21 May 1814, ADM 1/834/713A.

6. Renshaw to Officers, Officers to Renshaw, 1 Jun 1814, Renshaw to Jones, 18 Jul 1814, M148, R13/22, 127.

7. Renshaw to Jones, 18 Jul 1814 (quote), Vessels Captured and Boarded by the *Rattlesnake*, M148, R13/22, 127; Logs *Redwing*, *Conflict*, 9–12 Jun 1814, ADM 51/2065, 2199.

8. Renshaw asserted in his cruise report (M148, R13/22) that between 12 and 17 June, British frigates chased the *Rattlesnake* on four occasions, but Renshaw provided no details or specific dates. In addition, this author has been unable to find the British frigates in question. These encounters are quite questionable.

9. Renshaw to Jones, 18 Jul 1814, M148, R13/22; Testimony Lt. H. B. Rapp, CI *Rattlesnake*, M273, R8/204.

10. Testimony Lt. H. B. Rapp, CI *Rattlesnake*, M273, R8/204; Log *Leander*, 11 Jul 1814, ADM 51/2524; *New England Blockaded*, ed. Whitehill, 23 Jul 1814, 36–37; Winfield, *British Warships*, 122.

11. Log *Leander*, 11 Jul 1814, ADM 51/2524; Testimony Mid. W. Armstrong, CI *Rattlesnake*, M273, R8/204; Renshaw to Jones, 18 Jul 1814, M148, R13/22; Roosevelt, *Naval War*, 321.

12. Collier to Griffith, 11 Jul 1814, ADM 1/506/218A.

13. Verdict, CI *Rattlesnake*, M273, R8/204.

14. Report on State of Navy by Jones, 22 Feb 1814, *NASP Naval*, 4:198–201.

15. Morris, *Autobiography*, 66.

16. Morris to Jones, 29 Apr, 5 May, 22 Aug 1814, M125, R35/197, R36/17, R38/124; *DNI*, 18 May 1814.

17. Log *Barham*, 30 Apr, 2 May 1814, ADM 51/2185.

18. Logs *Barham*, *Statira*, *Forester*, 24–25 May 1814, ADM 51/2185, 2814, 2376; Morris to Jones, 22 Aug 1814, M125, R38/124.

19. Morris to Jones, 22 Aug 1814, M125, R38/124.

20. Morris to Jones, 22 Aug 1814, M125, R38/124; Logs *Eridanus*, *Tigris*, *Orestes*, 13 Jul 1814, ADM 51/2407, 2905, 53/938.

21. Log *Eridanus*, 13–14 Jul 1814, ADM 51/2407; Morris to Jones, 22 Aug 1814, M125, R38/124.

22. Morris to Jones, 22 Aug 1814, M125, R38/124. The identity of the first frigate is unknown. The *Tigris'* log mentions a second sail but does not identify her as a warship.

23. Log *Tigris*, 19–20 Jul 1814, ADM 51/2905; Morris to Jones, 22 Aug 1814, M125, R38/124; Sawyer to Croker, 26 Jul 1814, ADM 1/626/337.

24. Morris to Jones, 22 Aug 1814, M125, R38/124.

25. Morris to Jones, 22 Aug 1814, M125, R38/125; Morris, *Autobiography*, 75–76 (quote).

26. Morris to Jones, 22 Aug 1814, M125, R38/125.

27. Morris to Jones, 22 Aug 1814, M125, R38/125; Logs *Peruvian*, *Rifleman*, 18–19 Aug 1814, ADM 51/2658, 2770; Griffith to Cochrane, 9 Sep 1814, ADM 1/507/285A; Morris, *Autobiography*, 78. Morris contended that he had encountered the *Rifleman*. Though she was nearby, Morris had in fact encountered the *Peruvian*. Part of the confusion deals with the fact that both the *Peruvian* and *Rifleman* were *Cruizer*-class brigs.

28. Griffith to Cochrane, 23 Aug 1814 (2 letters), NLS, CP, MS 2335/67–68, 2327/80–81.

29. Barrie to Griffith, 3 Sep 1814, ADM 1/507/285A (quote); Griffith to Cochrane, 23 Aug, 9 Sep 1814, NLS, CP, MS 2335/67–71.

30. Morris to Jones, 20 Sep 1814, M125, R39/72.

31. Barrie to Griffith, 3 Sep 1814, ADM 1/507/285A; Morris to Jones, 20 Sep 1814, M125, R39/72.

32. Morris to Jones, 20 Sep 1814, M125, R39/72; Morris, *Autobiography*, 82.

33. Barrie to Griffith, 3 Sep 1814, ADM 1/507/285A.

34. David Milne to Home, 6 Sep 1814, HMC, *Home*, 165 (quote); *Portland Gazette*, 28 Nov 1814.

35. *New England Blockaded*, ed. Whitehill, 29 May 1814, 18.

36. Milne to Melville, 8 Sep 1814, NAS, GD 51/2/527.

37. Liverpool to Cochrane, 28 Sep 1814, NLS, CP, MS 2574/175–76.

38. *Examiner,* 9 Oct 1814.

39. Cochrane to Croker, 31 Mar 1814, ADM 1/505/139; Proclamation of Blockade, 25 Apr 1814, signed Cochrane, ADM 1/506/159A; Cochrane to Griffith, 2 May 1814, NLS, CP, MS 2349/38–39; Blakeley to Jones, 1 May 1814, *DNI,* 10 May 1814.

40. Blakeley to Jones, 8 Jul 1814, M124, R64/44; Captures by *Wasp,* 1 May to 6 Jul 1814, *DNI,* 11 Oct 1814.

41. Minutes of the Action *Wasp* and *Reindeer,* M124, R64/45A; Chambers to Domett, 7 Jul 1814, CM *Reindeer,* ADM 1/5444.

42. Chambers to Domett, 7 Jul 1814, CM *Reindeer,* ADM 1/5444 (quote); Lyon, *Sailing Navy List,* 140; Winfield, *British Warships,* 294.

43. Minutes of the Action the *Wasp* and *Reindeer,* M124, R64/45A; Bowers, *Naval Adventures,* 2:277–78 (quote).

44. Chambers to Domett, 7 Jul 1814, Testimony Matthew Mitchell (Master's Mate), CM *Reindeer,* ADM 1/5444.

45. Chambers to Domett, 7 Jul 1814, CM *Reindeer,* ADM 1/5444 (first quote); *The Hull Packet,* 26 Jul 1814 (second quote).

46. Geisinger Journal, 29 Jun 1814, LC; Testimony James Legg (Boatswain), CM *Reindeer,* ADM 1/5444.

47. Testimony John Simpson (Quartermaster), CM *Reindeer,* ADM 1/5444; Minutes of the Action *Wasp* and *Reindeer,* M124, R64/45A (quote).

48. Geisinger Journal, 29 Jun 1814, LC (first quote); Chambers to Domett, 7 Jul 1814, CM *Reindeer,* ADM 1/5444; Blakeley to Jones, 8 Jul 1814, Minutes of the Action *Wasp* and *Reindeer,* M124, R64/45 & A (second quote).

49. Geisinger Journal, 1–2 Jul 1814, LC.

50. Blakeley to Jones, 8 Jul, 10 Jul 1814, M124, R64/44, 47; British Vessels captured by the *Wasp,* 1 May to 6 Jul 1814, *DNI,* 11 Oct 1814.

51. *The Hull Packet,* 20 Sep 1814.

52. Board Minutes, 8–11 Jul 1814, ADM 7/266; "Capture of the *Reindeer . . .* by the *Wasp,"* London, 15 Jul, in *Baltimore Patriot,* 5 Sep 1814.

53. Croker to Keith, 14 Jul 1814, ADM 2/1380/263–64.

54. Blakeley to Jones, 27 Aug 1814, *DNI,* 23 Nov 1814.

55. Geisinger Journal, 31 Aug, 1 Sep 1814, LC; Logs *Armada, Strombolo,* 31 Aug–1 Sep 1814, ADM 51/2084, 2803.

56. Geisinger Journal, 1 Sep 1814, LC.

57. Grant to Croker, 8 Sep 1814, ADM 1/1861/202; Log *Armada,* 1 Sep 1814, ADM 51/2084.

58. Geisinger Journal, 2 Sep 1814, LC.

59. Sawyer to Croker 12 Aug, 13 Aug 1814, ADM 1/626/364–365; Log *Kangaroo,* 10 Aug, 1 Sep 1814, ADM 51/2505.

60. Arbuthnot to Sawyer, 1 Sep 1814, CM *Avon,* ADM 1/5446; Lloyd to Sawyer, 2 Sep 1814, ADM 1/626/426A; Log *Tartarus,* 1 Sep 1814, ADM 51/2876.

61. Log *Castilian,* 1 Sep 1814, ADM 51/2197; Arbuthnot to Sawyer, 1 Sep 1814, CM *Avon,* ADM 1/5446.

62. Minutes of the Action *Wasp* and HMS [unknown], 1 Sep 1814, *DNI*, 23 Nov 1814.

63. Testimony Lt. John Harvey, CM *Avon*, ADM 1/5446.

64. Minutes of the Action *Wasp* and HMS [unknown], 1 Sep 1814, *DNI*, 23 Nov 1814 (quote); Testimony Harvey, Arbuthnot to Sawyer, 1 Sep 1814, CM *Avon*, ADM 1/5446.

65. Lloyd to Sawyer, 2 Sep 1814, ADM 1/626/426A; Log *Castilian*, 1 Sep 1814, ADM 51/2197 (quote).

66. Lloyd to Sawyer, 2 Sep 1814, ADM 1/626/426A (all quotes); Testimony Harvey, CM *Avon*, ADM 1/5446.

67. Minutes of the Action *Wasp* and HMS [unknown], 1 Sep 1814, *DNI*, 23 Nov 1814.

68. Lloyd to Sawyer, 2 Sep 1814, ADM 1/626/426A (first quote); Testimony Harvey, CM *Avon*, ADM 1/5446; Admiralty's response to Sawyer to Croker, 6 Sep 1814, ADM 1/626/426 (second quote).

69. Blakeley to Jones, 11 Sep 1814, M124, R65/84.

70. *Examiner*, 25 Sep 1814.

71. Melville to Croker, 11 Sep 1814, Duke, Croker Papers, Box 7 (second quote); Extract of a Letter, dated 8 Sep, published in *Caledonian Mercury* (first quote), 15 Sep 1814; *Examiner*, 25 Sep 1814.

72. Blakeley to Jones, 11 Sep 1814, M124, R65/84.

73. Captures by *Wasp*, 11–22 Sep 1814, *DNI*, 23 Nov 1814.

74. Blakeley to Jones, 22 Sep 1814, M124, R65/100–101.

75. Letter from an Officer on board the *Wasp*, 23 Sep 1814, *DNI*, 14 Nov 1814. For the *Wasp*'s cruise, see Duffy, *Captain Blakeley*.

76. Extract, Journal on board the Swedish Brig *Adonis*, 9 Oct 1814, in Porter, *Journal*, 558–59.

77. *Columbian Centinel* quoted from the *DNI*, 26 Apr 1815. Duffy chronicles the numerous reports of the *Wasp*'s demise, and sheds light on those that are more plausible. See *Captain Blakeley*, 263–73.

78. Warrington to Jones, 1 Jun 1814, M147, R5/135; Jones to Warrington, 11 Jun 1814, M149 R11/338–39; Log *Majestic*, 10 May, 20–21 May 1814, ADM 51/2543; Master's Log *Morgiana*, 10 May, 20–21 May 1814, ADM 52/4190.

79. Journal of Rodgers, 4–5 Jun 1814, LC.

80. Logs *Majestic, Dotterel*, 4–5 Jun 1814, ADM 51/2543, 2294; Master's Log *Morgiana*, 4–5 Jun 1814, ADM 52/4190.

81. Journal of Rodgers, 17 Jun, 6 Jul 1814, LC; Warrington to Jones, 30 Oct 1814, M147, R5/147; Captures by *Peacock*, *DNI*, 3 Nov 1814.

82. Board Minutes, 2 Aug, 9 Aug 1814, ADM 7/266; Sawyer to Croker, 13 Aug 1814, ADM 1/626/365. This 38-gun ship was the British frigate *President*.

83. Warrington to Jones, 30 Oct 1814, M147, R5/147; Captures by *Peacock*, *DNI*, 3 Nov 1814.

84. Convoy Report for 1814, ADM 1/4359/314.

85. Warrington to Jones, 30 Oct 1814, M147, R5/147; Captures by *Peacock*, *DNI*, 3 Nov 1814.

86. Journal of Rodgers, 22 Oct, 29 Oct 1814, LC.

87. Captures by *Peacock*, *DNI*, 3 Nov 1814.

88. Board Minutes, 9 Sep 1814, ADM 7/266.

89. Bennett to Croker, 26 Oct 1814, ADM 1/3994; G. Stuart Bruce (British Consulate Tenerife) to Croker, 10 Oct 1814, ADM 1/3845.

90. Hope to Keith, 4 Jun 1814, NMM, KEI/37/9.

Chapter 13. "The Current Demands of the Service": An Appraisal of British Naval Operations, 1813–14

1. In July 1813 the European fleets in the Mediterranean, the Channel (Bay of Biscay), off the Texel (North Sea), and the Baltic contained 197 warships, compared to 112 in the three parts of Warren's command. See Ships in Sea Pay, 1 Jul 1813, ADM 8/100.

2. Ships in Sea Pay, 1 Jul 1812, 1813, ADM 8/100.

3. Black, *British Seaborne Empire*, 161–62.

4. Melville to Keith, 3 Sep 1813, NMM, KEI/37/9.

5. Bickerton to Officers, 5 Aug 1814, *Penguin* Order Book, USNA, MS 58.

6. Bowers, *Naval Adventures*, 1:279.

7. Melville to Cochrane, 10 Oct 1814, NLS, CP, MS, 2574/193–95.

8. Upton to Griffith, 22 Jan 1814, NMM, WAR/25/96.

9. *New England Blockaded*, ed. Whitehill, 11 May 1814, 12–13.

10. Hotham to Broke, 20 Nov 1814, SRO, HA 93/9/182.

11. Barrow to Hotham, 19 Dec 1814, Hotham Papers, HUL U DDHO/x1/7/71.

12. Glete, *Navies and Nations*, 2:376.

13. Dull, *Age of the Ship of the Line*.

14. Gardner, *Frigates*, 35–37.

15. Letter signed Albion, 4 Apr 1813, *Naval Chronicle*, 29:291–92.

16. Gardiner, *Frigates*, 52.

17. Melville to Broke, 23 Dec 1813, SRO, HA 93/6/2/65.

18. Melville to Warren, 4 Jun 1813, NMM, WAR/82/73–77.

19. Ships in Sea Pay, 1 Jul 1813, ADM 8/100; Admiralty Board Minutes, Late 1814, ADM 7/266.

20. Winfield, *British Warships*, 238–41.

21. Woodman, *Victory of Seapower*, 123.

22. Ships in Sea Pay, 1 Jul 1813, ADM 8/100; Admiralty Board Minutes, Late 1814, ADM 7/266.

23. Melville to Keith, 3 Sep 1813, NMM, KEI/37/9 (first quote); Melville to Wellington, 28 Jul 1813, *SDW*, 8:145 (second quote); Young to Foley, 14 Oct 1813, NMM, FOL/20B (third quote); Young to Foley, 28 Feb 1814, NMM, FOL/20C (fourth quote).

24. Melville to Warren, 3 Dec 1812, NMM, WAR/82/18–22.

25. The losses included the *Frolic* (though recaptured), *Peacock*, *Epervier*, *Reindeer*, *Avon*, and *Penguin*. The only British victory involved the *Pelican* over the smaller *Argus*.

26. Bowers, *Naval Adventures*, 1:243 (quote); Valle, "Navy's Battle Doctrine," 178.

27. Circular signed by Croker, 25 Nov 1814, ADM 2/1381/46–49.

28. Barrow to Hotham, 19 Dec 1814, HUL U DDHO/x1/7/71.

29. Melville to Croker, 11 Sep 1814, Duke, Croker Papers, Box 7.

30. Lloyd's to Croker, 19 Sep 1814, ADM 1/3994.

31. Statement Croker, 13 May 1814, HC, 27:869.

32. Lloyd's to Croker, 19 Sep 1814, ADM 1/3994.

33. Melville to Croker, 30 Apr 1813, Duke, Croker Papers, Box 7; Comparative Insurance Premiums, 1812 and 1813, NAS, GD 51/2/882/4; Rodger, *Command of the Ocean*, 569.

34. Statement Croker, 13 May 1814, HC, 27:869; Laforey to Warren, 14 Jan 1814, NMM, WAR/69/13–15.

35. Admiralty Board Minutes, late 1814, ADM 7/266.

36. Hope to Keith, 20 Jan 1813, NMM, KEI/37/9.

37. Statement Croker, 13 May 1814, HC, 27:870.

38. See Chapter 4 for details relating to tension between the Admiralty and Warren over the strength of his command.

39. Cochrane to Melville, 17 Jul 1814, Indiana University, War of 1812 Man.

40. Statement Croker, 13 May 1814, HC, 27:868.

41. See Chapter 5 for the American maritime infrastructure.

42. Comments on Blockade (circa 1813), Duke, Croker Papers, Box 1.

Epilogue. "A Wreath of Laurels . . . a Crown of Thorns": The Last Naval Campaign, 1815

1. Jones to His Wife, 6 Nov 1814, HSP, PWJ.

2. Jones to Madison, 25 Apr 1814, LC, JMP, Ser. 1, R16.

3. Jones to Madison, 25 Apr, 11 Sep 1814 (public & private), LC, JMP, Ser. 1, R16.

4. Jones to His Wife, [20 or 21 Sep 1814], HSP, PWJ.

5. Jones to His Wife, 6 Nov 1814, HSP, PWJ (all quotes); Jones to Madison, 26 Oct 1814, LC, JMP, Ser. 1, R16.

6. Jones to Madison, 15 Oct (first quote), 26 Oct 1814 (all other quotes), LC, JMP, Ser. 1, R16.

7. Biddle to Jones, 15 Oct, 19 Nov 1814, M147, R5/69, 82; Jones to Biddle, 19 Oct 1814, CLS, 188; Skiddy, "Ups and Downs," 1:60–61, Mystic Collection 304.

8. Jones to Decatur, 17 Nov (first quote), 23 Nov, Jones to Stewart, 29 Nov 1814 (second quote), CLS, 210–13, 217–218.

9. Jones to his wife, (20 or 21 Sep 1814), 6 Nov 1814, HSP, PWJ.

10. Madison to Rodgers, 24 Nov 1814, Spence to Rodgers, 13 Dec 1814, RFP, Pt II:4; Rodgers to Madison, 29 Nov 1814, LC, Rodgers Naval Papers, Box 2; Schroeder, *Commodore Rodgers*, 141.

11. *New England Blockaded*, ed. Whitehill, 20 Jul 1814, 36.

12. William Domett to Melville, 26 Jul 1814, NAS, GD 51/2/523/2.

13. Melville to Cochrane, 25 Oct 1814, NLS, CP, MS 2574/203–204.

14. Cochrane to Captains and Commanders near Antigua, 3 Nov 1814, NLS, CP, MS 2575/33.

15. Cochrane to Melville, 10 Nov 1814, NLS, CP, MS 2574/211–12.

16. Croker to Hotham, 19 Dec 1814, ADM 2/1381/80–82.

17. Croker to Griffith and to the Senior Officer at Bermuda, 26 Nov 1814, ADM 2/1381/52–53, 56.

18. Stuart to Griffith, 23 Dec, Stuart to Collier, 24 Dec 1814 (all quotes), ADM 1/1668/21A.

19. Griffith to Collier, 4 Oct (quote), 29 Nov 1814, Collier to Griffith, 24 Dec 1814, ADM 1/1668/21A.

20. Henry Jane to Hotham, 25 Dec 1814, ADM 1/508/21A; Stuart to Griffith, 23 Dec 1814, ADM 1/1668/21A.

21. Log *Constitution*, 24–26 Dec 1814, RG24; Log *Medina*, 1–24 Dec 1814, ADM 51/2556; Martin, Constitution's *Finest Fight*, 8–10 (quote).

22. Collier to Griffith, 29 Dec 1814, ADM 1/1668/21A.

23. Collier to Melville, 29 Dec 1814, NMM, AGC/2/18.

24. Griffith to Croker, 10 Jan 1815, ADM 1/508/27.

25. Admiralty to Cochrane, 27 Dec 1814, ADM 2/1381/92–95; Melville to Cochrane, 27 Dec 1814, NLS, CP, MS 2574/258–59.

26. Croker to Martin, 29 Dec 1814, ADM 2/1381/107–108.

27. Croker to Cochrane, 30 Dec 1814, Admiralty to Burlton, 6 Jan 1815, ADM 2/1381/109–10, 122–24; Admiralty Board Minutes, late 1814, ADM 7/266.

28. Admiralty to Caulfield, 24 Jan, Admiralty to David Lloyd, 25 Jan, Croker to Tyler, to Samuel Hood, 30 Jan 1815, ADM 2/1381/138–40, 147–50, 161–64; Bennett to Croker, 25 Jan 1815, and Admiralty response ADM 1/3995.

29. Croker to Collier, 26 Jan 1815, ADM 2/1381/152–53.

30. Evans to Hotham, 28 Jan 1815, entry 31 Jan, HUL U DDHO/x1/7/2.

31. Log *Constitution*, 8–9 Feb 1815, RG24.

32. Log *Constitution*, 21 Feb 1815, RG24; Stewart to Crowninshield, May 1815, M125, R44/93.

33. Remarks on board *Cyane*, 20 Feb 1815, CM *Cyane*, ADM 1/5449.

34. Ibid.

35. Douglas to Croker, 22 Feb 1815, CM *Levant*, ADM 1/5449.

36. Details for *Cyane* and *Levant*, ADM 7/556; James, *Naval History*, 5:32, 6:248; Testimony Falcon, CM *Levant*, ADM 1/5449; Hoffman to Sec. of the Navy, 30 Apr 1815, *DNI*, 14 Apr 1815. According to the British sources, the *Cyane* mounted a slightly different armament of 22 x 32-pound carronades, 8 x 18-pound carronades, and 2 x long 6-pounders.

37. Log *Constitution*, 21 Feb 1815, RG24; Testimonies Lt. John Henderson and James Stannus (Master), CM *Levant*, ADM 1/5449; Remarks on board *Cyane*, 20 Feb 1815, CM *Cyane*, ADM 1/5449.

38. Log *Constitution*, 21 Feb 1815, RG24.

39. Remarks on board *Cyane*, 20 Feb 1815, CM *Cyane*, ADM 1/5449.

40. Douglas to Croker, 22 Feb 1815, CM *Levant*, ADM 1/5449.

41. Falcon to Douglas, 22 Feb 1815, CM *Cyane*, ADM 1/5449.

42. Remarks on Board *Cyane*, 20 Feb 1815 (second quote), Falcon to Douglas, 22 Feb 1815 (third quote), CM *Cyane*, ADM 1/5449; Log *Constitution*, 21 Feb 1815, RG24 (first quote).

43. Douglas to Croker, 22 Feb 1815, CM *Levant*, ADM 1/5449. For the action, see William Dudley, "'Old Ironsides'"; Martin, *Fortunate Ship*, 195–200.

44. Douglas to Croker, 22 Feb 1815, CM *Levant*, ADM 1/5449.

45. Douglas to Croker, 22 Feb 1815, CM *Levant*, Testimony Lt. Alexander McKenzie, CM *Cyane*, ADM 1/5449; Stewart to Crowninshield, May 1815, M125, R44/93; Jellico to Collier, 12 Mar 1815, ADM 1/509/186A; Logs *Snake, Castor*, 16 Feb 1815, ADM 51/2327, 2226. The *Sir Francis Drake* was once a frigate, but as a store ship she carried twenty-two guns.

46. Collier to Griffith, 25 Feb, 12 Mar 1815, ADM 1/509/204A.

47. Log *Constitution*, 12 Mar 1815, RG24 (all quotes); Martin, Constitution's *Finest Fight*, 43–45.

48. Logs *Leander, Newcastle*, 11 Mar 1815, ADM 51/2524, 2589; Collier to Griffith, 12 Mar 1815, ADM 1/509/186.

49. Log *Acasta*, 11 Mar 1815, ADM 51/2102; Log *Constitution*, 12 Mar 1815, RG24 (all quotes).

50. Collier to Griffith, 12 Mar 1815, ADM 1/509/186.

51. Ibid.; Extract, Log *Levant*, 11 Mar 1815, *DNI*, 5 May 1815 (quote).

52. Collier to Griffith, 12 Mar 1815, ADM 1/509/186; Martin, Constitution's *Finest Fight*, 45–46; Malcomson, "Sad Case of Sir George."

53. B. T. Hoffman to Crowninshield, 10 Apr 1815, *DNI*, 15 April 1815.

54. Hotham to Cochrane, 2 Jan 1815, NLS, CP, MS 2327/114–15.

55. Ibid.

56. Hayes to Hotham, 9 Jan 1815, HUL U DDHO/x1/7/2.

57. Journal of the *Tenedos*, 13 Jan 1815 (quote), HSP; Hayes to Hotham, 17 Jan 1815, ADM 1/508/73A.

58. Decatur to Crowninshield, 14 Jan, 18 Jan 1815, M125, R42/41, 50; Newman, Mystic, Collection 51/Box 1.

59. Perry to Crowninshield, 28 Jan 1815 (first quote), attached letter from Decatur, M125, R42/82; Newman, Mystic, Collection 51/Box 1 (second quote).

60. Decatur to Crowninshield, 18 Jan 1815, M125, R42/50.

61. Hayes to Hotham, 17 Jan 1815, ADM 1/508/73A.

62. A. Lambert, "Taking the President," 101; Gardner, *Naval War of 1812*, 164.

63. Hayes to Hotham, 17 Jan 1815, ADM 1/508/73A; Journal of the *Tenedos*, 15 Jan 1815, HSP.

64. Decatur to Crowninshield, 18 Jan 1815, M125, R42/50; Log *Endymion*, 15 Jan 1815, ADM 51/2324.

65. Decatur to Crowninshield, 18 Jan 1815, M125, R42/50.

66. Newman, Mystic, Collection 51/Box 1.

67. Hayes to Hotham, 17 Jan 1815, ADM 1/508/73A; Details for the *Endymion*, ADM 7/556.

68. Newman, Mystic, Collection 51/Box 1 (first quote); Decatur to Crowninshield, 18 Jan 1815 (second quote), M125, R42/50; Log of *Endymion*, 15 Jan 1815, ADM 51/2324.

69. Newman, Mystic, Collection 51/Box 1.

70. Perry to Crowninshield, 28 Jan 1815, attached letter from Decatur, M125, R42/82.

71. Journal of the *Tenedos*, 15 Jan 1815, HSP (quote); Decatur to Crowninshield, 18 Jan 1815, M125, R42/50. For the action, see A. Lambert, "Taking the President"; Dunne, W.M.P., "The United States Frigate *President*."

72. Hope to Alexander Hope, 2 Feb, Hotham to George Hope, 23 Jan 1815, NAS GD 364/1/1267/23, 27; George Hope to Hayes, 15 Jan 1815, ADM 1/508/73A; Addendum to Decatur to Crowninshield, 18 Jan 1815, in James, *Naval History*, 6:241.

73. Black to Warrington, 26 Apr 1815, transcribed copy in Journal of Rodgers, LC.

74. Warrington to Crowninshield, 23 Jan 1815, M125, R42/65; Journal of Rodgers, 23–24 Jan 1815, LC.

75. Hotham to Cochrane, 12 Feb 1815, ADM 1/508/79A.

76. Biddle to Decatur, 25 Mar 1815, M125, R43/112.

77. McDonald to Croker, 3 May 1815, CM *Penguin*, ADM 1/5451 (third and fourth quotes); Biddle to Decatur, 25 Mar 1815, M125, R43/112 (all other quotes).

78. Biddle to Decatur, 25 Mar 1815, M125, R43/112; McDonald to Croker, 3 May 1815, CM *Penguin*, ADM 1/5451; Skiddy, "Ups and Downs," 1:69–73, Mystic Collection 304 (quote).

79. McDonald to Croker, 3 May 1815, CM *Penguin*, ADM 1/5451; Biddle to Decatur, 25 Mar 1815, M125, R43/112.

80. Biddle to Decatur, 25 Mar 1815 (second and fifth quotes), M125, R43/112; Testimonies McDonald and Lt. John Elwin (first quote), McDonald to Croker (third and fourth quotes), 3 May 1815, CM *Penguin*, ADM 1/5451; Silverstone, *Sailing Navy*, 47.

81. Journal of Rodgers, 24–25 Mar 1815, LC; Warrington to Crowninshield, 9 Apr 1815, M125, R44/32.

82. Hotham to Cochrane, 14 Feb 1815, NLS, CP, MS 2327/120–23.

83. Hope to Alexander Hope, attached to 8 Mar 1815 letter, NAS, GD 364/1/1267/25; Letter from an Officer on board the *Constitution*, 8 Feb 1815, *DNI*, 6 Apr 1815.

84. Griffith to Cochrane, 9 Feb 1815, NLS, CP, MS 2327/116–19.

85. Griffith to Hotham, 23 Jan 1815, HUL U DDHO/x1/7/2.

86. Treaty of Peace signed at Ghent, 24 Dec 1814, *Consolidated Treaty Series*, ed. Parry, 63:423.

87. Griffith to Cochrane, 9 Feb 1815, NLS, CP, MS 2327/130–31.

88. Cochrane to Croker, 24 Mar 1815, Cochrane to Hayes, 19 Mar 1815, ADM 1/509/34 and A.

89. "*Constitution* Frigate," originally published in the *New York Evening Post, Baltimore Patriot*, 18 May 1815 (all quotes); "Another Naval Victory," *Columbian*, 10 Apr 1815.

90. Biddle to Decatur, 10 Jun 1815, M125, R45/19; Log *Hornet*, 29 Apr 1815, RG24 (last three short quotes); Journal of Rodgers, 25–29 Apr 1815, LC (all other quotes).

91. Admiralty to Burlton, 6 Jan 1815, ADM 2/1381/122–24; Burlton to Croker, 17 Mar 1815, ADM 1/188/94.

92. Log *Cornwallis*, 27–28 Apr 1815, ADM 51/2046.

93. Skiddy, "Ups and Downs," 1:88, Mystic Collection 304; Journal of Rodgers, 29 Apr 1815, LC.

94. Biddle to Decatur, 10 Jun 1815, M125, R45/19.

95. Log *Cornwallis*, 29 Apr 1815, ADM 51/2046; Log *Hornet*, 30 Apr 1815, RG24.

96. Testimony James Newton, CI *Hornet*'s return, M273, R8/219.

97. Biddle to Decatur, 10 Jun 1815, M125, R45/19; Skiddy, "Ups and Downs," 1:93, Mystic Collection 304.

98. Warrington to Sec. of the Navy, 2 Nov 1815, M125, R47/2; Journal of Rodgers, 16–17 May 1815, LC.

99. Warrington to Sec. of the Navy, 2 Nov 1815, M125, R47/2; Journal of Rodgers, 14–30 June 1815, LC.

100. Journal of Rodgers, 1 Jul 1815, LC; *Nautilus* and *Peacock*, 30 Jun 1815, by Lt. Gov. in Council C. Assey, ADM 1/189/46A (first quote); Warrington to Crowninshield, 11 Nov 1815, M125, R47/17 (second quote).

101. Warrington to Crowninshield, 11 Nov 1815, M125, R47/17.

102. Warrington to Crowninshield, 11 Nov 1815, M125, R47/17; *Nautilus* and *Peacock*, 30 Jun 1815, by Lt. Gov. in Council C. Assey, ADM 1/189/46A; Journal of Rodgers, 1 Jul 1815, LC; Hughes, "Lewis Warrington."

103. *Nautilus* and *Peacock*, 30 Jun 1815, by Lt. Gov. in Council C. Assey, ADM 1/189/46A.

104. Warrington to Crowninshield, 11 Nov 1815, M125, R47/17.

Glossary

Abeam	The direction at a right angle to the ship's centerline.
Aft	The area toward the stern of a ship.
Back	To catch the wind in the sails in order to prevent a ship's forward movement.
Beam	The width of a ship. Also, the direction at a right angle to the ship's centerline.
Bend (sails)	To secure a sail to a mast.
Bow	The front of the ship.
Bower anchors	The largest anchors of a warship, carried near the bow. The "best bower anchor" was on the starboard and the "small bower anchor" on the port side of the ship.
Bowsprit	The spar protruding over the bow. Designed to secure various sails.
Brig	A two-masted, square-rigged vessel.
Bulwark	The solid railing around the uppermost deck of a ship.
Cable	A rope to which an anchor is secured.
Cannister shot	A tin with musket balls inside. When fired from a cannon, the tin splits open and the musket balls act like a shotgun.
Courses	The lower sails (the foresail and mainsail) on a square-rigged ship.
Dismast	The loss of a ship's mast.
Double-headed shot	A shot designed to cut rigging. The shot is similar in appearance to a modern dumbbell.
Fill	To catch air in the sails so as to propel the ship forward.

First rate	A three-masted, square-rigged ship of the line with three full gundecks, rated for at least one hundred guns.
Forecastle	The raised area between the foremast and the bow. This area was often armed with a combination of chase guns and carronades.
Foremast	The mast closest to the bow.
Fore and aft rigged	A type of rigging where the sails are parallel or nearly parallel to a vessel's centerline.
Foresail	On a square-rigged vessel, the lowest and largest sail on the foremast.
Foul	To collide, particularly this term refers to multiple ships being joined together through tangled anchors, cables, or rigging.
Frigate	A three-masted, square-rigged warship with one full gundeck, as well as a raised and armed quarterdeck and forecastle. Armaments varied widely for frigates in the War of 1812, but they were generally rated between thirty-two and forty-four guns.
Grapeshot	Numerous spherical balls often held in a canvas sack. Designed to turn a cannon into a massive shotgun.
Gundeck	A continuous deck, running the length of a warship, where the majority of the ship's guns were located. Frigates had one gundeck. 74-gun ships of the line had two full gundecks.
Hail	To speak across the water to another vessel.
Haul up	To trim sails to sail closer to the wind.
Haul off	To sail away from an object.
Headway	Forward movement of a ship.
Heave to	To bring the vessel to a stop.
Heel	To roll away from the wind.
Hold	The area below the waterline where supplies are stored.
Jib boom	A spar attached to the end of the bowsprit.
Larboard	A term used at the time of the War of 1812 to refer to the port side of a ship.
Lee	The lee side of a ship is the side sheltered from the wind. To be in something's lee means to be sheltered from the wind by the presence of land or another ship.
Lee shore	When the wind is blowing onshore. This wind is extremely dangerous for sailing vessels.
Leeward	With two vessels, the one to the leeward is the one farthest from the origin of the wind.

Luff	To cause the sails to cease driving the ship, generally by placing the bow into the wind.
Mainmast	The middle mast on a three-masted ship. The stern mast on a two-masted ship. Generally, the largest mast.
Mainsail	The lowest square sail on the mainmast.
Main yard	The yard to which the mainsail is attached.
Mizzenmast	The mast nearest the stern on a three-masted ship.
Ordinary	Keeping a ship in reserve, usually with the assumption that the ship is in a condition to be made operational.
Port	When facing the bow, the left side of the ship.
Private signals	Coded signals, often made with signal flags or lights, designed so warships could distinguish friend from foe.
Quarter	The stern section of the ship, used in combination with the side of the ship. Thus, the "starboard quarter" was the stern starboard section of the ship.
Quarterdeck	A partial deck toward the stern of the ship, above the highest complete gundeck. It is generally armed, and is where the ship's captain stands during an engagement.
Rake	To fire down the length of a ship. For example, "to rake from stern to bow."
Reckoning	Determining the position of a ship. "Dead reckoning" involves determining position from incomplete data, often meaning the absence of a clear lunar observation.
Rigging	Rigging comes in two types: Standing rigging are fixed lines that hold the masts and yards in place. Running rigging are lines that allow for control of sails.
Round shot	The standard type of artillery ammunition, consisting of a single ball of a diameter equal to that of a cannon's bore.
Royal poles	The small pole above the highest part of the rigging.
Schooner	A small vessel, favored by the Americans, having two masts and a fore and aft rig.
Second rate	A three-masted, square-rigged ship of the line with three full gundecks, rated between ninety and ninety-eight guns.
Ship of the line	Also referred to as a line of battle ship. Ships of the line were divided by size into first, second, and third rates.
Shorten sail	To reduce sail.
Sloop	A square-rigged warship smaller in size than a frigate. Brig-sloops had two masts, whereas ship-sloops had three masts.

Soundings	Using a line with a weight on its end to determine the depth of the water.
Spar	A generic term to describe poles to which the rigging is attached. The term can describe masts and yards.
Spar deck	A small deck connecting the quarterdeck and forecastle, giving ships with a spar deck a flush-decked appearance. American 44-gun frigates like the *Constitution* had a spar deck.
Sprung	The splintering, warping, or cracking of a spar or mast.
Square-rigged	A common rigging type for warships including all frigates and ships of the line. It involves placing yards horizontally across the masts.
Starboard	When facing the bow, the right side of the ship.
Stays	Often "in stays." To put the bow of the ship directly into the wind's eye, causing the ship to lose forward movement.
Stern	The rear of a ship.
Sweeps	Long oars designed to propel a small warship through the water like a galley.
Tack	To turn into the wind so that the bow of the ship passes through the direction from which the wind is blowing. Also, the course of a ship, especially with respect to the wind. The starboard tack indicates the wind is coming across the starboard side of the ship.
Third rate	Generically known as a ship of the line or line of battle ship. Specifically, a three-masted, square-rigged warship with two full gundecks, generally rated between sixty-four and eighty guns. The most numerous type of third rates were those rated for seventy-four guns.
Topgallant mast	Often preceded with "main" or "fore" to denote its placement on a ship. The mast stepped above the topmast.
Topmast	Often preceded with "main" or "fore" to denote its placement on a ship. The mast stepped above the lower mast but below the topgallant mast.
Topsail	The sail at the same height as the topmast. The sail above the mainsail.
Warp	To move a ship by placing an anchor in the water and having the crew use cables to pull the ship to the anchor.
Wear	To turn so that the stern of the ship passes through the direction from which the wind is blowing.

Weather	Typically, a ship weathers fixed obstructions like reefs and headlands by sailing far enough away from them to avoid getting driven onto the obstruction. Also used by some officers in the War of 1812 to mean to get to the windward of another ship.
Weather gauge (gage)	Being closer to the wind's point of origin than another ship.
Windward	With two vessels, the one to the windward is the one closest to the point of origin of the wind.
Yard	A horizontal spar to which a sail is secured.

BIBLIOGRAPHY

Archival and Manuscript Sources

Duke University, Durham, NC. Rare Book, Manuscript, and Special Collection
    Library, William R. Perkins Library
    Barrie, Sir Robert. Papers, Boxes 5, 7
    Campbell Family Papers, Box 2
    Croker, John Wilson. Papers, Boxes 1, 2, 3, 7
The Henry Francis Du Pont Winterthur Museum, Winterthur, DE
    Nichols, Francis. Journal of a Cruise on Board the U.S. Frigate *Chesapeake*, 1812–13, Doc 781
Historical Society of Pennsylvania, Philadelphia
    Begg, William. Journal of the proceedings of the H.M.S. *Tenedos*, 1812–15
    Feltus, W. William. Journal of Midshipman William W. Feltus
    Jones, William. Papers, U.C. Smith Collection
Hull History Centre (Hull University Archives), Hull, UK
    Hotham, Henry, Papers, HUL U DDHO/x1/7/2, 37, 71
Indiana University, Bloomington, Manuscripts Department, Lilly Library
    War of 1812 Manuscripts
Library of Congress, Manuscripts Division, Washington, DC
    Cockburn, George. Papers of, Container 9: Letters Sent, 3 Feb 1812–6 Feb 1814
    Evans, Amos. Journal of Amos Evans, Surgeon on board the *Constitution*, 1812–13
    Geisinger, David, Midshipman. Journal, Remarks and Occurrences on Board U.S. Sloop of
        War *Wasp* of 18 guns, Johnston Blakeley, Esquire Commanding, 2 May–23 Sep 1814
    Jefferson, Thomas. Thomas Jefferson Papers
    Lawrence, James. James Lawrence Papers
    Madison, James. James Madison Papers
    Porter, David. Porter Papers, Box 2

Rodgers, John. Rodgers Family Papers

    Letter and Order Books, 1811–12 and 1812–15, Pt III:38

    President's Journal, 9 Oct 1812–19 Feb 1814, Pt III:34

    Journal by M.C. Perry on board the *President*, 1812–13, Pt III:34

    Private Letters to Rodgers, Pt II: 3&4

Rodgers, John. Rodgers Naval Papers. Correspondence, Box 2

Rodgers, William. Journal of William T. Rodgers Midshipman U.S. Navy on board the *Peacock*, 1813–15, William T. Rodgers Papers

Shaw, John. Papers, Letterbook, Container 3

Mystic Seaport, Archive at the Museum of America and the Sea, Mystic, CT

    Newman, William D. First Hand Description of the Capture of the *President*, 1815.

        Newman Family Papers, Collection 51, Box 1

    Skiddy, William. "Ups and Downs of Sea Life." Vol. 1, 1805–39. Unpublished manuscript, Collection 304

National Archives, London, Admiralty Papers

    Letters from Commanders-in-Chief to the Admiralty

        Brazil, 1812–15, ADM 1/20–22

        Cape of Good Hope, 1814–15, ADM 1/66

        Channel Fleet, 1813, ADM 1/154

        Cork, 1813–14, ADM 1/625–26

        East Indies, 1815–17, ADM 1/188–89

        Jamaica, 1812–14, ADM 1/263–65

        Leeward Islands, 1813–14, ADM 1/334–35

        Leith, 1813, ADM 1/696

        Newfoundland, 1810–12, ADM 1/477

        North America, 1812–15, ADM 1/502–09

        North Sea, 1813, ADM 1/573

        Plymouth, 1813–14, ADM 1/833–34

        Detached Squadrons, ADM 1/3232

    Letters from Captains to the Admiralty

        Surnames, B: 1812, 1814, ADM 1/1553, 1556–57

        Surnames, C: 1813, 1815, ADM 1/1665, 1668

        Surnames, D: 1813, ADM 1/1735

        Surnames, E: 1813–15, ADM 1/1771

        Surnames, G: 1814, ADM 1/1861

        Surnames, H: 1813–14, ADM 1/1948–50

    Letters to the Admiralty from British Consuls, 1807–17, ADM 1/3845

    Letters from Lloyd's to the Admiralty, 1805–29, ADM 1/3993–95

    Letters from Secretaries of State to the Admiralty, 1812, ADM 1/4222

Secret Letters to the Admiralty, 1813, ADM 1/4359

Court Martial for the losses of the *Alert*, ADM 1/5431; *Avon*, ADM 1/5446; *Boxer*, ADM 1/5440; *Cyane*, ADM 1/5449; *Epervier*, ADM 1/5447; *Frolic*, ADM 1/5434; *Guerriere*, ADM 1/5431; *Highflyer*, ADM 1/5441; *Java*, ADM 1/5435; *Levant*, ADM 1/5449; *Macedonian*, ADM 1/5436; *Peacock*, ADM 1/5436; *Penguin*, ADM 1/5451; *Pictou*, ADM 1/5434; *Reindeer*, ADM 1/5444; *Southampton*, ADM 1/5434

Court Martial of Vice Admiral Charles Stirling, ADM 1/5442

Letters from the Admiralty Respecting Convoys, 1812, ADM 2/1107

Secret Letters from the Admiralty, 1812–15, ADM 2/1375–81

Admiralty Board Room Journal, 1812–14, ADM 7/262–66

Ship Details including manning and armament, etc., 1794–1814, ADM 7/556

Ships in Sea Pay, 1807–13, ADM 8/93–100

Admiral's Journal for Durham, 1814, ADM 50/77; Thornborough, 1813, ADM 50/70; Cochrane, 1813–15, ADM 50/122

Logs of the *Acasta*, 1813–15, ADM 51/2102; *Aeolus*, 1812, ADM 51/2106; *Africa*, 1812, ADM 51/2092; *Albion*, 1813, ADM 51/2104; *Albacore*, 1814, ADM 51/2100; *Alexandria*, 1813, ADM 51/2098; *Arethusa*, 1812, ADM 51/2122; *Armada*, 1814, ADM 51/2084; *Barham*, 1814, ADM 51/2185; *Bellerophon*, 1813, ADM 51/2024; *Belvidera*, 1812–13, ADM 51/2018; *Brazen*, 1812, ADM 51/2013; *Canso*, 1813, ADM 51/2217; *Castilian*, 1814, ADM 51/2197; *Castor*, 1815, ADM 51/2226; *Cherub*, 1813–14, ADM 51/2205–06; *Colossus*, 1813, ADM 51/2210; *Conflict*, 1814, ADM 51/2199; *Coquette*, 1813, ADM 51/2044; *Cornwallis*, 1815, ADM 51/2046; *Cressy*, 1813, ADM 51/2216; *Curlew*, 1813, ADM 51/2223; *Dannemark*, 1814, ADM 51/2302; *Dotterel*, 1813–14, ADM 51/2294; *Dryad*, 1813, ADM 51/2270; *Elephant*, 1813, ADM 51/2344; *Endymion*, 1813–15, ADM 51/2324; *Epervier*, 1813, ADM 51/2409; *Eridanus*, 1814, ADM 51/2407; *Fantome*, 1813, ADM 51/2295; *Forester*, 1814, ADM 51/2376; *Galatea*, 1812, ADM 53/582; *Garland*, 1812, ADM 53/572; *Hotspur*, 1813, ADM 51/2444; *Inconstant*, 1813, ADM 51/2487; *Indefatigable*, 1813, ADM 51/2463; *Jalouse*, 1813, ADM 51/2500; *Junon*, 1812–14, ADM 51/2465, 53/740; *Kangaroo*, 1814, ADM 51/2505; *La Hogue*, 1813, ADM 51/2527; *Leander*, 1814–15, ADM 51/2524; *Leonidas*, 1813–14, ADM 51/2522; *Loire*, 1813–14, ADM 51/2516; *Loup-Cervier*, 1813, ADM 51/2528; *Madagascar*, 1814, ADM 51/2551; *Majestic*, 1813–14, ADM 51/2543; *Marlborough*, 1813, ADM 51/2570; *Medina*, 1815, ADM 51/2556; *Medway*, 1814, ADM 51/2579; *Minerva*, 1812, ADM 51/2585; *Montagu*, 1813, ADM 51/2555, 4100; *Morgiana*, 1814, ADM 52/4190; *Moselle*, 1812, ADM 51/2572; *Mosquito*, 1813–14, ADM 51/2537; *Narcissus*, 1813–14, ADM 51/2609; *Newcastle*, 1815, ADM 51/2589; *Nymphe*, 1812–13, ADM 51/2590; *Orestes*, 1814, ADM 53/938; *Orpheus*, 1813–14, ADM 51/2615; *Pelican*, 1813, ADM 51/2660; *Peruvian*, 1814, ADM 51/2658; *Phoebe*, 1813–14, ADM 51/2675; *Pique*, 1813–14, ADM 51/2696; *Plantagenet*, 1814, ADM 51/2714; *Poictiers*, 1812–13, ADM 51/2694; *Queen*, 1813–14, ADM 51/2719; *Racoon*, 1813, ADM 51/2765; *Ramillies*, 1813–14, ADM 51/2027; *Rattler*, 1813, ADM 51/2775; *Redwing*, 1814, ADM 51/2065; *Rhin*, 1813, ADM 51/2743; *Rifleman*, 1814, ADM 51/2770; *San Domingo*, 1812–13, ADM 51/2834; *Saturn*, 1814, ADM 51/2789; *Shannon*, 1812–13, ADM 51/2861; *Shelburne*, 1813–14, ADM 51/2335; *Snake*, 1815, ADM 51/2327; *Spartan*, 1812, ADM 51/2812; *Spitfire*, 1813–14, ADM 51/2809; *Statira*, 1812–14, ADM 51/2814; *Strombolo*, 1814, ADM 51/2803; *Superb*, 1813, ADM 51/2051; *Tagus*, 1814, ADM 51/2873; *Tartarus*, 1814, ADM 51/2876; *Tenedos*, 1812–15, ADM 51/2909; *Thalia*,

1812, ADM 51/2077; *Tigris*, 1814, ADM 51/2905; *Valiant*, 1813, ADM 51/2941; *Variable*, 1812, ADM 51/2938; *Venerable*, 1814, ADM 51/2958; *Wanderer*, 1812, ADM 51/2971

National Archives, London, Colonial Office Papers

    Correspondence from Sierra Leone, 1814, CO 267/38

National Archives and Record Administration, Washington, DC

    Confidential Letters sent by the Sec. of the Navy, RG45

    Dexter, Daniel. Letter Book, RG45

    Logs of the *Congress*, 1812–14; *Constitution*, 1812–15; *Enterprize*, 1812–14; *Hornet*, 1812–15; *United States*, 1812–13, RG24

    Letters from the Sec. of the Navy to Congress, Vol. 2, RG45

    Letters Received by the Sec. of the Navy from Captains, RG45, M125

    Letters Received by the Sec. of the Navy from Commanders, RG45, M147

    Letters Received by the Sec. of the Navy from Officers below the Rank of Commander, RG45, M148

    Letters Sent by the Sec. of the Navy to Commandants and Navy Agents, RG45 M441

    Letters Sent by the Sec. of the Navy to Officers, RG45, M149

    Miscellaneous Letters Received by the Sec. of the Navy, RG45, M124

    U.S. Navy Courts of Inquiry and Courts-Martial, M273

National Archives of Scotland, Edinburgh, UK

    Papers of the Dundas Family of Melville, Viscounts Melville, GD 51

    Papers of the Hope Family of Luffness, East Lothian, GD 364

National Library of Scotland, Edinburgh, UK

    Cochrane, Alexander F.I. Papers, MS 2327, 2335, 2339, 2340, 2346, 2349, 2574, 2575

National Maritime Museum, Greenwich, UK

    Collier, Sir George, Letters to Lord Melville, 1814–15, AGC 2/18

    Dundas, Robert Saunders, 2nd Viscount Melville, Papers, MEL/101

    Elphinstone, George Keith, 1st Viscount Keith. Manuscripts, KEI/37/9, 40/4

    Foley, Sir Thomas, Papers, FOL/20B, C

    Hulbert, George, Order Book of Sir John B. Warren, 1812–13, Hulbert Papers, HUL/1

    Waldegrave, William, 1st Lord Radstock, Family Papers, WDG/11/13

    Warren, Sir John Borlase, Correspondence with Lord Melville, LBK/2

    Warren, Sir John Borlase, Papers, WAR/25, 30, 49, 54, 55, 69, 70, 71, 82

New York Historical Society, New York, NY

    Isaac, Hull, Letter Book

Suffolk Record Office, Ipswich, UK

    Broke, Sir Philip. Broke Papers, HA 93

    Log of the *Chesapeake*, 1812–13, HA 93/6/2/258

    Shannon's Journal, 1812–13, HA 93/6/2/112–13

United States Naval Academy, Archives, Annapolis, MD
    Log of the *Wasp* (Royal Navy), MS 157
    Penguin Order Book, MS 58
University of Michigan, William L. Clements Library, Ann Arbor
    Barrie, Sir Robert. Papers
University of South Carolina, Library, Columbia
    Hamilton, Paul. Papers
University of Southampton, Southampton, UK
    Wellesley, Arthur, Duke of Wellington. Papers

Books and Articles

A Narrative of the Capture of the United States Brig Vixen *of 14 Guns by the British Frigate* Southampton *and of the Subsequent Loss of Both Vessels . . . by one of the* Vixen's *Crew.* New York: Office of the War, 1813.

"Account of the Capture of the U.S. Ship *Frolic* by the *Orpheus* Frigate, Captain Hugh Pigot, 19 April 1814." *New York Public Library Bulletin* (August 1903): 278.

Adams, Henry. *The War of 1812.* Extracts from *History of the United States During the Administrations of Jefferson and Madison*, edited by H. A. DeWeerd. New York: Cooper Square, 1999.

Albion, Robert G., and Jennie B. Pope. *Sea Lanes in Wartime: The American Experience, 1775–1945*, 2nd ed. New York: Archon Books, 1968.

Bartlett, C. J. "Gentlemen versus Democrats: Cultural Prejudice and Military Strategy in Britain in the War of 1812." *War in History* 1 (1994): 140–59.

Bartlett, C. J., and Gene Smith. "A 'Species of Milito-Nautico-Guerilla-Plundering Warfare': Admiral Alexander Cochrane's Naval Campaign Against the United States, 1814–1815." In *Britain and America Go to War: The Impact of War and Warfare in Anglo-America, 1754–1815*, 173–204. Gainesville: University Press of Florida, 2004.

Bauer, K. Jack, ed. *The New American State Papers, Naval Affairs*, Vol. 1, *General Naval Policy and Defense* and Vol. 4, *Combat Operations*. Wilmington, DE: Scholarly Resources, 1981.

Baugh, Daniel A. "The Eighteenth-Century Navy as a National Institution, 1690–1815." In *The Oxford Illustrated History of the Royal Navy*, edited by J. R. Hill, 120–60. New York: Oxford University Press, 1995.

———. *British Naval Administration in the Age of Walpole.* Princeton, NJ: Princeton University Press, 1965.

Berube, Claude G., and John A Rogfaard. *A Call to the Sea: Captain Charles Stewart of the USS* Constitution. Washington, DC: Potomac Books, 2005.

Black, Jeremy. *The British Seaborne Empire.* New Haven, CT: Yale University Press, 2004.

———. *The War of 1812 in the Age of Napoleon.* Norman: University of Oklahoma Press, 2009.

Bourchier, Jane, ed. *Memoir of the Life of Admiral Sir Edward Codrington with Selections from his Public and Private Correspondence*, Vol. 1. London: Longmans, Green, and Co., 1873.

Bowers, William. *Naval Adventures During Thirty-Five Years' Service.* 2 vols. London: Richard Bentley, 1833.

Brannan, John. *Official Letters of the Military and Naval Officers of the United States During the War With Great Britain in the Years 1812, 13, 14, & 15*. Washington, DC: Way and Gideon, 1823.

Brighton, John G. *Admiral of the Fleet Sir Provo W. P. Wallis: A Memoir*. London: Hutchinson & Co., 1892.

Calderhead, William L. "U.S.F. *Constellation* in the War of 1812—An Accidental Fleet in Being." *Military Affairs* 40 (1976): 79–83.

Canney, Donald L. *Sailing Warships of the U.S. Navy*. Annapolis, MD: Naval Institute Press, 2001.

Carden, John Surman, and C. T. Atkinson. *A Curtail'd Memoir of Incidents and Occurrences in the Life of John Surman Carden, Vice Admiral in the British Navy*. Oxford, UK: Clarendon Press, 1912.

Chapelle, Howard I. *The History of the American Sailing Navy: The Ships and Their Development*. New York: W. W. Norton, 1949. Reprint, Konecky & Konecky.

Corbett, Julian S. *Some Principles of Maritime Strategy*. London, 1911. Reprint, Annapolis, MD: Naval Institute Press, 1988.

Crawford, Michael J. "The Navy's Campaign Against the Licensed Trade in the War of 1812." *American Neptune* 46 (1986): 165–72.

Crawford, William H. "The Journal of William H. Crawford." *Smith College Studies in History*, ed. Daniel C. Knowlton, 11 (1925): 5–64.

Crowhurst, Patrick. *The Defence of British Trade, 1689–1815*. Folkestone, UK: William Dawson & Sons, 1977.

Daughan, George C. *If By Sea: The Forging of the American Navy—From the Revolution to the War of 1812*. New York: Basic Books, 2008.

DeKay, James Tertius. *Chronicles of the Frigate* Macedonian, *1809–1922*. New York: W. W. Norton, 2000.

Denison, Charles, ed. *Old Ironsides and Old Adams: Stray Leaves From the Logbook of a Man-of-War's Man*. Boston: W. W. Page, 1846.

Dennis, D. L. "The Action Between the *Shannon* and the *Chesapeake*." *Mariner's Mirror* 45 (1959): 36–46.

Dillon, Sir William Henry. *A Narrative of My Professional Adventures (1790–1839)*, edited by Michael A. Lewis. 2 vols. London: Navy Records Society, 1953–56.

Dudley, Wade G. *Splintering the Wooden Wall: The British Blockade of the United States, 1812–1815*. Annapolis, MD: Naval Institute Press, 2003.

Dudley, William S. "'Old Ironsides' Last Battle: USS *Constitution* versus HM Ships *Cyane* and *Levant*." In *Fighting at Sea: Naval Battles from the Ages of Sail and Steam*, edited by Douglas M. McLean, 55–85. Quebec: Robin Bass Studio, 2008.

Dudley, William S., Michael J. Crawford, Christine F. Hughes, Charles E. Brodine, and Carolyn M. Stallings, eds. *The Naval War of 1812: A Documentary History*. 4 vols. Washington, DC: Naval Historical Center, 1985– .

Duffy, Stephen W. H. *Captain Blakeley and the* Wasp: *The Cruise of 1814*. Annapolis, MD: Naval Institute Press, 2001.

Dull, Jonathan R. *The Age of the Ship of the Line: The British & French Navies, 1650–1815*. Lincoln: University of Nebraska Press, 2009.

Dunne, W. M. P. "'The Inglorious First of June': Commodore Stephen Decatur on Long Island Sound, 1813." *Long Island Historical Journal*, 2 (1990): 201–20.

———. "The United States Frigate *President*: The Victor or the Vanquished." In *New Interpretations in Naval History: Selected Papers from the Eleventh Naval History Symposium, 1993*, edited by Robert W. Love Jr., Laurie Bogle, Brian VanDeMark, and Maochun Yu, 83–97. Annapolis, MD: Naval Institute Press, 2001.

Dye, Ira. *The Fatal Cruise of the Argus: Two Captains in the War of 1812*. Annapolis, MD: Naval Institute Press, 1994.

Eckert, Edward K. *The Navy Department in the War of 1812*. Gainesville: University of Florida Press, 1973.

Farragut, Loyall. *The Life of David Glasgow Farragut, First Admiral of the United States Navy*. New York: D. Appleton and Company, 1879.

Ford, Paul L., ed. *The Writings of Thomas Jefferson*. 10 vols. G. P. New York: Putman's Sons, 1892–99.

Ford, Worthington C., ed. *Writings of John Quincy Adams*. 7 vols. New York: MacMillan, 1913–17.

Forester, C. S. *The Age of Fighting Sail: The Story of the Naval War of 1812*, 1956. Reprint, Sandwich, MA: Chapman Billies, 2005.

Galpin, W. Freeman. "The American Grain Trade to the Spanish Peninsula, 1810–1814." *The American Historical Review* 28 (1922): 24–44.

Gamble, John. *The Memorial of Lieut. Colonel J. M. Gamble of the United States Marine Corps to Congress, 1828*. New York: George F. Hopkins & Son, 1828.

Gardiner, Robert. *Frigates of the Napoleonic Wars*. Annapolis, MD: Naval Institute Press, 2000.

———, ed. *The Naval War of 1812*. London: Chatham, 1998.

———. *Warships of the Napoleonic Era*. Annapolis, MD: Naval Institute Press, 1999.

Gates, David. *The Napoleonic Wars, 1803–1815*. London: Arnold, 1997.

Glete, Jan. *Navies and Nations: Warships, Navies and State Building in Europe and America, 1500–1860*. 2 vols. Stockholm: Almqvist & Wiksell, 1993.

Glover, Richard. "The French Fleet, 1807–1814: Britain's Problem; and Madison's Opportunity." *The Journal of Modern History* 39 (1967): 233–52.

Goldenberg, Joseph A. "Blue Lights and Infernal Machines: The British Blockade of New London." *Mariner's Mirror* 61 (1975): 385–97.

———. "The Royal Navy's Blockade in New England Waters, 1812–1815." *The International History Review* 6 (1984): 424–39.

Gough, Barry. *Fortune's River: The Collision of Empires in Northwest America*. Madeira Park, BC, Canada: Harbour Publishing, 2007.

Graham, Gerald S., and R. A. Humphreys, eds. *The Navy and South America 1807–1823: Correspondence of the Commanders-in-Chief on the South American Station*. London: Navy Records Society, 1962.

Greig, James, ed. *The Farington Diary*. 8 vols. New York: George H. Doran, 1922–28.

Gwyn, Julian. *Frigates and Foremasts: The North American Squadron in Nova Scotia Waters, 1745–1815*. Vancouver, BC, Canada: UBC Press, 2003.

Hall, Christopher. *Wellington's Navy: Sea Power and the Peninsular War*. London: Greenhill, 2004.

Hamilton, Stanislaus Murray, ed. *The Writings of James Monroe.* 7 vols. New York: G. P. Putman's Sons, 1898–1903.

Hattendorf, John B. "The American Navy in the World of Franklin and Jefferson, 1775–1826." In *War and Society: A Yearbook of Military History,* Vol. 2, edited by Brian Bond and Ian Roy, 7–19. New York: Holmes & Meier, 1977.

Hawes, Lilla M., ed. "Letters of Henry Gilliam, 1809–1817." *Georgia Historical Quarterly,* 38 (1954): 46–66.

Haynes, George H. ed. "Letters of Samuel Taggart, Representative in Congress, 1803–1814: Part II, 1808–1814." *American Antiquarian Society* 33 (1923): 297–438.

Hickey, Donald R. *The War of 1812: A Forgotten Conflict.* Urbana: University of Illinois Press, 1990.

Historical Manuscript Commission (HMC). *Report on the Manuscripts of Colonel David Milne Home of Wedderburn Castle, N. B.* London: HMSO, 1902.

Horward, Donald D. "British Seapower and its Influence Upon the Peninsular War (1808–1814)." *Naval War College Review* 31 (1978): 54–71.

Hotham, William. *Pages and Portraits from the Past: Being the Private Papers of Sir William Hotham, GCB, Admiral of the Red,* edited by A. M. W. Stirling. 2 vols. London: H Jenkins, 1919.

Hughes, Christine F. "Lewis Warrington and the USS *Peacock* in the Sunda Strait, June 1815." In *The Early Republic and the Sea: Essays on the Naval and Maritime History of the United States,* edited by William S. Dudley and Michael J. Crawford, 115–36. Washington, DC: Brassey's, 2001.

Inderwick, James. *Cruise of the U.S. Brig Argus in 1813, Journal of Surgeon James Inderwick,* edited by Victor Hugo Paltsits. New York: Public Library, 1917.

James, William. *Naval History of Great Britain: From the Declaration of War by France in 1793 to the Accession of George IV.* Reprint, 6 vols. London: MacMillan and Co., 1902.

———. *Naval Occurrences of the War of 1812.* London: T. Egerton, 1817. Reprint with new introduction by Andrew Lambert, London: Conway Maritime Press, 2004.

Jones, J. R. *Britain and the World 1649–1815.* Sussex, UK: The Harvester Press, 1980.

Jones, Wilbur D., ed. "A British View of the War of 1812 and the Peace Negotiations." *The Mississippi Valley Historical Review* 45 (1958): 481–87.

Kastor, Peter J. "Toward 'the Maritime War Only': The Question of Naval Mobilization, 1811–1812." *The Journal of Military History* 61 (1997): 455–80.

Keene, Joshua. "Notes on the Action between *Hornet* and *Peacock,*" edited by Hardin Craig Jr. *American Neptune* 11 (1951): 73–77.

Kennedy, Paul M. *The Rise and Fall of British Naval Mastery.* London: Allen Lane, 1976. Reprint, London: Ashfield Press, 1992.

———. "The Fortunes of War: Commercial Warfare and Maritime Risk in the War of 1812." *The Northern Mariner* (Oct 1998), 1–16.

Kert, Faye M. *Prize and Prejudice: Privateering and Naval Prize in Atlantic Canada in the War of 1812.* St. John's, NL, Canada: International Maritime Economic History Association, 1997.

Knox, Dudley W., ed. *Naval Documents Related to the United States Wars With the Barbary Powers.* Vol. 6. Washington, DC: U.S. Government Printing Office, 1944.

Lambert, Andrew. "Taking the *President*: HMS *Endymion* and the USS *President*." In *Fighting at Sea: Naval Battles from the Ages of Sail and Steam*, edited by Douglas M. McLean, 86–128. Quebec, Canada: Robin Bass Studio, 2008.

Lambert, Frank. *The Barbary Wars: American Independence in the Atlantic World*. New York: Hill and Wang, 2005.

Latimer, Jon. *1812: War with America*. Cambridge, MA: Harvard University Press, 2007.

Lavery, Brian. *Nelson's Navy: The Ships, Men and Organization, 1793–1815*. London: Conway Maritime Press, 1989. Reprint with revisions, Annapolis, MD: Naval Institute Press, 1997.

Leech, Samuel. *A Voice from the Main Deck: Being a Record of the Thirty Years Adventures of Samuel Leech*. Boston: Whittemore, Niles and Hall, 1857. Reprint, London: Chatham, 1999.

LeFevre, Peter. "Sir John Borlase Warren, 1753–1822." In *British Admirals of the Napoleonic Wars: The Contemporaries of Nelson*, edited by Peter LeFevre and Richard Harding, 219–44. London: Chatham, 2005.

Leiner, Frederick C. "The Squadron Commander's Share: Decatur v. Chew and the Prize Money for the *Chesapeake*'s First War of 1812 Cruise." *The Journal of Military History* 73 (2009): 69–82.

Lewis, Michael. *A Social History of the Navy: 1793–1815*. London: George Allen, & Unwin, 1960.

Lloyd, Christopher. *The British Seaman 1200–1860: A Social History*. London, Collins, 1968. Reprint, Rutherford, NJ: Fairleigh Dickinson University Press, 1970.

———, ed. *The Keith Papers: Selected from the Papers of Admiral Viscount Keith*. Vol. 3. London: Navy Records Society, 1955.

Lohnes, Barry J. "British Naval Problems at Halifax During the War of 1812." *Mariner's Mirror* 59 (1973): 317–33.

Londonderry, Charles W. Vane, Marquess of, ed. *Correspondence, Despatches, and Other Papers of Viscount Castlereagh, Second Marquess of Londonderry*, Vol. 8. London: William Shoberl, Publisher, 1851.

Long, David F. *Nothing too Daring: A Biography of Commodore David Porter, 1780–1843*. Annapolis, MD: Naval Institute Press, 1970.

———. *Ready to Hazard: A Biography of Commodore William Bainbridge, 1774–1833*. Hanover, NH: University Press of New England, 1981.

Lyon, David. *The Sailing Navy List: All the Ships of the Royal Navy—Built, Purchased and Captured—1688–1860*. London: Conway Maritime Press, 1993.

Mahan, Alfred Thayer. *Sea Power in its Relations to the War of 1812*. 2 vols. London: Sampson Low, Marston & Co., 1905.

Mahon, John K. "British Strategy and Southern Indians: War of 1812." *Florida Historical Quarterly* 44 (1966): 285–302.

———. *The War of 1812*. Gainesville: University of Florida Press, 1972.

Malcomson, Robert. "The Sad Case of Sir George." *Naval History* 24 (February 2010): 54–55.

Maloney, Linda. *The Captain from Connecticut: The Life and Naval Times of Isaac Hull*. Boston: Northeastern University Press, 1986.

———. "The War of 1812: What Role for Sea Power?" In *In Peace and War: Interpretations of American Naval History, 1775–1978*, edited by Kenneth J. Hagan. Westport, CT: Greenwood Press, 1978.

Markham, Sir Clements, ed. *Selections from the Correspondence of Admiral John Markham During the Years 1801–4 and 1806–7.* London: Navy Record Society, 1904.

Martin, Tyrone G. *A Most Fortunate Ship: A Narrative History of Old Ironsides.* Chester, CT: Globe Pequot Press, 1980. Reprint, Annapolis, MD: Naval Institute Press, 1997.

———. *The USS* Constitution's *Finest Fight, 1815: The Journal of Acting Chaplain Assheton Humphreys, US Navy.* Mount Pleasant, SC: The Nautical & Aviation Publishing Co., 2000.

Mayo, Bernard. *Instructions to the British Ministers to the United States 1791–1812.* New York: DaCapo Press, 1971.

McCranie, Kevin D. *Admiral Lord Keith and the Naval War Against Napoleon.* Gainesville: University Press of Florida, 2006.

———. " 'The Curse of the Service': Commissioned Officers, Advancement, and the First Lord of the Admiralty, 1793–1814." In *Consortium on Revolutionary Europe: Selected Papers, 2005,* edited by Frederick C. Schneid and Susan Connor, 225–36. High Point, NC: High Point University.

———. "The Recruitment of Seamen for the British Navy, 1793–1815: "Why Don't You Raise More Men?" In *Conscription in the Napoleonic Era: A Revolution in Military Affairs?* edited by Donald Stocker, Frederick C. Schneid, and Harold Blanton, 84–101. London: Routledge, 2009.

McKee, Christopher. *A Gentlemanly and Honorable Profession: The Creation of the U.S. Naval Officers Corps, 1794–1815.* Annapolis, MD: Naval Institute Press, 1991.

Memoir of Admiral Sir Henry Ducie Chads, G. C. B. by an Old Follower. Portsea, UK: Griffin and Co., 1869.

Morris, Charles. *The Autobiography of Commodore Charles Morris, U.S. Navy.* Reprint, Annapolis, MD: Naval Institute Press, 2002.

Morriss, Roger. *The Royal Dockyards During the Revolutionary and Napoleonic Wars.* Leicester, UK: Leicester University Press, 1983.

Muir, Rory. *Britain and the Defeat of Napoleon, 1807–1815.* New Haven, CT: Yale University Press, 1996.

Murdoch, Richard K. "A British Report on West Florida and Louisiana, November 1812." *Florida Historical Quarterly* 42 (1964): 36–51.

Owsley, Frank. "The Role of the South in the British Grand Strategy in the War of 1812." *Tennessee Historical Quarterly* 31 (1972): 22–38.

Padfield, Peter. *Broke and the* Shannon. London: Hodder and Stoughton, 1968.

Palmer, Michael A. *Stoddert's War: Naval Operations During the Quasi-War with France, 1798–1801.* Columbia: University of South Carolina Press, 1987.

Parliamentary Debates. From the Year 1803 to the Present Time, edited by T. C. Hansard. 41 vols. London, 1803–20.

Parry, Clive, ed. *The Consolidated Treaty Series,* Vol. 63 (1813–15). Dobbs Ferry, NY: Oceana Publishing, 1969.

Perkins, Bradford. *Prologue to War, 1805–1812: England and the United States.* Berkeley: University of California Press, 1968.

Petrides, Anne, and Jonathan Downs, eds. *Sea Soldier: An Officer of Marines with Duncan, Nelson, Collingwood and Cockburn, the Letters and Journals of Major T. Marmaduke*

Wybourn RM, 1797–1813. Transcribed by Emily Wybourn. Tunbridge Wells, UK: Parapress, 2000.

Pitkin, Timothy. *A Statistical View of Commerce of the United States of America.* New Haven, CT: Durrie & Peck, 1835.

Porter, David. *Journal of a Cruise.* 2nd ed. New York: Wiley & Halsted, 1822. Reprint, Annapolis, MD: Naval Institute Press, 1986.

Rodger, N. A. M. *Command of the Ocean: A Naval History of Britain, 1649–1815.* New York: W. W. Norton, 2004.

———. "Weather, Geography and Naval Power in the Age of Sail." In *Geopolitics, Geography, and Strategy,* edited by Colin Gray and Geoffrey Sloan, 178–200. London: Frank Cass, 1999.

———. *The Wooden World: An Anatomy of the Georgian Navy.* William Collins, 1986. Reprint, New York: W. W. Norton, 1996.

Roosevelt, Theodore. *The Naval War of 1812, The History of the United States Navy during the Last War with Great Britain.* New York: G. P. Putnam's and Son, 1882. Reprint, New York: Knickerbocker Press, 1920.

Ryan, A. N. "The Defence of British Trade with the Baltic, 1808–1813." *The English Historical Review* 74 (1959): 443–66.

Sainty, John C. *Admiralty Officials, 1660–1870.* London: Athlone Press [for] University of London, Institute of Historical Research, 1975.

Schroeder, John H. *Commodore John Rodgers: Paragon of the Early American Navy.* Gainesville: University Press of Florida, 2006.

Seiken, Jeff. "'To Strike a Blow in the World That Shall Resound Through the Universe': American Naval Operations and Options at the Start of the War of 1812." In *New Interpretations in Naval History: Selected Papers from the Fourteenth Naval History Symposium,* edited by Randy C. Balano and Craig L. Symonds, 131–46. Annapolis, MD: Naval Institute Press, 2001.

Silverstone, Paul H. *The U.S. Navy Warship Series: Sailing Navy: 1775–1854.* Annapolis, MD: Naval Institute Press, 2001.

Smith, David B. *Letters of Admiral of the Fleet the Earl of St. Vincent Whilst First Lord of the Admiralty.* 2 vols. London: Navy Records Society, 1922–27.

Smith, Joshua M. *Borderland Smuggling: Patriots, Loyalists, and Illicit Trade in the Northeast, 1783–1820.* Gainesville: University Press of Florida, 2006.

Stagg, J. C. A. *Mr. Madison's War: Politics, Diplomacy, and Warfare in the Early American Republic, 1783–1830.* Princeton, NJ: Princeton University Press, 1983.

Symonds, Craig L. *Navalists and Antinavalists: The Naval Policy Debate in the United States, 1785–1827.* Newark, NJ: University of Delaware Press, 1980.

Thompson, Neville. *Earl Bathurst and the British Empire.* Barnsley, South Yorkshire, UK: Leo Cooper, 1999.

Toll, Ian W. *Six Frigates: The Epic History of the Founding of the U.S. Navy.* New York: W. W. Norton, 2006.

Tucker, Spencer. *Stephen Decatur: A Life Most Bold and Daring.* Annapolis, MD: Naval Institute Press, 2005.

Tucker, Spencer, and Frank T. Reuter. *Injured Honor: The Chesapeake-Leopard Affair June 22, 1807.* Annapolis, MD: Naval Institute Press, 1996.

U.S. Congress. *American State Papers, I: Foreign Relations.* 6 vols. Washington, DC: Gales and Seaton, 1832–59.

———. *The Debates and Proceedings of the Congress of the United States [Annals of Congress].* 42 vols. Washington, DC: Gales and Seaton, 1834–56.

Valle, James E. "The Navy's Battle Doctrine in the War of 1812." *The American Neptune,* 44 (1984): 171–78.

Wagstaff, Henry M., and J. G. de Roulhac Hamilton. "The Harrington Letters." *James Sprunt Historical Publications* 13 (1914): 6–62.

Watson, G. E. "The United States and the Peninsular War, 1808–1812." *The Historical Journal* 19 (1976): 859–76.

Webb, Paul. "Construction, Repair and Maintenance in the Battle Fleet of the Royal Navy, 1793–1815." In *The British Navy and the Use of Naval Power in the Eighteenth Century,* edited by Jeremy Black and Philip Woodfine, 207–19. Atlantic Highlands, NJ: Humanities Press, 1988.

Wellington, Arthur Wellesley, Duke of. *The Dispatches of Field Marshal The Duke of Wellington: during His Various Campaigns in India, Denmark, Portugal, Spain, the Low Countries, and France, from 1799 to 1818.* 13 vols. Edited by John Gurwood. London: John Murray, 1837–39.

———. *Supplementary Despatches, Correspondence, and Memoranda of Field Marshal Arthur, Duke of Wellington,* edited by his son. 15 vols. London, 1858–72.

Winfield, Rif. *British Warships in the Age of Sail, 1793–1817: Design, Construction, Careers and Fates.* 2nd ed. Barnsley, UK: Seaforth Publishing, 2008.

Whitehill, Walter Muir, ed. *New England Blockaded in 1814: The Journal of Henry Edward Napier, Lieutenant in HMS Nymphe.* Salem, MA: Peabody Museum, 1939.

Woodman, Richard ed., *The Victory of Seapower: Winning the Napoleonic War, 1807–1814.* London: Chatham, 1998.

Newspapers

American Advocate, Hallowell, ME

American Watchman, Wilmington, DE

Baltimore Patriot & Evening Advertiser, Baltimore, MD

Boston Daily Advertiser, Boston, MA

Boston Gazette, Boston, MA

Boston Patriot, Boston, MA

Caledonian Mercury, Edinburgh, UK

City Gazette and Daily Advertiser, Charleston, SC

Columbian, New York, NY

Columbian Centinel, Boston, MA

Columbian Phenix, Providence, RI

Commercial Advertiser, New York, NY

Connecticut Gazette, New London, CT

Connecticut Herald, New Haven, CT

Constitutionalist and Weekly Magazine, Exeter, NH

Daily National Intelligencer [or *The National Intelligencer*], Washington, DC

Delaware Gazette and Peninsula Advertiser, Wilmington, DE

Eastern Argus, Portland, ME

Edinburgh Advertiser, Edinburgh, UK

Enquirer, Richmond, VA

Essex Register, Salem, MA

Evening Post, New York, NY

Examiner, London, UK

Federal Republican & Commercial Gazette, Baltimore, MD

Hull Packet and Original Weekly Commercial and General Advertiser, Hull, UK

Jackson's Oxford Journal, Oxford, UK

Liverpool Mercury, Liverpool, UK

Long-Island Star, Brooklyn, NY

Morning Chronicle, London, UK

Naval Chronicle, UK

Newburyport Herald, Newburyport, MA

New-England Palladium, Boston, MA

New Hampshire Patriot, Concord, NH

Newport Mercury, Newport, RI

New-York Gazette & General Advertiser, New York, NY

New-York Spectator, New York, NY

Niles' Weekly Register, Baltimore, MD

Portland Gazette and Maine Advertiser, Portland, ME

Portsmouth Oracle, Portsmouth, NH

Repertory & General Advertiser (or *Repertory*), Boston, MA

Statesman, New York, NY

Trewman's Exeter Flying Post or *Plymouth and Cornish Advertiser*, Exeter, UK

Times, London, UK

War Journal, Portsmouth, NH

Western Star, New York, NY

INDEX

ABOUT THE AUTHOR

Kevin D. McCranie is professor of strategy and policy at the United States Naval War College in Newport, Rhode Island. He specializes in the naval history of the Age of Sail. He is the author of *Admiral Lord Keith and the Naval War against Napoleon.*